Worldw

MW01599125

"This writing is what being brave is all about.
It brings up the kinds of things that are usually kept so private
that you think you're the only one who experiences them."

"Angel: The Complete Quintet"
International Edition Chosen Book of the Month
by *The Gay Times*, London:
"John Patrick is a prolific and prize-winning novelist whose
ability to crank out wide-ranging homoerotica is as deft and
sure as that of a dairy maid churning butter.
"In 'Angel' there is enough graphic sex of just about every
description to perk up even the most jaded imaginations.
Patrick knows how to mix 'n' match spicy combinations and his
enormous cast of characters includes porno stars, sleazy producers,
cute young studs with insatiable appetites (there's a bathhouse
scene that takes some beating) with sadism, degradation
and - improbably - love and affection."

"Tantalizing tales of porn stars, hustlers, and other
lost boys...John Patrick set the pace with 'Angel!'"
- *The Weekly News, Miami*

"...Some readers may find some of the scenes too explicit;
others will enjoy the sudden, graphic sensations each page brings.
Each of these romans á clef is written with sustained intensity.
'Angel' offers a strange, often poetic vision of sexual obsession.
I recommend it to you."
- *Nouveau Midwest*

"Self-absorbed, sexually-addicted bombshell Stacy flounced onto
the scene in 'Angel' and here he is again, engaged in further,
distinctly 'non-literary' adventures...lots of action!"
- *Prinz Eisenherz Book Review, Germany*

"'Angel' is mouthwatering and enticing..."
- *Rouge Magazine, London*

"'Superstars' is a fast read...if you'd like a nice round of fireworks
before the Fourth, read this aloud at your next church picnic..."
- *Welcomat, Philadelphia*

A Special Collection of Erotica Edited By
JOHN PATRICK

*All Boys
Are Not
Created
Equal.*

HUGE

*Every Man's Envy,
Some Men's Obsession.*

Books by John Patrick

Non-Fiction

A Charmed Life:
Vince Cobretti
Lowe Down: Tim Lowe
The Best of the Superstars 1990
The Best of the Superstars 1991
The Best of the Superstars 1992
The Best of the Superstars 1993
The Best of the Superstars 1994
What Went Wrong?
When Boys Are Bad
& Sex Goes Wrong
Legends: The World's Sexiest
Men, Vols. 1 & 2
Tarnished Angels (Ed.)

Fiction

Billy & David: A Deadly Minuet
The Bigger They Are...
The Younger They Are...
The Harder They Are...
Angel: The Complete Trilogy
Angel II: Stacy's Story
Angel: The Complete Quintet
Angel: The Complete Quintet
(Expanded International Ed.)
A Natural Beauty (Editor)
The Kid (with Joe Leslie)
Huge (Editor)
Strip: He Danced Alone
The Boys of Spring
Big Boys/Little Lies (Editor)
Boy Toy
Seduced (Editor)
Insatiable/Unforgettable (Editor)
Heartthrobs (including
The Boy from El Dorado)
Runaways/Kid Stuff (Editor)
Dangerous Boys (Editor)
WANTED: The Lusty Boys
Gorgeous (Editor)

Original Library of Congress Card Catalogue No. 90-070652
Expanded Third Edition ISBN No. 1-877978-63-9

Contents

"There are two things I hate: size queens and small cocks."
- Old Queer Saying

"There are two kinds of people: size queens and liars."
- Everett Quinton

Xenophobia

William S. Burroughs

"My cock is four and one-half inches and large cocks bring on my xenophobia.

"Like all normal citizens, I ejaculate when screwed without helping hand, produce a good crop of jissom, spurt it up to my chin and beyond. I have observed that small hard cocks come quicker slicker and spurtier."

- Excerpted from Mr. Burrough's jottings in "Interzone,"
published by Viking Penguin, Inc.

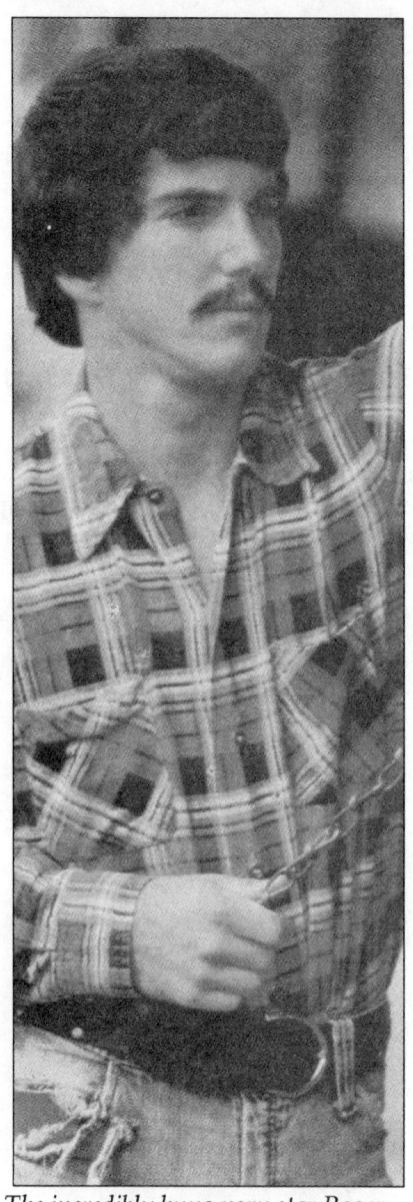

The incredibly hung porn star Roger,
at his prime in the late '70s,
posing for Blueboy Magazine.

Introduction:
The Cult of the Colossal Cock

John Patrick

I'm the first admit I've always been a size queen. There's just so much more to see.

I've tried to determine how this happened and, thinking back, I suppose it came about because my brother, seven years my senior, had such a big one compared to my puny one prior to puberty. When grown, my cock was actually bigger than his, which we proved one night when he was visiting from college, but that's another story.

While most men merely envy another who is well-endowed, for others, like me, it can become an obsession. For a long time, I felt I was one of the few people in the world who was obsessed in this way. Then, as I met more gays and read more books, I discovered I was hardly alone. As the writer Doug Richards observed, "Size fixation is certainly not without historical precedent. Phallic worship has existed since the Stone Age and continued unabated throughout the Neolithic Era and the Bronze Age. Phallic stone monuments from this latter epoch stand ten feet tall, direct fore-runners of the Washington Monument and Eiffel Tower. Artifacts from ancient Egypt, the Orient, Greece and Rome clearly show a preoccupation with the phallus. Among many awesome ex-amples, the Graeco-Roman deity Priapus, god of fertility, has always been represented with an oversized phallus. So modern day homosexuals are hardly the first to join 'The Cult of the Colossal Cock.'"

It was the late '70s before I was able to do much about my obsession. I bought a copy of *Blueboy* and fell hopelessly in lust with a model named Roger. Meeting him became a compulsion. I finally struck a deal with Roger's agent to have the star make a stopover in New Orleans on his way to Hollywood to make a film. During that long weekend in the spring of 1978, I was to observe the phenomenon of the big basket as I had never experienced it before. No one on the street recognized Roger, but the splendidly skin tight clothes he always wore clung enticingly to his bulging biceps and crotch, attracting the stares of men and women alike even in no-holds barred New Orleans.

He let me know right off that he didn't get fucked (he saved that for the screen and special occasions) but everything else was okay. I was so in awe of that mighty organ that all I really wanted to do was worship and adore it. It was the first time I had encountered one that large and I quickly discovered one of the problems a man so well endowed might have: it seems the meat rarely hardens to the extent it does with "normal" equipment. This is not much of a problem for these men when they are fucking women, cunts are designed to accept most anything, but for men with tight assholes, it can be an excruciating experience. After a few attempts to take Roger anally, I opted just to suck on it. Roger didn't have to but he eagerly got into a 69 position and proved a superb fellatist.

His posing for *Blueboy* pictorials led to a special issue devoted exclusively to him and inevitably came the films, most notably with Jack Wrangler in "Hot House" and "Sex Magic," and he became legendary to size queens all over the world.

Indeed, for us obsessed with size, it is to the field of hard-core video we turn for release. Golden Age porn star Luke said it best: "The three basics are the face, the body and the dick. You can get away with having two of them, or if your cock is abnormal enough in size, then just one will do. People really want to see those big dicks."

We are taught by mass media to admire bigness. The greatest, the grandest, the most beautiful. It makes sense that we should include cocks as an object of our esteem. The downside is that the person with whom you become obsessed can be reduced to a statistic. This was the opinion of Nick Jerrett, whom I sought out after he appeared in "Summer of Scott Noll." Nick said, "Psychologically, I don't think anyone minds having a big cock, but along with the benefits come the problems, like people looking at you just for that."

Dr. Charles Silverstein, in his book "Man to Man," agreed, noting that "in the gay world of today, the penis is revered. The big cock is the prize, adorned and adored, the possessor enormously attractive to the hungry hunter who wants to engulf it or be overpowered by it, with minimal regard for other physical characteristics, and none whatsoever for emotional or social ones." I understood Nick's position completely, that's why I preferred "dates" with the objects of my desire rather than quickie sessions.

And, thank goodness, even in an age when headline-hungry dinosaurs like Senator Jesse Helms (R-N.C.) would ban all discussion (even mention) of male sexuality, the porn producers persist. It's not the same as it was back in the golden age, when porn was chic and made with great care, but thanks to video, the good and the bad, the beautiful and the ugly, are all available to us for less than $3 a pop. Sex is so much trouble these days, porn has become a low-risk variant.

But, of course, it's not perfect. As critic Gerri Hershey says, "Orchestrated celebrity sex, however photogenic, can never approach the molten attraction of daily life passionately lived. It's ritual versus the real thing, and it's an apt metaphor for the uses of sex in our culture. Alas, we live in tepid times, and we've got more pandas than monkeys. The passionate are the endangered species. It ain't natural."

No, it ain't, but it'll do, until something better comes along. Like the right man.

By the very nature of the porn industry, there is a better chance of getting into bed with a sex performer than with a movie or rock star. Many have advertised liberally in gay publications. Others have depended on a network of wealthy gays to sustain themselves during lean periods. If you are lucky enough to live in New York, Hollywood, or San Francisco your chances of meeting a porn star are greatly enhanced, but there is always the option of traveling to them or having them visit you. This phenomenon of the "porn star fuck" is the basis of Dennis Cooper's novel "Frisk." "Everything I do is based on an urge that I don't understand, though I keep trying to understand it," says the character Dennis, as he flies from LAX to JFK to meet the blank-eyed young hustler/porn star of his current dreams, the one to whom he will explain: "You fascinate me so much that in a perfect world I'd kill you to understand the appeal."

"I can actually imagine myself inside the skins I admire," he confesses. "I'm pretty sure if I tore some guy open I'd know him as well as anyone could, because I'd have what he consists of right there in my hands, mouth, wherever." Dennis refers to his murderous compulsion as "religious," at one point comparing it to an Aztec sacrifice. Later in the book, Dennis concedes that the reality is always less than the fantasy and that resentment causes him to murder his dream dates.

"Desire," writes book critic C. Carr, "at its most extreme is tantamount to murder, a wish to possess or incorporate the love object, thus obliterating it."

Obliterating the objects of my fascination was never my intention. Over the years, I was able to arrange to meet porn performers and I always approached my time with them as an educational experience. Even though, most of the time, the actual event didn't live up to my exalted expectations, years later, I can still get off watching them on video, remembering my short time with them, editing out what one of my former lovers called all of the "idiosyncratic bullshit."

Yes, thanks to video, reality is enhanced. Thank goodness for Philo Farnsworth, the man who is credited with inventing the television set. His vision has enriched the lives of generations and has kept us informed and illuminated. And day after heartbreaking day, the TV is always there, now coupled with the VCR, ready to spring to life, offering up our idols. We don't even have to leave our bedrooms to enjoy them at their very best. Sex seems most perfect at one remove, unspooling in tape-loops and a VCR remote control is the perfect tool for watching these sexual legends. Ultimately, desire is expressed with the body but it begins in the mind and, in your fantasies, sex can be anything and everything you want it to be.

And those images, the author Dennis Cooper says, "can't lead anyone to a place where he wasn't headed for already. Fantasy becomes an end unto itself."

The most popular stars of video are generally those with the biggest endowments, from John Holmes (the biggest of all the white guys, at 8 1/2" soft), Clarence Thomas' favorite hero, Long Dong Silver (who was unbelievable at 18"), to Jeff Stryker (who posed for the world's most popular dildo, to which they added 2") to the current rage Ryan Idol (who weighs in with a reasonably paltry 8 1/2", but it's a groin that appears to have been "cut by a gemsmith," as one critic gushed).

These stars were following the advice a roommate gave beautifully endowed Matt Johnson, star of "Fever Pitch":

"He said, 'You only have one opportunity in life - if you've got it, flaunt it!' And he kept pushing me saying I could really be somebody in the porn industry, especially given the size dick that I have. I figured I had nothing to lose. If I got rejected, at least I'd tried. When I was growing up, I was embarrassed by the fact that my dick was so big. It wasn't until after I came out of the closet that I began to realize most guys are very appreciative of that. I mean, everyone is a size-queen. Everyone wants the biggest one they can find. But when they get it, being able to accommodate it can be rather difficult. Ten inches is probably not an everyday occurrence. If you do find someone who can accommodate it all, then you're afraid of him because anybody who is that large in rectal size has either been around an awful lot or is probably into a much heavier scene than I am."

Accommodation is only one problem associated with hugeness. One wag, in reviewing nicely long-donged Rod Garretto's performance in "Hombres," blamed the star's lack of hardness on what he termed the "Rick Donovan syndrome: a cock so big it can't stay hard." I was to observe this syndrome first hand and it is true, but still, just the sight of the famous appendage soft was enough to take one's breath away.

After seeing his incredible debut with insatiable blond bottom Leo Ford in William Higgins' "Sailor in the Wild," I sought Rick out and finally got him to agree to come to Florida. As I related in my book "Legends," some young men who had been invited as companions for other guests at a party I was giving in Fort Lauderdale joined me in my suite for drinks before dinner. Rick had been taking a nap in his own room before showering and getting dressed. The boys and I were in the living room talking when suddenly the star appeared, stark naked, a towel hanging loosely from one hand.

Conversation ceased. All eyes were riveted on the incredible appendage that hung lewdly between his legs. It was limp but it was the longest limp I'd ever seen. Addressing me directly, Rick asked, with a sheepish grin, 'Do you want me to wear a tie?'

I don't recall exactly how I responded; I think it was something like, "I don't think a tie would cover it, Rick. You'd better wear pants."

"Yeah, sure," he said with a smile and disappeared back into the bedroom wing.

"Is that for real?" asked one of my awed young guests.
I nodded and there seemed to be a collective "whew" hanging in the air.

While the reactions to his endowment amuse him now, in fact,

Rick never realized what he had until he was in his late teens: "Of course, I went through high school having sex with cheerleaders who always said, 'My God—you're SO big!' But my theory was, 'Well, how many cocks has she seen? One? Two? Five tops!' Secondly, girls are taught to think dicks are the size of a thumb, and anybody's is big compared to a thumb. And when I was in the military, there were prostitutes telling me how big I was. But I discounted that, too, because they're paid to tell you how big you are. My first lover was the one that convinced me I was big."

Unlike Roger, who had the biggest basket I'd ever seen, Rick showed nothing - and he loved it. "When I'm soft I don't show a basket," he revealed. "It's the biggest deceiver in the world. It's great because I know people are attracted to me, not my dick because they can't see it." (Can't you hear echoes of the poor little rich girl's lament, "I want a man whose interested in me, not my money?")

Rick played a super-macho role, which was fine with me. That's part of the fantasy with adoring a super-hung stud. Doug Richards of *Manshots* agrees: "The myth perpetuated by the onscreen persona of a mega-endowed star is that a man with a big cock is the quintessential man, and as such, never assumes what has become known as 'the female role.' The message that a big cock equals control, control means power and power is potency, sexual potency."

As he sailed from one hot video to another, Rick was dogged with the reputation that he couldn't get it up. The truth was, it took a long time for the monster to rise. He joked, "Sure, it does take me ten minutes to get a hard-on, but, Jesus, give me a break. It takes a half-pint of blood to get this thing up!"

He responded to his critics by reciting a litany of his finest screen performances, where he undoubtedly had the biggest hard-on most people had ever seen. He considered Matt Sterling's "The Bigger the Better" his best, and he liked "The Arousers," "The Biggest One I Ever Saw," and his debut film, "Sailor in the Wild." Rick's theory was that he had to be a star with his first outing. "The first thing you do sets the standard for good. I lucked out with William Higgins. He's a good filmmaker and he said I could choose who I wanted to work with and they would also want to work with me. And he offered me a lot of money. As it turned out, Leo Ford (his co-star) was a great guy to work with. Everything clicked."

Rick was not to have the same success with every video. In "Boys of Company F" he does a credible job of playing a hard-nosed sergeant but he doesn't have sex until the end and gets lost in the shuffle of the orgy. In "Bi and Beyond II," he's a sad sight trying to get an erection with a rubber slipped over his humungous equipment. He manages to get it into a girl and there are a few brief glimpses of him as he plows her, but, again, he's lost in the shuffle. After that video, Rick retired to teach scuba diving, then bounced back in Jerry Douglas' award-winning "More of a Man," in which he gets it on with Joey Stefano, although he doesn't fuck the infamous ass.

Falcon's "The Big Ones" demonstrates the reason Rick is legendary in porn circles. There he is, in 1991, still sporting a macho mustache, looking better than ever, reading lines with aplomb and fucking grandly. He even kisses his bedmate goodbye. It's a short peck on the lips but it's better than nothing. The only thing we found fault with was the fact that there was a noticeable lack of latex in his scene, odd for a star who has appeared in several "safe sex" entries in his lengthy (in more ways than one) career.

But the porn star by which all others are measured is John C. Holmes. He had an ordinary face, a skinny body and natural penchant for fucking but rose to the top of straight porn because of his incredible endowment.

In his September 7, 1987 tribute to John in *Screw*, publisher and Broward County sheriff wannabe Al Goldstein, wrote:

"It is the biggest cock in porn. Its eminence looms over the horizon of pornography and casts its mammoth shadow over the landscape of sleaze. Like Paul Bunyan, the cock is mythic, almost cosmic force that has a life of its own. It's a meteor piercing the sky. A rocket tracing fire into the heavens. The cock that defines pornography.

"It is an instrument of pain and pleasure. In itself, a metaphor for life. It is the MX missile of genitalia. As significant as man's landing on the moon, the Wright Brothers' first flight, the invention of the wheel and the discovery of fire.

"It's a bird, it's a plane - no, it's the cock of John Holmes! Appearing in thousands of porn films, porking thousands of women, it is the most legendary male member since Adam's fucked Eve. It is bigger than the sum of its parts. The cock of John Holmes has obsessed and fascinated me and captured the attention of the porno-goer since 1967. In paying our homage to John for being bigger than life, we commend him on his influence and contributions to male and female fantasy. We also take an existential pleasure in realizing that in spite of his gargantuan-sized cock, his life was riddled with drugs, pain, alienation and self-deprecation.

"What this means is that, indeed, the content and substance of life is more important than mere statistical data. The guy with a four-inch cock has no more or no less pleasure than the guy with a 14-inch prod. The number of women he has fucked, the quantity of sexual encounters one has had, have little value in the totality of what makes life significant. We salute John for what he is and what he proved to us he was not. We commend him and we take joy that we are not him."

In music, the King was Presley. In the parallel, subterranean world of porn, Holmes existed as a sort of scaled-down (in all respects but one) King. Both came from poor white trash backgrounds and both used a black man's weapons to rise to the top. For Elvis, it was rhythm and blues, for John, a huge cock.

Although he was the top stud in adult films, it never made him a wealthy man and because of his slippery, protean persona, you never knew where you were with him. John Holmes slid down the slope from sex to drugs to murder, aimlessly, without style, typical of a country boy who got in way over his curly head. In the end, he didn't know the truth about anything, much less himself. But he did make sexual intercourse look pleasant to millions of people, he showed care and respect for his partners, and he seemed to be able to laugh at himself. As epitaphs go, that's not bad at all.

Doug Richards commented: "Holmes had an ordinary face, a thin body and a certain skill, but he became the first male star of heterosexual pornography, strictly on the length of his dick. For many years, his was the standard by which all others were measured."

John came to Hollywood when he was already 27 and quickly made over 1,000 eight millimeter loops before being discovered by Bob Chinn and Richard Aldrich and cast as "Johnny Wadd," porn's parody of a hard-boiled Sam Spade-type detective. But he was never the swaggering, violent male chauvinist. Rather, he was quiet, gentle, almost artful when he fucked. He let his size do his posturing for him. In every film he made there was that sense of anticipation. We waited impatiently for him to unfurl his cock and let some bimbo try to take it all in one orifice or another. It was said to be a badge of honor in the industry to have taken John anally and lived to tell about it.

How big was it? John joked once, "It's bigger than a pay phone, smaller than a Cadillac." It was billed to be 14" long but some said it was really only 12 3/4". One report indicated it was 8 1/2" soft. I never measured it. Whatever his measurements, John was made to order for porn back in the '70s and came to symbolize the quantity-not-quality esthetics that had begun to typify America by that time. He was both the bane and the balm for the man who doubted his virility, the perfect "product" for a society of size-queens.

Industry sources have always contended that Holmes was "actively bi," that he would take a trick with a man any time if the price was right. Holmes once said, "I consider myself sexual." He admitted he'd had over 14,000 sex partners, including three governors and a U. S. Senator. "A happy gardener is one with dirty fingernails and a happy cock is a fat cock. I never get tired of what I do because I'm a sex fiend. I'm very lusty."

The truth was, his true love could only be bought by the gram. That love got him in trouble in 1981 when, early one morning, four people were brutally bludgeoned to death in a house in the hills above Hollywood. And the case got bizarre as the evidence came in. The house was the headquarters for a drug-and-burglary ring and a fringe member of the group was a drug addict by the name of John Holmes.

The police also knew that Holmes was a favorite of one of the men they believed engineered the killings, a Lebanese gangster named Adel Nasrallah, known in the states as Eddie Nash. Nash was a drug kingpin as well as a nightclub owner and when they raided his house they found cocaine worth $4 million on the street. Police theorized that Nash engineered the killings as revenge for a burglary at his house the week before, an incident some said was planned by John Holmes. To save himself, John led Nash to the burglars and left his palm-print above one of the victims. Police arrested him, grilling him for hours, but he refused to give them any information. He fled to Florida and worked at odd jobs but a few months later, he was extradited back to California to stand trial for the murders. The jury acquitted him.

In the aftermath of the trial, he appeared in a couple of trumped-up features but settled into a rut, taking whatever came along to support his cocaine habit. In 1985, one of the things that came along was Fred Halsted and Joey Yale's production of "The Private Pleasures of John Holmes," and even with the very accommodating assholes of porn veterans Joey (who also directed) and Chris Burns around for Holmes to fuck, it is a terrible film made all the more despicable by the sight of a star who was so obviously down on his luck.

Businessman Bill Amerson, his friend for over 25 years, took John under his wing and the star made some comeback films such as "Girls on Fire," "The Return of Johnny Wadd," and "Rockey X." He flew to Rome to make "The Rise and Fall of the Roman Empress" and "The Devil in Mr. Holmes," co-starring Italian parliament member Cicciolina.

Before John flew to Italy to make those last films, he was diagnosed as having AIDS. He consciously engaged in anal sex with Cicciolina as well as Amber Lynn and Tracey Adams, an act that some said was tantamount to murder. "He was chosen to get AIDS because of how he lived, who he was," said his wife Laurie (known in straight porn circles as Misty Dawn). She was divorcing him, repelled by his penchant for low-rent whores. She revealed that he would cruise the boulevards picking up the trashiest people he could find. His coprophilic obsession hinged on the "filthiness" of sex and he practiced it frequently over a period of years.

By October of 1986, the star was in noticeably failing health. He himself spread the word he had cancer. In *Screw*, Goldstein reported that fact and also the rumor that Holmes did indeed have AIDS. Finally, on March 15, 1988 in Los Angeles, Holmes succumbed to the disease.

As long as the human penis averages about six inches in length, the memory of John C. Holmes will remain well protected and highly profitable. The best of Holmes can be found in "Insatiable," with Marilyn Chambers, with the stud plugging the notorious Ivory Snow girl on a pool table. Critics picked "Eruption" (released by Cal Vista), a porn version of the thriller "Double Indemnity," as his best acting job and, filmed in Hawaii, his sex scenes with Leslie Bovee are appropriately volcanic.

John's legacy to gay viewers includes the inept Joey Yale vehicle,

"The Private Pleasures of John C. Holmes," as well as Falcon's treasures: the early loop "The Biggest of Them All" (Falcon Pac 16); "Black Velvet" (Pac 21); "Pool Party" (Pac 9).

The man is dead, but the product is immortal.

There are those who are not satisfied pursuing the big cock; they want one for themselves. A man who signed his letter, "Wants Ten Inches," wrote *The Advocate*: "I have always wanted a larger cock. When I was a kid, I was teased about my size and my foreskin. I was circumcised at the age of 22. I like the way my cock looks now. When it's soft it's only 3 1/2" in length and grows to 6 1/2 to 7" when hard. Is there any way to get my cock to hang longer when it's soft? I have been using a pump and the other day I pumped myself up to almost 8". But it only stays that size while it's in the pump. It was getting painful so I removed the pump and there was blood on the side of my cock."

The Sexpert advised: "Advocates of vacuum pumps say you may be able to slowly increase the size of your cock. I am skeptical, but if you enjoy playing with a pump, you might as well see if a few years of jacking off this way can make a difference, but stop pumping so hard! You run the risk of damaging the circulatory system that makes your cock get hard. I assume you'd rather have a 7" erection than no erection at all.

"Your cock is a perfectly fine size. Very few men have one that's bigger. It's easy to stay home, use the pump, obsess about your size, and blame it for the lack of sex in your life. But if you got out of the house and started chasing other guys, you'd soon find out that you've got all the equipment it takes to have a good time."

In *Wingspan*, the men's movement magazine, Greg Perry writes about how his shame over having what he calls a "tiny" penis drove him to overachieve, seeking "good grades, good drugs, and big money." Hung Jury, a Los Angeles dating service, accepts as members only men whose erections measure at least eight inches, and its founder Jim Boyd would surely agree with Perry's statement that "throughout the male culture, bigger is better and small is weak." Boyd insists that "most American women want a well-endowed lover" and that "there's a shocking correlation between penis size and the divorce rate in this country that no one wants to talk about."

The novelist David Rees, in a chapter of his book "Dog Days,

White Nights," titled "Cock," says: "To discuss the sexual and esthetic appeal of cock, to introduce the subject of cocksize, opens up a whole can of writhing gay worms. We all have opinions on these matters, mostly very firm opinions; and we only agree on one thing -that size, shape and esthetic appeal bear no relationship whatsoever to performance. Some men say, quite sincerely, that they never even think about it.

"But most of us, if we are honest enough to admit it, do find that the shape of another man's cock is of some relevance. A straight friend of mine said that this was beyond his understanding; the vagina was of no concern to him in thinking of a woman's sexuality. 'A cunt is a cunt is a cunt,' he said, 'and that's all there is to be said about it.' I think he was ignoring the fact that a woman's sexual organs are hidden, whereas nothing is more visible than an erect cock.

"Size doesn't interest me much, despite my memories of a seventeen-year-old with an eleven inch cock, but I would be a hypocrite if I said that a very minute cock was not a disappointment. I can't say what an acceptable minimum or maximum would be; I've never thought about it. To me, some cocks are ugly and some are attractive, but their esthetic appeal hasn't been a part of any decision I've made concerning whether to go to bed with a man a second time, or to go to bed with him repeatedly; and I find those who say cock size is their sole criterion in gauging sexual charms are quite incomprehensible."

I would have to agree with David that to make it a sole criterion in gauging sexual charms is a mistake, but when taken as part of an entire menu, size is a huge bonus. After all, like I said, there's just so much more to see.

I.
Tales of the Humungous

*"All honesty, we must remember,
is in the tongue of the teller."*
- Mary Gordon

Mightier Than The Sword...

Donald Vining

Gideon found himself getting more confused every day he was around these movie people. It was culture shock enough for a boy from Central Pennsylvania to find himself working in sunny Spain, without having all this other confusion.

He had grown up on movies in which Archer Carmichael, as the villain, made you want to hiss him, yet in person he was the nicest, kindest member of the company doing yet another version of "Robin Hood." On the other hand, Gideon had adored Dennis Manley in many a heroic role, had jacked off many times looking at pictures of him torn from fan magazines, but now that he knew the man, what he'd like to thrust into him wasn't his cock but a sword.

Villains being kindly, heroes being bastards and a film about Robin Hood being shot in Spain instead of England seemed typical of a topsy-turvy business and he wished he were out of it. But that would mean giving up Ivan.

And Ivan, thrilled to be the fencing coach and director of the sword-fights in the film instead of the fencing coach at the university when Gideon met him, was far handsomer than Dennis Manley had been even in his prime, which wasn't exactly yesterday.

Gideon remembered what high adventure it had seemed when Ivan told him that one condition of his contract was that Gideon be hired as his assistant and perhaps be given work as a bit player. He would have been thrilled even to have a job as garbage collector if it meant being close to Ivan.

It was the influence of all those Dennis Manley costume dramas in his youth that led Gideon to select fencing as his sports activity in college. At that point he hadn't laid eyes on the new fencing coach, who had defected to America competing in the Olympics. Fencing was not one of the things TV ever bothered to show during the Olympics. Lots of track and field, tiresome amounts of basketball and boxing, both of which Gideon loathed, but never two seconds of fencing. So when he first reported to class and saw how handsome and sexy his instructor was, his legs had gone weak. The pictures of Dennis Manley got thrown out, displaced by one of Ivan that appeared in the college newspaper alongside an article about his Olympic medals and his defection. Film star Dennis Manley, Gideon thought, was part of his past.

With all the films Dennis had made during the last cycle of costume dramas from Hollywood, what did he need with private coaching from Ivan? True, Manley had lately been cast more as debonair jewel thieves and con men, but was his swordsmanship so rusty that he needed every moment of Ivan's time not taken up with directing the fights? Gideon felt sure Dennis spent most of his private fencing lesson on his back with his legs in the air. As for Ivan, he could be put in the Guinness Book of Records not only for his fencing awards but also for the size of what dangled (or reared) between his muscular legs. He had told Gideon that those that really knew him called him "Ivan the Terrible" and now he understood.

Gideon felt as bad now as during those frustrating days at college when he was consumed with lust for Ivan but was kept at arm's length by his thirty-year-old dream-boat. Fencing classes had been delicious agony as young Gideon's hard-on strained his jockstrap from the first bell to the last.

"It won't do for an instructor to become involved with one of his students," Ivan told him.

"Ha!" Gideon responded, "I know three girls who are fucking their Psychology professors."

"Oh, well, that's the Psychology Department for you," Ivan said dismissively.

Then came the budget crunch and the administration cut many of the sparsely attended courses and extra-curricular activities. Fencing was the first to go.

"What will you do now?" Gideon asked.

"A dancer friend of mine has suggested I come to New York and teach dancers and actors dueling. He says I can have some space in his dance studio."

"Are you and he...?" Gideon's voice trailed off.

Ivan smiled. "No, never. He's got a boyfriend in the ballet."

Agonizing months passed until the college year ended for Gideon and he decided to take a summer job in New York and it wasn't long before he came to call on Ivan at his studio. The older man seemed delighted to see him.

"I'm not your student anymore, so..." Gideon said, letting the sentence fade away, but his hungry eyes completed it.

"True, though I think you should take lessons this summer. You're very talented."

"No, no lessons, because then you'd tell me again I was your pupil and you can't get involved and I - "

Though Ivan still had occasional trouble with English, he understood the body language of his former pupil. "But it is different with private lessons."

And he took Gideon in his arms willingly at last.

In his private lessons, Gideon was soon to discover that sex wasn't all cock, but when it came to cock, Ivan had more cock than the student had ever imagined existed, and the skill to use it. Thrusting it between Gideon's legs, he would make frottage as exciting as being fucked by anybody else and when he finally was able to fully accommodate Ivan, being fucked by him was the greatest high the slender boy had ever known. Gideon's throat wasn't deep enough to take all of the shaft for the head alone was a mouthful, but licking the long, thick shaft was ecstasy.

Now, the memory of those wonderful days in New York were all he had since they had come to Spain. Ever since Manley laid eyes on Ivan he had commandeered all of the instructor's time when he wasn't directing frays between Robin's merry band and the deputies of the Sheriff of Nottingham or King John.

The misnamed Manley had married and divorced twice with much publicity but it was all a front because, as far as Gideon could see, he had no interest in any of the women on the set. And dozens of nubile female fans put themselves in his path, hoping to be deflowered by the star, only to go home as virginal as they left. Even the director's wife, less sophisticated than she liked to imagine, had used all of her wiles to lure Manley to her bed, partly to arouse her preoccupied husband, but mostly because what Dennis displayed in his forest green tights was on the epic scale of the production. Manley's response to the bosomy lady's seductiveness was chilly enough to turn that hot corner of Spain into a setting for "Nanook of the North."

After his first lesson from Ivan, suddenly Manley was a perfectionist, wanting more and more private coaching and Gideon, in a new and strange business in a new and strange land, became more and more lonely and forlorn. Archer, the eternal villain with a profile so sharp you could shave with it, seemed to understand and sympathize with the fencing coach's young assistant.

"Manley is usually quite fickle," he assured Gideon, as if he were reading his thoughts, "and by now he'd have worked his way through the entire merry band and half the crew. Normally, I'd say you'd have Ivan back in a day or two but he must have some special hold on Manley."

"He does. The gossips on the wardrobe crew have told me that half the bulge in Manley's tights is padding but all of that in Ivan is real."

Though no one was allowed in the hastily-constructed temporary building where Ivan gave his coaching lessons, Gideon was able to sneak around back and listen. The walls were fairly flimsy compared to the thick ones on the huge castle set and Gideon's ear, pressed to a crack in the boards, heard very little clanging of steel on steel. Instead, he heard much slapping of skin on skin and Manley grunting and gasping, followed by huge moans and finally sighs. Then Manley said, "God, look at that, even now that it's soft again, you make Jeff Stryker look puny."

"Who is this Stryker?"

"Let's just say he's an ex-champion now. Another American product who has lost out to foreign competition."

Then there came a loud knocking on the door and an assistant director called out, "Duel at the drawbridge coming up, everybody on the set."

Gideon scurried away from his listening post and hastened to the set. In time, Manley, with a star's deliberateness, joined them, his face showing the smugness of the well-and-thoroughly screwed. As Ivan gave the crew instructions for the sword-fight, Dennis threw him a look of proud possessiveness that made Gideon want to throw up, preferably on the both of them. He felt sick; how could he hope to compete with a major star, one who, although a bit shopworn, was still staggeringly handsome and rich.

After the scene, Gideon approached his lover and mentioned how impressive Manley's basket was. "Is that for real?" he asked. Ivan simply shrugged his shoulders and turned his attention to the next scene.

As the director called for action again, the cameras rolled and Gideon plunged into the fray with his sword, madly attacking the

Spanish extra who was cast as his foe. Having disarmed him as he was supposed to do, he turned his attention to the star, beleaguered by several swordsmen just as the great drawbridge to the castle began to be lowered by a member of Robin's band who had infiltrated it. Instead of the easily parried thrust Gideon had been told to give, he suddenly slashed with his blade at the wad of padding at Dennis' crotch, the tip tearing across it. Cotton batting spilled out. Startled, Dennis took a panicky step backward, protesting loudly, and tumbled into the moat surrounding the castle.

"Cut!" the director cried. The other swordsmen, Robin's enemies as well as allies, went quickly to the spluttering star, threshing around in the shallow, muddy water. While the sudden conversion of the enemy to rescuers delighted Gideon no one else seemed the least but amused. A nonplused Ivan, on the sidelines, glared at his lover.

"Get off the set and don't come back," the director shouted at Gideon.

Archer came to Gideon's defense. "These things will happen in the heat of battle - "

"Not on my set!"

Hauled red-faced out of the moat, his toupee askew, the soaking star threw Gideon a look he clearly hoped could kill. "Amateur!" he sneered, that being the worst epithet he could think of.

Gideon, hit by the realization that he had lost his job and quite possibly his lover would send him back to America, tried his best to look repentant, but like Ivan he was an unconvincing actor. He waited in vain for Ivan to come to his aid.

"If you're really worried that Kevin Costner's Robin is going to get to the theaters before this one, you'd better not waste time looking for a replacement for this kid."

The wardrobe and makeup people swarming around him, Manley spat, "I want that little shit out of here by the time I get back, " his voice was so high in his hysteria that it would have disillusioned his fans the world 'round. He all but stamped his foot as he said it.

Gideon cast a pleading look towards Ivan, who stood abashed, clearly prey to conflicting feelings.

"I say, give the boy another chance," Archer said.

"Well, what you say doesn't count for much - " the director said.

"I'm not the star, I'll admit, but a hero doesn't look like much without a villain for contrast."

Gideon didn't care for the job itself, he had already discovered making movies involved more tedium than glamour but if he was ready to say goodbye to his brief career in films, he was far from ready to say goodbye to Beau. His heart ached that his love was saying nothing, making no move in his defense and he started to leave the set dejected. Finally Ivan, a bit shamefacedly, said, "I can fix it so that Gideon doesn't attack Dennis at all. Someone else can disarm him."

"I doubt that'll satisfy Dennis," the director said.

"Oh, I handle Dennis," Ivan said with a broad smile.

The director nodded, perfectly aware, as the whole company was, of the relationship between the two of them.

"So handle him," Archer said sharply.

Ivan came over to Gideon at the edge of the set and under his breath said, "And no more nonsense from you."

"At the time, I thought it was worth it."

Ivan's eyes widened in surprise at the hurt and anger in Gideon's voice but he went about the business of choosing another man to join the fray against the star at the drawbridge and Gideon was instructed to fall to the sword of the man he had formerly bested.

"He's still here?" Manley shouted as he returned to the set newly-costumed.

"I have changed things. He's out of it early," Ivan said.

"Not good enough. I want him out of this production, out of Spain!" This time he actually did stomp his foot.

"All right, Dennis, whatever you say," the director said.

After a long, painfully indecisive moment, Ivan said, "If he goes, I go, too."

Dennis blanched. Gideon glowed. It had taken Ivan too long but at last he was taking a stand.

"If I said the word, and the studio offered enough money, I'm sure my former coach could be lured out of retirement."

The director shook his head. "By the time we contacted him and flew him over here, we'd be way behind schedule and Costner's Robin'll be in release. Let's just everybody calm down and get on with it."

"Yeah, let's get on with it," said the rotund actor playing Friar Tuck, who had obliged so many of the women Dennis disappointed that behind his back the company referred to him as "Friar

Fuck."

Dennis took a stubborn stance and shook his head.

"It's as important to you as it is to me that this 'Robin' comes out first," the director said. Everyone knew none of Manley's recent pictures had done well, either financially or critically.

"Well, all right," he said grudgingly, "as long as that amateur doesn't come within twenty-five yards of me."

The drawbridge was drawn up again and the scene started over. Gideon let the Spaniard run through him with a thrust to his armpit which would look as though it passed through his body in the quick glimpse the audience would have of it, if it didn't blink. He fell to the ground and heard the clash of swords grow more distant as they approached the drawbridge. Finally the director yelled "Cut!" and seemed satisfied. Dennis, Gideon noticed as he picked himself up from the ground and dusted himself off, had flounced off to his dressing room.

Gideon approached Ivan contritely. "I'm sorry," he muttered. "You should be."

"I've just been feeling so deserted. He's taken you over night and day."

"Gideon, what can I do? He is the star."

"But I'm horny all the time and I have to sit around while Dennis has all the fun."

"Soon it will be over," Ivan said, and walked toward his trailer. Gideon followed and as they reached the door, he pleaded, "Can I come in awhile?"

"What if Dennis finds out? That's all we need after that scene you made."

"Fuck Dennis!" Gideon screamed and turned on his heel. "I'm going back to America where I belong."

"Wait. I've been cruel. Come inside. Who cares what Dennis thinks?"

Ivan pulled Gideon, not at all reluctant, into his trailer and closed the door. Gideon put his arms around the older man's muscular torso. "I've missed you so."

"And I miss you, I didn't realize how much till now, holding you in my arms again."

Their bodies pressed together, Gideon felt the phenomenal cock swelling till it seemed as though it might grow too big for the trailer to contain.

Then there was a knock on the door. "Mr. Manley wants you in his trailer at once." Ivan recognized the voice as that of Dennis' personal dresser.

"Not now, I'm busy," Ivan said, rather unintelligibly since Gideon was pressing his lips against his.

"Right away," the voice outside said peremptorily.

"I'm busy," Ivan said as Gideon's hands were busily lowered Ivan's tights, and pushing jockstrap aside to reveal the knob of the great cock.

"Oh, Mr. Manley won't like this," said the voice outside, clearly dreading returning to Dennis with bad news.

Gideon lowered Ivan's jockstrap and ran his tongue along the great cock, then took the large loose balls and fondled them just as there came a furious rapping on the trailer door.

Dennis' voice, high with hysteria again, screamed, "Ivan, how dare you! I can make or break you - " He paused, listening. "I hear slurping. Who's in there with you?"

"I'll see you later," Ivan called to him, his head thrown back in enjoyment as Gideon's mouth swallowed as many inches of the cock as were feasible.

"You'll see me now or you'll never work on a movie again."

"This is worth it," Ivan said as Gideon bent his head and took first one, then both of his balls in his mouth.

"Ivan, please," Dennis whined.

"Don't let people hear you beg," Ivan said, lifting Gideon up from his knees. "Think of your image."

Gideon lowered his tights in anticipation and bent over. Ivan spread the asscheeks wide.

"I'm not about to lose you to a silly nobody," Dennis hollered, rocking the trailer in his fury.

The rhythm fitted with the gentle, steady slide of Ivan's cock up Gideon's ass. After Gideon's muscles became adjusted to all they had to accommodate once again, Ivan put his arms around the boy and his huge cock slowly went ever more deeply inside of him.

Then the trailer began to rock even more violently and Gideon wasn't sure if Manley was doing it or if it was the result of the stepped up thrusting of "Ivan the Terrible's" swift sword, but by then he had ceased to care.

The Boy Who Broke My Sister

John Patrick

My sister's cunt always seemed to start trouble. Guys took dibs on who would go first on Friday nights, the night my folks bowled in a league. Often, fights broke out.

I would crouch at the top of the stairs, watching. The boys stood around the living room, their dicks in their hands, whooping and hollering. My sister's power, I could see, came from between her legs; one guy put his hands there, shoving them up under her skirt. That started it. I thought how powerless they were against her.

One by one, she held their cocks in her hand, her power over them increasing with each stroke. Their faces contorted, they moaned and groaned as she stroked them. Some of them came right then, others, they waited, waited for her to go to the sofa. Finally, she made herself comfortable, lifted her skirt and, her crotch at the edge of the cushion, spread her legs. They got on their knees in front of her, the ones who hadn't come already and even some who had, hard again, overwhelmed by her power. And it would begin, one after the other, invading her.

And they hated her for it. One day, I was in the locker room after football practice and overheard them talking. There was laughter.

"She's a whore," one guy said. "How can you stick your dick in that whore?"

"The rubber oughta break just once, the slut deserves it," another one said.

"Yeah, but where else would we get it?"

A week later, they saw me, on the landing, just as I went into my crouch. I was barely into my teens and just had my first real orgasm a couple of weeks before, thinking about what would happen Friday night.

"Hey!" Bruce yelled. "Joey! Come here!"

My sister laid her arm over her eyes. "Joey, stay away," she screamed. "Go back to your room."

"No, you're a big boy now, you want your share, don't ya?"

I didn't say anything, I just stood on the landing, staring at them. But my boner gave me away.

"Hey," Bruce yelled, "Joey's got a hard-on!"

They all chimed in and I held my hands over my ears, shaking. Three of them ran up and grabbed me, dragged me down the stairs, and pushed me in front of the sofa. They pulled my pants off me. My sister screamed. Two guys held her down, Bruce and another guy shoved me towards her.

She kicked at them, at me, and the harder she fought, the heavier they were with both of us.

Soon, I was just like one of them, just one more prick.

But that's not the way Bruce saw it.

"God, look at that kid, he's bigger than two of us put together!"

Bruce took my penis in his hand and stroked it. I had noticed that he was the only one who ever touched any of the other guys.

My sister uncovered her eyes and stared at me, at my equipment. "God, Joey!"

Before, I had been ashamed of my cock. It was so puny when it was limp, with the foreskin hanging over the head and I thought it was the ugliest thing I'd ever seen. I didn't take a shower at school because I would have to expose it. But as I got older and my cock got hard, it was a different thing altogether. Now I was discovering just how different.

I was terrified but I liked what Bruce was doing, sliding the skin back and forth the same way I did three, four times a day, sometimes more. Bruce brought it to the lips of my sister's cunt.

"Verna's gonna love this one," he laughed.

"Shit, he's her brother, man," another guy said. "She *been* lovin' it!"

Two guys held her down again and Bruce shoved me from behind. I closed my eyes, pretending it wasn't anybody I knew, just a whore.

"Shit, look at him go!" Bruce yelled. "He's probably been doin' this more than we have!"

Bruce's hands clutched my ass, pushing me, lifting me. I was in where their dicks had been only I was in deeper than any of them. I began to shudder. Bruce wouldn't let me free. I came.

*

Verna had the abortion in a little town about forty miles away and never came back. After that night, the boys never came back either.

I went to see her and she told me I could fuck her but I didn't want to. She knew a guy who worked at a gas station and I stood in the hallway outside her bedroom and jacked off listening to them fucking.

Several months after Verna left, Bruce came to the house. I had avoided him a couple of times on my way home from school. But soon he was a senior and I was a freshman and we were in the same school. He asked me if he could stop by and I said sure. I didn't even ask why. I guess I hoped I knew why.

And I was right. He started by asking for a Coke and when we were in the kitchen, he talked about that night, how much fun he'd had. He didn't apologize and I suppose I didn't expect him to. Finally, he touched my crotch and asked, "How long is it anyway?"

"I don't know really. I mean, I've never taken a ruler to it or anything."

"Well, why don't we?" He stroked it wildly.

I smiled and shook my head.

"God, maybe it could be in the Guinness book of records or somethin'!" He started to unzip my pants.

"Oh, I doubt it."

"C'mon, let's find out." He had pulled my zipper all the way down before I could say anything, not that I wanted to. And there, on the kitchen floor, he undid my belt, knelt down and pulled my pants down around my knees. Just as he began slipping my shorts down, my cock stirred and roared up into his face.

"Shit, what a piece of meat!" he cried, staring at it. "I've never seen one that big."

"How many have you seen?"

"Oh, a lot. You know, we've been fuckin' whores for five years now. Your sister wasn't the first and won't be the last, and I've seen lots of dicks, man, but yours is awesome!"

I just stood there, beaming.

I knew he couldn't help himself, he'd have to touch it. What I hadn't expected was that he would kiss it. "Do you think if I suck it, it'll get even bigger?"

"I don't know, I've never had anybody suck it."

"You mean Verna never blew this baby?"

"Verna never did nothin' with my dick."

"Smart kid." He held my ass and slowly slid the head and a couple of inches of it into his mouth, then drew back, admiring it again. "It even tastes good, Joey." And then he took as much of it in his mouth as he could. He choked, then continued. I couldn't help myself, I came but he could feel it and pulled it out just as I started to come. "See, it is bigger! And shit, look at that load!" He caught most of it in his hand and slid the sticky substance between his fingers. Then he took it back in his mouth and unzipped his own pants and pulled out his cock. With the cum from my cock coating his fingers, he jacked himself off. I got hard again very quickly and he stood up and asked me for a ruler. All we could find in the kitchen was a yardstick and he held it out and measured me.

"Eleven! Fuckin' eleven inches, man! I bet it'll be a foot when you're my age."

"No, I think I'm finished."

"Well, I'm not," he said, shaking it. "I'll be back. And let's just keep this our secret, right? Just like with your sister."

"Yeah, just like with Verna."

*

By the following Friday, I had it all worked out. He arrived just as my parents were leaving.

"Have a nice night, boys," my mother said, swinging her bowling bag.

"We will," Bruce smirked.

No sooner had the door closed than Bruce was down on his knees, unzipping my pants. "I gotta see it."

He sucked on it for about five minutes and I thought I'd come but I managed to pull away.

"What's wrong?"

I stroked my cock, teasing him with it. "I think I'd like to fuck."

"Well, who wouldn't? But your sister's moved away and we ain't found anybody else yet."

"Maybe we could fuck each other."

"You crazy, man? Guys don't fuck each other."

"Some guys do."

"Queers. We ain't queer."

"Still, I'd like to try it."

"You'd really let me?"

"Yeah, if you'd let me."

"I don't know." He stroked my cock. "That'd kill me."

"I heard tell that big ones feel better 'n little ones."

"How can that be?"

"Dunno. That's just what I heard."

"Shit, man, I just don't know."

I agreed to let him go first. And his little pecker hurt. At first it was a sharp pain, as if I was being torn apart. I gasped as he continued to poke and jab and, mercifully, he came.

He tried to weasel out of the bargain but I wouldn't let him. He said if he had to do it, he had to have a drink. I found Dad's whiskey bottle and he took some long swallows from it. By the time we got back to the living room he was staggering.

"Just sit there," I said, pointing to the center of the couch. I knelt on the floor in front of him and hoisted his legs over my shoulders.

"Oh, god," he kept moaning, over and over.

I greased it up and started in. He didn't know what hit him. The more he fought me, the harder I shoved it into him. I don't know where I found the strength to hold him down but I did.

And as I deposited my seed deep inside the boy who broke my sister, he screamed, "You're gonna kill me," and started bawling like a baby, which seemed, under the circumstances, entirely appropriate.

It Had to Be Huge

Joe Leslie

"You don't need to do this, you know. I'll give you a passing grade just on general principle."

He had dropped to his knees, unzipped my trousers and was licking the head of my prick, still semi-hard because I was fighting it. I wanted to surrender to him but I was terrified. Who would believe my story? It was his word against mine. A jury would always believe the boy. I would be ruined. Yet, I remembered, he was of legal age, even though he was still in high school, still looked as if he were 16.

"Yeah, I know, I know," he chuckled, playing with my balls. "Shit, Joe, I've known about ya for a long time."

Watching my cock grow to half-mast under his machinations, I asked, "Oh? What have you known?"

"That ya liked me. Shit, man, I caught ya lookin' at me dozens of times. Nobody's ever looked at me like you've looked at me!"

"Well, I've never seen a basket like yours before!"

"Like it, eh?"

"Oh, it'll do."

He proceeded to pull my trousers down around my ankles and then return his hands to my crotch, where he massaged my balls, then worked them over with his tongue while his hands moved eagerly over my chest.

"I guess," I sighed, "I'm not as adroit at hiding my feelings as I thought."

And with that, my cock grew to its full strength. He was immensely pleased with himself and began sucking in earnest. His zeal made up in good measure for what he lacked in technique. I suddenly wondered where he learned to do this. I wanted to know yet I didn't. I took his head in my hands and steadied it. When I was close, I cried out but he didn't pull it out in time and I ejaculated onto his cheek.

Wiping his face, he cried, "Shit, man, what a load!"

"...Sorry about that," I said handing him a washcloth.

"I'm not," he laughed.

I stood outside the door of the tiny bathroom as he finished washing his face, then stepped over to the toilet, unbuttoned his 501's and pulled out his cock. Even in the dim light, I could see it was semi-hard.

"Ever try to piss with a hard-on?" he asked.

I knew it was a cue. If I know nothing else, I know cues. After all, I write plays, mostly unproduced, except by our little workshop. But this was hardly a play. It was more like a scene in one of the X-rated movies I rented some weekends when there was no action. I remembered one scene that had two studs giving each other golden showers after some hot and heavy tearoom action, one sitting on the toilet, the other flanking him. I grew hard again just thinking about it. I stepped over to him and touched his hand, the hand holding the shaft of his cock, the cock that I knew would be huge. It had to be huge. The bulge was prodigious. What the fabric of his jeans hinted at had to be extraordinary. I took it in my hand and, feeling the heft of it, I suddenly felt ashamed, ashamed that my own dick was so puny compared to his. Randy's sex was not only long but it was also a beer bottle of a cock, so thick I feared I could never get it into my mouth. But I did. I leaned over and took it, halfway, into my throat, then maneuvered myself onto the toilet seat. He began thrusting his hips almost immediately, sending my head crashing back against the wall, and I sat there, obediently taking it, all of it. With the sweaty palms of his hands pressed against the wall, he face-fucked me so intensely that I began to choke. The more I fought him, trying to keep from gagging on it, the harder he plunged his meat into my mouth and throat. I grabbed his ass, squeezing the cheeks, hanging on as he climaxed. It was a ferocious orgasm. As Randy's sperm gushed from his cockhead, the organ slipped from my mouth, and juice rolled down my chin and splattered on my own rejuvenated sex.

After catching his breath, Randy reached down and coated my cock completely with his juice, then knelt down on the cold bathroom floor and blew me again.

*

"What, I wore ya out?" He was laughing at my elation as I lay on the bed with my eyes shut, spent but perfectly content. I had come twice. I hadn't done that in years. "I'm an old man," I mumbled.

"Old shit! You're what, thirty?"

"Thirty-five. But right now I feel ninety."

"Well, I guess I'll just have to go out and give this to somebody else."

I opened my eyes. His cock, semi-hard again, was swaying seductively above my head. He was now nude and I was shocked at how emaciated he was. His cock was enormous in proportion to the rest of him. I vowed to get him to eat properly. I ran my hand up his hairless leg and started to play with his furry balls, the big balls of a bull.

"Randy, I don't want you to ever give this thing to anyone else again without my permission!"

He laughed heartily then gleefully set his cock in motion, dancing crazily before my eyes. When he climbed over me, his knees pressed to the mattress, his hands clamped behind my head, guiding my lips to it, I felt it was time for me to set down some guidelines.

"We shouldn't be doing this, you know that."

"No, no, we shouldn't, but what the hell - "

And then he proceeded to ram his cock into my mouth. I gasped for air as I went down.

*

When I awoke the next morning, he was still cradled in my arms, almost tiny, except for the cock that somehow had lodged itself between my thighs, touching my balls. I vaguely remembered his being on top of me, dry-humping me with it, shoving it between my legs and coming again. I had been so exhausted I had practically passed out. I felt the sheet; it was still damp. I pulled away from him and went to the bathroom. When I returned, he was awake, playing with his splendid sex.

"God, doesn't it ever go down?" I asked, wrapping a towel around me.

"Not as long as it has an audience."

Seeing how extraordinarily beautiful his cock was in the day-light, I became aroused again. I sat on the bed and wedged myself between his thighs. He permitted me to stroke it, tease it, examine it thoroughly.

"God," I said in awe, "you could kill a girl with this."

"Na. None of 'em'll let me near 'em."

"That's what you get for being the baddest boy in school."

"Yeah, I got a helluva rep, ain't I?"

"Yes, and if they knew this about you — " Eagerly I kissed the shaft of his cock and worked my way up to the glistening purple head.

"Nobody knows nothin', except Ron. Ron and I, well, we taught each other stuff. That was when I first moved here, before he really discovered girls. What he sees in those cunts I'll never know, but he can't forget me. I won't let 'im."

Ron! I should have guessed. Just talking to Randy gave Ron a hard-on. I'd always wondered about the quiet ones, the ones who just stayed at their desks, never caused any trouble, what were they thinking? Imagine, I gasped, Ron was not thinking about pussy. He was thinking about the same cock I had in my hand, the magnificent one I was about to devour!

"You're cool, Joe, ya know?"

"Hmmm, I thought I was hot. Oh, and call me Mister Leslie," I teased.

"Yeah, Joe! Okay, Joe! Yeah!" he cried.

The end of my weekend with Randy touched me deeply because, when I left him a couple of blocks from where he lived with his mother, he gave me a quick buss on the cheek. "See ya in school," he said, slinging his jacket over his shoulder and trotting down the street. I sat in the car for a few moments to savor the wondrous sight of him as he disappeared from view as if he was a mirage, merely a figment of my lurid imagination.

The next day, as I was unlocking my classroom door, he suddenly appeared and reality, the reality that he indeed was not a mirage but one of my students, kicked in.

"Ya got time for a quickie?" he whispered.

"I'm afraid you'll have to wait till Friday," I said, switching on the light.

"Friday! Shit!"

I turned around and he was gone. I stepped out into the hall to see him disappearing among the students racing to get to their first period class.

I didn't see him again until the sixth period and he barely acknowledged me. I called on him twice and he was attentive and knew his lesson. He had a talent for acting, I decided.

After the bell rang, I approached him. "We're starting rehearsals for the senior plays this afternoon. Would you like to try out for it? I think you might enjoy it."

"Na, that's sissy shit," he said, grabbing his books. "But," he smiled, "thanks for the offer, ah, Mister, Mister Leslie."

*

I straddled one of the folding chairs in the gym and began listening to one of the ingenues read when I noticed Randy, barely inside the door, slouched against the wall. I let him stand there for a while, absorbing things, then called him into the group. As if we had already agreed he would play a role, I handed him the script. "You'll only have two scenes, just a couple of lines in each, but these are important roles."

He said nothing, just nodded and took the script. I had marked the scenes and had written his name across the binder. He smiled when he saw it and stepped off to the side, listening as other people read. When I dismissed them, I told Randy to stay behind.

"I thought we could just run through it together," I said, turning the pages of my own script.

"You mean we're gonna do it here, right in the gym?"

"Ha! Don't I wish."

"Hey, man, I'm not gonna be able to wait till Friday. That's why I came here. Not to be in this play or nothin', but get it on, right here."

Slamming the pages of the script together, I stepped away, fearful he would reach out to me, touch me. "I was afraid of this. I've made a terrible mistake."

He stopped abruptly. "I'm sorry," he said, his voice taking on a softness, a gentleness I had not heard before. He moved closer but I backed away again, my hands gripping the script tightly, as if I was preparing to strike him with it.

Sensing my fury, he said: "Oh, shit, I shoulda known better. I didn't want to make ya angry." He stepped away, as if about to make an exit. I waited for the line and it came, on cue: "Hey, it's cool. I'll wait'll Friday. I'm not as bad a boy as people think I am."

I couldn't haven't written the lines better and it was in that moment that I surrendered to him completely, falling, inexplicably, hopelessly in love with him. My arms ached to hold him; my lips hungered to press against his. But instead, I swallowed hard and said: "Okay. Let's go over your lines."

I instructed him in the scene and he read, very badly at first but promisingly, while I read the other part.

When we were finished I said: "You know, Randy, a person should be able to get away from life and go into a dream. That's what playwriting and acting is to me, going into a dream. When you're reading some of the great plays, when you do that, you sort of take up with the writer of those plays and something magical happens."

"Kinda like when we got together, eh?"

"Sort of. Think of it like this: if I were a musician, I'd want to be involved with Mozart. For me it was a guy named Mark Davis. He was an old playwright when I was a boy, younger than you. He had six plays produced in his lifetime. Nothing anybody remembers now but he taught me so much. I've always wanted to teach someone else everything he taught me."

"Yeah, I'll bet," he snickered.

"No, seriously, not just about sex but about everything. About life."

"So why didn't you?"

"Fear. I was afraid of becoming involved with one of my students. I mean, before now."

"Why now?"

"I can't tell you why this has happened, I just know I'm glad it did. I don't regret it."

"Shit, I don't either, Joe. And I'll never forget it neither."

"Either."

"Either! Me neither!"

"You're hopeless!"

"Yeah, you'll see just how hopeless I am - on Friday night!"

"It's a date."

*

"So, ya think ya can turn me into an actor in three months?" he asked, idly rubbing my naked chest.

"Look what you've done to me in a week! That's the least I can do for you." I held my hand over his, gently stroking the tender young flesh.

"Shit no, Joe. Ya got it all wrong."

As his head fell to my chest, I began caressing his hair, matted with sweat after our first sexual bout of the night. "Oh? How so?" I asked.

"Well, you're the one that's really done somethin'. For the first time in my life, you've made me feel really wanted."

I suddenly felt ashamed; so accustomed was I to one-night stands and going home to Mother every week I had not fully comprehended what I had initiated. In my lust for him, I had foolishly ignored the consequences.

"It works both ways, you know." I kissed the top of his head. "I want to try it again."

"But I don't want to hurt ya."

"I'm relaxed now. Very relaxed. Let's try. Please." My hand gripped his glorious erection, swelling to maximum strength with the promise of more action. He was truly amazing.

"Okay, it's your funeral," he chuckled.

I had tried on a couple of occasions to take him anally, first on my back, then doggie-style. Neither worked. I just couldn't handle the width of it. He would get it part of the way in and then, seeing I was having difficulty with it, he would go soft. But I was determined; I wanted to feel him deep in me, hard, thrusting to orgasm and, once I had, perhaps he would be willing to surrender to me. He had shown no desire for it; he seemed fixated on oral gratification. Perhaps the idea of anal sex was repugnant to him, although he did say, with a sly smile, his green eyes glittering: "I never tried that with Ron. He told me he couldn't imagine anyone being able to do it so I didn't even try it."

As I got on my knees, bending over, resting on my elbows, he prepared my asshole with grease, then coated his hard cock. Slowly, he inched it into me. The shaft was fatter near the base and when he finally had most of it in I thought I had been gorged. I bit the pillow and ran my hands up and down his flanks as he began fucking me in earnest.

"Oh, yes, Randy, yes," I cried in sublime agony. "Oh, god! Oh, god!"

It seemed he instinctively knew how to screw. I could hardly believe it was his first time, so proficient was he. "Born to fuck" was the only epithet that came to mind. He never pulled completely out until he came.

"Oh, yeah!" he cried. "Fuckin' A, man! Fuckin' A!"

He permitted his heavy teenager's load to spurt onto my balls and slide onto the bedsheet, then slid the slimy cockhead back into me. I jacked off and was pleased with myself that I had matched him, orgasm for orgasm, so far that weekend. But I could feel his erection returning and I resigned myself that it was going to be a long night.

*

Over the next few weeks, he became adventurous, wanting to screw me in every imaginable position. His favorite became my favorite and the very first sex of our weekends: As soon as we entered the room, I would lower my trousers and boxer shorts. Silently, I would kneel on the mattress at the foot of the bed, spreading my legs wide apart. He would grease me and then his cock, kneel down and begin, penetrating me slightly, then deep, deeper. It would be swift, his first orgasm of the weekend, gushing into me, filling me. Then he would roll me over, push me up into the center of the bed and fuck me wildly again as I jacked off, often cumming again himself. It seemed he could usually manage two orgasms for each of mine.

I found him to be a boy who did not know how to play games of either children or grown-ups, but he was quick to learn sexual games: how to tease and how to taunt, and, especially, how to flaunt his obvious gifts. He said he dreamed of having an older man, a man who would teach him things, a friend, a real friend who could understand him and whom he could understand. He said he had found that with me and, again, I felt ashamed, ashamed because of the terrible passion I had for him. I loved him, true, but my concern was selfish, I had only lustful thoughts. I could never get enough of him and his magnificent cock.

Billy Couldn't Believe It

Michael Taylor

Billy found himself in Times Square again, seeking out Vinny, driven by the urgent need to kill his pain by practiced means. Vinny would know where he could go.

"Hey-aye! Been a while!" Vinny was delighted by the surprise. "Where in hell have you been, Billy my boy?" He abandoned his task of re-stacking a pile of *Playboys* at the side of the newsstand.

"Away. Far away," Billy said evasively.

"That far, aye? Well, looks like you're back. And you're lookin' better'n ever, Billy Boy."

"I ain't feelin' better'n ever, Vinny." Billy looked seriously into Vinny's familiar old face and whispered confidentially, "I gotta get off, man." Vinny looked away, scratching at the stubble on his chin. He took the butt of the cigar from his mouth and looked Billy hard in the eyes.

"That bad, huh?" Billy nodded and shuffled his feet. "Ya don't need that junk, kid, ya know that." Billy nodded. "You're all cleaned up now... look at'cha, I never seen ya lookin' so good."

"Vinny. I need it, man." His deep blue eyes pleaded, working on Vinny as he'd always been able to. "Where's the action now?"

Vinny relented, scribbling a number on a scrap of paper. "Sammy. Tell him Vinny said you're cool."

"Thanks, Vinny," Billy said, already hopping away, "I knew you could help me."

"Sure," Vinny muttered, shaking his head. "Anytime, kid."

After calling Sammy from the nearest pay phone, Billy hurried to the address he was given. The apartment was at the top of a dim, narrow staircase. As he knocked on the door, Billy grimaced at the stench of urine in the hallway littered with trash.

"You Billy?" Sammy asked. Billy nodded, forcing a smile. Sammy slid the chain in its track on the door and let the boy in. "I didn't know Vinny knew any cute kids." He grinned with satisfaction as he looked Billy over.

"Only one," Billy quipped. Sammy was certainly right about that, Billy thought, if this guy was any indication of the other boys

Vinny knew. Billy guessed Sammy to be in his early 20's, scrawny, with a pock-marked face and greasy, slicked-back hair.

"You trick?" Sammy asked, his eyes riveted on Billy's crotch.

"Not today, man. I got cash."

Sammy shook his head. "You got thirty? That's what it's gonna cost ya."

"I got it. And for thirty you gotta hit me." Sammy nodded and Billy followed him to a table near a window and sat in one of the three mismatched chairs.

Sammy pulled the window shade, plunging the room into near darkness. "Thirty." Billy pulled a wad of bills from his jeans pocket and dropped them on the table. "And now you're broke, huh?"

"No," Billy said.

"Sure you are, kid. Why don't you just hang on to your money and pay me in another way?" He caressed the smoothness of Billy's cheek.

"No." Billy eased his head back from Sammy's reach. Sammy shrugged his shoulders and sat in a chair opposite Billy.

He pulled a tiny white packet from his shirt pocket and slid it across the table. Billy picked it up, smelled it, and took a taste on his finger while Sammy stuffed the bills into the pocket of his slacks. He walked across the room, returning with a disposable syringe sealed in a plastic wrapper which he placed on the table along with a brown rubber tourniquet, a stub of a candle in an ashtray, and a tarnished spoon. As he prepared the dose, Billy rolled up his sleeve. Sammy glanced at the boy's arm and read his scars like a palm reader. "Been away from it awhile, eh?" Billy nodded and wrapped his bicep with the strip of rubber. He focused on the bubbling white formula cooking over the flame and then examined his arm, touching a vein.

When Sammy was ready, he pulled Billy's arm across the table. The tip of the needle slid into the vein effortlessly. Billy felt nothing prick him. He stared at the one tiny drop of blood being drawn up into the syringe and then pushed back into him, followed by the liquid. The taste immediately shot through his mouth and a rush went from his head through his body and then back up again in one hot flash. The drug began to flow through his veins, numbing him. His head became fogged, his limbs heavy.

Sammy stood and the squeak of the chair across the dirty linoleum floor reverberated in Billy's ears. Sammy put his arms around Billy and led him to the couch near the door, laying him on it, placing his head on the cushioned couch arm. One of Billy's heavy arms slid from his side, his hand coming to rest on the floor.

"Mmmm, you are a pretty one, all right," Sammy said, kneeling beside the couch. "Especially this..." his fingers traced the outline of the bulge in Billy's jeans.

"No," Billy said groggily, his words hardly formed, his tongue so thickened by the drug. "Leave me alone." He tried to roll away.

But Sammy rolled him back and unbuttoned his shirt. His hands began working over the hard, hairless chest. Soon his lips were licking the flesh, working their way to the nipples. As he began chewing on them, Billy tried to push him away but he had no strength. Sammy just chuckled and continued with what he was doing, tugging at the zipper of Billy's jeans. Billy struggled to raise his legs in an attempt to kick his attacker, but he was powerless, his own body not at his command. The zipper was lowered and Sammy's hand fumbled with Billy's limp sex as he left drool along Billy's pecs, licking and sucking the skin of the boy's throat, chest and shoulders. The scene in which Billy found himself helpless was making him sick. The sweet smell of the pomade in Sammy's greased hair assaulted Billy's nostrils. And Billy couldn't control it, he wretched, covering Sammy with it. Sammy jumped to his feet, screaming curses at his visitor, and the blows to Billy's head did not stop for several minutes.

*

"You always been some kinda trouble," Vinny said, turning the shower on full blast. Billy woke with a start as the cold water came cascading over his naked body. He screamed and jumped up from the big old white bathtub. Vinny chuckled and pushed him back down. "Gotta getcha cleaned up there, Billy Boy. You're one dirty little fella. Dirty, alright." The water became warm and Vinny started scrubbing the boy with a bar of soap. Billy pulled the soap from Vinny's hand to wash himself without his help.

"Where the hell am I?"

"My place." Billy squinted up at Vinny, recalling the events leading him to Vinny's bathtub. "I didn't know what else to do witcha, after Sammy come an' dump ya right down on my newsstand. He was pissed as all hell."

"*He* was pissed..." Billy's anger overrode his agony.

"Well shit, ya puked all over him."

"He shoulda just left me alone. I *gave* him his fuckin' money."

"You too good for the likes a' Sammy, I see. Acquired some pretty high standards since ya been away, aye Billy Boy?" Vinny said, leaving the room.

Billy ignored him, now enjoying the bath, soaping, scrubbing, massaging. As he cleansed his cock, he realized Vinny had gotten him naked and put him there. He wondered about Vinny. He was friendly with the street kids but always talked about his wife who died years ago, and his daughter who lived in the Bronx. No, Billy decided, Vinny couldn't care less.

Vinny returned to the bathroom with a fluffy bathrobe. "Wrap yourself in this, Prince Charming," he chuckled, draping the robe on the toilet seat, along with a towel. "We'll see if we can find ya somethin' to eat. 'Fraid I'm all out a caviar and champagne, though. Looks like you'll have to make do with ham 'n' cheese and a beer."

Billy stared at him blankly. "Yeah," he said, "fine." Vinny shook his head and closed the door behind him.

Slipping on the robe, three sizes too big for him, Billy saw his reflection in the mirror. Sammy had been quite thorough with him; he'd have a couple of shiners by morning. His street career was over for a few days at least. He was furious, but all he could do was cry.

*

While Billy nibbled at his sandwich and sipped his beer, Vinny pulled the mattress from the sofa in the living room. "I'll sack out here. You can have my room. Least I can do for a prince."

"What's with the prince shit?"

"You," Vinny said with a smile, "you got class, kid. Nothin' but the best for Billy Boy." Billy puzzled over Vinny. "Too classy for Sammy."

" 'Cause I didn't do him?"

"He said you insisted on payin' cash instead." He fluffed the pillows and mumbled as he shook his head, "just don't understand ya sometimes, kid. Might not a gotten your face all smashed up..."

"He was gross, Vinny. I didn't want to do him, okay?" Billy snapped at him.

Vinny sat on the edge of the bed smiling at Billy's angry young face. "I kinda like that," he said, "you not goin' for just anyone who comes along."

As Billy finished his beer, it was as if he was seeing Vinny for the first time. Vinny had always been like a fixture on that street corner, always there to shoot the breeze between johns, either bundled up against the chilled winds of the New York winters, or in Hawaiian shirts and baggy slacks each sticky summer. Now Billy found himself sitting in Vinny's home, watching the man prepare for bed, wearing only his boxer shorts. Billy could see, although heavyset, Vinny was very strong, he'd probably been a jock in school, and his belly and legs were covered with spidery black hair. Yeah, Billy thought, he'd been with tricks that were older and a whole lot uglier. Besides, there was something about Vinny that always drew him back to the newsstand. A twinkle in his eye, a long funny story about the old days in Sicily, and if he was ever short, Vinny was good for it.

Billy looked around the apartment. It was cozy, stuffed, as if Vinny had moved from a ten-room house to these two little rooms. Suddenly, Billy felt at home. His belly was full, he was clean, he was warm. And Vinny was getting ready for bed. "I'll just watch a little TV, it'll put me to sleep in a hurry," Vinny said, slipping between the sheets. "You make yourself at home in the bedroom, kid."
Billy walked over to the couch and smiled down at his host. "Thanks, Vinny. I can always count on you." He brought his hands to his hips in a movement that caused the robe to part, exposing his body, the sex he was so proud of. "How come you're so good to me?"
" 'Cause you're such a cute little bugger," Vinny said. " 'Least you were before ya puked all over Sammy. Now look atcha." He shook his head and turned his attention back to the TV at the end of the bed. "Go to bed, Billy. You're in need of your beauty sleep."
Billy smiled. "If anyone needs beauty sleep it's you." And he ran to the bedroom and shut the door.
"Ungrateful little shit!" Vinny called after him.

Billy sat on the edge of the unmade bed. Vinny's room was a mess, the poor man needed a maid. Billy decided he'd have to make the bed before he could sleep in it. He picked up the clothes he found lying about the room and gathered and stacked the newspapers and magazines neatly. If Vinny kept his newsstand this messy, he thought, he'd never sell a single magazine. When he was finished, he was immensely pleased with himself, and he wanted to show off his accomplishment to his host. He returned to the living room, the TV was still on, but Vinny was already fast asleep. Oh well, he thought, he'd show him in the morning. Billy picked up the remote control to turn off the TV and go to bed, but lowered himself to sit gently at the edge of the bed, mesmerized by the picture. An old Tarzan movie was on, and Billy loved Johnny Weissmueller; he became horny just watching him. Now that was a man, he thought, and his cock sprang to attention.

Vinny stirred and his foot bumped Billy's butt. Billy turned his attention from the screen and leaned back on the mattress. Vinny had twisted the sheet off his body and Billy could see his pubic hair pushing out from the gap in his boxer shorts. His horniness got the best of him; he wanted to get off but he didn't want to get off alone. He wanted to suck on a dick while he jacked himself off, and since Johnny Weissmueller was just a phantom on the screen, Vinny would have to do. Besides, nobody in New York had been as nice to him as Vinny.

Billy popped the top snap of the boxers and peeled the fabric away. Slowly, gently, he slid his fingers in. A swift yank and the cock was free. Vinny stirred again and Billy quickly clamped his mouth on it and began sucking.

"What the fuck?" Vinny mumbled. Billy's nose was buried in the clump of dark pubic hair, his tongue swirling around the head, then the shaft of the prick as it hardened. Vinny started to push the boy away but stopped himself. What the boy was doing felt so good that he relaxed and closed his eyes, deciding to just lie back and enjoy it.

Suddenly Billy had a mouthful. He pulled the cock from his mouth and stared at it. It seemed Vinny went from four inches soft to eight or nine hard and still growing. Billy couldn't believe it. When Vinny was erect, the foreskin seemed to disappear and Billy slid it back and forth, holding the cock, admiring it. He'd sucked many a penis throughout his career, but Vinny's was easily one of the biggest and most perfect he'd ever seen; his own paled by comparison. Big veins snaked along the sides and across the broad back of the shaft. He wrapped both of his hands around it and touched the glistening knob with his tongue. Vinny was starting to leak. Billy took a deep breath and eagerly took it back into his mouth and nursed it, Vinny groaned softly. Billy forgot all about his own erection, wanting nothing more than to bring this glorious thing off. Using every little trick he had learned on the streets, he had Vinny groaning in ecstasy in no time. When he felt the explosion was near, he withdrew the mighty cock and sucked the ballsack. Vinny's come spewed all over his face but he kept sucking, chewing, driving Vinny crazy.

Finally Vinny pulled Billy up by a shank of his long brown hair and chuckled, "Now look at whatcha gone and done. You gonna have ta take a bath all over again."

Billy smiled, "Only if you take it with me."

"In a minute," Vinny sighed, closing his eyes and pushing Billy's head back down into his crotch again.

The Delivery

John Patrick

The storm clouds had been building up all day and by evening we were having a thundergust typical of Florida in mid-summer, the kind of place where even the weather overdoes it. I decided to stay in, order some chicken. A few minutes later, I heard a car door slam, footsteps, a yell, then a dull thud. I opened the front door and there he was, lying face down in the courtyard, the bucket of chicken soaked and smashed on the threshold.

"Oh my god," I cried, stepping out and helping him to his feet.

"Shit," he sputtered. "I'm sorry."

"I'm the one who's sorry. It's those bricks; they're very slippery when it rains like this." I stepped back. "Are you hurt?"

"I don't think so, but my pants —" His khakis were soaked and filthy. "And I've got a date tonight."

"Come in — "

"Oh, god, the chicken!" He stepped over the bucket.

"Forget it."

"No, I'll go back and get you another bucket."

"No, no. I'm really not hungry. I'm more concerned about you."

Concerned was putting it mildly. A month before, after a long day at the office, I had ordered chicken and this new boy, Denny, a dark-haired collegiate-type with a huge basket, had delivered it. From then on, I ordered a bucket at every opportunity, hoping he would deliver it. Each time, I made him wait while I found change. I offered him a Coke. I gave him a big tip. But he resisted me. He always had more deliveries to make. One night, he told me he worked until ten. Tonight I called at 9:15.

Now this.

"Shit," he said, standing in the middle of the living room, rubbing his thighs. "I've really fucked up. I'm sorry."

"No, no. It's my fault. I'll tell you what - why don't you slip out of those pants and I'll throw them in the wash. That way you won't have to go home and change for your date."

His frown twisted into a slight smile. "No, I don't think that'd be a very good idea."

"Don't be silly. Here, you can change in the bathroom and slip into my robe."

I stood at the entrance to the hallway, beckoning him.

"Look, I'm not stupid. I know that you —" He hesitated, shuffled his feet.

"That I what?"

"Let's put it this way, that you like me."

"How could you tell?"

"I've been around," he smirked.

"Well, liking you has nothing to do with your pants —"

I couldn't keep a straight face. "Well, maybe a little."

He chuckled and shook his head. His hands slid down the soggy trousers, stretching the fabric so that his crotch was prominently displayed. "Yeah, I've gotta get outta these wet pants."

"My sentiments exactly."

He grinned and followed me to the bathroom. I handed him the robe and closed the door behind him. In moments, he was back in the living room, bundled in my robe, which was a size too big. He had left his baseball cap in the bathroom and his long hair cascaded over his face, making him appear younger and more adorable than ever. His eyelashes fluttering with embarrassment, he handed me the pants.

"Hurry, okay?"

"Right."

When I returned to the living room, he was reclining on the couch with his hands behind his head, watching "Days of Thunder" on cable. "I like this movie. Seen it a dozen times," he said.

"I don't care for the movie but I like Tom Cruise. You kind of look like him," I said, lowering myself to the couch beside his feet. "Same nice smile."

"Don't I wish."

"You do. Except you show more."

"Show more?"

"Well, you know, where it counts."

"Oh, where's that?" He moved slightly, permitting the robe to part right where I wanted it to. I caught the sight of the head of his cock peeking out. He saw where my eyes were as I turned towards him and leaned back against his feet. He brought his hand to the edge of the robe and pulled it back a bit more, then more, until I was staring at the thickest cock I had ever seen. As it lay limp against his thigh, it was not exceedingly long but the circumference thrilled me.

He chuckled. "You're an okay dude, ya know?"

"Think so?"

"Yeah, you know how to treat people right. I could tell right off."

"I try," I mumbled, my hand drifting down towards the object of my desire. It had a pronounced upward curve and, when he tweaked it, it grew harder.

"Yeah, you sure do try, I've gotta give ya that. Every time I delivered here, you tried everything you could to get me to stay."

His cock began to thump and seemed to rise of its own accord to meet my fingers. I caressed the shaft gently, then worked my way to the head. I could barely fit my hand around it. The balls were full, round, and I stroked them. He wriggled his hips so that he was lying flat on the sofa. I moved to the floor, positioning my head at his crotch. He leaned into me and guided his cock towards my lips. As big as it was, I managed to get my mouth around it. His hand went to the top of my head and steadied me as he rammed his hard sex into me. Attacking my mouth furiously, he cried, "Oh, yeah, suck that dick."

His cock began to throb, pulsating wildly. I took it as deep as I could and held the base with my hand. My other hand clutched the robe and held on. Then, with the sounds of Tom Cruise roaring around the racetrack in the background, Denny came in a thunderous orgasm. As he bucked and reared in ecstasy, I pulled back and brought the robe up to the heart of the action, catching most of his load on it.

"Oh, yeah," I moaned.

"Wow," he panted as I pressed the cock tightly, squeezing every drop of juice from it.

Unwilling to give up the prize, I went down on him again and, as "Days of Thunder" was reaching its inevitable climax on the tube, I reached my own with the delivery boy's splendid sex deep down my throat.

Later, when he came back into the living room wearing the khakis fresh from the dryer, I smiled, and handing him a twenty, I said, "That chicken was delicious." And I smacked my lips.

Grinning, he just shook his head, stuffed the bill into his pocket and, as he raced from the front door to the car, there was a thunderclap so loud it shook the house.

Angel In The Flesh

Alfredo Villanueva-Collado

Yesterday, today, or perhaps tomorrow, I have put on Raimundo's clothing, those tight jeans full of holes, hugging my ass and thighs, making me look thinner, perhaps more desirable, and the yellow shirt he received in the mail for having given his father a grandson. I have chosen Adrian's walk and Paolo's expression and gone out into the street with my eyes wide open and my gaze suggesting things to men who go by without dreaming.

Looking is all important in this game, to perceive peripheries, move your eyes up and down quickly from the crotch to the face and back to the crotch, stopping by a thick hairy arm or an archangel's lips, on a body moving towards who knows what zone of boredom and pain. It always hurts to know that it is already late, that no watch will stop so that the other may turn around, so that I may signal to him, so that we may find a doorsill, an alley where we may crush each other and make each other come in just a few moments. The advantage of being a man is to be able to fuck and piss standing up and anywhere, then pull up your zipper and walk away, with a certain swing, a certain thrust to the knee and the hip indicating a degree of satisfaction, but never fullness.

With popper in my pocket and a couple of joints, I move slowly towards the bus that will take to the movie house where other players await. I sit by a window to amuse myself watching Turks and Colombians selling junk on the streets and in stores, the multicolored crowd streaming in and out of shops where everything can be acquired at a discount, everything but what I want to buy. Each one has it, shows it, hides it, touches it, loosens it.

The movie house is packed. I feel a cold sweat sensing that with so many surely there is one, perhaps a married man with a family, who might feel the need to calm the itching that nothing calms by the simple operation which he will perform before the screen where he looks at his own fantasy. When the man comes atop the woman, he will feel as if he himself had been the recipient of the scarlet caress and will drip with joy, his orgasm coinciding with the actor's, without realizing that he has come responding to a male's coming, that the female could very well have been a young man or a piece of melon, the important thing being to penetrate and to share in the outward flow, to soak.

I stay on the ground floor, getting used to the dark. Many already have their hands inside the pockets of their pants. Some cover their faces with their hands, some chain smoke, some let their hands rest against their seats. There are those who remain like that for hours, rejecting, some indignantly, any proposition. I have heard many of those, the same ones I heard when I was ten, pursuing me when school let out or, when I was fifteen, the slap in the face from the man whom I had just jerked off. But today it does not matter for I have Adrian's face, and I move with a great cat's grace, studying each one sitting against the wall, careful not to lose my balance and fall into whirlpools of sea urchins.

I move to the balcony, sit in the back. An enormously fat man jerks off looking at me. Raimundo, Adrian or Paolo would not go near him but I am going to play with his toy. I throw myself at his knees, an appropriately devout gesture, and I humiliate myself pantingly, thinking this-is-what-I-am, we-all-do-this. I smell the nitrate, try not to think. Its flame possesses me, I accelerate my rhythm and the fat man pushes me away. Not yet, he says. I have just come in, he says. I get up, straighten my pants. I wish to withdraw gracefully but I stumble, and he extends one hand and helps me out. I do not look at his face. As I turn my back to him, I get lost among the bodies glued to the back wall waiting.

There are those who hunt motionless and there are those who roam. I belong more to the second than the first category, and the game often does not work. I get tired, bored, tell myself I must get my money's worth, two shots at a dollar fifty each. There is nothing so cheap in the shops on Fourteenth Street. Any of the Colombians or Palestinians would be worth more, perhaps a knife thrust.

Discouraged, I sit in the middle of a row, away from the corners already occupied. I smoke, rest a bit. I look at the movie. Poor whores with their jungle red lips, with their long nails, dressed only in bracelets and earrings. Nobody pays any attention to them. Suddenly, one makes me sit up. She takes her labia and ties them into a knot. This I have not seen before. It looks difficult, like a guy giving himself a blowjob. Abruptly, I realize I am still in the same place, the circus. I am still at the circus.

To my right, a slender dude. Closely cropped hair. Intense, dark gaze.

In front of him, a line of black men, some drunk, with huge blood sausages dangling from their flies. Grass turns me into a philosopher and I think it is just for them to be done by a white. But even when giving them pleasure, he is using them, as they were used on the plantations. As every Tom, Dick and Harry uses them. White is not less white for sucking black cock. Black sperm does not stain black. Black sweat does not absolve from guilt.

The whites play with the men in the line, one after the other. No one comes.

One face begins to interest me. Handsome. He is in seventh heaven. Stretched on his seat, pulled back, eyes closed, his body undulating with the rhythm of the sucking. Happily, he has reduced the game to its components. I stare at him. He pushes the cocksucker away and returns my stare. Come play with me, he seems to say.

He pulls his pants completely down. I do the same. I take the nitrate, give him some. Neither of us seems to be in a hurry. I begin to caress him. He relaxes. Another player draws near. I look up and there he is, already attached, his cock in my man's mouth. I replicate his rhythm. I begin to open up, once in a while I surface, gulp for air. My man opens his eyes and looks at me, a mouthful of smiles. I begin to experiment, bite his hard stomach, spit on him, jerk him off with both hands. He no longer does anything with anyone else; rigidly arched, he surrenders completely, begins to whimper, low, then high. I don't even touch myself but begin to feel myself straining to shoot, a furious pounding beginning in my temples. He howls repeatedly, comes in great spurts, squeezing his thighs. I take the huge cock back into my mouth and continue. He laughs. Everyone is looking at us. As I suck, lick, love, he says, "A man after my own taste." Laughter bounces, distracts, angers, hurts. But we don't care.

Ceremoniously, I clean him with my handkerchief and we put on our clothing. "Well done," he says. I move my head affirmatively, look at him one last time. He does not seem that attractive now; he seems older, used and, perhaps, in a year he will be dead. Like me. Like the others.

Big Top Men

Donald Vining

Serving the circus folks in their commissary, Hank concluded, wasn't all that much harder than waiting tables at the Central Cafe back home, which he had done for almost a year before he tangled with the law. Even though the employees and performers ate in two shifts, the commissary tent had to be a lot larger than the cafe. And as the newest employee, Hank had been given the tables farthest from the kitchen tent, but he didn't mind the extra legwork. He was, after all, young and healthy and lucky not to be behind bars.

Hank would have preferred to serve some tables of roustabouts, those muscular types who set up and took down the tents at each city on the circus' tour, or the tables where the daring young men on the flying trapeze sat, rather than those who were in the side show. Still, the sideshow people were interesting, certainly not the sort of persons one ran into at home.

It was perhaps, after all, a lucky day when the police found him going down on that man in the men's room of the station. The john in the john had turned out to be an advance man for the circus, in town to place ads in the paper and put up three-sheet posters on billboards for the coming extravaganza. He had the glib tongue to convince the judge that Hank had seduced him, horny after weeks away from his wife, and to make it plain he'd be leaving town the next day anyway to ballyhoo the circus at its next stop. For Hank, known in the town, it had been more embarrassing and difficult, with the vice squad snickering as they testified.

"Oh, he was going at it," one said to the judge. "His head was bobbing and he was having a ball."

"Having two," the other policeman said with a leer, "Had 'em both in his mouth when I pulled open the door of the booth."

"You said a mouthful," agreed the first cop. The policemen could have been trying out to be clowns with the circus, Hank thought, but he couldn't deny any of it. The publicity man had great pendulous balls which he'd pulled from his pants along with his cock while enticing the easily enticed Hank as they stood side by side at the urinal. It was the balls as much as the cock which made

Hank easy to lure into one of the booths. He often cruised the men's room at the station and had scored with commuters returning late from the city to wives they were in no hurry to come home to. But he had never come across any man with balls to equal those of the circus flack. What a pity he'd always be out in advance of the troupe so that Hank was denied a return engagement, uninterrupted by cops who should have more important things to do.

After the judge ordered Hank to serve time or get out of town, he faced a quandary because he had little saved to finance a move. It was the advance man, as they left the courtroom, who tipped him off that he should apply for work with the circus when it arrived. Perhaps he felt guilty for having blamed Hank as the aggressor. People were always finding the work too hard or the constant traveling tiresome, he said, and would quit, leaving the circus short-handed.

As it turned out, Hank's experience as a waiter was just what the circus employment office wanted.

Leaving home didn't bother Hank. His aunt and uncle had always rather begrudged having to bring him up after his parents died. Besides, the town was in deep doldrums. Factory after factory had closed and there was a limit to how many could successfully be turned into shopping malls if nobody had work and money to spend. Life with circus, on the other hand, Hank reasoned, promised to be lively.

Hank was astonished at how little the five hundred and fifty-five-pound Miss Dotty Dainty ate and the way Elijah the Living Skeleton wolfed down his meals. Why she didn't get thin and he get fat Hank couldn't understand. He liked the buzz of high-pitched sound at the table where the midgets and dwarfs ate. They had their own table; as if, they'd have been disadvantaged by the boarding-house reach of the longer-armed. They didn't seem an unhappy lot despite the bad deal some might think they'd gotten out of life. Hank guessed they felt lucky to have work in the side show and as clowns, just as he felt lucky to have his job in the commissary.

If he didn't get to wait on any of the many male beauties in the troupe, the top men of the big top, at least his path from the kitchen tent to his assigned tables took him past some of them, including the German lion tamer. As he passed, Hank could see the roots of the great mane of blond hair -meant to match those of the lions, were dark, but what of that? A lot of circus was just glitz. The guy's name wasn't really Leo Felix either, but Klaus Fuchs, which the well-named Randy Mann loved to pronounce Fucks. Even without his tight-fitting gold performing outfit, Leo-Klaus was quite a spectacle. The specialty of his act was the moment he put his head in the lion's mouth and Hank dreamed of the way when the great Leo might put his smaller head in Hank's mouth.

By the time the noon meal was cleared away and the trestle tables set up for dinner, Hank was as tired as he'd ever been. He retreated to his bunk in one of the dormitory tents to recoup some of his energies before the whole process of feeding the troupe began again after the matinee. He didn't realize he'd closed his eyes and dozed off until an oily voice penetrated his consciousness. Opening his eyes reluctantly, for he had been dreaming the lions had torn Leo's clothes off, leaving him naked in the center ring, Hank saw Randy Mann, his only obnoxious teammate, standing at the foot of his bed almost drooling at the sight of Hank's tight young ass.

It didn't take Randy long to zero in on Hank but Hank wasn't interested. There were perhaps two dozen men in the troupe for whom he'd have performed any sex act known to man but Randy was not one of them. Somehow he reminded Hank of the hyena in the menagerie. Randy wasn't the type to be easily discouraged, however. Every time he got Hank alone, the talk turned to sex, with Randy hoping to raise Hank's temperature to a point where he'd succumb.

"You resting? I thought maybe you'd like to meet some of the more interesting members of the company. A bumpkin like you can use a little guidance and I can provide it."

"I'd like to meet Leo."

"Mr. Fucks? He's probably busy teaching his lions new tricks. Or if not, he's tied up with Gino, from the Italian tumbling troupe. They've been quite a pair the last few months, although I've heard he's getting tired of Gino's jealous scenes. He even gets jealous of Leo's female fans."

"But that tumbler's so small," Hank said, wrinkling his nose.

"Not where it counts, baby. When he gets that thing hard, we could use if for the center pole of the main tent!"

"I've heard that small men - "

"On the other hand, you know Rollo the Giant? Nothing! Just nothing! You have to go looking for it in his bush and then you're not sure it isn't just a pimple!"

"Poor shit."

"So he rolls over. Rollo the Rollover we call him. Of ass, he's got plenty."

"So Leo goes for big cock?"

"Doesn't everyone?" Randy leered. "Although the dwarfs and the midgets have their admirers, too. One thing you learn in the circus, kid, is that no matter what sort of deck Mother Nature dealt you in the way of a body, she also saw to it that it has its fans. Even Miss Dainty. Would you believe that one of the dog trainers thinks she's the most?"

"The most is a good way to put it - five hundred and fifty-five pounds!"

"He's crazy about her. And he's a little guy, hardly bigger than her left tit."

"I'm glad for her. She seems very nice, and smart, always reading."

"Then they're the midgets. Now Tiny Tom is really a good-looking man but I mean he is little. But Vivienne the Equestrienne thinks it's just too adorable the way his pretty little mouth comes just to the level of her cunt."

"You seem to know all about everybody's sex life."

"I make it my business. Now for instance, the contortionist. You may have seen what he can do in the side show but he can do things we dare not show in public. That man can not only bend over and suck himself off, which a lot of us have tried with limited success, but he can put his head down between his legs and come up behind himself to rim his own ass!"

"I'd just as soon not see that!"

"Oh, we've got some extraordinary people with this company." "Now, if we only dared show it in the sideshow, we've got what has to be the biggest cock in the world on one of our roustabouts. Practically as big as an elephant's trunk!"

"Now you're exaggerating."

"Not much. Women have fainted at the sight of it. Couple of guys, too. And foreskin! That guy has so much foreskin you could dock a transatlantic liner in there and still have room for a tugboat!"

Hank laughed and said, "I think I'll go for walk and get some air after that."

"Getting a bit hot and bothered?" Randy asked hopefully,

stroking his crotch.

"Just bothered, not hot," Hank said, leaving the tent.

Randy, however, was not so easily shaken off. He fell in step with Hank. "Someday I'll get our tattooed man to take off the briefs he has to wear in his act. Underneath are really dirty pictures. For one thing, there's this snake that's made to look as if it's crawling right into his asshole."

"Thanks but that's enough of this kinky shit. Leo's more my type."

Randy snorted. "Oh, nothing but the best for the new boy, eh? Well, you talk about kinky, Leo's right in there with the kinkiest. You tangle with him, you gotta tangle with Simba too."

"Simba?"

"His oldest lion."

"I don't want to hear any more."

No doubt Randy's story wasn't true, but Hank didn't think he had the courage to run the risk. He would have to forget Leo and turn his attention to less glowing stars, though he had seen nobody who even approached the magnificence of the lion tamer.

Without the dream of making it with Leo to sustain him, Hank soon found it had been an illusion to think he'd see a wider world once he left town with the big top. What with serving three meals a day in two shifts and cleaning up afterward, there was little time to go sightseeing. The little bit he saw of Battle Creek looked much like Toledo, which looked like Gary, Indiana. Also growing tiresome was Randy's never-ending pursuit, though he began to play the pimp more than the suitor.

"The Siamese twins have the hots for you, kid," Randy would say, "Any time you want a double-header."

"No, thanks. I'm not into freaks."

"Look, Uno and Nono can't help being joined at the hip. And they're not as freaky as Leo and his threesomes with Simba."

"You know, I don't believe what you say about Leo. Miss Dainty says he's a great guy."

"What would she know? She doesn't see that side of him."

"I suppose not."

"You did notice that Gino is temporarily out of the show?"

"No, I don't watch the show any more. I've seen it too often."

"The guy's done up in bondage. I guess Simba got moody again."

This much Hank could at least confirm. The next time he served a meal he looked over at the table where the tumbling troupe sat and Gino was indeed sporting bandages and, Hank noticed, eating standing up as though it were painful to sit. He was so busy noting that, he didn't see the excitable Rumanian tightrope walker - who was always having political arguments with his tables - jump up from the table and shake his fist at an adversary. The tray full of bowls of hot soup that Hank was carrying spilled, scalding both Hank and the tightrope walker, who were quickly dispatched to the infirmary for treatment, cursing Hank in his native Rumanian. When they arrived at the infirmary, the tightrope walker insisted on being treated first and Hank put up no argument. While he was waiting, Gino came in.

"What happened to you?" Hank asked. "Did Simba get out of hand?"

"Simba? Hell, I'm not the lion tamer, I'm a tumbler. I don't get within ten yards of a lion if I can help it. This is all the result of a nightmare."

"A nightmare?"

"I have the top bunk and in this dream I was trying out a new tumbling trick and the next thing I knew, I had fallen out of my bunk and landed on the spurs of the rodeo rider who sleeps underneath me. That woke him up and he thought somebody was trying to steal his boots so he grabbed for them and yanked those spurs right across my backside. It's all because of those clams.

"I went out for clams after the show the other night. They didn't agree with me and that caused my nightmare."

The pain of Hank's burns almost entirely disappeared when he realized Randy had been lying, that Leo indeed did not insist on a threesome with Simba. Perhaps, after all, there was a chance for him.

As he left the tent, Hank came upon Leo sitting on his bench in the commissary. The lion tamer had apparently seen the collision or heard the Rumanian's complaints and asked, "You going to be all right, kid?"

"Sure," Hank said, stopping in his tracks. "And my name is Hank."

He looked Leo squarely in the eye and noticed that he was being appraised top to toe. He paused long enough to let Leo get a good look at his trim torso and the German's gazed definitely lingered on the crotch. He winked at Leo and suspected his buns got well inspected as he walked away.

Shaking off the persistent pursuit of Randy, Hank began to spend what little free time he had hanging around the lion cages. As he expected, this led eventually to an encounter with Leo, who asked him, "You got a particular interest in lions."

"More in their tamers."

A smile crossed the blondined German's face, softening its sometime severity.

"Actually, the lions frighten me. That's why their tamers impress me."

"You're wise to be frightened of lions. I don't relax my attention a second when I am in the ring with them, much as I love them and they me."

"How did you start in the business? There are no lions in Germany."

"Of course there are, not in the Black Forest, but in zoos and circuses. But if you want the story of my life, you must give yours, and for that I think we should go to my trailer."

Hank's smile spread from ear to ear as Leo led the way. As a star attraction, he did not sleep in the tent dormitories but in an elaborate trailer. Unlocking the door, he ushered Hank in.

"You don't want to hear the story of my life, do you? I mean, it's all in the publicity and you must have read it, how I was adopted by a circus owner and..."

"Yes, I've read it," Hank said nervously.

Leo took him in his arms. "Okay, then, I think it would be more fun to do this - " And Leo kissed him, a bit paternally at first, but then with increasing passion. Hank felt his cock hardening as Leo pulled him closer and could feel a similar hardness in Leo's tight pants. With increasing intensity, they brushed their crotches together.

Soon Hank's hands were undoing the buttons on Leo's form-fitting shirt.

"I've got a scar or two on my body," Leo said.

"Your body is beautiful, scars or no scars," Hank gushed.

"Yours certainly is."

They quickly undressed and when Hank removed his shorts, his cock popped upright like one of the clown's jack-in-the-boxes.

"What a schwanz!" Leo cried.

"A what?"

"Schwanz. That's German for cock, and I'd say yours is a Superschwanz!"

"You match me inch for inch," Hank said, reaching out for it.

"Perhaps. Let's measure." And Leo stood close to him, their cocks sliding together, very well-matched, except that Leo was not circumcised, although fully erect no one would have known.

Hank dropped to his knees and, grasping Leo's heavy balls, began sucking the cock till his lips were lost in the generous outcropping of dark pubic hair. As his head bobbed up and down, savoring Leo's cock, he began to feel little flicks on his buttocks. Looking up, he saw that Leo had in his hand one of the smaller whips he used to keep the lions under control. Without viciousness he was applying it in little slaps and Hank twitched with delight. Leo stepped up the strokes and Hank began to think of him as Klaus, the star in the center ring.

"A rosy pink butt is very pretty to fuck," Leo said.

Hank ran his eager tongue down the seam of the great cock in front of his face, then flicked it at the hairy balls. He was about to take the great orbs fully in his mouth when Leo laid the whip aside, pulled Hank up and laid him across his naked lap. There was a great noisy slap on Hank's left buttock, Leo rubbed the rounded mound of flesh before delivering a similar blow to the other cheek. As Leo spanked and rubbed, spanked and rubbed, Hank began to wonder if this was not what he wanted all his life, if he hand't missed something because his father died when he was so young. He whimpered a bit because he thought he was expected to, but inside he had a glow to match the one on his ass.

Leo lifted him off his lap, laid him facedown on the cot and straddled him. Hank braced himself for the penetration by that huge cock whose entire length his mouth had explored. When it didn't immediately occur, Hank turned and saw Leo was pulling a lubed condom over the shaft, throbbing like one of the circus animals that couldn't wait to perform. Finally Hank felt it being pushed inside him, slowly at first, and then, as he relaxed, steadily faster.

As the German's body lay full on his and strong arms enveloped him to grasp at his cock, it felt so much better than the quickies in the terminal back home. Leo's tongue licked at his ear, burrowed in, and Hank's breath began to come in short gasps. Soon Leo too was gasping and Hank could feel him quivering on top of him, then being shaken by spasms as he shot his load. After the last spasm, Leo did not pull out but rolled to the side, pulling Hank's body with him, holding him close. Leo worked Hank's cock until the boy shot his load and then allowed Hank time to recover before he finally pulled out. He leaned over and kissed the boy, then said, "You must call me Klaus from now on."

"That's the way I've begun to think of you."

"We must see each other again."

"What about Gino?"

"Ha! Too tempermental and unruly." He ruffled Hank's hair and chuckled. "But you, yes, you I will be able to teach tricks I never taught him."

Hank smiled.

"And you must meet Simba. You will love Simba and he will love you."

The Monster

William Barber

As they walked through the park in the center of the Square, Jamal's strong arm brought comfort to Marty. They crossed to North Main Street and continued walking toward the hill. Jamal kept up a conversation with Marty, telling him about growing up in the Harlem projects, about how tough life was in New York City, about music and museums filled with beautiful works of art and about the opera. Jamal loved opera. Marty looked at him strangely when he told him that. Marty only knew opera from the Three Stooges, and he thought it must be as ridiculous as anything could be. But Jamal assured him it was beautiful. He told him about Madame Butterfly, and Marty listened as Jamal described how tragically Butterfly stabs herself to death at the end of the opera, singing her guts out, because Pinkerton had not been true to her.

When they got to Hill Street they began to climb. At the top of the hill stood a big old Victorian mansion that had been divided up into a rooming house. The place had once belonged to one of the richest families in town, but time and the turning of luck had brought it now to its shabby, faded grandeur. The family was all dead now except for a niece who inherited the place and rented out the rooms. All the tenants called her The Witch. She would come around and bang on your door if you were ten minutes late with the rent. Jamal made sure he was never late with the rent.

Jamal led Marty up the long cement and stone stairs that led to the house. There they climbed another long set of wooden steps that took them to the wide porch that ran all around the house. Jamal took Marty over to the banister and pointed out toward the city below them. From this vantage, they could see the entire city.

A few long blocks away, Marty could see the tree tops of the Square. Even the First National Bank Building, which was eight stories tall, was not as high as they were.

"Wow," Marty said with wonder. "That's awesome." The night twinkled with a thousand stars and a nearly full moon shown its light down on them from above.

Marty stared out into the night and tried to locate places that he knew. He could see all the way across town to where he had grown up, but he could not quite see the actual house. Everywhere below, car lights moved through the streets of the city. A light breeze made the porch a pleasant spot.

Jamal stood back and admired the beautiful young man. There was something about Marty that was appealing to him. The long ringlets of blond hair turned him on, that was for sure, but it was more than that. It was more than the peaches and cream complexion, and the tiny boyish wisp of a mustache that was hardly visible on his upper lip. It was his eyes, big and blue and so inquisitive, like a child. That was it, Marty was like a young boy, with such an innocent expression on his face as if he had yet to discover all the wonders of the world around him. Jamal felt a pang of sadness, wanting to keep this boy from ever having to know the real pain that life contained as well. He did not know yet that Marty had already experienced a great deal of life's pain. But that pain did not register in Marty's expression and that amazed Jamal. He wanted to throw his arms around the boy and hug him. It made him sad to know that Marty had to work the streets to stay alive.

Jamal led Marty around to the side of the house to a door. Inside, they climbed the stairs to the second floor and then on up to the third. There was a long hall that led to another door which Jamal opened with a key. Inside that door was another flight of stairs.

"My God!," Marty exclaimed, "do you climb this far every day?"

"Two or three times a day," Jamal answered. "That what keep my legs in such good shape," he laughed. He let Marty walk ahead of him up the last flight, and watched as Marty's pretty little melon shaped butt churned with each tread. It was a great little ass and Jamal sort of licked his lips thinking about how much he'd like to shove his dick up between those solid cheeks and take a ride. If only his dick wasn't so goddam big.

When they got to the top of the stairs, Marty couldn't believe his eyes. The apartment was one large room that once had been the ballroom of the mansion. It was a giant space, which Jamal had fixed up very nicely, a living room area on one side, a small galley kitchen in the corner, and a huge brass bed sitting in a bay window, with a view of the river and the big marble bridge that was downtown. The walls were adorned with posters from the Metropolitan Museum in New York City as well as the various operas that Jamal had been to. In the center of the room was a big white bearskin rug.

"I calls the place 'Heaven' cause it's so high up in the sky," Jamal said with a smile.

"Wow!" Marty said again. "You live like this just from hustling?" he asked.

"Shit," Jamal said. "I only hustle in the evenings. Days I work my regular job installing car stereos and alarm systems."

Marty took a good long look at Jamal. He was impressed. This handsome strong black dude really had his shit together. For the first time in years, Marty felt safe, away from the constant danger of the streets and the awful fear he'd felt when he was in jail. This was a harbor in the middle of the sky and he felt comfortable in Jamal's company.

"Less get you cleaned up," Jamal said. He went into the bathroom and began drawing a tub full of water. He came back into the room and opened a drawer. When he turned around he had a joint in his hand.

"You smoke?" he asked, lighting up. Marty smiled and took a hit. What a great smile, Jamal thought. This boy couldn't be prettier if he tried. Jamal took Marty into the bathroom and told him, "You take off your clothes and put them in this chair. I'm gonna scrub you down myseff."

The thought of having Jamal's big black soapy hands running all over his body kind of gave him a thrill. He dropped his pants in a hurry and pulled his shirt up over his head. He scrambled out of his sneakers and turned around completely naked.

"Now hop in the tub," Jamal instructed. "I'm gonna take my clothes off too so's I don't get wet when you start splashin'"

Marty climbed into the tub and sat down in the hot water. It felt terrific. He ducked his head under the water to wet his hair. When he came back up for air and wiped the water out of his eyes, he saw Jamal just unzipping his fly. As Marty watched with apprehension, Jamal began sliding his denims down his strong black legs. As they went down, Marty saw the base of Jamal's cock appear, black as pitch and wide as Marty's arm. Slowly the denims continued down, exposing more and more of the shaft until the pants came off completely and Marty was staring at the longest and blackest dick he'd ever seen. It was like a foot or more of radiator hose, perfectly shaped and hanging there between Jamal's muscular legs. The head, which swung there almost to Jamal's knee was covered in thick black foreskin.

"Jesus!" Marty exclaimed, "what do you do with that thing?"

"Juss about anything you want me to, sugar," Jamal said with a big smile. He sat down on the side of the tub and picked up a bar of soap. He scrubbed Marty's shoulders and chest and back. It felt good having Jamal wash him and Marty closed his eyes. Even with his eyes closed he kept picturing Jamal's enormous black cock. What could he ever do with that thing, he wondered. It would probably kill him if he sat on it, and surely he'd choke to death if he tried going down on it. Still, it fascinated him and he wanted to see more of it.

"Stand up," Jamal instructed, and Marty stood. He was embarrassed that his own average size dick was now standing straight up in the air and hard as a rock. Jamal smiled, and soaped it down good. He washed Marty's balls and then turned him around and soaped out his asshole good.

"You want to get real clean?" Jamal asked. Marty shrugged and watched as Jamal produced a hose that attached to the faucet. He got a jet of warm water running and then told Marty, "Bend over and hold on to the end of the tub."

Marty did as he was told, and soon he felt the rush of warm water on his asscheeks. Jamal rinsed the soap from Marty's firm little ass and slowly applied the jet of slow running water to the crack. It was a sensual feeling and Marty bent over further, spreading his legs at the same time. Jamal guided the hose to Marty's asshole and slowly began to shove it up Marty's ass an inch at a time. Marty reached back and spread his ass cheeks with both his hands. The hose slipped further in.

Jamal let the warm water fill Marty's intestines. He would need to be cleaned out good if he was going to take The Monster. When he felt Marty'd had enough water, Jamal told him to sit on the toilet and drain it out. Jamal did as he was told. When he had flushed himself out good, Marty climbed back into the tub and they repeated the process. Seeing the douche hose shoved up the sweet little butt made Jamal's tremendous penis begin to swell. Marty looked back and saw it, sticking farther out from Jamal's body than before, getting longer and fatter. Again Marty sat on the toilet and let the water drain until he was completely clean. He climbed back in the tub and Jamal soaped his ass again and rinsed him off. He pulled the plug on the tub and helped Marty step out. He dried him off with a large clean towel and then Jamal led Marty by the hand to the big brass bed.

Marty was in a dreamlike state, transfixed. They lay down on the bed side by side and began to kiss. The fat, wet sensation of Jamal's tongue filled Marty's mouth as he sucked it. Was this really him? Kissing a black guy? It felt so good and he was so hot for Jamal. Marty ran his hands through Jamal's tight kinky afro and held him tightly. Jamal's tongue continued licking his face and pushing itself between Marty's swelling lips. The giant penis began to push against Marty's belly and he reached down to grasp his hand around it. His small fingers could not get all the way around the shaft of black steel so big and heavy in his hand. Marty jacked his hand up and down on the thick flesh.

"Let me see it," Marty whispered harshly. Jamal rolled over on his back and Marty slid down beside him until his face was even with the fat head of Jamal's pulsing cock. Marty crouched there, staring in awe at The Monster. Never before had he seen anything like it, not even on a horse. It lay across Jamal's hard muscled belly and the foreskin reached all the way to Jamal's tight little nipples. Marty laid his head on Jamal's strong chest and lifted the python dick and placed it next to his eager lips. He opened his mouth and slowly took the foreskin in to suck on. Guiding it down until he had swallowed the whole head of Jamal's meat, Marty began to suck in earnest. He jacked his hand up and down on the wide shaft and kept on sucking. His whole face was full of cock and foreskin. He reached his other hand down and placed it around the column further down and jacked him now with both hands. Still, neither hand was bumping into the other, there was so much cock. Marty stared down the wide black shaft as he sucked it. It seemed to weigh about ten pounds and still seemed to be growing while Marty slurped on it, sucking the juices, chewing down on the thick foreskin.

Jamal began mumbling sweet nothings and encouraging Marty to swallow even more of his throbbing hardon. Marty got on his hands and knees and swung his body around. From that position, with Jamal's dick still firmly planted in his mouth he began to slowly crawl toward Jamal's legs. The giant shaft slid into Marty's throat and started down.

Marty kept crawling until he couldn't swallow any more. He let his throat do a milking action on the tube of flesh until he started to gag. Marty backed off and the huge slab came up out of his throat. "God!" he said, "I just can't possibly take any more of that giant down my throat." Jamal understood. There weren't too many guys who could, but there were a lot who would be willing to die trying.

"Thass okay, baby," Jamal whispered. His huge cock bounced up and down on his belly with an aching need.

"Maybe I can take it up my ass instead," Marty offered.

"Go for it," Jamal agreed.

"Have you got any lube?" Marty wanted to know. Jamal reached into a drawer beside the bed and produced a tube of K-Y. Marty took the tube and applied a big gob of it to his asshole. He pushed some up inside. Then he took the whole tube and shoved it inside his asshole and squeezed. That ought to do it, he thought. He hoped. Then he took the rest of the K-Y and massaged it all up and down the fat black shaft he was going to try to sit on. He made damn good and sure that Jamal's Monster was as lubed as he could get it. His hand slid easily up and down the slippery shaft until that little tickle in his asshole was driving him crazy again and he needed a big cock up his ass. Ever since jail, with all those black guys fucking him again and again, he had not been able to satisfy that little tickle that kept gnawing at him from inside. He knew now that it was black cock that he needed, and as much of it as he could get. And here it was, all lubed and ready and just waiting for him to use it.

Marty got up and straddled Jamal's body like a jockey mounting a stallion. Jamal pushed his enormous hardon up and Marty reached behind himself and grabbed it. He lined the puckering foreskin up against his eager asshole and wiggled it up inside. From that position he was able to pop the whole head of Jamal's dick through his tight sphincter. Marty gasped with pain for a moment but refused to remove the shaft. He took several deep breaths and twisted his little ass around until the pain began to turn to pleasure.

Marty slowly began to back down on the greasy shaft. Squatting like he was gonna take a shit, he backed himself down a little at a time. He held his grip on Jamal's column to help guide it in, and twisted his body from side to side to ease the passage. The huge cock began to fill his whole inside and still he kept sliding down, two more inches, and two more inches. He got to the point where whatever big black cocks had fucked him before, they'd never gotten past that point to where the tickle was. Marty bent his knees more and let his asshole slide down the greased pole that was skewering him. Yes! Now it was feeling good, now he was reaching the tickle! He squatted more and held his breath. He rode up and down a little to get things started. He rode it there, about halfway down and it felt so damn good up his ass. With his strong leg muscles he began to bounce up and down on the Monster, forcing it up his ass harder and harder, riding it like a cowboy chasing a buffalo. Up and down he went riding off into the sunset, up and down. He'd reached the tickle at last. Finally he'd found a guy with a dick big enough, and hard enough and, yes, black enough to satisfy him. And then he just closed his eyes and took a deep breath and impaled himself on Jamal's massive cock. He let his legs completely bend and sat right down, all the way.

The fact that Jamal's tremendous shaft of pitch black flesh did not rip Marty right in half was amazing. He ground his little hips around in circles. He yelled for half the saints in heaven to witness this miracle. He got it in and he intended to keep it there. He wiggled his ass like a duck and bounced some more. He started yelling "Fuck me! Fuck me! Fuck me!" He was out of control. If he was a jockey he had just gone from trot to gallop and still he could not get enough. Jamal hung onto the mattress and let him ride, pony, ride.

Marty felt himself erupting. His hard little dick throbbed like it was cumming, but nothing shot out. He had so much dick up his asshole that nothing could shoot out. His dick throbbed just like he was having an orgasm, but he realized that he was having that orgasm deep up inside himself somewhere, in some distant spot where the tickle had once been. His sphincter snapped and crackled all around the shaft of black steel, but still no cum came out. It was an outrageous sensation and Marty gasped for breath, hanging on to Jamal's wide chest for some control until the throbbing began to ease a little and he could catch his breath.

"Oh, baby, thass good, thass fine," Jamal cooed beneath him. "Baby take the big black dick all the way." Oh, god, Marty thought, this is the best fuck I've ever fucking had!

They rested like that for a few minutes, but still Marty refused to come up off the dick. It was in him where he wanted it and he had no intention of letting it go. So he just sat there, with the silliest grin on his sweet little face and giggled and cooed and made funny noises in his throat while Jamal smiled up at him.

For Jamal it was like having this sweet little blond angel descend from heaven in his lap. The Monster pulsed deep up inside the boy and waited for more action to start. Jamal was built to go on for hours like this, but he'd never met anyone who could take it as long and as hard as he liked to dish it out. Until Marty. Here was this gorgeous little white boy who looked like the kid who came over to mow your grass, and he got himself all the way down on your big black cock and juss can't seem to get enough. Um, um, um.

Marty began to slowly move his ass up and down. After a short rest he was ready to go again. This was Jamal's cue. The first time, that had been for Marty, just so he could get used to a real mansize penis inside him. This time, it was going to be Jamal's turn.

"This time you gonna fucked, baby," Jamal said, and Marty just closed his eyes and whispered "Yes!" Placing his big black hands on Marty's small white hips to hold him in place, Jamal rolled the white boy over on his side and came around with him. He continued around with Marty still impaled on his huge cock until his rose up on his knees and bent the boy in half like a folding lawn chair. Marty's feet spun in little circles in the air and his knees were pressed right down into his own shoulders. Jamal placed his hands in the crook behind each of Marty's knees to pin him tight and spread his legs apart. He raised himself up off the bed and began to slowly thrust his hips.

Marty was bent so far in half that his asshole was now pointing toward the ceiling with Jamal's wide black shaft still all the way inside. Jamal began to pump that asshole harder, pinning the white boy right to the bed and holding him there where he could really get at him. Marty just gave it up, he surrendered completely, throwing his arms out wide like Jesus and whispering, "Go ahead, dude, rip my ass in half."

"Yeah, I gonna rip your white ass to shreds," Jamal said harshly, picking up his cue from Marty. Then like a locomotive starting up, the wheels slowly grinding more and more as it picks up speed, Jamal's hips began the ancient labor of the fuck, pushing and pulling, thrusting the pelvis faster and faster, plunging his giant shaft in to the hilt time after time. Marty went crazy.

Marty looked down and saw the massive bulk of Jamal's black

You Should Have Seen My Father's

Leo Cardini

"That's nothing! You should see my father's!"

Those were the words that began it all, spoken with a smile and a wink by the blond, young Adonis who had just stripped off his jockstrap, revealing a cock that looked several sizes too large for him as it hung down heavily between his legs under the lush forest of his pubic hair.

I was so stunned I just sat there on the bench that ran the length of the row of men's lockers in front of me as he disappeared around the corner, towel in hand, heading for the showers.

This was last July. I was over at the Riverside Health Club, just down the street from my house in Linden, New Jersey. It was a Tuesday night around eleven o'clock, predictably deserted by that hour, which I always preferred. I mean, after a day's work, who wants to go to a crowded, noisy health club? Besides, I had learned many years ago that if there was any successful cruising to be done in a health club, it was to be done when it wasn't very crowded. Not that I ever had any success at the Riverside. I mean, the Riverside Health Club in Linden was a far cry from the health clubs in the Village, where I lived for about ten years before moving out of the City.

So there I was in the men's locker room, stripping down for a shower and evaluating my body. When I had everything off but my jockstrap, I ran my right hand across my chest, checking out the muscled, twin-mound firmness of my pecs, and the soft forest of short, black hairs that lightly covered them, before descending across the flat, taut-enough terrain of my abdomen, incapable of resisting the temptation to continue further below, slipping my hand into my jockstrap and grabbing a generous portion of soft, warm cock and balls.

Nope, not a bad body for a guy forty-ahem-something years old. And I was proud of it. You see, when I turned forty, I felt very, very old. And it really got me down. All my friends said I looked fine for my age. For my age - that made it even worse. I mean, you don't look at some young guy and say he looks fine, "for his age," now do you?

It got to the point that whenever I looked in the mirror it seemed all I ever saw was the young man I would never be again. Yes, I would never again be that teenager who lured so many of his classmates into clandestine encounters, addicted to smooth, young bodies pressed against my then equally smooth, young body, and overwhelming, uncontrollable orgasms, as only the young seem to have, when great gushes of adolescent cum spurt forcefully out at such astonishing distances as to make such activity worthy of the Olympics.

Nor would I ever again be the collegiate in a dorm room with a dorm mate who, late at night after a few beers, was willing to succumb to my desires, as long as I conveniently forgot all about it on the following day and never mentioned it again. Though there was many an occasion when this same guy would seek me out to get drunk again on the next weekend.

Yes, all of that was behind me.

Well, one day a couple of years back I decided to make the most of what I had. That was around the time I moved out of the Village and bought a house in Linden, which is just eight miles West of New York City. I joined the Riverside Health Club, I exercised regularly, I watched my diet, and, in general, became non-fanatically health-conscious. Soon, I could look in the mirror and see a noticeable improvement in my appearance. Though I might have a few gray hairs among the black, at least I still had a full head of hair, and though lines had appeared on either side of my mouth, I would always be a handsome fellow with a killer of a smile. Besides, those lines gave me "character."

But I was still fortysomething, longingly watching the youth of Linden exercising at the Riverside, or playing basketball outside the high school, or hanging out on corners dressed in sweat pants that couldn't conceal their firm butts or those spontaneous, uncontrollable hard-ons that are the curse of youth and a blessing to men with interests such as mine. And though I was driven to distraction by all those bodies I longed to touch, to kiss, and to experience in the throes of orgasm, I knew there was nothing I could do about it. But anyhow, back to that night at the Riverside. There I was, stripped down to my jockstrap, my hand assessing its contents and toying with the titillating temptation to see if I could get away with jacking off right then and there, when I was interrupted by the sudden appearance of the only other guy who'd been in the

Nautilus room at that hour.

I quickly pulled my hand out of my jockstrap and fiddled with the contents of my locker as he passed behind me, stopping at an upper locker four to the right of mine.

As he worked the combination on his lock, I glanced over at him, thanking whatever god looks after the fortunes of men like me who admire the bodies of boys like him.

I'd seen him several times before working out at the Riverside. He had blue eyes, and blond hair that obscured his neck in back, and inched down over his forehead in front; he was lean and well-muscled, the way a runner is; he was handsome, with gentle features and a fair, unblemished complexion; and his lips were full and sensual, always parted in a slight, pout, which made me ache with desire to slip my tongue in between them.

But what I couldn't help noticing whenever I saw him work out was that prominent bulge in the crotch of his spandex shorts. At first I thought it had to be stuffed, but believe me, Linden isn't the kind of town where you exercise with stuffing in your crotch, if you know what's good for you.

But as I'd watched him go through his Nautilus workout on earlier occasions, he seemed so artless and so focused on what he was doing that I felt sure whatever was there had to be real. He didn't seem like the kind of kid who'd resort to artifice.

The thought of him - that smooth-skinned, lean-muscled, fair young man with the intriguing bulge that tortured the crotch of his spandex shorts - got the cum spurting out of my cock, hot and abundant all over my chest on more than one evening before falling asleep.

He now had his locker open and went rummaging through its contents. Then he opened the lower locker, kicking off his sneakers and tossing them in.

I needed something to busy myself with - an excuse for lingering while he stripped down.

"Shit!" I said under my breath, just audible for him to overhear, as I pulled one sneaker out of my locker. The knot in my shoelace that had I cursed earlier that evening now presented me with just the pretext I needed.

I sat down on the bench, still wearing nothing but my jockstrap, and picked at the stubborn knot.

I watched out of the corner of my right eye as he peeled off his white, loose-fitting tank top. In doing so, he exposed his left armpit to my sidelong view. I saw the abundance of bristly, blond hairs damp with sweat, and I longed to inhale their pungent odor as I ran my tongue across the warm cavity of his armpit.

He dropped his limp tank top on top of his sneakers. Balancing himself with his right hand pressed against the lockers, he pulled off one sock, then the other, tossing them on top of his tank top. Oh, how I longed to bury my face in his discarded clothing and smell that wonderful blend of body sweat and foot odor, the precious byproduct of his workout that probably meant nothing at all to him, but oh so much to me.

He faced his locker again, hitched his thumbs into the hipsides of his black spandex shorts and peeled them off, his bikini-brief tanline and cream-colored asscheeks slowly coming into view. When he had the shorts down to his ankles, he sat down, pulled his feet through their legholes, and threw them on top of the pile of his other gym clothes.

My fingers were still on the knot in my shoelace, barely going through the motions of solving the problem it presented as I watched him stand up again and reach into his locker, wearing nothing but a swim-style jockstrap.

From my angled view I admired his slim waist and flat, tight abdomen. A narrow highway of short, blond hairs ran down from his chest, crossed his navel and descended into his jockstrap which sagged at the waist some several inches below his navel, pulled down by the demands of that over-burdened crotch it was privileged to serve.

He pulled a towel out his locker, turned until he was facing me, and placed it on the bench. Then, without turning back, he hitched his thumbs in the elastic waistband of his jockstrap.

I was helpless to resist staring at his crotch.

My fingers ceased their work on the knot as I watched him pull on the elastic waistband, one hand on either hip. From the angle I was sitting at, I watched as he revealed the full overgrowth of his blond pubic hair and, at last, that long, fat, cut cock, which plopped down, finally free and unencumbered, heavily between his legs. I was amazed, for he had an absolute monster of a cock, looking several sizes too large for him, as if it had drained every bit of excess from his body, enlarging itself while sculpting a lean, lightly-muscled masterpiece of a physique.

I was suddenly aware that I had abandoned my application to my shoelace. My mouth hung open in amazed interest, and the growing bulge in my jockstrap reflected my preoccupation.

I attacked my shoelace again with a desperate attempt at concealing my profound fascination, but my eyes immediately returned to his huge, soft cock in mesmerized attention.

He turned to the lockers again, tossing his discarded jockstrap onto the pile of his other just-removed gym clothes. Then, after securing the combination lock on the locker above, he turned until he was facing me again and grabbed his towel off the bench. His huge cock hung dangled just inches in front of my face as he raised his left leg, planting it on the other side of the bench, that huge prick and balls swinging like an erratic pendulum in the fork of his legs. That's when he said, "That's nothing! You should see my father's!" Then his right leg joined his left and with a smile and a wink, he headed for the showers.

His acknowledgement of my interest happened so suddenly and unexpectedly that I sat there in stunned silence. Out of habit, my right hand moved down to the elasticized pouch between my legs, slowly massaging my half-hardness.

I thought of joining him in the shower. Thank God the Riverside has a shared shower instead of those individual stalls, which might be good for jacking off, but sure as hell are frustrating for a dirty fortysomething-year-old man like me. But I knew if I did join him, I wouldn't be able to keep my eyes off him - so young, so smooth-skinned, and so well-endowed. And I would get a hard-on, of course. Which possibly he might not mind.

Alone in the locker room, considering what course of action I should take, my eyes fell on the pile of his discarded gym clothes. There they were, damp with the sweat of this young, blond man with the lean, hard body and that great big cock. Yes, there they were, thrown so carelessly together after intimate contact with him as he worked out on Nautilus equipment, his muscles straining, forcing his attire to conform to the contours of his body.

There was that cotton tank top that had felt the brush of his chest hair the stab of the tight nubs of his nipples as he went through his routine. There was that pair of black spandex shorts that strained against the contour of his butt and muscular thighs. And there was his jockstrap, that article of cotton and elastic that was privileged to mold itself around the demanding dimensions of that fat, pale-brown cock with the purplish-pink cockhead that looked like an exotic, oversized mushroom, and those two big balls that hung so heavily in his ample ballsac. Yes, there they were, unappreciative of this tantalizing intimacy, never to know how much I envied them, how willing I'd have been at that moment, in the men's locker room at the Riverside Health Club in Linden, New Jersey, at a little past eleven on a Tuesday night just before closing time, to strike up any bargain the devil would offer me, with no negotiation whatsoever, to be merely one article of his clothing for the time span of just one workout with this blue-eyed, blond-haired Pan.

His jockstrap rested on top of them, arresting my spellbound attention, inviting me, daring me. I knew no one else was in the locker room, and that Raoul, the cleaning attendant, would be in the swimming pool area at this time of night.

I slid over on the bench until I was in front of his lockers. I spread my legs apart. My cock insistently pressed against my jockstrap like it was begging me to free it from its confines so it could join in my fascination with the contents of this lower locker.

I leaned forward and picked up his jockstrap. I moved it towards my face, pressed its pouch gainst my nose and inhaled. Like a powerful aphrodisiac, its heady aroma overwhelmed me, clouding my mind with a dizzying collage of the sights, sounds and smells of countless locker rooms where an infinite number of noisy young men, full of the bravado of youth, stripped down in each other's presence, making crude jokes about sex to cover their uncertainty, bragging about their exaggerated exploits, sometimes grabbing their cock and balls to make a crude point, and punctuating their conversations by snapping towels across each other's bare asses. I felt the dampness of that small, precious area where the ass straps joined the pouch, just under his balls. I felt the ribbed elastic of the pouch press against my nose where just minutes before it had pressed against his huge cock, holding it in, imprisoning it, an envied jailer put to a difficult task.

I slowly rubbed his jockstrap across my face, inhaling its odor as I repositioned my own jockstrap down below my balls and slowly stroked my erect cock, lost in a timeless moment of perfect bliss. Then I saw out of the corner of my eye that someone was watching! He was standing there several yards away from me at the end of the row of lockers. He was still totally naked, holding his towel in one hand. What had happened to his presumed plan to shower?

I knew there was no excuse in the world that could explain away my behavior. So I lowered his jockstrap from my face and repositioned my own to cover what I could of my hard-on as I sheepishly smiled at him and waited to see how he'd react.

He returned my smile with a mischievous one of his own, like we were co-conspirators. At the same time, he absentmindedly clutched his cock, tugging it to one side.

"When I was in high school - I just graduated last June - I used to go crazy in the locker room because I really had...well, have...this thing about jockstraps. And I'd always try to be in there alone when all the other guys were taking their showers, just so I could look at their jockstraps and touch them and...well...I had all kinds of fantasies. You'd probably think I was a real crazy sex fiend if I told you about all of them."

He took a step towards me.

"And when I could get away with it, I'd steal one of their jockstraps. Yeah, I know that's wrong and kind of perverted, but it was like I just couldn't help myself. Like the jockstrap was ordering me to ignore the way my heart was beating and pick it up and slip it into my gym bag. The rest of the day in school I was scared stiff I'd be caught. I mean, could you imagine if someone discovered I'd stolen his jockstrap?"

He was now casually stroking his lengthening, impossibly long cock.

"And all the way home, I'd keep thinking about that sweaty jockstrap that wasn't mine. I'd get a hard-on and I'd have to try to think about something else so it'd go away before anyone saw it. But my mind would keep going back to that jockstrap and...well, it's a miracle none of my friends ever caught me with a hard-on."

He pointed at his jockstrap, which I was still holding.

"Rub it against your crotch, huh? Please?"

I pulled my jockstrap down below my balls again and satisfied his request.

"Oh, yeah. That's what I'd do once I got home and into my bedroom - rub it against my cock until I got nice and hard. And then...well...I hope you don't think this is strange, but what I'd do is start to fantasize about the guy's...father.

"I mean, that's what I'd always do, look at the guys in my school and dream about their fathers. You see," he confessed, "I've always had a thing about older men...like you."

With this, he sat down next to me and rested his right hand on my left thigh.

"Do you mind?" he asked a bit anxiously.

I nodded no, continuing to rub his jockstrap on my cock with slow, jackoff strokes.

"Oh, by the way, my name's Bobby," he said. "Bobby Malone."

"Bill. Bill Caroline."

He slid his hand across my inner thigh until the back of it brushed against my ballsac.

In response, his cock gave a massive twitch.

Staring at it, I couldn't help but ask, "Your father's. Is it really bigger than yours?"

"Oh, I just say that as a joke because people are always staring at my cock and it makes me feel self-conscious. Actually, my father's...not around."

The note of sadness in his voice convinced me not to sk why.

"Maybe that's why I, like older men. You know, father figures?"

"Uh-huh?"

"And I make up stories about him...like I'm looking through his bureau, examining his underwear. Then I try on one of his jockstraps, and just as I'm looking at myself in the mirror he walks in one me. He tells me I shouldn't do things like that, and so I won't forget he has me take it off and spanks me on my bare bottom. Then he makes me...well, do other things."

Did I detect a slight blush at the thought of "other things"?

I dropped his jockstrap to the floor and continued jacking myself off with long, slow strokes, sublimely sensitive to the back of his hand brushing against the steady rise and fall of my ballsac.

By now his cock was also almost fully hard. It stuck out long, thick and heavy between his legs, the sheer weight of it forcing it to hang down slightly, acknowledging defeat to the law of gravity. He wrapped his left hand around his cockshaft and began to slowly stroke it.

His eyes became heavy-lidded with pleasure and his hand resting on my thigh tightened.

"Here. Let me help you with that," I said, reaching over to wrap my free hand around his cock.

"Wait a minute. I gotta tell you something first. I've never done anything like this before. Never. I know a lot of my friends fool around with each other sometimes, but they're really straight and that's just what it is...fooling around. I was always afraid if I joined them they'd somehow notice that I liked it more than I should, or liked in the wrong way. You know? So you gotta understand, if I act like I don't know exactly what I'm doing, it's because I'm..." He gave a little laugh.

"...a virgin."

"I'd say you need an older guy to teach you the ropes."

"Yeah."

I reached over for his cock and rubbed my fingers against the underside of his fat, flaring cockhead.

"Ohhh!"

He closed his eyes, inhaled and lowered his head in ecstasy. But no sooner had he allowed himself this first indulgence in man-to-man, or rather man-to-boy sex than he suddenly straightened up again and opened his eyes.

"S'posin' someone sees us!" he whispered.

"The shower," I said, surprised at how hoarse and urgent my voice sounded. "The private one."

This was a large, tiled, shower cubicle set apart in its own recess, easily accessible to those with limited movement, and concealed by a shower curtain.

He brightened. A look of devilish anticipation came over his face.

"You slip in first," I directed.

"Yes, sir!"

He stood up, held his towel in front of his crotch in a nearly successful attempt to lose his cock in its folds, and slipped away, giving me one last, smiling look.

As I dropped his jockstrap back onto the pile of his gym clothes and grabbed my towel, I heard the sound of the shower curtain hooks screech open and close, followed by the noisy cascade of the shower water.

I made my way to the shower, concealing my own cock with my towel, and slipped in after him.

He was facing me, the shower water hitting him on the back of his neck and his shoulders, rivering down his body, a great stream of it networking down his cock, forming a huge waterfall at the tip of it and splashing loudly on the tiles below.

He extended his open arms towards me. I stepped forward and we joined in an embrace.

"You ever have a guy's tongue in your mouth?"

"No. I really am a virgin. I mean, in every which way."

And with this he closed his eyes and tightly puckered up his lips.

"Relax," I said.

"Like this?" he asked, untensing his lips.

"Um-hmh."

I pressed my lips lightly against his, feeling their warmth and softness.

I slid my tongue between his lips. He acknowledged its entrance by wrapping his arms tighter around me and melting his chest against mine.

My tongue probed inside his mouth. His tongue greeted it and they playfully sparred with each other like two familiar friends. From below, I felt his huge cock hardening again pressing stiff and heavily against my right inner thigh. My own cock had risen to its full eight inches, hard and unyielding as a rock as it curved upwards, halted in its ascension by the fork of Bobby's two legs. I shoved my ass back to create a small space between our two bodies and up it popped. Then I pressed myself against Bobby again, trapping my cock between our two lower abdomens.

He withdrew his lips from mine and whispered, "Jesus. You're so hard. Do you mind if I touch it?"

In answer, I took a step back.

He reached for my cock and wrapped his fist around it, gently squeezing it.

"Wow! And it's so warm. Can you believe it? I've never touched another guy's cock before."

Awkwardly, he began tugging at it.

Though his technique left something to be desired, I groaned at his welcome touch.

Then he got down on his knees. His face wasn't more than six inches from my cock. His open-mouthed expression was one of absolute fascination. How I wished, in my jaded middle age, that I could once again have his freshness of experience.

He reached up with his right hand and cupped my balls in his palm, like he was weighing them. My cock twitched in response, competing for his attention. Watching it close up, he said "Wow!" again to himself.

Then he stuck his tongue out and began licking the underside of my upward-curving cock with slow, tentative strokes. Every time the tip of his tongue reached my piss slit, my cock twitched, jumping up off his tongue to his obvious fascination.

Then he wrapped his lips around my cockhead and looked up at me as if to say, "Alright?"

I looked down at him, captivated by the image of this young man on his knees with the shower water hitting him on the back of the neck as he slowing stroked his cock while holding my own in his mouth and looking up at me for approval.

In response, I nodded back at him. He slowly moved his lips down along my cockshaft. His warm, moist mouth sent a wave of pleasure coursing throughout my body. But he descended no farther than maybe three or four inches down my cock when he gagged. He quickly removed his mouth from my cock, turned his head to the right and coughed several times.

I put my hands under his armpits and pulled him up until he was standing again.

"It's not that I didn't like the feeling of having you in my mouth. I just couldn't stop myself from coughing."

"You'll get used to it."

"Assuming I have someone to practice on."

"I think that can be arranged."

"I was hoping you'd offer."

And to seal the contract, we embraced again. This time, his tongue took the lead and eagerly probed between my lips.

I slid my hands down and over his nicely-rounded asscheeks, savoring their mirror-perfect proportions. Then I slipped my fingers between his asscheeks, gently pulling them apart.

He moaned as he pushed his ass outwards.

With my right forefinger, I explored the rim of his tight asshole. He removed his lips from mine and let out a low, prolonged groan. "Last winter," he said, "I bought this vibrator on Forty-Second Street, and when I'm all alone at home I play with my asshole. It really feels good. I've been practicing for the real thing, if you know what I mean. I'm all ready, condoms and all. Though I'm a little nervous about the first time. Like s'posin' it's too big for me and it hurts?"

"You need someone to massage your asshole first and get it nice and relaxed."

"You have someone in mind?"

I kissed him on the neck as I inserted the first digit of my right forefinger up his asshole. An involuntary "Ah!" escaped his lips. I carefully explored his asshole. He rested his head against my shoulder and moaned in response to my probing.

"I think I'm going to need a lot of massaging."

"That's okay, I'm very patient."

"I was hoping you'd say something like that."

I slowly removed my finger and then slapped him on the ass. "We'll get back to your butthole some other time. But for now, you just relax and let me take care of that cock of yours."

I kissed him on the throat and made a gradual descent, a slow, worshipful pilgrimage down his chest, between those two pecs with the slight forest of blond hair between them. Then I digressed to his nipples, first one, then the other, gently sucking them into my mouth and teasing his nubs with the tip of my tongue, playfully bending them like they were small rubber prongs. I eventually resumed my journey down his chest until I was traveling across the flat terrain of his abdomen, ultimately passing below his navel and reaching his pubic hair.

I got down on my knees in front of him. With my hands on his calves I indicated he should spread his legs apart. He did, looking down at me with an eager half-smile on his face.

"Now, you just relax and enjoy yourself," I told him.

"I can't believe this is finally happening to me!" he whispered, just loud enough for me to hear. "And in a shower! See, that's another one of my fantasies." He laughed.

"I guess I've always had a lot of fantasies about a lot of things."

Oh, that I could be the one to initiate him into every single one of them!

His thick, long, whopper of a cock was now fully aroused and pointed practically straight out at me just a few inches from my lips, attempting unsuccessfully to curve upwards. I opened my mouth, stuck out my tongue and licked the underside of his cockhead, just below his piss slit.

His cock squirmed like a sleepy monster.

I licked again. And again. And again...countless times until I had I had his cock bobbing up and down in front of me like, a helpless, willing slave to my fond attentions.

I looked up. He was smiling with delight at this little game.

Then I captured his cock in my mouth, trapping his fat swollen cockhead in mid-bob.

"Oh!"

Holding his cockhead in my mouth, I put my hands on his asscheeks and continued to tongue him under his piss slit. I felt his cockhead repeatedly swelling up in response.

Then I slowly descended on his cock, feeling its remarkable thickness. Soon his cockhead pressed at my throat, but there was still so much more of him to go.

I relaxed my gagging muscles and with a slight shove I got most of his cock in my mouth. But I knew that no matter how much I longed to get all of him in me and bury my nose in his pubic hairs, there was no way I'd be able to, though that sure didn't keep me from trying my damnedest.

"Oh!" again from above.

I slowly worked my mouth up and down the length of his cock, deliciously traveling every inch of it that I could fit inside my mouth.

Soon I had established a rhythm; up and down his cockshaft, one moment just his cockhead in my mouth, my tongue flitting across his cockslit, the next moment that same cockhead down my throat until I could take it in no further.

At some point, I had taken my hands off his asscheeks. My right hand played with his enormous, loose balls while I used the left to jack myself off.

Finally I felt his cock thrust forward and I knew he was tensing his ass and leg muscles in anticipation of shooting his load.

I stood up on his right, letting his cock slip out of my mouth and into my right hand, replacing my suckstrokes with jackoff strokes. His left hand reached for my own cock, grabbed it out of my grasp and tugged on it while I pulled on his.

I slid my left hand around his waist, feeling the tenseness of his body as he arched forward and finally, as a low, urgent, prolonged "Ahh!" emerged from his throat, shot out spurt after spurt of cum in huge jets that flew across the cubicle, landing in large, slowly dripping wads on the shower curtain.

I could no longer hold off my own orgasm. I felt my left leg shake uncontrollably, which it often does when I'm standing up and my cum is on the verge of spurting out. And then I felt it - wave after wave of cum, urged out of my cock by this inexperienced hand that instinctively knew just what to do when it really mattered. My breath came in short gasps as my cum joined his on the shower curtain.

When we were done, he said, "Wow! You sure shot a lot of cum. I wanted to get down on my knees and surprise you by taking your cock into my mouth at the last moment, but then I thought I'd fuck it up and make a real mess of things."

"Like I said before. You need practice."

He slipped his arm around me.

"Yes, I do. From someone older, with more experience."

I slipped my left hand into his asscrack.

"Now, about breaking in that tight little hole of yours."

"Yeah?"

"What are you doing tomorrow night?"

He wrapped his hand around my cock and leaned over to kiss me on the cheek. But before he did, he said, "Paying a visit to my...Uncle Bill, I think."

"Good boy. You think right."

*

Later, after we had dried off and dressed, he asked, "By the way, how old are you?"

"Oh...Fortysomething."

"I'm glad. But you're not going to tell me exactly how old?"

"Oh, I don't know."

He kissed me on the cheek, fondled my crotch and said, "I'll bet if we took a walk in the park down by the river right now I could get it out of you."

"I can be pretty stubborn, you know."

"Good! Let's go, huh?"

Piece Officer

Mark C. Canterbury

Rush hour traffic in South Florida sucks. And not in the best sense of the word either. The only redeeming factor of being stuck in the state's largest outdoor parking lot is the opportunity to cruise - and fantasize about - some of the hot- looking guys trapped in neighboring vehicles.

Such was the scene as I creeped and beeped my way home from an ill-fated job interview. Good job - no money. What crap. Some people think they're doing you a favor by 'letting you' work for a gay company. Puh-leeze! As for the 'alternate route' suggested by the talk radio traffic 'copter - bigger crap! Thanks to the misinformation, I was now trapped in a massive gridlock. Ah, for those carefree days in Key West when a working wage was only a brief bicycle ride away, even in the rain.

So 'Car Window Cruising' becomes the pastime of choice in these situations. It can be tricky, though. The mustache that looks so good in the rearview mirror of the car ahead can sometimes be attached to a real oinker! Other times, luck looms and the randy radar tracks in on a real daddy type - complete with a station wagon full of rug rats.

"Hmmmmm. I'd like to make him happy for an hour," I mused, noting a real head-turner one auto over. "He's just my type." Your type, my friends would counter, is pants and a pulse. What can I say? I was gifted/cursed with a hyperactive sex drive.

"Whoa! Hold the phone!" Just ahead, in full straddle over his lean, mean moving machine, was one of Fort Lauderdale's finest . . . with a capital FINEST. This guy had shoulders out to there, tapering down to a gym-trim waist, his torso framed by a black patent leather bandoleer. Gun belt, helmet and knee-high official issue stompers made the picture perfect from my vantage directly behind the hot cop. My car's air conditioning didn't work. No matter: nothing could've cooled me off at that point. And I just had to see more.

"C'mon, c'mon, give me room!" I was talking to myself, directing traffic if you will, in an attempt to pull alongside this fantasy on wheels. If he looked as good from the front as he did from the back well, the masturbatory possibilities were boundless.

Slowly, the cars inched forward. After what seemed like an eternity, an opening appeared and my 'Bird changed lanes, allowing me the privilege to gain on my goal.

To say it was as if I'd gone to heaven, that he was a perfect '10,' that he was a centerfold come to life, would all be cliche . . . and true. Man, this guy was flawless. His tattooed biceps put Popeye to shame! His tan looked like a month spent in Rio. And his jet-black Fu Manchu framed a face that should have been staring from pin-up posters everywhere.

"This guy is breathtaking!" I panted. You could tell that he knew it too. In that cocky, cop kind of way. Aggressive, not arrogant, though. It all looked great to me.

Due to a shift in traffic patterns, I ended up driving behind the gorgeous gendarme again. "Hey, no problem," I thought. "All the better to check out his beefy butt!" Oh, what I wouldn't have given to be that bike seat. Or at least the opportunity to 'play Portnoy' for a while.

THUMP!

"Oh, shit! NOW I've done it!" Pretty stupid, Alexander.

While my mind was wafting away on the wisps of wonderment, my car was tailing too close to the man of my dreams. It is definitely not cool to hit a police officer on a motorcycle. No physical damage was done; we were traveling too slowly for that. But a ticket and a lecture - at the very least - were in my immediate future.

"License, registration and proof of insurance, please." The request came in deep, well-modulated tones, but this was still one lousy way to meet your fantasy face-to-face. Why not in seductively stretched Speedos on the beach, or at a small, dimly-lit bar in skin-tight 501s? Sheesh!

"Is it too late to just apologize, officer?" I tried, figuring I had nothing to lose and a citation to gain. "I guess I got, er, distracted." What the hell. My come-hither glance worked well at the levi-leather bars - except that with this guy, the leather 'drag' was authentic!

"I appreciate the apology, sir, but I still need to write this up. Is this your correct name and address?" he asked referring to the information on my driver's license. Even with those mirrored aviator shades I knew this guy - Officer Masters, his badge read -

had steel blue eyes and I knew they were glaring at me.

"Excuse me." His voice interrupted my reverie. "May I borrow your pen?," Masters asked, pointed to the writing instrument in my pocket. "Mine seems to have run out of ink." Great. Now he was going to write me up with my own pen! My mind raced to the calendar. "Is it a full moon?" I wondered. "No, it's not, but my birthday is tomorrow." What a present!

While the peace officer wrote me up I stared at him, imagining what he could do to me on, over, or under his motorcycle. I'd give him a 'piece' all right - a piece of my mind, a piece of my heart, a piece of my . . .

"Here you go. Sign here, sir." What a set of pipes. "Thanks for your cooperation. Drive more carefully in the future and when we meet again it won't be by accident like this." Sigh.

I slowly slipped my car into gear and eased back into traffic. "God, that man was unbelievable!" I oozed. "Let me write his name down and when I get home I'll see if he's listed in the phone book." There was an empty place in my shirt pocket. "Damn! He didn't give my gold Cross pen back! A citation AND a missing pen. Cripes!"

When I got home I tried to take my mind off my depression afternoon by watching the tube. The entertainment decision rested between "Elektra Glide in Blue" on video tape or a rerun of "CHiPs" on the cable. Neither grabbed my attention - or my balls - like the thought of Officer Masters.

"C'mere, boy. You like what you see?" It was Masters standing before my mind's eye, staring holes through me. "I saw you eating me up with your eyes. Now it's time to try it with your mouth." His bear-sized hand pushed down on my shoulder, forcing me to my knees. I knew what was expected of me in this position.

My face was now level with the steaming blue-covered crotch. Although my new master allowed me to unbuckle his belt with my hands, I was required to unzip his trousers with my teeth. I did so without complaint. As his pants slid to his ankles - not an easy thing to do over those monster, hairy thighs - I attacked the massive mound in his snow-white briefs with my mouth. I licked the roundness in the middle, making love to each precious orb. The long, fat tube that stretched the length of his shorts became shockingly longer with this attention. For a brief moment I became apprehensive. Could I get this monster in my mouth, let alone my ass? Well, I'd go down trying!

I continued my oral expertise by lowering his jockeys with my teeth and setting upon his superman-sized cock with my mouth. I'd had some big ones in the past, but this thing was huge. So huge it couldn't be measured in just inches. This male monument was over one foot long with a giant mushroom head cap and a shaft that got even fatter as you went to its base. The piercing below the glans attracted me like a magnet. Masters' cock was a real ass-spliter - and a personal challenge.

I set upon it like I was a condemned man and my last meal was tube steak. Even from my kneeling position and Masters' desire to show no emotion, the tension in his leg muscles told me of his pleasure. I got most of the shaft in my mouth and worked all of it with my tongue. From the piss hole to the crown all the way down to the base of his massive member, I sucked this man to his molten core.

Slowly, from somewhere at the back of his throat, a low growl began. His grip on my shoulders tightened. I knew to get ready for the white-hot flood that was coming my way. Dipping and sucking even more, the growl became louder when . . .

RRRRRING!

Suddenly I was sitting bolt upright on my sofa, with my pants at my knees and my own oversized erection in my hand. The ringing in my ears was actually the ringing of the doorbell. My memorable moments with Officer Masters had only been in my mind, dammit! I organized myself as best I could, running a hand through my hair and attempting to arrange my cock so that it wasn't quite so obvious - not an easy thing to do. I wasn't expecting anyone - my 'surprise' party wasn't until tomorrow night, so who could this be?

"Mr. DeGrate? Officer Masters. I stopped you earlier today, remember?" How could I forget? Even though I'd only seen him wearing sunglasses, I'd have recognized those eyes anywhere. "I deliberately took your pen this afternoon so I'd have an excuse to see you alone. May I come in?"

Could he come in? Was he kidding? Could this be happening?

"From the look in your eyes today, I could tell you were pretty interested in me. Well, you look pretty good yourself. Looks like you've spent a little time in the gym too. I like that in a guy.

"I also like that you didn't try to fuck me over with some bullshit sob story today, trying to cry your way out of a ticket. You took it like a man. But your cooperation didn't give me an opportunity to show you a quaint police procedure we employ. It's called a 'strip search.' If you cooperate, I won't have to use these handcuffs . . ." Masters jingled the metal bracelets for emphasis.

I put up one helleva fight - and thus began a beautiful relationship.

I also discovered that I was psychic. Every throbbing inch of my earlier fantasy measured up.

"Happy birthday to me, happy birthday to me, happy . . . "

Night Off

Edmund Miller

The guy was one of those hot little numbers who never lose their high school glow--the Billys and Bobbys and Richies and Dougs. This Billy had all the usual stuff--the hair a little too bleached and the soft touch of restlessness that always gets its own way in the end. Not quite handsome, he had the good, regular features of tradition and the pale translucent skin that comes from spending too much of his outdoor time at night. He also had the faded blue-gray eyes of dreams--just the usual hypnotic, pale blue-grays. And, yes, he knew he would do; he certainly would do; he certainly knew.

But as Billy had a chance to note while surveying the few customers, this was not going to be a busy night for the paraphernalia shop in the backroom of Houston's famous Maryjane's. "It looks like everybody's resting up for New Year's tomorrow," he thought. He yawned for a big effect and shifted his perfect little buns on the high stool he was perched upon behind the counter. But then he saw something to sit up straight for. He had spotted a Dark Stranger with a great curling handle-bar mustache; the muscles of his ass were straining against his jeans as he reached up to unhook a sample black leather jockstrap from the ceiling display. Billy's ass strained a little too.

As the Dark Stranger held the thing out to Billy, his eyes asked, "How much is this?" Bill hated to admit he could not satisfy this perfectly reasonable inquiry.

"We don't sell many of those. You don't want all that leather hanging around when you're getting down to business," he said, running his hand over the wide waistband of the jockstrap in question and then in rapid succession over his own midriff and the Dark Stranger's, where it paused to explore the remarkable definition in the abs. "We've got some great ones with just a leather pouch and thong." But the Dark Stranger was not ready to get down to it. He gently removed the hand of the solicitous clerk from where it had come to rest with a finger or two intertwined in his beltloops. Still, Billy was not to be put off so easily. Outrageous eagerness was the tone he was striving for.

"Perhaps I can interest you in something else," he said, running his palms slowly over the contours of the Dark Stranger's chest from nipple to waist and a bit lower. This time the Dark Stranger did not stop him, although he did laugh a bit--or at least he smiled. "He's hooked," Billy thought. "Do you want to try this on? No? Ah, come on. I'll try one on if you will."

The Dark Stranger looked around the shop as if to see how much of all this the other patrons were taking in. Billy followed his glance boldly. Two browsers seemed to be following the one-sided conversation with considerable interest. "We can try 'em on," Billy suggested, "and those two guys can shout encouragement."

"It's too big," the Dark Stranger seemed to suggest as he held the strap up against himself and gauged the free play in the waistband.

But holding the thing out at arm's length and stretching the waistband fully, Bill gave it his expert scrutiny. "Oh, I don't know. I think you can probably fill it out," he said. He popped his fist into the pouch and gave the outer surface a professional caress. Then he held the jock up against the Dark Stranger's crotch. He did not fail to make the most of the opportunity of running his hand over the hard muscles behind.

The Dark Stranger shook his head and then, tossing the jockstrap on the counter, again removed the roving hands--with growing reluctance, it seemed to Billy.

Then Billy ran his palms over the course of the Dark Stranger's chest for one last try, more rapidly this time, and left the fingers of his right hand to linger just inside the waistband of the Dark Stranger's jeans. "I think I have just what you need back in the stock room."

The Dark Stranger crooked a finger in Billy's general direction and shifted his eyes toward the door. Then he started to leave.

"Hey, wait a minute! I can't just wrap it up and take myself home."

The Dark Stranger turned back slowly and stared.

"What I mean is, if we still feel this way at two when I get off, why sure I'd love to go home with you and all."

But the Dark Stranger shrugged and looked away.

"And, of course, I don't really have a place I can take someone."

But the Dark Stranger turned back toward the door and started to go again.

"Hey, wait. Maybe I could just get somebody to cover for me.

Hey Scott! Scott! Where is that guy when you need him?"

But it was too late. The Dark Stranger was gone.

"Well, what about the stock room?" Billy asked no one in particular and without much conviction. The two browsers certainly had no answer to his question. "I don't deliver, do I?" thought Billy, sadder but wiser. "I didn't even get an affectionate pat on the butt out of that."

This abrupt end to the affair was not exactly what Billy had planned. There was, he reflected, a certain excitement in turning 'em on and then turning 'em off. But this number had been a keeper. Teasing is all very well for a while, but sex is a lot better. It had not even been Billy's intention to add the spice of inaccessibility to his charms this time; it had just sort of happened. He had fallen for his own sales pitch, he thought, fingering his own upper lip and thinking about the great restraint the Dark Stranger had evinced by all that silence. They always take you too seriously. But the evening's adventure was over.

Later that night Billy stood under a cold shower trying to get the Dark Stranger out of his system. But the firm abs and hard butt he had touched so briefly kept coming back to mind. He licked his lips just thinking about the serious work that the stiff bristles of that big mustache could do in his crack. He massaged the leathery rope of his cock, and it grew moment by moment under his familiar touch. He poked his index finger into his ass, and his cock sprang out in a large arc, flinging soapsuds all over the shower stall. He reluctantly pulled his finger out so that he could steady his cock with both hands. He ran his two hands out along the length of the shaft, savoring the agonizing stiffness. He leaned back against the tiles and closed his eyes as cold water lashed at his chest. He reached down to his balls where the skin was stretched with unusual tightness. There was only way to relieve the tenseness he felt: he had to come. He lathered up his cock with both hands, at first slowly, then faster and faster. He felt the thick veins throbbing through the slick surface. He felt his cock reach for that last bit of firmness. And then suddenly he blew--all over the walls of the shower stall. He even hit the ceiling in one place. There was come on his chest and in his hair. And he simply could not stop coming. It went on and on, even as his cock started to go down. There was come all over his feet, oozing between his toes. Finally he was standing in a pool of come; the drain was clogged with the swirling stuff.

He felt faint. He was still breathing heavily. Somehow he rinsed himself off and dragged himself into the bedroom, where he flung himself on the bed still ringing wet. But he did not pass out. He lay there exhausted with his eyes closed and tried to sleep but could not. As it was, he had to lie on his back because his cock was still semi-hard. But even with the lights out and his eyes shut tight, he could still see the vision of the Dark Stranger's mustache brunching between the cheeks of his ass. He could feel it. He arched his legs up in the air. He spread his ass so the Dark Stranger could get in closer. He was sweating. He reached up to the headboard for the lubricant. He fumbled with the dispenser, but at last he got a good glob of stuff. He rushed to cool off his little hole. He stuck his index finger in and hit the spot right off, and his cock sprang to new attention. He let it bounce in the air although the heavy weight was painful to him. That was what the Dark Stranger would have done. Billy stuck a few more fingers up his ass, and then finally like Little Jack Horner he popped in his thumb. The skin was taut on his cock by this time, and the cock itself had reached its full eleven inches again. His asshole was still aching for the Dark Stranger. Reluctantly, Billy slipped his fingers out: perhaps there was another kind of relief at hand.

He reached back up to the headboard. After a moment of two of fumbling around, he found what he was looking for. It was the twenty-inch double-headed hard rubber dildo he had borrowed form the paraphernalia shop. He rubbed the head at one end with the lubricant that was still on his fingers. He flopped the thing on the bed between his legs with a heavy wonk as he thought about the Dark Stranger. He felt the firmness of the thing. He thought how wonderful it was that he could not even quite touch his fingers together when he hefted it. It must be a good nine inches around--just the way he imagined the Dark Stranger's cock. He spread the cheeks of his ass and arched his legs up a bit more. And then he began pushing. His cock was arched over his chest and dripping pre-come down his chest and on to the sheets as the head of the thing slipped in with his fist thrust. He groaned and then groaned again and then reached down with both hands and got a good grip on the thing about half way along its length. He urged it forward. He felt his insides being wrenched open. He wanted it. He needed it so much. And then suddenly he gave way, and eight or ten inches of the thing shot up inside him. He screamed. The pain was too much. Slowly he eased the thing out although even then the muscles of his ass were reluctant to let go. But little by little it moved back. Then as at last the rim of the head popped out, he shot again--all over his chest and face, all over the sheets and the floor. He missed the ceiling this time, but he was gasping with exhaustion once again. He was too tired to clean anything up. He rolled over into a pool of cool liquid and fell immediately to sleep. He slept soundly and peacefully. He slept late.

The next evening all the closets emptied into the bars since it was New Year's Eve. When Billy got to work he found himself hard-pressed, even with Scott helping out, to keep up with the brisk sales in decorative inhalers, color-coded handkerchiefs (he remembered he needed to order another gross of red), and tee-shirts proclaiming humorous half-truths.

Then, just after midnight, while the champagne glasses were still raised in the air all over the complex of bar, garden, and shop and while balloons were still floating down from the ceiling and had not yet started to pop as they got trampled by the crowd, then, just then Billy felt a familiar firmness behind him and squirmed a bit to see whether he could bring the owner of this familiar thing more specifically to mind--or at least to the point. He could do neither. And when he turned to check the inventory, he found himself getting a New Year's kiss from his dream man, the Dark Stranger. The kiss knocked the wind out of him. The Dark Stranger's tongue was reaming his mouth thoroughly before Billy quite realized what was happening. But he soon had the presence of mind to send his own tongue dancing back. And he also improved the occasion with roving hands, discovering to his delight armpits thick with the damp silk nature intended them to have. Except for his tongue and the chance rasping of his mustache against Billy's smooth upper lip, the Dark Stranger was less demonstrative. Allowing Billy to come up for air at last, the Dark Stranger stepped back and smiled.

Billy was not about to make the same mistake he had made the might before. As the Dark Stranger slipped his hands down over Billy's buns, Billy guided the fingers to places conveniently worn through. The Dark Stranger examined what he found with care. The Dark Stranger's fingers surveyed a smooth and hairless terrain, and then one of the fingers found the sensitive pucker, which of course gave way before it instantly. As the Dark Stranger began some leisurely thrusts with the index finger of his right hand, he put his left hand under Billy's shirt and began to pluck at the nipples. These responded at once by dilating. By the time the Dark Stranger had pulled off Billy's vest and shirt, his nipples were inflamed and raw from the attention they were being given.

It was time, Billy thought, to retire to the stock room to take a full inventory. Assuming that Scott could mind the counter during the slow period that would follow the noisy ringing in of the new year, he led the Dark Stranger from the shop, holding on to what handle he could while he worked his way through the dense holiday crowd. With some effort fighting against the weight of the crowd, he pried open the door to the stock room, but it snapped shut behind him almost as soon as he was inside. When the Dark Stranger did not reopen it and follow him in, Billy pushed his way back out again and, not seeing the Dark Stranger anywhere nearby, adjusted his basket for more public business and set off on a circuit of the bar.

Wherever it was that the Dark Stranger had gotten himself carried off to by the currents of the crowd, Billy could not find him. After fifteen minutes of search and several checks in the stock room, Billy returned to the paraphernalia shop, puzzled. His ardor was cooler--his nipples were cooler--as he picked up his tee-shirt and vest to put them back on. As he hoisted the tee-shirt over his head, a slip of paper floated out of it, cutting a zig-zag descent that Scott stopped just short of the floor. But even before Scott handed him the note, Billy could see his own familiar message written on it: "No sale."

II.
Odyssey

**One Man's Pursuit of the Colossal Cock
A Sequence of Stories By John Patrick**

*"Travel, in the younger sort, is a part of
education; in the elder, a part of experience."*
- Francis Bacon

Bull

"...That's a hundred for the first half hour, fifty for each additional half hour," the woman on the other end of the line says, faintly bored.

"Fine," I stammer. "I'm at the Doral on Park, Suite 540. I'll expect her in, say —"

"An hour, maybe less. I'll call you right back and verify."

While I wait, I leaf through the latest issue of "Screw." On one of the many pages of little ads offering sex for sale, one dominates, heralding: "The Gayety Boylesk Presents Bullwhip Drummond...In Person!"

What a calamity; the King of Porn has been reduced to flashing it for queers. Disgustedly, I push the newspaper off the bed and lower my head to the pillow.

Across the room, the late news flickers on the TV but it is Bull's image I see...in the last scene from "Belle Du Bois."

The water gently ripples in the villa's brightly lit pool, surrounded by the terrace and lush tropical foliage, indirectly lit. On the edge of the pool Bull is waiting.

"Mah, oh, mah," Carole sighs as she enters the scene, her eyes riveted on the prodigious bulge in his red swim suit.

"Off goes the robe, Carole baby," Cash Stevens, the director, barks.

Slowly she slips each arm from the robe and then haughtily drops it behind her. Now wearing only her pink panties, she lowers herself to the edge of the pool and folds her arms across her wondrous chest, covering her nipples and pushing her tits together.

"Okay, Bull," Cash directs. "I want you to run your hands up her thighs. Work her over real good." He hesitates, waiting for Bull to get into position. "Okay, now, we're rollin'."

As his hands grapple at the panties, Bull kisses Carole's thighs and she closes her eyes. Cash tells her to lean back on her hands and thrust out her pelvis. Bull tugs at the panties with his teeth, then works his way into her crotch until the fabric is soaked with his spit. Carole puts her hands behind her, flat on the deck and lifts herself up. Bull slips her panties from her body, then spreads her thighs. His tongue darts avidly in and out of her vagina. Languidly, Cash pans up Carole's body as she groans in pleasure.

"Okay, Bull, sit next to her."

When Bull is in position, they embrace. As they kiss deeply, Bull begins fondling her breasts and toys with her cunt. After a few moments, Cash hollers, "Okay, Bull baby, we all wanna see it!"

The stud stands and turns, his back to Carole. As he begins to remove his trunks, Carole brings her tiny hand to her brow as a shade and looks directly toward me. The intense lights blind her. As she attempts to locate me, I step further into the shadows ("Act like I'm not even there," I told her. "Give yourself up to the moment."). Not seeing me, she shrugs her shoulders and turns her attention to primping her hair, then picks up her panties and dabs perspiration from her forehead and upper lip.

As Bull tosses his swim suit onto the deck and turns to face her, Carole's eyes widen and her gasp is audible. The video I had shown her could not have adequately prepared her for the sight of the King's appendage in the flesh and at full potency. Cash has anticipated her reaction and turned his camera on her face. I am glad he doesn't have it trained on my face. Embarrassed, yet unable to avert my eyes, I mumble, "Jeezus."

"Take it to her, Bull," Cash orders. As Bull steps toward her, Carole instinctively reaches up, her quivering hand tentatively touching the tip of perhaps the most photographed cock in the modern world. In its engorged condition, the foreskin of the meat is pulled tight onto the shaft, revealing a huge, purplish knob about the size of a small fist.

The stud brings his hand to the back of Carole's head and gently pulls her forward. She hesitates. I know what is going through her mind. "Simulated," I had told her. But Bull had done his number on her cunt and she didn't seem to mind that. Certainly she could reciprocate. In fact, because I knew how responsive she was to any kind of stimulation, it was obvious to me he had brought her to orgasm.

Yet now she resists taking his cock in her mouth. But the more she fights, the more Bull pushes. He has been on hundreds of shoots. He knows his job. This is for real. But this is Carole's debut. And I had lied to her; I had told her it was all make believe.

Finally, realizing she is being confronted by an inevitable situation, her jaw goes slack. Her lips begin to quiver. Cash edges into position as first the tip, then the entire head of Bull's cock enters her mouth. One, two, three inches of the thick shaft follow. Carole's eyes begin to water. Bull lets go of her head to bring both of his hands to the base of his cock, straightening the arc of it as he thrusts it deeper into her throat. I have benefited from Carole's preference for giving her male partner head. She prefers it to vaginal intercourse, being more able to control it. But now it seems she has no control. Bull totally dominates her.

Cash cuts to a high angle shot from above, showing Carole struggling to take in the last inches of it...and failing. Bull withdraws and starts again.

"Bring her down," Cash orders. Bull brings his hands to Carole's shoulders and presses her down. He keeps the head of his cock in her mouth as he lowers her onto the edge of the pool. He brings his hands flat against the deck and begins face-fucking her. She gags several more times but Bull is relentless. Cash whirls around them, shooting from a variety of angles.

"Super!" I say, loud enough for Cash to hear.

"Okay, now to Position Three!" he yells. Cash and Bull have conspired their own code and Three is what Cash ungraciously calls "the tit fuck."

The stud begins sliding his cock in and out of her cleavage. On each upstroke, she takes the tip of it between her painted lips. Then his cock caresses her nipples, pushing the tip of them into the opening of the urethra. He squeezes the heavy breasts around his penis and begins thrusting back and forth slowly, his saliva acting as a lubricant. Slowly, gradually he increases the tempo, playing with the erect nipples as he fucks.

After a few moments, Cash says, "Okay, Bull, on to Four." The stud drops to his knees and takes Carole's ankles in his hands, forcing her legs up into the air. He hoists her legs over his shoulders, then firmly plants his sweaty hands on her soft, thick ass.

Cash climbs onto the platform and shoots across Carole's body, aiming up at Bull. Showing the cockhead and then the shaft slowly disappear inside Bull's sex partner is one of Cash's favorite scenes. Screen One shows the action in tight close-up.

I look to the pool to see Bull arcing his back like a loose-limbed acrobat, permitting Cash full access to the action. Cash straddles Carole, his crotch in her face. She has ceased to be human, becoming nothing more than a pliant receptacle for the stud's sumptuous meat. ("What they do in these movies isn't love-making," I told her. "It's play acting.") She screams. Cash pulls back to get a close up of the look of agony on her face. "I can't," she cries. "This is just too much. Please, don't." She stretches her arms toward Bull. He draws her tight to his body, hugging her as she begins to weep.

He seems, after years of fucking girls fresh off the boulevards, charmed by her, by her naivete, her lack of professionalism.

Carole sobs as Bull enters her. Perhaps it is more a cry of desperation than of pain. I have violated her trust. But I feel, when it's over, she will *appreciate it. After all, she as being paid handsomely for getting the fuck of her life.*

Bull is gentle; he takes his time. I have always thought it was not just the length of the member but the thickness, the excessive width of it, at the head and on down the shaft, splitting them open, that frustrated women, and Carole moans deeply. She is in pain and Cash cuts to a close up of the desperation in her face. With her mascara streaking down her cheeks, she looks as ugly as I have ever seen her, but, since she is playing a washed up blue movie actress, it is perfect.

As the stud begins pulling Carole up and down on his cock, Cash hovers over them like a locust, the camera becoming an invader and a recorder of the most sacred, private moments of two peoples' lives. They fuck for five minutes, Carole continually whimpering.

"Great, Bull," Cash finally says, "Just a couple more jabs."

Carole wraps her legs around Bull as he lowers himself onto her body, kissing her tits, then her mouth. Bracing himself on the edge of the pool again ,perspiration drips from his furrowed brow as his body tenses.

"Yeah, it's comin!" he cries.

"Hot damn!" Cash hollers, scurrying to get into position again, holding Bull in a medium one-shot as the stud pulls out of Carole and perches his cock, distended and quivering, over her belly. His hands do not touch it for a few seconds, allowing Cash to zoom in for an extreme close up. The stud's head flips back and his entire body shudders. Juice spews from the head of his cock in a turbulent arc, forming a sticky puddle at Carole's navel. Soon he brings both of his hands to the base of the shaft, gripping it like a golf club, then flogs her tits with it, the finale to the patented Bull Drummond money shot.

"Jee-zus!" I laugh, shaking my head in wonderment.

"Money in the bank," Cash yells. "Money in the fuckin' bank!"

My left hand grips my erection. I stroke myself. The phone rings. I stroke myself one last time...semen covers my hand.

I let the phone ring until it stops.

*

"...I couldn't fuckin' believe it really was you in the crowd, man," Bull laughs, answering my tap on the dressing room door. "I mean, you of all people."

"Me of all people? Hell, I'm just one of the idolaters, coming to worship at your altar! And you of all people should know I'd get some kind of perverse pleasure out of coming here."

He smiles. "Got that right."

The Gayety Boylesk is a hastily constructed "theater" on the second floor of an aging building. A theater ticket brokerage and a dry cleaner are on the first floor. After paying $5 to get in, I gingerly made my way through the dingy, shadowy labyrinth designated by a crudely lettered sign as the "Hospitality Area." It is adjacent to the rest rooms and men loiter there, sipping soda pop and cruising. The area spills out into a long, narrow room with about a hundred shopworn theater seats jammed into it. The seats face a raised platform and soiled brocade curtains have been hung at one end, parted to reveal a small screen.

When I entered the viewing room, an absurdly amateurish loop was winding down, depicting a dozen grungy young men listlessly performing oral sex on each other. It was enough to give porn a bad name. As showtime approached, men seemed to appear out of nowhere, streaming in as if they were extras from "The Night of the Living Dead."

There were four boys on the bill ahead of the star, thugs who lackadaisically pranced around on the platform. As the climax to each of their dances, they slipped through the guys sitting ringside, wiggling their cocks in their faces. A couple of the boys let some of the men cop a feel and were rewarded with sawbucks. One inventive lad went so far as to permit a balding, bespectacled man to kiss his limp cock.

Suddenly, the house went dark. A startlingly young Bull Drummond (billed in the credit crawl as "Big Bill Thompson") appeared on screen dressed as a sultan in a red satin robe and matching turban with a huge faux jewel in the center, permitting a scrawny, unkempt "slave" boy to fellate him.

After what seemed like an eternity, the reel Bull reached his climax and the film stopped. A tiny blue spot was thrown onto center stage and there he was, in person, squatting, his naked back to the crowd, obviously masturbating. The spotlight enlarged and Bull slowly turned to face the crowd. Over his groin he held a turban much like the one in the loop and, to the inspired accompaniment of Frank Sinatra singing "You'd Be So Nice to Come Home To," he cavorted around the stage, teasing the men in the front row, letting them peek behind the turban. Some tried for more but he adroitly pulled away. As the last notes of the song were being played, he resumed center stage and the spot gradually diminished until it was solely on the turban. For a fleeting moment, the stud lifted the turban to reveal the world's most celebrated tool in what I knew to be only a half-mast condition.

As I was making my way out of the theater, the dancers were beginning to circulate in the catacombs, hypocritical sycophants, doing anything to cadge drugs or cash, their eyes vulturously searching for the next score. One of them approached me saying "Mr. Drummond" would like to see me in his dressing room. I followed him with great reluctance, feeling perhaps Bull would think I had overstepped my bounds, making myself a witness to the extent of his decline.

But now he acts genuinely pleased to see me. He opens the door wide for me to enter and I realize just how emaciated he has become. The sheik mustache he has affected makes his face appear older and uncharacteristically sinister. His wild brown curls are matted to his head with sweat. His cheeks are chalky pale, his lips chapped, turning orange. He's wearing his usual lived-in clothes: baggy chinos and sneakers with no socks. He pulls on a cashmere sweater that looks as if it had been picked up off the floor which, of course, it had.

"Sorry about the mess," he says with a chuckle, "but the maid service in this joint sucks."

"Ha! At least you have the star dressing room."

He shakes his head in dismay. "Star, shit, man, this is the only fuckin' dressing room! It's supposed to be for everybody but since I really am a fuckin' star for chrissakes, the rest of 'em have to dress in the hallway behind here."

I look about the squalid room. A single soft white bulb glows weakly over an old dressing table littered with trash. The stench of stale tobacco, Lysol, and amyl nitrite assaults my nostrils. A narrow bed has been jammed against the wall. Clothes have been strewn flagrantly on the bare mattress. It could just as easily be a jail cell.

Seeing my eyes fall to the bed, he says, wearily: "I catch cat naps there. You know how it is." I flinch at the thought of his grueling schedule, dancing five shows a day and turning tricks in this pitiful room.

"I was amazed to see you in a gay loop," I say, stepping over to the bed and lowering myself onto an available corner.

"God awful, ain't it? Yah can tell old Cash baby didn't do that! And did you see how young I was? Shit, I was barely street legal then!" He exuberantly pulls the straight chair over to the edge of the bed and straddles it, folding his arms along the back of it. "But most people don't recognize me with that robe and turban ."

"C'mon! How could you hide it? Get serious!"

"Whatcha mean?" he asks, jumping up. "When that boy opens my robe?" He demonstrates with his hands and a thrust of his pelvis.

I nod. Even in baggy chinos, the bulge of his crotch cannot be denied and, gulping, I avert my eyes.

"Yeah," he says, chuckling, flopping down on the chair again. "But, hell, I was just plain old Bill Thompson back then."

"Big Billy Thompson, but he's gone forever...long live the King!"

"Yeah, well, I'm not so sure how long the King's gonna live at this rate." His eyes turn cold, desperate. "God, I could use some blow. You bring any blow?"

"I thought you'd never ask! You know the way it is, an eight ball a day keeps the doctor away!" We share some of the half a gram I brought with me and I leave the rest for him.

"Ahhh, this is Florida's finest," he says, sniffing loudly. "You can always get the best. Hey," he says, bringing the coke spoon to his nose again, "maybe I should go down to Florida when this fuckin' thing is over."

"Tricking?"

"Hell, no, I wouldn't wanna be doin' no five tricks a day. I mean a real vacation, like go see you."

"It's got a certain charm but it's boring as hell."

"Well, we'll fix that!" he laughs, cupping his balls.

"Haha! You've just been through a helluva ordeal. Cash told me it was all for nothing, that they never got any testimony out of you."

"Shee-it, John, they couldn't. I mean, what was I gonna tell 'em about them murders?" He averts his eyes. "But I don't wanta talk about that." He lights a Kool. "I'm sick of thinkin' about the past. I gotta move on, get my career back in gear, you know what I mean? Shit, it's been from gigolo to curio in one big slide!"

"I know," I tell him. "In fact, Cash has been talking about another James Bond parody. I think he's gonna call it 'Thunderballs.'"

"Cute. But I gotta do a guest shot in a gay flick for somebody the

"Cute. But I gotta do a guest shot in a gay flick for somebody the first week of February." He flinches. "Oh, don't worry. Nothin' any worse than you just saw. I mean, just a guy or two goin' down on me. Hell, it was the only offer I got and it'll be just a day's work."

"Queen for a day?"

"Cute. You've become a fuckin' comedian!"

I reach into my breast pocket, withdraw a hundred dollar bill and hand it to him. "Try that for laughs."

He stares at the C-note. "Now, that ain't no laughin' matter."

I hand him another. Then three more. "No, no laughs, just lots of fun." I pause. "You have no idea how much fun." I hand him another one. "And here's to a lot more fun in the future."

"Hell, John, you kept me alive in that fuckin' jail. You don't need to do no more."

I break into a cold sweat. My head begins to throb. I wipe my brow with the back of my hand. "God, it's hot in here."

"Not as hot as it could get in Florida," he says with characteristic gusto, groping himself again. His face twists into a lecherous smile. "Ya know what I mean?"

Could it be he is aware of my inchoate fantasy? No, it is more likely I tantalize him because he has to prove no one, absolutely no one, is immune to the charms of the King.

I gaze at my freshly shined Gucci loafers, then look up, into his bloodshot eyes. "Perhaps you could come down," I say, the answer hanging like a temptation.

"Fuck yeah," he says, jumping up. "You know, one thing I always wondered was why the hell you had to bring your old lady — " he hesitates, as if he's straining to remember her name, then, with a slow grin, continues: "Carole, yeah, Carole baby...god, what tits." He smacks his lips. "Anyway, why the hell you brought old Carole in on it, I mean, just to make a movie with me, I could never figure, but the more I get to know you—" He touches my arm gently. "You got nothin' to fear, John. Believe me, I've seen it all. First you want to watch, now you want to touch. If you want it, you can have it. I can handle it. Man, it's just that simple."

"Nothing is ever as simple as it may seem, Bull." I leave it that way, if it makes him happy.

Standing at the door shaking his hand, I feel scores of beady, sewer rat's eyes staring at us covetously. Impulsively, he hugs me and, for a moment, there is a genuine connectedness that I haven't felt with him before. It's as if he is reassuring me that, yes, whatever I want to do will be all right with him.

And, as I step away from the door, heading for the exit, his fans move in, a marauding horde, converging to pick the carcass.

I pull my overcoat snugly around me and, in the lengthening afternoon shadows, I begin the long walk back to the hotel. The blustery wind swirls huge wet snowflakes into my face but I cannot help but smile.

*

"...Sleep well?" I ask Bull as he slides into the chaise longue next to mine on the beach.

Nodding and stretching his long legs out in front of him, he says, "Yeah, man, I needed a good rest." He has slept for almost twelve hours...in the guest bedroom. He lights a joint and inhales it gratefully. He offers me a toke.

"No, thanks, I'll stick with my vodka." I lift my glass in salute.

There is dull thunder on the horizon. The leading edge of a distant maelstrom is swiftly rolling toward us, an eldritch pile of clouds, suffused with ethereal pink, as if ominously lit from within, the shade of pale blood, the final glow of the sun. The water of the Gulf becomes a mirror, reflecting the tempest above it, its color changing from green to gray, winds thrumming its surface, roiling first in wavelets, then churning heavier, slamming as whitecaps against the shore. Gradually, the sun is consumed, leaving a sky of solid slate. As the first raindrops strike, we scurry into the house. The windblown rain, flamboyant in its utter insistence, at once splendid and terrible, slashes at the house.

"It's almost a summer storm," I say, stepping behind the bar in the now somber living room. "It'll probably be over as quickly as it came up."

"Scary," he says, lowering himself into one of the suede bar chairs. The mirror with the coke on it has been left on the bar from the night before. He picks up the razor and lackadaisically toys with the powder, chopping it and forming several long, skinny lines. "You really get off on this shit, don't yah?" he asks in a faintly bored voice.

"It makes the sleaziest whore look glamorous and the dumbest conversations seem very profound. I guess you could say it camouflages a multitude of sins."

"Yeah, I remember. You and me, we got sleazy whores in common."

I nod. "Can't get our fill."

We share an affinity for the kind of tarts Cash always says men would drunkenly debauch and soberly ditch: Rock slut hairdos, trim butts, the vulgar innocence of corrupted youth and the willingness to bend for it, lie back for it, or squat down and squirm for it like dogs with their feet in the air.

"Got any Percs?"

I shake my head.

"Oh, don't you worry none, I don't do as many as I used to," he goes on, "just on special occasions, yah know?"

"I never got into it," I say, bending over to do some lines. "Coke's enough for me, really."

"Yeah, it'll do. I guess it's gotten down to me doin' whatever's handy, if you know what I mean." He brought his old briefcase with him. "Carry it with me everywhere," he said. Inside are his drugs, his glass pipe, baking soda, a petri dish for cooking cocaine powder into rock base, a bottle of 151 rum and cotton swabs for lighting the pipe.

"Aren't you going a bit too far?"

"No," he says, preparing the pipe. "How far you goin'?"

I snicker. How far? I have much evidence of how far he is willing to go. He seems to have a penchant for, and incomparable competence at, anal sex, most notably in his last appearance with Candy Kane in "Rear Entry," a parody of Hitchcock's "Rear Window." It must have been agony for her.

"How far is far enough?" I say, dismayed.

"Hey, you didn't bring me down here to talk in fuckin' riddles. And I know you weren't all that shot in the ass havin' me just hang out here on a vacation." He screws up his face in another of his patented lecherous smiles and smooths the fabric of the swim suit I loaned him, giving obscene definition to the crotch. "Naw, the way I figure it, Johnny, you didn't wanna come right out and do it. You're a shy kinda guy, really hung-up on sex and shit, so you figure out a way to do it through the old lady, but then that ain't enough. Fuck, it's never enough. There's always gotta be more."

I regard his crotch closely and suddenly realize he is regarding me. I stammer, "You're quite the amateur psychologist, aren't you?"

"Yeah, that's me, Doctor Drummond."

"Well, Doctor, I guess you have analyzed it better than I have. Maybe I'm too close to it. I don't understand why I should feel the way I do. I just know that I am constantly in awe of your astonishing prowess. Like all great actors, you make it look so easy. I envy that. I'm just so inept."

"Fuck, it's easy after you've been doin' it for as long as I have."

"But so much of it is, well, what most people consider a perversion."

"Like what?"

"Well, what you did with Candy in 'Rear Entry.' I mean, the anus is an exit, not an entrance. Like Emerson said, `There are many things of which a wise man might wish to be ignorant.'"

"Hey, my motto is, if it feels good, go for it."

"I know, I know. But I've always wondered how a person must feel when they get plowed by that piece?"

"Hell, what they tell me is that when I do it, it's like gettin' a massage in there."

"Perhaps. I know it belongs in the script, everybody wants to see it. But you really can't script it, you just wing it like the rest of it. No motivation, no dialogue. Just sex. But if I had to, I could never really write about it convincingly." I sip my drink.

"Oh, I get it now," he chuckles. "You gotta justify everything. Like you're havin' sex with me would be like," he pauses, "what do you people call it? Research?" He laughs. "Yeah, that's it, research!" Grinning broadly, immensely pleased with himself, he jumps up. He has become as insistent as the rain that continues to slash the house. He strokes the mammoth bulge in his swim trunks. "Hey, c'mon. You've made me so fuckin' horny, I can't stand it. We might as well get this research over with."

Do I want to agree with Voltaire: if you try it once you're a philosopher? If so, I must accept its corollary: if you do it twice, you're a pervert. So when I do it, it's got to be perfect because I intend to philosophize about it for the rest of my days. I have reasoned it would have to be done in private. I could not endure it in a group or on a movie set. I would need to concentrate, to fully appreciate the pleasure of it, of a degradation so bizarre it is incomprehensible. If I were to go that far I could leave nothing to chance, I would have to put myself in the hands of a professional, a true master of the art. And a man who was at one time perhaps the world's highest paid hustler is standing in front of me at this very moment, stroking the world's most photographed cock, telling me how horny he is...

"...Believe me," he says. He is alive to his fingertips, playfully applying the lubricant, preparing me for the grand assault. He told me to lie flat on my back, with my legs straight up in the air. "It's the easiest way," he says in a cadenced, poetic lilt, nearly crooning the words. He is methodical, gentle, thoughtful. He breaks an amyl nitrite capsule and hands it to me. I bring it to my nose, sniff deeply. He takes my other hand and places it on my groin. "Just keep jerkin'...don't stop, no matter what. And keep sniffin' that shit. That'll help, too."

Grinning sheepishly, he stands up and turns his back to me. I remember Carole, on the set of "Belle Du Bois." Different swim trunks, the same lewd bulge. That was a dress rehearsal, I chuckle to myself. If Carole could see me now! Bull lowers his trunks and steps from them.

Slowly, he turns toward me. While I was awestruck by the gigantic size of Bull's organ the first time I saw it in the flesh, it seemed somehow soft and pink and harmless, almost a ridiculous prop nature had playfully stuck onto a gangling, hollow cheeked kid. But now with the storm letting up and the glow after sunset filling my bedroom with eerily opalescent light, the King's cock takes on an altogether different aspect, becoming far more pernicious than anything I had ever imagined. It takes on an intense animal magnetism of its own, somehow removed from its owner, as if Bull himself was strangely separated from the scene. He kneels on the bed. He doesn't touch the frightening member, letting it speak eloquently for itself. I squint in disbelief at the flaming, fearsome menace. Bull cups my ass in his calloused, bony hands and, as he lifts me up, I squirm higher onto the pillows to get a clearer view of the action. He shoves a pillow under my ass and licks and tongues my asshole, driving me to a new threshold of pleasure. When he slowly, deftly begins to insert the head of his cock, I am glad I had moved next to the bed the little camera I used to film Carole. When this is over, I will have preserved this moment forever. The head of his cock is completely in. I shudder. The pain is overwhelming. Tears come to my eyes. As he presses into me,

I wince. My cock is losing its hardness.

"No, no...please, I can't," I stammer breathlessly, tears rolling down my cheeks.

"Just keep jackin' off," he says authoritatively. For every inch he withdraws, he pushes forward two. Unstoppable as the storm that slashed at the house, he has become a machine. An immense, ferocious fucking machine. I am overwhelmed by a sense of outrageous shame. I regret having started it but, simultaneously, I crave it, eagerly desiring the successful completion of the act. Finally, he has all of it in and his practiced thrusting becomes rhythmically regular. He lets go of my ass and grabs the inside of my ankles, shoving my legs onto my torso. I gasp as he pulverizes my anus but when I can feel completion must be imminent he suddenly pulls out.

"No, no," I murmur, "let me feel you coming inside of me, please. I'm only going to do this once. Let me make the most of it."

"But," he says, hesitating. But then, nodding resignedly, he closes his eyes and invades me again. I cringe in pain as I feel the full extent of it deep within me. The final fucking lasts only a few moments when the explosion comes, engulfing me as only a plenary indulgence could. The echo of Bull's orgasm hums in my body, mingling with my own.

I clasp my hands onto his buttocks and press him against me. I never want the joy of this moment, of having him holding me, coming inside of me, to end.

His smile is odd, pained almost, as he withdraws his drippy cock and brings it to mine, squeezing them together and letting the last of the juice gush from each of them.

In a haze of weariness and thirst, I stumble from the bed and retreat to the privacy of the shower to wash myself. I flinch as I notice the blood trickling from my ass is washing down the drain.

*

The beach is deserted. The storm has passed. The full moon is reflected on the gently rippling water as I float on my raft, sensing a sadness in the rhythm of the stars as they dance their last flickering recognition of the night. The lights of the fishing boats out in the Gulf look like unfabled constellations.

I have been unable to sleep, ruminating over the assault. It had been a grand display, enormous in its intensity, yet strangely unfulfilling, leaving me spent but unsatisfied, as if I had just made a stop on a grand tour and I am suddenly eager to experience new sensations, sensations I have only begun to formulate in my mind.

The stories "Bull" and "Snake" have been adapted from material originally appearing in "The Bigger They Are...," the first book in "Angel: The Complete Quintet," published by STARbooks.

From New York to Hollywood.

Snake

I.

The man I had come to see appeared at the finale of the Rialto's show, when the three women, two whites and a Latin, and the two white men that make up the cast had finished their act. The men wandered off into the wings, leaving the three women alone on the darkened stage. Suddenly, a tiny spot started searching the floor until it found Snake, off to one side, reclining as if he was asleep, a faux snakeskin loincloth wrapped around his slim waist. Like a strange creature from a distant world, he pretended his sleep had been disturbed by the light. He stretched, stood, then started dancing a variation of the limbo, hopping, jumping, swooping around the girls as they giggled. He did a split, splaying his arms and legs as if they were dislocated, shaking and shimmying simultaneously, moving like a snake. The tempo of the music grew more and more upbeat, until it seemed as if instead of Snake moving to the music, the music was coming from his body. His movements became so fast I could not decide what was happening.

And when he suddenly cast aside the loincloth and was naked, he became, for me, a revelation, so lithe, so absolutely sensual, epitomizing a new frontier. He had become the force I wanted to invade me: dark, tormented, savage. He lifted his arms above his head and did a variation of the belly dance, with hips, stomach, and rump moving violently. The spot narrowed, centered on his crotch. His cock was at last erect. He took it in his hand and stroked it. The spot pulled away and hit the faces of the three women, permitting the audience to share their joy in seeing this miraculous organ in all of its glory. He danced around them and jiggled it in their faces. They touched him, but briefly. One girl opened her mouth very wide and acted as if she were ready to receive it, but Snake pulled away and danced across the stage. They never risked offending the sensibilities of their audience.

A drumroll began and the spot returned, enlarged now to reveal most of the dancer's body as he threw his head back and finished masturbating. There was a crack of the cymbals and the spot went out.

When I ventured into the theater I was repelled by it, by the smell of it, but I couldn't leave. There was something horrifying about the setting which helped create the epiphany I had sought. As sordid as it was, something told me I had wait for Snake's part of the show. And my patience was rewarded. I longed to record what I had just seen, to keep it forever, to play and play again, to evoke and reflect on the spirits that enchanted me.

II.

"...Concept. I'm talking concept," I told Sol Weintraub as I slid into the bright red banquette across from him at the Russian Tea Room.

"Yeah? What's the concept this time?" he asks, lighting a fresh Marlboro with the butt end of the last.

"Black and white."

"Like 'Citizen Kane?'"

"No, like in man and woman."

"Oh, shit."

To a "Russian" waiter named Salvador, dressed in a red tunic, we placed our order: The blinis with caviar for Sol, the chicken Kiev for me.

"See," I went on, "I know this gorgeous stripper in L.A. She does a splendid thing with rhinestone snakes..."

"What's that got to do with anything?"

"I'm getting to it."

"Hey, Johnny, it's like I tell my wife, I don't have all day," he chortled. His head was proportionately larger than his body and when he laughed he tended to bump up and down in his chair, his belly heaving against the edge of the table.

"Okay. She needs somebody to dance with. Somebody like Snake Russell."

"What about him?"

"Well, yesterday I saw his show at the Rialto."

"Doesn't interest me," he said, scratching his salt-and-pepper beard.

"But he's good. You've gotta admire the man's perdurability."

"I'm sure I should, if I knew what the hell it meant."

"His staying power. He's everlasting."

"Shee-it! You never cease to amaze me." He shook his head in mock desperation. "But to be truthful," he went on, almost in a whisper, "about eight years ago it must be now, I tried to get Snake for some loops when we were still makin' stuff here. He was buildin' quite a rep for himself in stuff for the old Ramrod company and I thought it'd be kinky to put him in something with a little class, as a novelty you understand. There is a market for that oreo cookie stuff. Small, but...well, anyhow, by the time I tracked him down he'd gone to fuckin' Tinseltown."

My eyes flashed. "Do you have any of the things he did out there?"

"Hell, they'd hardly qualify for our `Golden Age of Smut' Library, Johnny!"

"That's us, the golden-agers." I chuckled. "I think it's still a viable idea, as a novelty, of course. A little pepper with the salt."

"Suit yourself, Johnny. It's your money, but he may play hard to get. I heard he had some trouble while he was in L.A., but I'm sure your checkbook can cure any reluctance he may have. You know how niggers are."

I nodded but I really had no idea how niggers were but I was willing to learn.

Later, in my suite at the Intercontinental, Snake asked me, "That motherfucker Weintraub never wanted me in movies before, why now?" He inhaled deeply on a joint he brought with him and leaned back into the plump cushions of the floral-print sofa.

"No, Sol wanted you," I told him matter-of-factly. "He really did, you'd just left town —"

"That's really bullshit, man, but it don't matter none now." His face was rugged, the cocoa skin drawn taut over handsomely high cheekbones, the nose, shapeless, a bit homely, the lips thick and full, but not unseemly so. He offered me a hit.

"No, thanks. Grass puts me to sleep. I prefer champagne. In fact, would you like some?" I opened my briefcase and pulled out the little leather coke kit.

"Naw, I'll stick to this." His drawl was rich, confident, calm.

"Well, I enjoy this...recreationally, of course."

"Yeah, now recreation's somethin' I can get into, you know what I'm sayin'?" His words tended to run together in a slow, mesmerizing way. "Seems like there's been a lot of that goin' on all of my life!" He smiled slyly.

I took my sunglasses off and laid half a gram on my hand mirror. As I began cutting some lines from the pile with my gold razor blade, he stretched his long legs under the coffee table and finished his joint. "So," he said, "you doin' this gig in L.A.?"

"Yes," I said, doing two lines and throwing my head back and shaking it as I sniffed loudly. "We hope to start shooting in a couple of weeks."

"I hate them motherfuckers in L.A., man, you know what I'm sayin'? They tried to nail me for possession, somethin' that'd never happen here. But I beat the beef. Yeah, the big city's where it's at. You know, years ago when I was just a kid in Atlanta a dude tells me, `The thoroughbreds is in New York,' he says. 'You go there and see what kinda thoroughbred you is.' Well, I showed 'em all!"

"Yes, you did. I've seen your show and you're a true thorough-bred." I stared at his crotch.

"Yeah," he chuckled, "it's tough bein' the best or biggest of anything. But I can handle it." He couldn't have been more than 25 but he appeared as if he was really old; a man who had packed two years of living into every year he'd been alive. "Yeah, I got a grip on it. I mean, I can haul out my ego when I need to, but I keep it under control."

"I'll bet you do," I mumbled.

"What?"

"Nothing. I was just thinking about how those girls must feel up there with you. You simulate it so beautifully— "

"Hey, man, I ain't fakin' it. I get off at every show. Four times a day sometimes." He shook his head in wonderment at his own prowess. "Damned if I don't."

"Well, I for one was in awe of your dancing...to say nothing of your dexterity. The pace you set as you're getting off is slow, deliberate, very effective. God, you're really a master of your art!"

"Nice of yah to say so, but it's all a joke, you know what I'm sayin'? Ya gotta find it funny, all those people payin' to see me dancin' around on the stage and then jackin' off. Shit, it's just amazin', man. Fuckin' amazin'."

"Yes, amazin'. And," I went on, "I'm betting people will find you just as amazing on film."

He straightened up on the couch, preparing to leave. "Yeah, well, I gotta be getting back to the theater soon." He looked deep into my eyes. "Ah, I know ya paid just to got me up here, you need an audition or anything?"

"I set it up as a trick for you so I wouldn't involve the theater in our negotiations for the movie."

"Yeah, that was a good idea. They don't need to know nothin'. The guy that runs the joint thinks he owns me. Nobody owns me." He grinned.

"Exactly."

"But I mean, if you wanted somethin', I'm here to oblige," he said with a broad grin. "I know how the shit's supposed to come down, man. I mean, like you paid for whatever turns you on."

"Oh, but my intentions are strictly honorable." Champagne. More champagne. I needed more champagne. I returned to the mirror and chopped some more lines.

"Ain't nothin' dishonorable about gettin' your rocks off. Shit, I do it three, four times a day. Like the wise man says, `If it feels good, go for it."

I did another line. Then two. How far could I take this? The temptation was overwhelming but I told myself that I must have patience. I sniffed loudly and said, "Yeah, a friend of mine has a saying, `If you're scared to go too far, you haven't gone far enough.'"

"I'd agree with that," Snake said, jumping up abruptly and beginning to sway back and forth in front of me, almost dancing to the tune that had started on the radio, "It's Too Late To Turn Back Now." I laughed at the absurdity of it. Even though he was wearing a loose-fitting, sleek silver Nike running suit, the ebony vine plainly, perversely was inching down his left pant leg. It was as if he was calling it to action, yet he couldn't have been horny. But, then, I remembered someone once telling me blacks were always horny.

I sat there, inert. He saw my eyes were riveted on the obvious bulge. "I'll admit it's very tempting but, well," I stammered, "perhaps some other time."

"Well, I gotta get movin' anyhow. And thanks for the five bills for tonight "

"A down payment, Dwayne," I said, rising to let him out of the suite.

"Russ — " he said, extending his hand.

"Okay, Russ," I said, giving him a firm handshake. "We'll just call it a down payment."

"Yeah, sure."

III.

"...The ease with which you do it is remarkable," I told him as he stretched his long body across one of the huge couches in my suite at the Bel-Air. We had just returned from eating prime rib at Lawry's and he was finishing a joint. "Like all great actors, you make it look so easy."

"Shit, it's easy after you've been doin' it for as long as I have, man." He leaned back into the plump cushions of the pumpkin-hued sofa. "Yeah," he sighed. "It's nice bein' rich."

"Well, if you're going to have a pied-a-terre in LA, you couldn't do much better than the Queen Anne suite."

"Yeah, couldn't do much better," he said, leaning back and rubbing the bulge in his jeans. It was as if he was reading my mind. "Well, when you gonna do somethin' about that down payment?"

"Eh?"

"Yeah," he went on, languidly stretching and bringing his feet to rest on a corner of the coffee table. "Like I was wonderin' what I was gonna have to do to collect the rest. And if I could get any tips. Sure could use some tips right now."

"Could be," I said. He watched me keenly as I opened my wallet and dropped five crisp hundreds on the coffee table between us.

"Bless yah, brother," he chuckled, leading me to the bedroom.

"...This is the best way," he said softly.

He had told me to lie flat on my stomach, with a pillow under my groin. I had moved the wardrobe mirror near the bed so that I could watch the event. On the other side of the bed, I positioned a video camera on a tripod, trained directly at the heart of the action, but angled   so that my face would be hidden. As I watched him over my shoulder, he lowered his jeans and stepped from them, then slowly turned toward me. It was all I could do to suppress a moan of admiration. I had seen him perform on stage but there was something magical about the long cock in the dim light of the luxurious bedroom. It took on an altogether different aspect, brutish, slithering in and out of his tight fist, appearing very much like a snake; I almost expected a tongue to come hissing from its monstrously flat, purplish head. He knelt on the bed and slipped a black lubricated condom on it, then he took the cheeks of my ass in his strong hands. His elegantly tapered, dark fingers spread my cheeks. I hit the remote control and the camera began to whirr. First he brought his tongue to my anus, sending me close to orgasm with his teasing. Then he inserted his thumbs into my moist hole, paving the way for the entry of the dark serpent. As the head of his cock entered me, he removed his thumbs. When he began shoving inch after inch of his cock into me, I winced. My cock was losing its hardness.

"No, no..." I stammered, tears rolling down my cheeks.

As he pressed into me, I smelled something sweet. Coconuts, I decided. He smelled like coconuts. Sweet, much too sweet. In the beginning, the pain threatened to overwhelm me, but after a few moments, as he was rolling across my body, with his hands planted firmly on the mattress, the pain gave way to a strange sense of well-being. I orgasmed without touching myself, soaking the pillow beneath me.

Ever the formidable, seasoned performer, he suddenly withdrew, slid the rubber off and dumped his load across my bare ass.

I lay on the bed, listening to him wash himself in the bathroom and when he returned to the room I called to him. He stood at the head of the bed, his hands on his hips. He smiled but said nothing. I wrapped my arms around his waist and hugged him. My lips brushed his pubic hair and I kissed the semi-flaccid shaft of his cock. The fragrance of coconuts lingered, not as sweet, but still pungent. Still potent.

"Okay, man, it's gonna be real easy," he said, soothingly, yet commandingly.

The hard black flesh slammed against my cheek, then hit my chin. Soon he was banging my lips, demanding me to let him enter. I knew the second I did, there was no retreat. I prayed for a tear in the momentum. A pause, as a consolation to see the crude shambles that a sequence of events can lead to.

A sissy's tears came to my eyes as I opened my mouth. "No," I stammered, wishing to postpone, delay, regroup. But he was insistent. He could not be denied this victory. Then the incredible organ entered my body again, this time in another orifice, a place far better equipped to deal with the gargantuan size of it. Yet I choked. I cursed my ineptitude. My lack of athletic ability. I could not even do this without fouling it. But he put his hands on each side of my head and pressed his thumbs on my cheeks. He was showing me the way. I was, after all, being taught by the master. Slowly, deliberately, he slid his sex back and forth into my mouth, a little deeper each time. Soon he began to thrust his hips in an urgent, forbidding rhythm. I gagged again, but he did not pull back. If anything, he jabbed himself deeper into my throat. Tears began to flood my eyes again. I lifted my arms so that I could grasp his biceps and push him away. I struggled, but the more I did, the more insistent he became until, finally, at the point of his extraordinarily intense orgasm, he released me. As he withdrew his cock, his juice surged from the head of it, slathering down my chin and splattering my chest.

He went into the bathroom again. I rubbed the sticky substance from my chin and mingled it with my own juice that soaked my robe. Again I orgasmed without touching myself. I followed him to the bathroom and found him drying himself with one of the hotel's huge bath towels. He smiled and seductively rubbed the towel up and down the shaft of his cock. I could not help myself. I wanted to touch it once more. Just once more. Inexorably, my hunger had not been quenched. I dropped to my knees before him. He wrapped the towel around my shoulders and began to bend his brutish, insistent cock to meet the lips of his willing slave. I kissed it. First the shaft, then the sack, then the head. I kissed it as if I was saying goodbye. It was getting to be too much of a pleasure. Perhaps an addiction. Like chocolates.

IV.

I found Snake's new show even more disgusting than the last because they had done away with the stage and sealed off that part of the building. ("Urban renewal," the ticket seller told me.) Snake and his partners were forced to cavort on gym mats in the center of a large room, with lights brightly piercing the dark, the audience standing about it in the shadows in total awe, like the apes surrounding the monolith in "2001." But Snake carried it off with dignity, like a heavyweight champ coming in and out of the ring. A tired looking young blonde with a rose tattoo on her ass writhed on the mat to the accompaniment of "She Works Hard for the Money," removing her bra and panties. She fingered her slit as

Snake entered from the wings. He dropped to his knees, made intimations toward cunnilingus, then laid over her body, thrusting gratuitously as the girl moaned and groaned. After a few moments of this, Snake jumped up and pranced off the "stage."

Moments later, he was leading me to the dark, narrow, smoky storage closet that passed as his dressing room. Laconically, he wiped his body with a sperm-stiffened towel and we talked about his returning to California. "...Only if I can stay with you at the Bel-Air," he laughed.

"Of course," I said, lowering myself into a folding chair just inside the door.

I told him of my attempts to find a suitable co-star for his next video and my various ideas for a script. I assured him I would sign him to a two picture deal worth at least three grand. We shared a couple of spoonfuls of coke and then, suddenly, he slammed the door, plunging the acrid room into darkness.

"...I know, man," he said, as supremely authoritative as ever. "I know what you're wantin'. There ain't gonna be another movie, man. But you, ya couldn't stay away, could ya?"

Coconuts. The smell grew heavier as he stepped closer. He pressed his hands on my shoulders and shoved his crotch in my face. As the silkiness of the codpiece caressed my cheek, I could feel his weapon, still coiled inside the G-string, beginning to harden. He pushed me down and the old chair collapsed behind me, my knees hitting the floor.

"Yeah," he deadpanned, "I know what ya need. You're always gonna need it."

"I— " I stammered.

"Well?" he asked, his voice rising.

"No," I sputtered, tilting my head back and looking up at him. "Don't do this. Not this way."

He clamped his powerful hands to the sides of my head and forced me forward into his groin.

"No — " I said, my mouth slammed against his silky skin.

"Hey," he laughed, "the answer's yes, motherfucker. Once you've had it, there ain't no end, you know that."

I opened my mouth to speak but I choked on the words.

"Lick it," he said, his voice rising again. He applied his thumbs to my jawbone and forced my head back. My eyes began to tear.

"Oh, god," I grumbled helplessly.

He laughed and shoved my head down again, my nostrils filling with his pubic hair. I concentrated on the smell. Vulgar, yet heavenly. I closed my eyes. He used one of his sweaty hands to snap the button of his G-string and, as it fell away, the mammoth organ banged against my cheek, free at last to lodge its final, most devastating assault on my being. I shook my head, desperate to move away from the pain this closeness was inflicting upon me. But he brought both of his strong hands to my head and steadfastly refused to release me. The head of his cock bumped my lips, then careened off and slammed into my closed eyelids. He moved one hand to the back of my head and the other grasped the shaft of the terrible black dick.

"Open," he said without a trace of emotion.

My jaw went slack and I started, awkwardly, apprehensively, to take the head of it in my hopelessly eager mouth, running my tongue over it, gauging once more the outrageous extent of it. I gagged. He wrapped one hand around the base of hard shaft and I could feel him straightening it as he shoved it into my mouth. I gagged again and he withdrew some of it, but then shoved it back even further, until I thought I was going to choke. Suddenly, he pulled it completely out, leaving it to vibrate in front of my face, taunting me. He passed the head of it across my lips, again and again, tantalizing me, making me beg.

"Kiss it," he ordered. He slapped my face with it, first one cheek, then the other. I kissed it and when I did, he pushed the shaft along my lips. "Kiss all of it," he barked. Then he presented his heavy sack for me to adore and glorify.

"No, no," I pleaded, sounding like a bullfrog gulping for air. "Not like this. Come back to my room."

"No time," he purred as he slid the member back into my mouth. I felt an incredible tension. I feared that once it was in my mouth I would choke on what would come gushing from it.

"Now," he said, drawing it back for the final assault.

And as his warm come entered my throat, I knew there could be nothing more, that this was the ultimate degradation, the ultimate sensation.

My search had ended.

Until tomorrow.

Lancelot

There was no sky, just a colorless clay-like mass hanging overhead. At least in wasn't raining. It had rained in New Orleans every day for weeks. The pungent smell of garbage hauled to the curb reminded me of Rome. When in Rome, I thought, and prepared to visit New Orleans' version of the Spanish Steps, on St. Louis, nearly out of the Quarter, where the hustlers hang out, near the Corner Pocket bar on the corner of Burgundy. Money saves you from a lot of little deaths.

I stopped at a corner grocery about three blocks from the bar and bought an apple juice. A young black, buying groceries, cruised me. He was short, well groomed and moved with assertiveness and intention as he left the market. I followed, attracted by his sinewy body and his blackness. At the age of forty, I met a black man who taught me what I had been missing for the 25 years I had been out, and now I searched for black power in every city I visited.

"Hi." His smile was dazzling; the teeth were white, perfect.

I melted. "Hi." I looked up. The dirty whipped cream sky seemed to be blowing away like smoke. "It looks like it might be a nice night after all."

"Yeah. 'Bout time."

I followed him eagerly. I told him I was visiting the city on business; he told me he was an artist.

"I live in the next block."

"Does this mean you're inviting me up to see your etchings?" He grinned.

Soon he was unlocking the door to the quaint apartment house and we entered a tiny corridor. As we stepped up the dusty old iron staircase leading to the third floor, I inhaled the wonderful smells, of old wood, disinfectant, and upon entering his suite, the smell of paint, freshly applied. I stood before the canvas on the easel in the main room, looking for clues to my host's inspirations. I wondered about the wild slashes across an otherwise tranquil scene.

He put his groceries in the pullman kitchen and came back into the main room, sliding behind me, enveloping me with his strong arms, his hands working their way to my crotch. He pressed his own crotch into my buttocks.

"What do you think?" he asked.

"I like it."

I craned my neck to look at his face and he kissed me full on the mouth.

"...Don't you think I should know your name? I mean, we have kissed, felt each other up —"

"No, it adds to the mystique," he chuckled.

"Very well."

"Seriously, it's Lance."

"Lance?"

"My mother teaches English. She loved the stories of Camelot. She said if she ever had a boy she was going to name him Lancelot. I just shortened it."

"I love it."

"This is what I love," he said, slipping my erection out of my jeans. He bent over and licked the head of it. "God, this is one of the biggest ones I've seen in a long time."

"Bullwhip Drummond I'm not, but I'm glad you like it."

"I told you, I love it." And he engulfed the flesh right down to the pubic hairs in one gulp.

"...Safe sex?" I asked as I climbed onto the bed and he took my rigid sex in his hand again.

"Doesn't really matter," he said, "as long as you pull out in time."

I thought of pre-cum but didn't pursue it. I worried about pulling this off; all of the other black men I had known had been the aggressor, stunning me with their prowess, but now Lance was preparing himself to be bottom, on his back, spreading his legs.

"Don't you fuck?" I asked him.

"I'm not good at it."

I cringed. A black man not good at it?

I prepared my cock but it was futile; I went soft. His disappointment was obvious; he had a cigarette while I played with both of our cocks.

"I don't like black guys, just white guys," he said between puffs. "Older white guys know what they're doing."

"Normally," I shrugged.

"Relax."

"Yeah." I took his dark cut cock in my mouth and deep throated it. It grew enormously under my pressure. I wanted it so badly, I would take it any way it was offered. It was not unusually large but, in proportion, I thought it humungous.

I could feel my own sex come around slowly until, finally, hovering over him, blowing him, I moved into position between his legs. I was conditioning myself that, to please him, I would have to assault his anus. He put his cigarette out and slid his legs over my shoulders. In a comfortable position again, he lifted himself to meet my prick and it slid in, to the full length, without stopping. He gasped and brought his hands to my balls, playing with them as I fucked him.

Then he took his cock in his hand and jacked off while I plunged into him. Seeing the joy on his face as he came made me move faster, harder, until, finally, I pulled out and my own cum joined his on his belly.

I lay quietly on the bed, on my stomach, recovering. He came from the bathroom with a wet cloth. He got between my legs and parted them, seizing my sex and wiping it. It grew hard again as he lovingly stroked it. "Hmmm," he murmured, lifting me up further. I could hear him applying lube to his cock. My asshole began to quiver in anticipation. The sheer force of his penetration sent me flat to the mattress and he climbed over me, his hands flat on either side of my head. He teased me, pulling out almost all the way, then slamming it back in again to the hilt, over and over, until I screamed for mercy. He kissed my ears and I found his mouth. We kissed as he started to cum again. He pulled out and sat up, cumming across my ass. Without saying a word, he wiped me clean again with the damp cloth.

"Hmmm," I murmured, running my hands up his thighs. "Nothing like a good lancing."

He chuckled then kissed me.

"...You know, you shouldn't wear that Rolex on this street," he said as he kissed me goodnight. "Guys'll rob you just to get it, hock it and buy more crack."

"Thanks, I appreciate that."

"Yeah," he grinned, "I think I saved your life tonight."

"Yes, you did. You surely did."

Stepping out onto St. Louis, I slid the watch off my wrist and dropped it in my pocket. As I began the long walk back to my hotel, I looked up. The sky had cleared completely and New Orleans was covered by a blanket of bright stars.

The Wounding Prick

"There is never any ending to Paris and the memory..."
- Ernest Hemingway

It was on the Quai Voltaire I first encountered him, among Parisian toughs of various ages and origins, several Arab, one striking Negro. He was a smooth blond young man who in America would have been considered a boy, where manhood does not begin until the age of 21. The youth looked at me with a great deal of hostility, something I had grown to expect since I had been in the country to attend the film festival. I was staying outside Cannes at the Hotel du Cap Eden Roc, in a bungalow near the sea, and it was restful, too restful. I went to Vallauris to see all the Picassos and to la chapelle that Jean Cocteau painted in Eze. Still, I was bored and took le train bleu at night to Paris. The cabin was very nice but I was alone. I had come to France to write, not only about the festival but about men who would please me by fucking me. But I met no one at Cannes about whom I could write, because I can write only about what I love and what I love is large and punishing. Now, in Paris, from the size of the blond's big basket, things were looking up.

"You're beautiful," I told him in my best French. "I bet you make a fortune here."

He just chuckled, shrugged and turned away. I followed him. When he stopped, I stopped. Finally, I offered to buy him coffee and as we walked toward the Champs Elysee, a dusty wind stirred our hair. On me, it was a nuisance; on him, it was becoming. Having done the Musee du Quai d'Orsay, the Musee Picasso, and the Musee Rodin, then walked around the Louvre, I was tired but I didn't mind walking with him at my side. I soon discovered he spoke English; indeed, he had been born in America. When his mother, who was French, left his father, she brought him with her to her native land. He was passionate about his desire to return to America one day.

"How about the next flight?" I suggested as we took seats at a table in Lilas cafe.

"What?"

I chuckled. "Nothing, just wishful thinking."

"Careful what you wish for," he muttered, motioning the waiter.

As we sipped our un demi, he looked at me intently, steadily. He asked me where I was staying. I told him the L'Abbaye St. Germain, a charming little hotel on the Left Bank. I proposed that he accompany me there and I would make it worth his while. It was hardly a smile, but he nodded his agreement.

His name was Paul and his large pale moon face soon became the most entrancing of all my visions of Paris, far more beautiful than the city's colored walls, its gray skies that change from milk to pearl, the wet green of the gardens, the reflections in the Seine. And in the twilight hour, as we walked back to the hotel, the metallic glow of the sky, a sky different from any other, gave my companion an incandescent glow.

As his voice became more soothing and gentle, my passion for him was like a flame that burned steadily; he paused now and then, expecting that I would seize the occasion to inject a word or two, but I remained silent, simply nodding, as if in a trance, and his hostility fell away more and more.

By the time we reached the hotel room, I was ready for a glass of eau-de-vie. I poured drinks for both of us, then as I put his drink in his hand, I winked happily. I sipped my own drink, the colorless alcohol feeling good on my tongue and it was still in my mouth when he wrapped his arm around my waist and drew me to him. It was an unexpected gesture, followed by a long, breathless kiss and I surrendered to him completely. "Oh, fuck me," I breathed.

He took his time undressing me, pushing my hands away as I reached to remove his clothing. He pinched my nipples, fondled my balls, beat on my cock, testing me. As his fingers probed my anus, I groaned in ecstasy and he chuckled.

Then he ordered me to lie on the bed, face down. The hostility had returned. I realized I was naked in my hotel room with a stranger who was fully dressed; I had lost control. I reclined on the bed and reached out to him as he stood over me, hands on his hips. I stroked the now enormous bulge in his tight trousers.

He stepped back. "You want it?"

"You know I do."

"Face down," he commanded.

Obediently, I nodded and rolled over.

He massaged my buttocks, then pushed my thighs apart and brought his mouth to my anus, spitting eau-de-vie into it, then forcing his finger in, then two fingers, finally three. I fought him and he was forced to secure my arms behind my back with the bedsheet. After filling my crack with spittle and more eau-de-vie, he spit on my balls, then propped me up and slid his hand under me so that he could coat my cock with saliva and jack me off. He did this as he penetrated me with his fingers. I writhed uncontrollably and came. That should have been enough, but it was not. I heard a zipper being lowered. By then it was dark but with the light from the street streaming through the windows, when I strained my neck to look behind me, I was able see what he was taking from his trousers. It was what the French call a wounding prick. I moaned as he climbed over me. I lifted myself so I would watch as he began jamming it into me.

The pain excruciating, my head fell to the pillows and I pleaded, "No, no, please, no, no."

He pulled out savagely, took a kerchief from his back pocket and stuffed it in my mouth.

He stripped off his trousers and mounted me again. I craned my neck to continue to watch the spectacle as the throbbing flesh was again inserted into me. Only once before had I experienced one nearly as large. I was in Miami and I called a number in an ad in the weekly gay newspaper. My date was large, black and, a practiced whore, his fucking of me was slow, methodical, almost magical in the way he turned pain into pleasure. He had only a few inches of it in me before I came and when I did, he pulled it out, finished.

But now because I had already come, the intensity of Paul's pressure on my anus caused me to cry out uncontrollably.

"Does it hurt?" he sneered, "Oh, good, good. I'll make it hurt more. That's the whole point, isn't it?"

As he plunged the long, thick, very pink rod into me to the hilt, I tried to move up on the bed, but he pinned my legs with his own. It was like a virgin happening and that seemed to please him. The more I squirmed, the harder he fucked me until I could feel him start to come. He yanked his cock from me and rolled me over on my back. His thighs straddling my head, he held the mighty cock over my face and came. The gobs of cream hit my eyes, my hair, my cheeks. He battered my head with it until he squeezed the last drops from it. Then he yanked the kerchief from my mouth and commanded me to lick his cock clean.

I trembled all over in anticipation and took a deep breath as he held my head with his slender hands and guided me to it. His fingers moved to my cheeks and the head of his cock slid into my mouth. At first I tongued it, savoring it, and he let me, but then he screamed, "You love it too much, too much!"

The prick began to lose its hardness and he withdrew it and began whipping my face with it. Soon it was firm again and he began edging it back into my mouth.

"Take it all or I'll piss on you, pervert."

I did my best but I had trouble handling even the head of it.

"You can't take it all up your ass, you can't take it all down your throat. What the fuck good are you, anyway?"

"No good," I murmured, the head of it still in my mouth.

The pee started, then stopped. He withdrew, then began peeing again, soaking my face, my hair, the pillows. I closed my eyes and began to cry hysterically. Laughing, he hoisted my legs over his shoulders. "Now you're going to take it all!"

Somehow, I did.

*

We entered the tiny Bar Hemingway of the Hotel Ritz from the rue Cambon through a revolving door. On the wall to the right they had hung a portrait of an older Hemingway and on the bar stood his bust. We took two of the four stools and Paul ordered us a cocktail called The Hemingway, consisting of lemon, Drambuie and bourbon, a mixture Papa undoubtedly would never have touched, and the bartender told us how the famous author used to keep his own bottle of gin there for martinis.

The black leather chairs at the six cocktail tables, the teal brocade carpet, and the wood-paneled walls made the place feel very masculine, very British. As we drank our Hemingways, Paul told me about a bullfight he saw in Spain and I remarked as how I now knew where he'd pick up his techniques. He laughed and said, "Now I'll take you to the place where Papa really got drunk."

Obediently, I followed. Just after we had entered Harry's Bar through the saloon-style swinging doors, someone brought his dog in and the bartender approved with extravagant laughter. A man in shirtsleeves made room for us at the bar and the bartender brought a generous scotch for me and a demi for Paul. My date started to talk about America again, his early life in Baltimore. I brought up my desire to see him if he ever came to America. "Oh," he said dreamily, "I would like to go back but I would miss Sundays on the butte at Montmartre, picnics in the Bois de Boulogne, the carousels in the Tuileries, the lake in the Luxembourg where the children sail their little boats."

"Yes, it is lovely here. Certainly a world away from Baltimore. But I live a world away, too, in Florida, on the Gulf."

"It is pretty there, I have heard. But not like here. Here we have great lovers."

"So I've noticed."

"Yes, I would miss all the lovers. The French, they make love everywhere."

"And you, Paul, do you ever make love?"

"What we did, that wasn't love?"

I blanched. In the loud bar, I wanted to feel his beauty had paled, to feel he was nothing more than a prostitute, an enthusiastic amateur blessed with a voluptuous physical gift, and a bit too aware of it and what it all meant and how it all looked and how well he performed, enacting fantasies merely dreamt by others. And I had to admit he did it damned well but when he quoted me a price to spend the rest of the night with me, I demurred, "Enough is enough."

With that, the hostility returned and he spun on his heels and left the bar.

Later, I crossed the Seine by the Louvre to see the Pyramide, beautiful at night, then ate Breton oysters at La Coupole and, even though it had started to rain, I decided to walk back to the hotel.

In the quiet of the night, walking the fabled cobblestoned streets, I was restless, my heart full of passion, and I cursed myself for hungering for the wounding prick.

And then, through the drizzle, I saw Paul, standing outside my hotel, waiting.

The Innkeeper's Lover

"I was always attracted to jocks younger than myself," Danny, the innkeeper's lover, told me, "but when I met Paul I realized there are the things you lust after, the things you want, and the things you need. I decided I needed Paul more than anything."

Meeting Danny's needs seemed to be what Paul was born to do. A robust, jovial man with curly sandy blond hair, Paul was a striking contrast to his pencil-thin, prematurely gray 25-year-old lover. Over the wine and cheese they served, late in the afternoon, I revealed I was working on a new book about porn stars and Danny began quizzing me about my relationships with them, especially the hung ones.

Paul chuckled, "Yeah, Danny's got this thing about size."

"Don't we all," I muttered.

Danny said there were two other guests, a traveling salesman and his lover, but they spent most of their time elsewhere. Suddenly they came charging through the door, toting shopping bags overflowing with packages. I was introduced to Joseph, a short, plain-looking, nervous type in his early 30s, and Robby, his dark-haired, farmboy lover. They declined an invitation to join us and disappeared into their room. Danny whispered, "I think they're having problems. Joseph's putting Robby to work dancing in the bars while he's here. Can you imagine?"

"No, I can't."

"And you'll love this: yesterday when I cleaned their room I found the black G-string he wears with the big pouch."

"I can see you," I chuckled, "fingering it, holding it up to your nose - just one whiff and you were in heaven!"

Danny grinned.

Things were beginning to get interesting. After weeks of flooding rains, the skies had cleared and it was bright and sunny in Dallas. When I arrived at the Inn, a lovingly restored colonial residence on a quiet street five blocks from the center of gay life on Cedar Springs Road, the top was down on Danny's red Mustang convertible parked in front of the Inn. He promised me a ride. It was only a matter of time, I thought.

That night I picked up a little black boy at Big Daddy's. Not only was he achingly cute and cuddly, he was the epitome of sartorial splendor in a black suit, white shirt, and red polka-dotted tie.

"You wear that outfit to work?" I asked.

"Oh, no, just when I go out. I like to look nice."

"You certainly do."

He had been out only a short time and I noticed with chagrin he couldn't keep his eyes off the musclebound dancers that gyrated on the tiny stages in the middle of the room. After an hour of conversation, I coaxed him to join me at the Inn but he demurred, saying he had to get up at 5 a.m. to go to his job as an assistant manager at K-Mart. He did, however, accompany me to my car and, once there, he was all over me. His kisses were like little sucks on my lips and tongue and I grew hard immediately. I reached between his thighs to find under his impeccable black trousers his cock was ensconced in a jockstrap; he was hard as well. Before long, I was able to snuggle between his thighs and kiss the bulge at his crotch.

"No, no," he kept saying, trying to push me off.

I returned to his face and quickly found his ears were vulnerable, and I kissed and tongued ferociously. His body shuddering, I went back between his thighs and managed to slip his hard-on from its captivity. I sucked it through the cloth of his trousers. He tried to escape.

"I must go -"

"No, you must come," I joked.

"Really, I must go."

The harder he fought, the stronger his erection - and the more determined I was to have it. I kept sucking it, sheathed in the silky fabric. He held my head down; he lifted my head up; he shoved it back down. Soon his jism soaked the fabric.

"Oh god," he groaned one last time.

*

By the time I awoke the next morning, Danny had already laid out the complimentary breakfast rolls and fruit but was nowhere in sight. I remembered they had mentioned Paul would be gone for a few days on a buying trip for his antique business and Danny would be taking him to the airport early. As I poured coffee, I read a note from Joe left on the table for Danny; Robby would be dancing at Zippers that night starting at nine. I made my plans.

*

Arriving early at Zippers, a narrow, dingy little bar in a seedy section of town, I became entranced with a dark-haired youth in a black leather jacket and black shorts playing pool by himself. I stood off to the side sipping my beer, watching him intently. A tall musclebound young man with curly blond hair strutted by carrying a duffel bag. "You dancin' tonight?" he drawled to the pool player.

"Yeah," the boy replied, making his shot.

The blond entered the closet that doubled as a dressing room and turned on the light. As he stripped for action, I could see the clothes dropping to the floor through the vent in the bottom of the door.

"When do you have to start dancing?" I asked the pool player.

"Around ten."

"Then there's plenty of time to have a little fun."

"No, I can't. Once I get here I can't leave."

"Oh," I shrugged.

I began dreaming about the closet, that perhaps there was room for two in there, when Danny came up to me with a drink in his hand. "Did you have a nice day?"

"I live for the nights."

"Smart man."

Joe and his lover were right behind him and before long, Robby had replaced the blond dancer in the closet. When he came out, I gasped. His baggy clothes had hidden a flawless jock's body and when he mounted the tiny stage near the entrance to the bar, I pointed to his magnificently shaped ass and sighed to Joe, "You must love plugging that."

He shook his head sadly. "No. He's straight. The most I can do is eat it out."

"Pity, but at least that's something."

"He dances like a straight boy," Danny said.

I took this to mean that he was like the others, not putting much into it, just gyrating a little, flexing, and spending most of their time standing still so customers could feel their skin and slide money into their pouches.

After the second drink, Danny said he had to leave and I walked him to his car. "What's the rush?" I asked.

"Oh, with Paul gone I'm going to finish the video I started."

"Video" always being a cue for me, I pressed on, "Oh?"

"That's the way my ex-lover and I communicate. He's in California and we swap tapes. He always wanted me to bottom for him but I never would so now I'm going to send a tape of me and the dildo."

"Why a dildo? Why not the real thing?"

"If I could find eight inches or more, I would."

"Now I know why I came to Dallas."

"You?"

I nodded. "More."

He shook his head. "I guessed as much." He rolled his eyes heavenward, then down to my crotch, then directly into my eyes. "But I don't think so."

"Hey, aren't you a member of the Chamber of Commerce?"

"Of course."

"Well, then, it's your duty to welcome visitors to the city."

He chuckled.

"Yeah, it'd be a menage a' trois, you, me and the dildo."

"I've never had a three-way. It would be better if it were you, me and one of those dancers. Like Robby."

"Hell, you'll never get Robby or any of those dancers tonight. How about one of the kids along Throckmorton?"

He thought a moment. "I wonder if Eric's gotten out of jail."

"Eric?"

"You'd love him. He's straight but he digs getting fucked."

"I love it already."

"Blond, beautiful hairless body."

Smacking my lips, I said, "God, let's go."

We found Eric standing on the corner in cowboy boots and a black cowboy hat over his long blond hair. His white jeans clung tightly, invitingly to his firm buns. He had gotten out of jail the day before; a possession charge. He was already back on the crack and anxious; it was easy to get him for the bargain street-rate of $30, times two.

Danny had set up the camera at Paul's warehouse near the World Trade Center, a few blocks from the Inn. He had focused the camera on a couch with large fluffy cushions in Oriental design.

Eric appeared to be on a tight schedule; he shed his clothes immediately and dropped onto the couch on his stomach. He lived up to his billing in every way and I lusted for him but I agreed to the scenario my host painted as we traveled to the scene: "After the camera's rolling, I'll do Eric, then you come in with the dildo, then...well, you know."

All went smoothly to begin with, Danny's thin six-incher sliding easily into the hustler. But Danny resisted the dildo; I could only get a couple inches of it in before he'd swish me away. He was incredibly tight.

"Bring that big dick of yours over here," he ordered, pointing to the end of the couch in front of him. He leaned over Eric and started to play with my balls.

"God, you weren't kiddin' were you?"

I beamed. I love it when they love it.

Soon he was licking my balls, working his way to the shaft, then to the head of my cock. He continued to pummet Eric as he began sucking me. I steadied his head with my hands and closed my eyes. He clamped his hands on my ass and brought the sucking and the fucking into a perfect harmony. When I felt myself close to cumming, I pulled away and climbed over the two of them. Slowly I slid my sex into Danny. He groaned but finally relaxed enough to let me get the head and a couple of inches in, then he climaxed. He couldn't take any more and I let him get up. As he returned to the camera, I invaded Eric. I no sooner began than I was ready to pop.

Even with a rubber on, the hustler didn't want me to come inside of him. "I wanna see it," he groaned, lifting his ass to meet my final thrusts.

My body heaving, I pulled out, slipped off the rubber, and came all over his face. "He saw it all right," Danny yelled, joyous that he had captured it all on tape.

The next day, when I was checking out, Danny handed me a bill marked "Paid in Full."

"But -" I started.

He grinned. "This one's on me, big boy."

*

A few months later, while visiting the back room at my local video store, scanning the section where the new releases were haphazardly tossed on a table, my eyes focused on a coverbox with "Danny Does Dallas" in big block letters. The naked youth with the cowboy hat on the cover, superimposed over a scene of Dallas by night, was unmistakably Eric. It was one of a series titled "America's Sexiest Home Videos." I rushed to the counter and rented it.

After a segment of Danny masturbating, there was Eric, on the couch, on his stomach, being fucked by Danny. I waited patiently. My hands entered the frame, the dildo was inserted. Mercifully, as I walked in front of the camera and took my place at the end of the couch, I was trimmed at the waist but in the final few minutes, as I slammed into Eric, despite the atrocious lighting, I was readily identifiable. Danny, on the camera, zoomed in on my climax. It was the best scene in the movie.

The next day, I went back to the store and paid the owner the $59 he said the tape cost him; I told him it was awful, not to buy another one. Back at home, I labeled the spine of the contraband: "Souvenir of Dallas, TX" and slipped it into the stacks on the shelves, between "Something Wild" and "Stallions."

The Boy Back Home

When I spotted him, he was lying on the beach in a secluded area of the little dunes. Even from a distance, I could tell he was young, blond, well built. I walked further up the beach, then turned around. When I approached the spot again, he'd moved, up closer to the water. I waded into the warm water of the gulf and my feet sunk into the sand like roots. I was stalling for time, gathering my courage. Although I had always been reluctant to approach anyone so close to home, the bulge in his little blue bikini was too inviting to dismiss lightly.

Suddenly, a squad car was charging along the path behind the little dunes, a usual occurrence in the afternoon, just checking on the activity. The car stopped and the cop got out. He surveyed the scene for a few minutes, got something out of the trunk, then left. The action held the boy's attention, held it far more than I did. He was paying me no mind.

As attracted as I was to his build and the sun-bleached hair that hung enticingly over his eyes, I decided to give up the fight, to continue walking south. But as I started to take a few tentative steps in that direction, he stood, shook the sand from his towel, picked up his gym bag and began his retreat into the woods. It was as if he had challenged me. I hastily left the water and followed him.

I had only walked the paths in front of the woods a few times, too timid to venture into them. I feared the police and, besides, I had no reason to, never having seen anything go in there that captured my fancy. But the blond was something to be captured.

I pursued him until I came to a fork in the path. I was confused, having lost sight of him, and I didn't know which way to turn, but then I glimpsed his bikini through the pines. He was actually standing still, as if he was waiting for me.

I took the long way to the thicket where he had laid out his towel. The gays had, over the years, taken branches and built little private tanning areas about four foot by seven foot here and there throughout the woods. The boy had laid his towel in the middle of one of them and was sitting up, smoking a cigarette, as I approached him.

He ignored me. I stopped at the branches surrounding the area he had staked out and stared at the bulge between his thighs. Now he noticed me. As our eyes met I asked, "You ever done any modeling?"

"No. Never thought about it. Why, you a photographer?"

"No, but I know people who are. And when I see somebody I think they could use, well, I guess you could say I'm sort of a scout for them."

"You think they'd like me?"

"I'm sure of it. You have everything...the hair, the eyes, the build, and," I gulped.

He smiled.

"Yes, your smile. Teeth are very important."

"I had braces."

"They did a good job. Yes, you're quite perfect."

I entered his domain and lowered myself onto his blanket. "Mind if I sit down?"

He nodded.

"Are you visiting here?" I asked hopefully.

"Nah," he chuckled. "Born here, man."

"Born here! I've never met anyone who was actually born here!"

"Yeah, I love the place."

"I've never seen you here at the beach."

"Usually I just come down here on the weekends."

"I avoid the weekends. Too crowded."

He shrugged his shoulders and smiled.

"But you wouldn't mind traveling, on modeling jobs and so on?"

"Guess not. I haven't had a vacation in years."

"Oh, I must ask. Are you 18?"

He laughed.

"You could pass for sixteen."

"Yeah, ain't it a bitch? Maybe when I'm forty I'll only look thirty."

"I'm sure of it." I smiled and reached into the pockets of my swimsuit, demonstrating they were empty. "God, I wish I had one of my business cards."

After he tossed his cigarette away, his hand fell to my groin. "I'll bet this is the only calling card you ever need."

"I was thinking the same about you," I said, moving my hand onto his bulge.

"We shouldn't," he said, his hand leaving my bulge and clamping over my hand. "The cops may come back."

The summer showers always seem to start around three o'clock and I heard a drop of water, small and flat, and then the next sharp drop struck the blanket, as if to put an end to something and begin another thing.

"Let's make a dash for it," he said. "I'm parked close by."

The rain became a sign, reminding me that love had not yet died not even in the years since I first drove south through raindrops that slicked the road, my convertible cutting straight as a knife's edge through the sad and baleful beauty of the countryside and then, as the skies cleared in Florida, it seemed to be the golden after-light of life's recurrent possibilities.

*

"Hey, this is a neat house, man," he said, as he came in after me.

"Thanks. Care for a beer?"

"Yeah, really. It's hot out there." He dropped onto one of the bar stools and watched me fix drinks.

"See," I went on, "what I'll do is take a few pictures of you to give them an idea and then we'll just see what happens. Won't take long. We can do it any day you're free."

"I didn't think you were serious about that shit. I don't know that I could go out to California." He picked up his pack of cigarettes. "Hey, I need a smoke. I'll go out on the deck."

"It's still raining. You can smoke in here."

He nodded and lit up. I touched his leg and left my hand there. He didn't move. "Yeah, I'm really into magazines and videos," he said after taking a long drag, "but I've about worn mine out."

"I just got a new one from the people in California I was telling you about. Would you like to see it?" I asked, my hand sliding up and down his naked thigh.

"I guess I got a little time," he said, bringing his hand to my crotch.

I went into the bedroom, switched on the TV and shoved a cassette into the deck.

He bounced down on the edge of the bed and I lowered myself down next to him, bringing my hand around his body and hugging him lightly. He finished his cigarette.

The video was one by Kris Bjorn and the natives were huge. "God, look at that!" he cried. "Yeah, I like 'em big."

"So do I. " My hand moved to his bulge again. I began stroking the hardness I found there and he began exploring me.

His urgency overwhelmed me and soon I was leaning back, letting him pull my trunks down. As my erection slid into view, he gasped. "Shit, you're bigger'n all of them. They should take movies of you; I've never seen a bigger one."

"But you've never left this town."

"Never had any reason to," he gushed, stroking it. Then, staring into my eyes, he began licking the head of it and said, "Yeah, sooner or later, everything comes to you."

III.
Fables And
Other Flights of Fancy

"My uncle Billy has a ten-foot willy -
Showed it to the girls next door;
They thought it was a snake
And hit it with a rake
And now it's only four foot four."
- Edna O'Brien

The Ceremony

Kyle Stone

The low-lying sun gleamed on the tips of weapons and metal helmets as Attlad rode into camp ahead of his men, leading his naked young slave, Micah, on a horse behind him. A section of the vast open area was crowded with colorful tents, the insignia of the different leaders flying from the center poles. Nearby, horses were tethered and, in another spot, men in brown uniforms were setting up trestle tables and preparing great fires laid in pits dug deep in the ground. Where Attlad's dragon pennant unfurled in the breeze, at the largest tent, made of green and black silk, they dismounted and while the leader talked to his men, Micah stood quietly by his side, watching him closely, waiting for the hand signals he had come to know well. All around him, the strange language he still could not understand slid back and forth between the men. While outwardly attentive, his mind worked on the possibilities for escape presented by the sprawl of the encampment and the river he saw glinting in the distance. When Attlad gestured to him to take two pails and get water for the horses, he felt a rush of rebellion. He, too, was a respected young warrior! He might be a slave, for now, such were the fortunes of war, but he was not a menial servant. He stared back at the leader defiantly.

"You do not obey?" Attlad's hands sliced the air, the signs clear as any spoken words.

Micah trembled with anger but it was his duty as a soldier to escape and the chance to reconnoiter was more important than his pride. Setting his jaw, he picked up the wooden buckets that stood by the hitching post and started for the river.

When he returned, Kee, the handler, was waiting. "Come, I will prepare you," Kee signed, leading the way to a small hut nearby. After they were inside, he pointed to a table in the middle and told Micah to get naked.

As he lay down on the table, Micah asked, shaping the signs carefully, "What will happen?"

Kee paused in his work to sketch the words in the air. Micah watched avidly, trying to follow. "Your master will display you to the men. You will show every part of yourself for their enjoyment.

I will tie back your hair so they can see your face all the time, as well as your cock and ass. All will want to touch you for the last time because, if tonight he gives you the rings, you are his, and only his, forever. Understand?"

Nodding, Micah winced as Kee slapped his penis from side to side then began trimming his pubic hair. He closed his eyes. He knew this to be another test and his pride made him want to acquit himself to please his master. He blushed as Kee spread his legs and washed his cock and balls then began rubbing him with scented oil. His cock began to stir to life. Kee chuckled and applied more oil. Micah was proud of his cock and opened his eyes to see it, strong, hard, glistening.

He was equally proud of his long blond hair, how it fascinated the swarthy men, how they played with it endlessly, doubting it was real, but Kee grasped it in one hand and twisted it out of sight under a tight leather cap. Next, he fastened a leather collar with large silver spikes around Micah's neck and secured leather bracelets to his ankles and wrists.

When Attlad strode into the hut, he seemed to fill the tiny space. Kee stepped back at once and Micah stood up, awaiting his hand signals. The leader took a small bottle from the pouch at his waist and pulled out the stopper. He dabbed the red-brown liquid on Micah's nipples and they became hard as Attlad's rough fingers stroked them. The master then rubbed the liquid on the underside of Michah's penis, smiling when he saw the cock obediently spring to attention. He stepped back, took a swig of wine from a bottle that had been on the table, and admired his slave. Setting the bottle back down on the table, he took Micah in his arms. He kissed him on the mouth, forcing Micah's mouth open and the wine flowed between them. Micah swallowed greedily, his lips clinging to his master's. Then Attlad clipped a leash o his slave's collar and led the youth from the hut.

By this time, it was dark and great flaring torches cast an eerie light over the camp. From the meadow below came the sound of a large group of men talking and laughing together. Attlad leapt easily onto his mount, twisting the leash around his hand. He started off at brisk trot. Micah, his arms cuffed behind him, his head held high, jogged beside him. But soon Attlad gathered speed and his slave had to run fast, afraid of losing his balance and being dragged into the gathering.

A cheer went up as they appeared at the amphitheater where trestle tables had been set up. They stopped at a small stone platform, lit by a circle of torches. Chains hung from a scaffold high above them and a fire flared down below.

Attlad, at ease on his nervously prancing steed, turned his horse to face the assembly and began speaking. Micah was hoisted up onto the stone platform and stood catching his breath, awaiting a signal from his master. When it came, it shocked him. "Display yourself," Attlad's hands said.

The slave glanced about, frantically searching for a way out, but Attlad flicked his stinging whip across the youth's firm buttocks. In a reflex action, Micah thrust his hips forward, bending his knees.

"More!" Attlad commanded.

As the crowd hooted with pleasure, Micah pumped back and forth, ashamed of his lewd gestures.

"Turn around, open yourself up to them!"

Obediently, Micah bent, parting the cheeks of his ass, but Attlad reached over and forced his legs even wider apart. The crowd cheered. Micah closed his eyes and tried to ignore them.

When Micah was allowed to straighten up, Kee attached chains to the bracelets on his ankles and wrists. When Kee gave the signal, the chains were tightened, raising Micah into the air. As the slave was hoisted above them by his arms, a tremendous shout went up from the crowd. The slave's legs were slowly raised until his feet were level with his hands and his body was bent double like an animal suspended in a pit for roasting. The chains moved gently, swinging back and forth, creaking slightly in the breeze. The men laughed at the sight and, as they began to eat and drink, every few minutes the length of the chains was altered so that at times Micah was stretched almost taut, the manacles on his wrists and ankles cutting into his skin. Then the chains would lengthen and move close together so that his ass was split wide open, exposed to their further scrutiny. Then he was abruptly lowered and his feet swung around and up again so that he hung facing the crowd, his arms pulled back behind him, his cock pointing down toward the crowd.

As the men feasted below him, some climbed up on the tables, trying to touch the slave with their filthy, sweaty hands. As he struggled to cope with the torment, each new position increasing his threshold for pain, time seemed to cease for Micah. By the time he was lowered to the stone platform and unshackled, he could hardly stand; the muscles in his arms and thighs screamed in protest.

A frenzy of shouting and hand waving broke out below him. His master was making another speech and Micah was taken to his side. When Attlad finished talking, he held up both hands, his fingers spread. Ten. To his horror, Micah realized he had been auctioned to the men at the front table for ten minutes. Panic beat at him, but Kee was already thrusting him towards the rowdy group. The man nearest him grabbed his arm. Another jerked off his leather cap and tugged at his hair. His captors made him kneel on the table, his forehead pressed against the wood, his ass high in the air, and the whipping began. "Dance!" one of the men shouted. "Make your ass dance for me!"

In spite of himself, Micah began to wriggle, trying to avoid the sting of the whip but that only made his tormentor beat him harder and faster, screaming at him to dance. The slave jerked convulsively, emptying his mind of everything but his desire to avoid pain. But he could not escape the sound of their rude laughter, the clinking of the bottles, the belches.

Now they pulled him by the hair until he was upright, his knees splayed wide, his cock arching towards them. They began tormenting his penis, flicking it lightly, then squeezing it with their hands, pulling back as he sought release. Their fingers pushed and poked at his balls, explored his anus. Finally, one of the men climbed onto the table and opened his pants, pushing himself into Micah's ass, showing no mercy. He was so drunk that he could not stay in, toppling off the table onto the ground amid the cheers of the men. Then Micah felt the nozzle of a wine skin shoved up his hole and the wine squirted inside him. Hot tears of pain and humiliation stinging his cheeks, he sought to find Attlad in the sea of faces but he could not. Soon another man invaded him. This one came quickly, but so violently, they both fell off the table. Micah on top of the warrior, straddling his chest, dumping a mixture of cum and wine on it. Rudely, the man pushed him down, forcing him to lick up the mess.

Suddenly, time was up and Attlad pulled him off the man and held him for a long, comforting moment. Cum and wine still oozing from his mouth, Micah felt the fingers on the palm of his hand tell him with signs, "You did well. I am pleased."

Something stirred in Micah, something deep and unacknowledged until now, and he raised his master's hand to his lips and kissed the hard, callused palm.

"Come," Attalad said, "time for the rings."

The rings. Micah shivered, but he longed to have the approval of his master.

As Attlad led his slave back to the fire at one side of the platform, a tense silence fell over the assembly. The bottom of the scaffold holding the chains where Micah had been hung was shaped like a square and the slave's wrists were attached to the top corners, his ankles at the bottom, so that his aching body was stretched to form an X. Two bare-chested men took positions, one in front, one behind, and began to beat him with long, flat, pliable paddles. Writhing desperately, Micah cried out as each blow landed in a slightly different area of his flesh so that no part of his body went unpunished. Finally, when Attlad gave the sign, they stepped back, leaving Micah gasping in pain. The leader stepped close and took the instrument handed him on a silver tray. Micah tensed again but he was not prepared for the hot, excruciating jolt of agony that was afflicted on his right nipple when Attlad touched it. Micah screamed and began to struggle desperately, twisting and turning against the restraints. He knew it was useless but reason deserted him. Then Attlad brought the instrument to his slave's left nipple and Micah screamed again. Next Attlad lifted the boy's stiff cock and pressed the instrument to its root. Mad with the pain, it took the slave a while to realize that Attlad had stopped and was pressing a soft cloth dipped in wine to his parched lips. He sucked it gratefully. In the flare of the torchlight, his naked body gleamed with sweat, his face red, slick with tears. But Attlad was not finished; he reached up and pierced the slave's right ear. Micah lost consciousness for a moment but he stirred when he was finally taken down. The slave fell into his master's strong arms, clinging to him. Then Attlad's great black horse was brought before them and after he vaulted easily onto its back, Micah was hoisted up in front of him and they rode out of the feasting area to Attlad's tent. There, Micah was thrown on the bed. He lay on his back and his master sponged him off with a steaming liquid, his hands sure, possessive. When it was over, Micah rested his head on Attlad's chest and sipped wine from a golden goblet. When his master stroked his hair and began fingering his pubic hair. Micah spread his legs wide. He winced as Attlad touched him where the fire still burned.

"Come," Attlad gestured, "look at my love slave."

Micah was led to a large mirror that had been propped up in a corner of the tent. He was startled by the image before him, the gold rings in the reddened nipples and from the chain between them dangled a gold disk with Attlad's symbol emblazoned on it, and the gold earring with red teardrop suspending from it. His master turned him around and pushed his head down so he could look between his legs and see his own ass. He saw the gold ring that gleamed under his cock and hanging from it a red tear drop like the one in his ear. As Micah straightened up again, Attlad, moving his hands slowly, explained, "No one will touch you now, you are mine."

Micah nodded. Attlad pointed to the wine and Micah poured it. Attlad stretched out on the bed and had Micah lay beside him, his head resting against his thigh. He gave him sips of wine as he talked in his own language with its clusters of harsh consonants. As Micah listened, he nuzzled his master's crotch. Soon Micah was straddling him, licking his master's skin. Attlad, his eyes soft, let his slave cover him with wet kisses and suck on the hard nipples. When Miach moved down the muscular torso, his master made himself vulnerable to him for the first time. Micah pulled the cloth away from the crotch and his eyes feasted on the hugeness of what was revealed. As he began to take as much of it as he could in his mouth, he moaned. He sucked it tenderly, careful to shield the skin from his sharp teeth. Soon Attlad pulled away and told Micah to lower himself onto it. Micah carefully balanced himself over his master and brought his ass onto the great cock, wincing with the pain as it slowly entered him. The tender skin around the ring and its jewel at the base of his own cock rubbed and stretched. He strained to take all of it inside him, the bed creaking with his exertions. Attlad arched his back and the tendons stood out on his neck as he began to groan. Now Micah redoubled his efforts, sweat standing out from his taut body, his own cock beginning to jerk wildly. When Attlad came, Micah sat still, daring not to move. Attlad lifted his slave from his body and smiled, "Good. You are good. Lie down."

Micah obeyed.

Attlad sipped some wine and soon was ready to take his slave again. "Hold your ankles," he ordered.

Micah lay on his back, his legs in the air, and held his ankles. Attlad pushed his legs wide apart and knelt over him, his member swelling enormously again as he stroked it. The slave moaned and gasped for breath as his master thrust deeply into him, trying hard not to cry out as Attlad's body banged against the soreness of his own genitals but after several minutes of furious fucking, it was too much and he began to whimper. Attlad pulled him to his chest and exploded inside him again. For a moment, they lay still, catching their breath. Then Attlad rolled Micah back so that the wet eye of his ass was more accessible and he saw that the slave still had an erection. He kissed the base of it and his lips were cool and soft against the burning tenderness there. Micah cried out with pleasure, his jock jerking suddenly, releasing a pearly stream of come that spurted onto the chain joining his nipples. Attlad laughed and allowed him to bring his legs down. The master took a cool cloth and wiped off his slave, then himself and laid back down on the bed. He hugged Micah to his chest and entered him again, but did nothing more.

And as they fell asleep, the master's huge cock in the slave's tight ass, Micah no longer dreamed of escape.

The Prince's Jewels

Jamoo

At dusk the jungle birds ceased to sing and, peering out from his hiding place near the old, vine-covered temple, Laloo felt his heart beat frantically because coming down the road was the one he longed for. There was barely enough light to see the vigorous young man clearly but a light breeze off the Ganges brought his scent of ghee oil mixed with clean sweat and perfume to Laloo's nostrils.

Late every afternoon, Laloo would watch the young god walk by after his bath in the River, then go to his bed of straw and dream of sharing kama, the joining of two bodies, only to awake the next morning with a wet mess between his legs, feeling even more lonely than the day before. But dreaming was all he could ever hope to do because the young man, Prince Abdulla, a nephew of the Sultan, was not of his class or even caste. Yet the Prince's features, emerald eyes, light olive skin and aquiline nose, gave away a shameful heritage. Nearly twenty years before, a general in Alexander's army came to the palace and had a liasion with Princess Zaydah, who died giving birth to the boy. The Prince's past made him even more attractive to Laloo because he, too, was of mixed blood, the son of a pale-skinned Moslem father and a Negress. But he was nothing more than a mulatto, fit only to clean out the stables at best.

On this starry night, as the Prince drew nearer, Laloo looked down to see the bulge poking out of the vasana, the skirt-like garment he wore. When he hurriedly stepped back to hide in the darkness, he slipped and sent stones bouncing in front of the young prince.

"Who goes there?" Abdulla asked.

Laloo stepped onto the path, his brown eyes looking out from under long black lashes. The nostrils were flared and quivering from fear, the prince thought, and the mouth was large, full and red, parting to draw in a quick breath. Above the smooth forehead, Abu could see the dingy folds of a cloth turban. In the darkness, he could not tell if it was a boy or girl.

"I frightened you," Laloo said, looking up at the prince, laughing nervously.

"You did. You should not be playing in this place so late. Come along, I'll walk you back to the city."

"But this is my home."

"Little liar. Stop playing games, now come along."

"But I do live here. Come see, if you're not afraid, he who jumps at a pebble in his path!" Laloo cried, dashing into the mouth of the shrine, the Prince at his heels.

"See, this is where I sleep," Laloo said, standing before the bed of straw in a corner of the stone room at the very back of the crumbling temple.

"How wretched it is, so damp and cold."

Laloo nodded. "Not like your apartments at the palace."

"You know who I am then?"

Laloo nodded again, leaning down to light a fire in the pit he had dug out.

"Then why do you not bow to me?"

"Why, what has His Highness ever done for me?"

"You push stones in my path, now you insult me! I should have you killed."

Laloo stood again. "I can think of no better way to die than at your hand."

"What?"

"I watch you every day. Once I followed you to the river to watch you bathe."

"And I suppose you were the one who stole my clothes, leaving me with only a loincloth!"

"Yes. You have many clothes and I sold them to buy food. I didn't want to. I wanted to keep them, wear them, sleep in them, because they were yours, but I had to sell them."

"I will have you put to death for stealing! I may kill you myself!" He drew a dagger from his sash.

"Go ahead," Laloo said, ripping the thin white vest he wore, revealing his smooth, hairless chest. "Stab me. That's all you know, you barbarian! Yes, I know who you are and what you are. You're no better than me. You're the son of a barbarian."

"Ha! So, tell me, little thief, did you like what you saw at the river."

Laloo blushed and looked away, mumbling, "Yes, your Royal Highness."

"Then you like barbarians?"

Laloo's eyes returned to feast on the handsome young prince and he smiled. "Only one."

"And I like what I see now. I swear you are prettier than any girl in the palace." He stepped closer and loosened Laloo's turban, then casted it on the ground.

"You disgrace me," Laloo cried.

Abu took one of the soft tendrils of the boy's hair and twisted it with his finger. "No, it is a disgrace to cover such beautiful hair. You are very fair to look upon. What is your name, little thief?"

"Laloo."

"So, Laloo, what would you say if I said you have found favor in my eyes, that I shall spare your life?"

"I would be most grateful, Your Highness."

"And what if I said you make fire in the blood of my veins?"

"I would say you do the same to me, Your Highness."

"And would you please me?"

"I swear by the gods of both my father and mother I would please you as no one ever has."

Abu tossed his dagger on the ground and removed a large emerald ring from his finger and held it up to the firelight. "With this ring you would be a wealthy thief indeed."

"Yes," Laloo cried, his eyes sparkling. "It would buy me anything I desired."

"If you please me, I will give you this and all the jewels I am wearing."

"All of them?"

Abu nodded and took off his silk turban. Out spilled black curls that cascaded past his shoulders. Shaking his mane, he tossed the turban to the ground and dropped the ring into it, followed by all the gold and silver bangles encrusted with diamonds from his dark, thick, hairy arms. Then he took the three-inch-long amethyst earrings from his ears and the two strands of black pearls from round his neck and added them to the mound of jewels in the turban. Last of all, Abu removed the small gold hoop from his right nostril and the diamond stud from his left to drop into the cache of gems. Laloo reached for the turban, but the Prince's slipper pushed it away.

"They are not yours yet, little braggart. First you must please me." Abu unbuttoned his knee-length coat, which was the color of ripe corn, and untied the indigo sash from round his waist. After pulling the coat open and casting it off, he slowly ran his hand over his naked chest. "What is wrong? You were all talk and bragging a moment ago."

"All that hair, the Prince must be half ape," Laloo whispered with a shy grin. He stepped forward and placed a hand on the hard chest, then moved it to the hair that circled the navel. "I thought you'd have a jewel hidden in here as well," he joked.

"There's only one jewel I have left to give," the Prince said.

Laloo's slender hand moved down to the bulge in the black silk of the Prince's vasana.

"Yes, that is the one," the Prince groaned.

Laloo kneeled before the Prince and drew the skirt down. With every inch, he gasped as the tremendous phallus was revealed. Finally, it was set free and bounced into Laloo's face. He was speechless. The phallus was almost as dark as his own but twice the length. As he ran his fingers through the tight, fleecy curls that surrounded the base, the Prince thrust forward and the organ bumped Laloo's lips. He opened them and kissed the mushroom-shaped head, which was oozing hot, salty seed. As he lowered the vasana to the ground, he nipped and licked at the dark testicles hanging below the organ.

After Abu stepped from the skirt, he stretched out on the straw like a panther. Laloo bent over him and planted wet kisses on the Prince's thighs, then moved up to his stomach and chest where he ran his fingers through the spiraling black curls till he came to the copper nipples and licked them as his fingers explored the matted, wet hairs under Abu's arms, inhaling the scent of ghee oil and sweat. Abu groaned and Laloo brought his lips to the short goatee, then to the Prince's lips. The Prince embraced the boy and they kissed passionately, their crimson tongues becoming like liquid flames. So sweet were the kisses that burned Laloo's lips that he trembled in a violent fit of lust. Abu rubbed his strong hands over Laloo's moist back, tracing the line of his spine as it led to his tailbone. Thrusting his hands under the vasana, he squeezed the round buttocks and let his fingers wander into the hair-dusted cleft between them. As he probed up into the sensitive flesh, Laloo cried out. The Prince grinned and slid his hands around the boy's slender waist and lifted him. He sat against the wall with his knees drawn up and leaned Laloo against them as if they were a cushion. With the boy in his lap, he leaned over and began to suckle the tiny dark brown nipples as his fingers toyed with the wiry patches of hair growing under the arms and they kissed again.

"Your kisses are sweeter than dripping honeycomb," the Prince said, then opened his legs and, with no support behind him, Laloo fell into the straw. Abu descended upon him, the huge phallus in Laloo's face, and he drew the youth's head to it and the sucking of the giant prick continued for several minutes. It seemed Laloo was worshiping the cock and the Prince rejoiced in it, moaning again and again how much the youth was pleasing him.

"Are you ready for the greatest pleasure of all?" Laloo asked, looking up into the prince's face.

"Oh, yes," the prince sighed. "You can tell how ready I am."

Laloo got on all fours in order to fully accommodate the Prince. When Abu spread the boy's brown buttocks and thrust his tongue between them, Laloo moaned. Having prepared the way for his cock, Abu grinned as he began furiously spearing Laloo's tight opening with the head of it. The boy worked himself into such a frenzy that his own member became hard and quickly shot its discharge onto the straw. But Laloo screamed for the Prince to keep on, to go deeper, and he did, clawing at Laloo's shoulders, until, at last, with his large balls slapping against the youth's thighs, he was all the way in. Then, as the Prince increased his strokes, Laloo began to cry until the semen was soaring into him. "By the gods, little Laloo, you earned your jewels," Abu panted.

Then he rolled off the boy and pulled him next to him. Laloo snuggled deep into the crook of Abu's sleekly muscled arm and breathed, "It wasn't those jewels I wanted, it was this one."

And as the little thief's hand stroked the mighty organ, still swollen, the Prince smiled, "If that is all you want, then it is yours, forever."

The Orphan: A Fable

John Patrick

To a temple built on the sides of Mount Lugh there came an old woman and a young boy who had been orphaned when his parents were killed by bandits. The priests and priestesses took the old woman into the temple and as she lay dying, they agreed to care for the child and find him a good home.

But the residents were soon captivated by the boy's quick wit and athleticism, as well as his spectacular beauty, his golden hair and sapphire blue eyes. They came to feel the youth had been sent to them by a higher power who was rewarding them for their good service in his name. So it came to be that the youth spent his boyhood at the temple and became a favorite of the high priest, Sinh.

It had been Sinh's fate always to have worshiped youth from afar, to never be able to act upon his desires; the youths he admired were always someone else's children. But with the arrival of the orphan, whom he named Ryun, Sinh felt that the higher powers had granted his lifelong wish to have a boy to whom he could devote his life, teaching him everything he needed to know to succeed.

Some years later, when Sinh was returning from a prolonged trip, he came upon Ryun swimming alone in the grand pool of the temple. Sinh was stunned by the youth's exuberance. He swam and swam and, when his young energies were finally spent, he pulled himself from the water and reclined on the grass. Sinh hid behind a tree so that he could continue to watch the youth in private. He was astonished at the richness of the naked flesh before him; it was as if he was seeing the boy for the first time. Ryun's skin shimmered in the ruddy light of sunset and he breathed heavily, his chest rising and falling. Sinh noticed his muscles had become well-formed, due to his careful diet and exercise, and only the merest golden down was visible at the base of his stomach. Then when Sinh's eyes settled on the youth's sex, he discovered Ryun had come of age, with an organ of monstrous proportions.

As the boy rolled over and laid his head upon his arm to sleep, Ryun's buttocks loomed before the priest. It was a sight even more breathtaking than the youth's sex. The ass was perfectly formed, with the tiniest golden hairs now sprouting between the cheeks. The old priest was spellbound, aroused beyond anything that he had known.

He closed his eyes and begged forgiveness for the thoughts that entered his mind. But when he opened his eyes again the boy was still there and, as the priest shifted to a better vantage point, the lad's eyes opened and sparkled with surprise. Beckoning him, he moaned, "Oh, Father."

"Yes, my son."

Rubbing a spot above his ass, Ryun said, "Please, I think I pulled a muscle climbing from the pool. Will you rub it for me?"

It was as if his prayer for forgiveness had been answered with a sign, a sign that what Sinh had desired was not a sin after all, that it was merely an extension of the education process begun years before.

The priest's hands, large-boned and strong, moved with great tenderness, gliding up and down across Ryun's smooth back to settle on the spot the youth had pointed to. Applying heavy pressure there with the palm of his hand, the holy man said, "Feel better?"

"Oh yes," the boy groaned, "oh, yes." And he began undulating his hips in a way that Sinh took as another sign and he bent forward and kissed first one asscheek, then the other, his tongue occasionally sliding between them. The youth groaned softly but did not attempt to move away or prevent Sinh from making love to his flesh.

The priest's hands crept lower and lower until his fingers fluttered up and down the smooth insides of the youth's legs. At this probing, the youth allowed his legs to part and his balls to become visible. The priest's hand reached under Ryun and stroked the sack, then moved deeper to find a member that was now hard and its incredible heft amazed him. His own sex, he realized, was barely half the size of his young charge's. Sinh felt each had been blessed, the youth because of his endowment, he because he had been chosen to be the first to experience it.

Ryun began to writhe against the grass, his hips rising against the probing of the priest's mighty hands, his moans now coming in a steady tempo, his golden locks flashing. Finally, the priest could stand it no more and brought his lips to the boy's sex. Soon his mouth had opened and the hugeness of the youth began to fill him, slowly, inch by inch, until the priest realized he merely had to hold himself still while the boy released himself of his passion. When the boy ejaculated, it was an incredible moment as the fleshy tool was being thrust deep into the throat of the priest, Ryun heaving enormous sighs.

When the priest lifted his head away, the youth rolled over and sat up, hugging the kneeling priest. His trembling young hand fell to Sinh's lap and confirmed the priest also had a need to be addressed. The boy gazed steadily at Sinh, who sighed at the sight of the youth's eyes, even more enchanting in this dusky light. Ryun's hand gripped the swollen tool and began rapidly pulling at it. He was amazed at the heat of what he stroked. Soon, Sinh was shuddering and moaning and his milky seed was covering Ryun's hand. Impulsively, the priest hugged Ryun tightly to him and kissed his naked shoulder.

They stayed there, in the garden, at the end of the pool, hugging each other, for several more minutes, then the priest invited the youth to his private quarters. There they took their evening meal, with puzzled servers coming in and out. After dinner, the priest invited the youth to stay and Ryun gleefully accepted. W h i l e he had been in the front room on several occasions, the lad had never entered the priest's bedroom. With moonlight streaming through the stained glass windows, casting a dazzling rainbow of hues across the large bed, it was a chamber more befitting a king than a humble priest. Ryun lowered his naked body to the edge of the silk-covered bed and watched as the priest slipped from his robe.

From the beginning, Sinh was Ryun's favorite priest because the man's mouth always seemed ready to curve into a smile at any moment, as if he were teasing him, and now, the priest's face seemed to be breaking into the biggest, most provocative smile the youth had ever seen. And when the priest was naked, the youth felt him too slender and supple to be a man, yet he had powerful legs, a flat stomach and a mat of soft, brown hair mingled at the navel, seeming to point to the sex, which was in perfect balance with the rest of him. As Ryun began to take note of his own development, he felt his cock overpowered his body, drawing attention to itself, impossible to ignore. Yes, the youth thought, the priest was in every way perfect, as if his body had been formed in one quick, sure stroke by the higher powers. And his eyes lingered on the beauty of the priest's cock, rising to hardness as the man approached the bed. The lad reached out and took it in his hand and began stroking it. The priest stood before him and placed his hands on either side of the youth's head. Ryun took his time exploring the entirety of the priest's sex, fondling, stroking, probing with his fingers before he finally began to kiss the swollen member and take it into his mouth. He had discovered his own sensitivity years before and how he responded to the slightest touch. Thus he seemed to intuitively know just what pressure to apply, taking his cues from the moans and groans of the priest. He watched with fascination as the priest's cock gushed forth cum in a climax even more grand than the one he had enjoyed before their meal.

But so strong was the passion of the priest that his cock remained hard as the youth drew him onto the bed and permitted him to lie across his body as they embraced.

Ryun's own huge, hard sex was pressed against the priest's and they moved heavily together and eventually came again, one after the other. Ryun fell asleep, kisses still damp on his face, and slept deeply through the night. The priest could not rest, so intense was his pleasure. The night he had dreamed of so often had finally arrived and he didn't want it to end.

And at dawn, Ryun awoke to kisses traveling the length of his body.

*

As the days passed, there seemed to fall upon the priest and the orphan a pattern: after prayers and studies, a late afternoon swim followed by dinner alone together, and then Ryun would spend the night.

After a few weeks of this routine, Sinh schooled his young charge: "Be honest and frank in all things. Give willingly and happily as you receive. Inflict no pain or anguish on others." So it came as a surprise to Ryun when, as they entered the bedchamber, the high priest told him, "Tonight, my son, there may be some pain to you, but it will pass and such pain will become a pleasure."

Confused, Ryun remained silent as Sinh tenderly massaged his body as he so often had. "In time you will become, like me, the instigator. But for now let me bring to you, to both of us, the greatest joy of our love."

And with that, he rolled the boy over onto his flat stomach and spread his asscheeks. As it had on that first day, the priest's tongue worked gently over the boy's skin but now it found its way to the virgin anus and his hands quickly began skimming lightly across his shoulders and down his sides.

Then the priest lay across his young pupil and he began to undulate his body against the youth's. The weight of the priest upon him made Ryun short of breath, but he felt an overwhelming desire to possess the priest, possess him as he never had before. His thighs parted and the priest knelt between them and guided his cock toward the damp rosebud.

As the hardness entered the youth, Sinh felt Ryun's body stiffen. His face twisted in pain. The priest paused. "I know I am hurting you."

"No, just a little. Pray, continue."

With great care, Sinh pressed slowly downward, stopping, then starting again as Ryun adjusted. The youth seemed to crave the pain the priest was inflicting, as if he were a child knowing he had done wrong and unable to rest until he had been punished. The priest, it seemed, was rough and gentle at the same moment. "Push harder," Ryun said, and soon the priest was completely inside his lover and his teeth were biting Ryun's naked shoulder.

When the thrusting began in earnest, Ryun responded to the rhythm of the assault. Soon they were moving together, Ryun's fingers finding his own cock and stroking it so that he could have release at the precise moment his aggressor did. When Ryun began to feel he could contain himself no longer, the final thrust came and they both cried out so loudly the priest was afraid they would awaken the others. When at last they were quiet, the priest held the boy in his arms all through the night.

Following that blissful evening, Ryun would not sleep until the priest had made love to him in this way. And after he had taken his pleasure, the priest would not rest until his mouth had slid up and down the outrageous length of the grand muscle Ryun possessed and the explosion had come into his throat.

Eventually, Sinh told his faithful lover, "I cannot in good conscience seal you off completely from the rest of the world. You have been mine and mine alone for many, many months, but your education must be considered. Knowledge is the mightiest weapon you will ever possess. For this reason, I must share you with all of those at the temple who had been so anxious to know you as I have known you. And," he winked," some you will want to know as I have known you. You are ready for it."

And although there seemed to be no pattern or scheduling of their assignations, eventually the youth had shared his bounty with each of the priests at the temple.

Before long, the spectacular charms of the youth became known to the priestesses and they asked Ryun to visit them in their beds, after which they too sang his praises as an incredible maker of love, insatiable but careful not to hurt them with the exceeding size of his member.

Shortly before Sinh's death, Ryun promised his mentor to continue his noble work. For his part, Ryun knew that the priests were not cold and calculating villains who sought to take advantage of youths. Their code was, rather, systematically and logically evolved, demonstrating exceptional imagination, sensitivity and courage.

Eventually, Ryun confirmed to all how important his mentor's work had been by deciding to remain at the temple, studying and devoting himself to caring for orphans, several of whom, it was said, were his own children, the result of his frequent assignations with the priestesses.

Although there were those who were to eventually turn against him, jealous of his attentions to others, those Ryun had pleased unfailingly overcame them and conspired to make the beautiful young man a priest, a honor bestowed upon him shortly before his own untimely death. One grateful priest echoed the sentiments of the others who had many times shared their bed with the young man some had come to regard as a god: "He not only has enriched my life with his own presence, he has attracted many dozens of beautiful youngsters to the temple, educating them in the manner of Sinh. To Ryun we will be forever grateful."

Ryun's consecration, his loyal followers knew, was vital because legend has it that shortly after a priest dies his soul transmigrates into the body of a cat and upon the cat's death, the transition of the priest's soul into heaven is accomplished. And for seven days the cat with the soul of Ryun refused to eat. On the seventh day, he died and suddenly, all the cats in the temple had a golden mantle and their gold eyes turned sapphire blue.

The Obelisk

Leon del Ciervo

Then came a new arrival,
very tall, very thin.
He, too, was very handsome.
"This is my friend Mohamed,"
said Mustafa,
"and he wants to have sex."

I was a little tired,
but...How could I refuse?
A menage a trois in Egypt...

With the speed of lightning
Mohamed stood naked
and how can I describe
the sight that hit my eyes?
Begging Puccini's pardon
I paraphrased Des Grieux:
"Cossa non vidi simile a questa!"

I had made a discovery,
Right in front of my eyes
was Aswan's greatest obelisk,
twin brother to Paris',
to Cleopatra's Needle and to Rome's.
The long lost obelisk
believed lost at the sea.

While I feasted my vision,
the obelisk came to life,
all by itself,
defying gravity,
immense in all its glory,
throbbing to reach its size.

And what a night that was!
There is no place like Egypt
where pleasure flows freely,
full of humor,
among beautiful men.

Mohamed performed well;
a virtuoso performance,
a man who knows his instrument
and plays to the sublime.
Mustafa, Mohamed and me,
three live serpents
coiling around each other.

Chef's Surprise

L. Amore

Dice the celery. Chop the onions. Julienne the carrots. But, I quickly learned, carrots can be a problem if your knife is dull. Bingo. Blood. "Oh, shit." I grabbed a towel.

Chef John rushed over.

"You okay?" he asked, gripping my finger and applying pressure.

"Yeah." I looked into his eyes. I wanted to cry. Not because of the cut finger but because I was trying so hard to make a good impression. Jobs for novice chefs are hard to come by and getting a chance to apprentice under the universally renowned Johnny Finegullo was a chance of a lifetime. Then, when I actually laid eyes on him, I couldn't believe my good fortune. As I walked into his office, he flashed his big smile on me; his face opened up and I forgot what he looked like, really, and the room kind of got brighter. I don't even remember what I said in the interview, but whatever it was, he must have liked it. His green-green eyes aimed right at me, he said: "You'll do fine."

Later, I heard he had recently been divorced. It seemed he came home and found his wife in bed with another man. As farfetched as that seemed, considering how handsome John was, I considered it another lucky break for me: Perhaps he would need someone to console him in his loneliness.

Now this. His long fingers gripped mine. In that moment, I wondered if, as I'd always heard, finger size really was an indication of the size of one's penis. If so, John was endowed beyond my wildest dreams. I had never seen such long fingers.

"I have a box of bandages in my office. Come with me."

"...I'm sorry," I said as he grabbed a bottle of spring water and began washing off my finger. "I know how rushed we are with the banquet for the *padrino* tomorrow."

"You'll make up for it. You're a good worker. I've been watching you."

"Oh?" He had me sit in the chair in front of his desk and he was standing before me in his black and white plaid culinary pants, the ones that were too tight on him, accentuating his muscular thighs and big basket. I thought about fainting right then, doing a nosedive right into his crotch, but he stepped away and began rummaging through his desk until he found the bandages. After applying a thick piece of gauze and then a bandage, he again began going through the drawer until he found something that looked like a tiny condom. He proceeded to unwrap it and roll it over my finger.

"You are quite a doctor," I said. "You must have seen a cut finger or two in your time —"

"In my time?" he laughed.

"Oh, I didn't mean — "

He chuckled, "Oh, I know. I don't mind. If you wish to learn, you come to the *padrino*, right?"

"Yes. I know there are so many things I have to learn."

"Yes, many. But I've noticed that you learn very quickly. Nothing like learning on the job. And you'd better get back to it."

"Yes, sir," I said, rising from the chair.

"Will you be able to work overtime tonight?" he asked, smiling that big smile as I opened the office door.

"Of course."

"Good."

*

Everyone had gone except Chef John and me. While he finished cutting the last of the filets mignon, he told me to make sure all the doors of the restaurant were secured. After making the rounds, I returned to the kitchen to find him in a highly agitated state.

"There's no more plastic wrap! I asked them to stock more what with the banquet and all, but no! Idiots!"

"We'll find something," I said as he went on cursing the help in Italian. "You're just tired."

"Yes, I've lost my patience completely. And my back is killing me."

"Here, let me rub it."

"That's not necessary."

"You bandaged me up this morning. It's the least I can do."

"But— "

Before he could say any more my hands were massaging his

neck, his shoulders, the small of his back.

"Ah, that is wonderful. Masseurs could take lessons from you."

"Some have."

He chuckled. "You are a boy of many surprising talents. I've been watching you, remember."

"Yes, I know."

"Ever since that first interview, I have had a feeling about you."

"Oh?"

He was responding to my heavy stroking, the stress leaving his joints.

"Yes. And now I am sure of it. I think I know what you like. As you said, in my time I've bandaged many a wound."

I chuckled. "And I've given many a massage."

My hands drifted down, slowly but surely, to his crotch. When I got there, I found what I was doing was pleasing him even more than I thought. He let his head drop back onto my shoulder as I massaged his groin. Before long, I worked the zipper down and released his cock. I could feel the evidence that the theory about long fingers was, in this case, true and I wanted to see it. He turned his body slightly and I knelt down. It was a cock and a half. It didn't curve up or down, just jutted straight out. I made a clean sweep with my tongue on the underside of it, then the tip. Precum oozed from it. I held it, admiring it. He moaned. I went down on it, as much of it as I could take. My breathing was cut off as a rush came to my ears. I saw spots. I wasn't really aware of how huge it was until I tried to get it all down my throat.

He started moving his hips. Slowly, rhythmically he sent it in and out of my mouth, all the while my tongue doing its thing. From the moans and whimpers he was making, I knew I was doing something right.

I worked his ballsac loose and licked the balls. I stuck each of his testicles in my mouth in turn and sucked gently while I continued to stroke the monstrous meat. The musky scent of his sweaty balls sent shivers through me.

Suddenly, with insistence, he took my head in his hands and began fucking my face.

I could feel the eruption was imminent and I struggled to set it free. He grabbed my shoulders as the penis slid from my mouth. Cum seemed to fly out of it. So much cum that I knew he hadn't had a good orgasm in weeks. When he was finished, I laid my head against his groin, not wanting to leave it. Even in its now nearly flaccid state, it was the most splendid organ I had ever seen. He ran his hands through my hair and hugged me to him. "Oh, I needed that."

I moaned.

Then he started to chuckle. The chuckling gave way to a guffaw. He let go of me and I looked up. He pointed to the filets. He had come all over them.

I stood up. "You really only got two of 'em," I laughed, separating them.

"Leave them there," he said, zipping up his pants, "and put the rest in the refrigerator."

After sliding the tray of beef into a space in the walk-in refrigerator, I turned to see him standing at the back door, a brown bundle under his arm. "Let's go," he said. "It's been a long day."

I nodded. I was quiet all the way out to where our cars were parked. "Why don't you follow me?" he said finally, as if he was reading my mind.

*

He apologized for the cheaply furnished rented room. "Even in my situation, the wife gets everything," he explained. "All I kept was my portable CD player."

I told him all I cared about was the bed. But all I really cared about was him. Seeing him naked, having him kiss me, kissing him back.

But once in bed, he descended on me like Genghis Khan on Asia. He kissed my neck and bit my skin as he went after my nipples. Preceded by his warm tongue, his grand, bushy moustache tickled and scratched its way down my pelvis, leaving a wet trail over the muscles of my abdomen, halting at my pubic hair. He held my buttocks with his hands and examined my groin as if it was something he was going to serve his guests. My hard-on bobbed in front of his face. I felt terribly small compared to him, but he winked and said, "Not bad."

What wasn't bad was his sucking of it. He pulled my foreskin back and ran his tongue around the glans, then deep throated me as if he had been doing it all his life, which maybe he had, wife or no wife. I was too busy coming to ask any questions. I couldn't hold it. I had many wet dreams of what that moustache would feel like wrapped around my cock and I shot all over his face. Now he looked as if he had tears running down his cheeks. Laughing, he went to the bathroom and when he returned, he was carrying a wet towel. After he wiped me clean, I took the towel away from him and made him lie back. I rubbed his cock clean, then applied my mouth to it. It rose mightily again and I was awestruck. Incredibly, it looked even larger now than it did in the kitchen of the restaurant. I sucked and licked and sucked some more. As he went wild under me, I flung his hairy legs over my shoulders and proceeded to lavish my attention on his ass. Each time my tongue tried to pry open his anal lips, they would pucker and he would moan.

Eventually, he relaxed and my tongue invaded him. I held his prick with one hand while I brought mine to the crease of his ass. I placed the tip against his bud and felt it tighten with apprehension. From the way he had sucked me, I doubted he was a virgin but I took it slow just the same. Soon he was grinding his ass against my groin. I let go of his cock and fell on top of him. Keeping a slow, steady rhythm as I fucked him, I kissed his forehead, his cheeks, and sucked on the mass of hair that was his moustache. Then we kissed. His tongue met me half way. It was like a hot Popsicle only tastier. I felt the bumps on the roof of his mouth.

I stepped up my assault on his asshole and he lost all control. If it weren't for his having put Anita Baker on the CD player when we arrived, I'm sure his new neighbors would have called the cops. I pulled back and spit on his cock, then stroked it to orgasm. His semen spurted out with each whack to his prostate. I started to come myself and pulled out just in time to leave my load mingling with his on his chest. I collapsed on him and he wrapped his arms around me. The CD stopped playing and, finally, with my hand grasping his cock, we slept.

*

When I awoke in the morning, the chef was in the tiny kitchen. I got up and followed the aroma of coffee brewing. The table was set and John was standing over the stove with only an apron on. I came up behind him and hugged him.

"Mornin', baby," he said.

I kissed his naked shoulder.

"Feel like steak 'n ' eggs?"

"Do I ever."

As we were eating, he asked if I liked the beef.

"It's great."

He smiled that big smile. "It has a special sauce."

"Oh?"

"Yeah, it's been marinating in it all night."

"What do you call it?"

He grinned. "Chef's surprise."

I'm Not A Size Queen

"Sex with the young can be fun if you're in the mood. One of the best experiences I ever had was with a teenage boy. He was Puerto Rican. He was uncircumcised...it was really awesome because he was so young and so in wonderment of it all. He was fearless. He would do anything. He wasn't very big. He was just a baby. See, I'm not a size queen. But it was excellent."

— Madonna, in the book "SEX"

"The Monster of His Cock"

A Review by John Patrick

William Tester's debut novel, "Darling," is a study in forced outrageousness and, being the story of a consummate love affair between a boy and a cow, to excerpt certain passages from it seems a fitting way to end this trip down fantasy lane.

To set the scene, we quote a review in *The Village Voice*, by Katherine Dieckmann: "Skipping back and forth between child-hood barnyard reveries and a present-tense, increasingly drunken showdown in a New York apartment, Tester tells a classic tale of sibling rivalry between two former farm boys: our narrator, Bubba, and his older brother and nemesis, Jeab. Even though Bubba is ostensibly the focus here, it is Jeab's character that is etched most clearly. He's the kind of callous, possibly satanic, youth who burns down a barn on Christmas, shoots stray dogs for kicks; and grows up to be a Navy bomber pilot. Bubba hates him for this, plus all the usual reason a younger sib resents an elder -for being there first, for being more savvy, for being bigger."

This "bigger" part, however, carries a certain specificity in Tester's universe, as this boyhood recollection from "Darling" reveals:

> *I saw Jeab dancing in our shower water naked in the steam.*
> *"Hey, Bubba, check this mother out!" he said.*
> *The monster of his cock between his shower-watered legs.*
> *I turned and toweled into my corner where I washed hid off from Jeab.*
> *I want to bash my brother's head in. Scoop my spoon into his perfect eyes and blind him, grinning here. I think my brother might read my mind.*
> *"Like I did what?" is what Jaeb says, facey.*

Dieckmann notes that this passage establishes early on Bubba's penile fixations and his tale never stops rotating around the question of dick. "Sometimes," Dieckmann states, "this emphasis is more affecting than annoying, especially when we're privy to Bubba's fears of inadequacy."

A wonderful example of this is the following passage:

Swollen as a garden hose, my mean and greasy pistol, like a cock, begins to twitch.

Near the end, we finally are treated to the revelation that Bubba got to the cow first, before Jeab did, and his descriptions are graphic, rapturous and highly unsettling:

Her conch shell. Hide split like a mango is her place behind my cow. Her place, like something from the water, something plopped beneath the ocean shelled and shapeless on a rock. She looks like that, well, more or less. I pet and stroke my chest at her...
Some monster.
Now I get it in...
I put myself behind of her.
I plug my awful hard-on in this sweetly feeding doll.
I pull her rubber folds apart and put myself in hers.

And just as Bubba grabs the udder and starts to squirt, his milk pail clanks.

What Is a Size Queen?

H. Max

What is a Size Queen?
On super size he's super keen;
He hunts big dick;
It must be super thick;
And almost as long
As the dong
Of King Kong.

But always remember what the wise man said:

> *"It's not the tractor,*
> *it's how long it stays in the*
> *field plowing."*

Afterword:
"The New Penis?"

John Patrick

A frank new, unashamed male sexuality is on the rise. That's the opinion of *The Village Voice's* columnist "Ven Detta."

"You spot one every day," Ven claims. "Framed by well-washed jeans. Profiled through cotton sweats. Shrinkwrapped in Lycra. There's another now on the IRT, straining against the inseam of a Brooks Brothers wool blend. Perhaps it's pressed against your leg."

What is it that Ven's spotting? Why, the penis, of course. The New Penis. "It's urgent, surprising," Ven says. "Yet shy. And suddenly, it's in the news.

"What is it about this insignificant flesh cylinder that's giving fashionable people pause? Is it biology or culture that's propelled the male member to the forefront of style?"

Ven answers these questions by quoting Jason Kanner of Boss Models, Inc., who revealed in *People* magazine that "men are more body-conscious these days."

Yes, finally, it seems, the penis, is undergoing a social emergence. What was once "coyly buried in folds of Eisenhower era surge" is far more visible, but the penis for the '90s isn't the chaste James Dean bulge of "Rebel Without a Cause," or the raunchy outline of Joe Dallesandro's hefty tool used on the cover of the Stones' "Sticky Fingers" album.

"It's an amalgam," Ven insists. "Assertive, informed, utilitarian, presenting itself with Horatio Alger optimism: buoyant, modest, but all there."

Ven credits style-setters like Bruce Weber and poet Robert Bly for bringing the penis out of the closet. Superstar examples of this New Penis are Marky Mark with his pants down and Jason Priestley in his crotch-clutching jeans, but you can see examples in everyday life. Ven tells about meeting a salesman at a Gap store who resembles a young Warren Beatty and wears his pants at fashionable flood-level: "His balls are tucked in on either side of the rise. The penis points upward to noon. The effect is eye catching, well balanced, sprightly. 'I always wear it this way,' he claims."

And now to the point. Whereas this book has been about men's obsession with size, Ven says that's old hat. The new thinking is that "a Harry Reems thumper is as relevant today as the running board on a DeSoto. It ruins the line. The pumped-up porn penis of the demented disco decades now carries other connotations. And in the latex age, no one wants to be around when the Ultra-MAXXX goes pop."

Oh yeah?

Just ask writer Jim Shelley. He says, "This may be the New Age, but the penis is stubbornly lagging behind. There is nothing modern about the penis (you can't teach an old dog new tricks, as they say), and men are still very attached to them.

"Does size matter?

"Size, believe me, matters (it matters to me that I've got a big one). 'Size doesn't matter' is what men with small penises say. The point about penises is: They are never big enough. After all, anyone who says it's fine to have a small one has small one. Anyone who admits he's got a small one is a wounded wreck and actually has a very small one. Anyone who says he's got a big prick is a big prick, and obviously has an even smaller one. Anyone who won't say he's got a big one definitely has a small one. Fact.

"This means, logically, that all men have small penises. But men, being the incredible species they are, have not only convinced themselves that this isn't true, but that in fact all men have big penises — all men except them.

"Men, let's face it, are right to be hung up about what hangs down. Can you think of anything better to be obsessed with?

"Men's paranoia about penises is so sophisticated that if you have an eleven-inch dick, it still gets you (somewhere deep down) that some other man has twelve inches. It's not even that your girl might know or meet him, it's just the knowing. The wondering. Men never grow out of the fascination with their penis. They are so paranoid about size, they'll do anything for a woman who tells them they have a big dick. Size matters. Men like big things: big cars, big tits, big cigars.

"Men even end up with names for their penises. (Mine, I hasten to add, has a very long name.) But names strike me as ridiculous. Some men name their penises after movie stars (as in 'Suck my Marlon'). Then there are names like Dinkle, Dingle, Winkle, Todger, Tadger — baby names. Others are more bizarre: Pork Sword, Big

Eddie, Little Elvis, Mr. Ferret, the Heat-Seeking Moisture Missile, Beef Bayonet. The personification of the penis is not for nothing. A man's penis is his god. When men are led astray by their willies, they call it 'he:' 'It was beyond my control. He did it.'

Anka Radakovich, sexual correspondent for *Details* magazine, says that, to women, "the penis is a peculiar organ. We believe that man's best friend is actually his penis. Like a dog, it is always happy to see us, enjoys being petted, and often rubs itself against our legs. When we are not calling it 'it' or 'he,' we use pet phrases. An English friend likes to call his 'Nigel' or 'Cedric'; Marla Maples probably calls Donald's 'The Donald' or 'Trump Tower'; I like to call them 'Bob's Big Boy,' or 'The Violator.'"

Anka says that she was thirteen before she really started to understand penises, thanks to her brother's friends, who were always trying to get her to touch theirs or put them between her legs. "That is when I realized," she admits, "that the penis has a mind of its own. As I grew up, I understood it's the mind of a perpetual adolescent.

"It's no secret that most men either brag or exaggerate the size of their maleness. (I once overheard a group of guys discussing a friend who was a 'two toweler,' meaning it was so gigantic that he could hold up two wet bath towels with it when erect.) According to *Harper's* Index, American men claim the average length of their erect penis is ten inches. American women, however, estimate four inches is more like it. Most women say a six- to eight-incher is most desirable. Over ten inches requires a shoehorn, and a foot-long needs a crowbar.

"Men with enormous endowments think that women worship them. But we cannot idolize an organ, especially if it is attached to someone we can't stand.

"...Most women say that a man with a bulge in his Calvins is sexier than one who's nude. If women really thought penises were as important as men think they are, we would be reading magazines with names like, 'Penises Today,' or 'The Scrotal Review.'

"Ultimately, it's not what's in the pants that counts but how it's used. Friends have told me they've had such unsatisfying sex with guys of all sizes that rubbing against a corner of the couch does a better job."

New penis or old penis, man's cock is always good for a laugh. Even in the Old West. In his delightful novel, "The Man Who Fell

In Love With The Moon," Tom Spanbauer endows his hero with a suitably heroic cock. The half-Injun boy grows up in a whorehouse and sleeps with the madam until, one night, the boy's hard-on pokes her. The hero remembers:

"...Ida jumped out of bed. She lit the kerosene lamp, turned the wick up, and lifted the covers.

"Then she lifted the nightshirt.

"Ida looked under my nightshirt for a while and said, 'Look at the size of that one, would you?'

"No more sleeping with Ida."

Oh, but it wasn't what you're thinking. The reason the boy couldn't sleep with Ida was that poor Ida could never sleep if there was a hard-on in the room. She tells it: "When I lifted that boy's nightshirt — there it was. Needed a double mule team to drive that thing home."

The boy goes on to say: "...Every time Ida told that story, my dick got bigger. To listen to her tell it, my dick was bigger than a grizzly bear's. Bigger than Paul Bunyan's. Bigger than his blue ox's. Big as the state of Idaho. That's how I got my other name, the name that all of us used to laugh at: 'Out Of His Pants,'" which was later enlarged to "Way-Out-Of-His-Pants."

Yep, as the old cowhand says, when all's said and done, New Penis or Old Penis, it's just never big enough.

Rapper and underwear model Marky Mark Wahlberg bunches it, as recorded for posterity in the best-selling book "Marky Mark," by Lynn Goldsmith, published by Harper Perennial, and available by mail from STARbooks Press. The book carries a caution label.

The New Balls:
Does Marky Have the Most?

"Testicles represent one of the most puzzling paradoxes of the human anatomy," jouranlist John Berendt tells us. "They are the core of masculinity, yet they render a man agonizingly vulnerable. To this day, scientists cannot agree why the testicles of some mammals have evolved in the perilous scrotal position, as ours have, while those of elephants, gorillas, and whales are tucked up in the relative safety of the abdominal cavity. Elephant balls don't clang, so why should ours?"

No one is sure why, but as long as the balls are clanging, we're listening.

And these days who has the most "balls," in every sense of the word? We would argue it would have to be the hottest gay icon of the moment, Marky Mark, known more for his underpants than his rapping, who began 1993 by showing up in music and department stores all over the planet promoting Calvin Klein underwear. Sometimes the boy even had the clothes designer himself, now much married and drug-free, in tow, beaming delightedly as Marky scrawled his name on anything and everything that had the CK logo.

A spy on the scene in San Francisco at Macy's department store reported the rapper was "flirting outrageously with all of the guys." When someone asked him if he'd ever wear Fruit of the Looms, Marky said, "Well, I ain't gonna say while I'm sitting here next to Calvin Klein." Calvin just smiled. (I mean, if you were Calvin, wouldn't you be smiling?)

Marky is "New Kids on the Block" star Donnie Wahlberg's baby brother and both have pulled themselves up to incredible celebrity status after years of struggle on the mean streets of Boston. Despite his heady success, brother Donnie says Marky "doesn' t take himself too seriously, to a point where he's like, 'I want to be a star.' He just wants to have fun."

Well, FUN is what his fans are having! And lots of it. At the beefcake boy's San Francisco appearance, kids started lining up at 8 a.m., but it seemed no coincidence, Jim Provenzano reported, that the first in line was an older gay man, Tony Bruno, who had actually seen Marky at a concert at the Warfield Theater. "He's great," Bruno said. "He shows he's non-judgmental, no matter what you are, your race, your sexuality." Bruno confided that he was not going to wear his Marky-autographed briefs, he was going to "frame it." Provenzano said that a small herd of gay men showed up about an hour before Marky's appearance. "We 're devoted but not demented," one fan said. Another fan reported that Marky's famous bus shelter posters (featuring him holding his crotch in his CK briefs) were a hot item in S.F. "The one at Castro and Market was broken into twice." Then the fan revealed, "It's an Allen wrench that you need."

Another fan called Marky "homo-positive. For somebody that's such a street tough, he's sending a really good image."

And, yes, image is what he has — in spades. At the signing, Provenzano reported, Marky flirted outrageously, pulled up his shirt to show the trim of his Calvin Klein undies under his baggy pants, and spoke semi-intelligible phrases about the "good people comin' to support the Funky Bunch." (His other band members were cordoned off to one side.) Marky obliging signed the packages of underwear presented by the first 200 people in line, who, Provenzano joked, were rushed by like political deportees. A gang of hired goons kept the photographers at bay.

After the signing, Marky and Calvin were rushed to a waiting stretch limo and, as they sped away, Marky leaped up through the sun roof, ripped off his shirt and hat, and exposed his torso "like a beefy young Pop Tart." A young gay fan was assaulted by a bunch of girls when he managed to catch Marky's cap.

And now the teen idol fan magazine Tutti is offering up "Marky Mark's Undies" in what it is heralding as the "Contest of the Century: We See London, We See France, We See Marky's Underpants! It's Completely Gross! Yes, we here in Tuttiland are known for being on the edge of everything. And it is for this reason that we are proud to announce that for the first time ever, this magazine is giving you the chance to win a pair of Marky's underwear! That's right, a pair of actual MM undershorts! Just think how cool it would be to own an actual pair of these in-demand undergarments. You'd be the envy of all your friends and relatives. People will want to know you. They'll want to be your friend. It'll be great! Even filling out this coupon will put some zest in your life."

But, in an italized note, the magazine's editors were compelled to assure their young, impressionable readers that: "Marky owned and touched the underwear we're giving away but he never actually WORE them. So all you hygiene freaks out there can relax." Well, shucks, that did it for us! We wouldn't want the undies UNLESS Marky had worn them! And, even better, if he'd spilled a little of his cum on 'em. Or, at the very least, sweated in them! Indeed, the sweat off Marky's balls should be bottled and sold.

Anyhow, when he wasn't signing underwear (or touching it for contests), Marky (now immortalized by the teen fan magazines as simply "MM"— the once definitive MM, Marilyn Monroe, is probably turning in her grave) was performing at gay clubs. Dish diva Michael Musto journeyed to Marky Mark's first concert in a gay venue (at the Boys' Bump Night at USA in New York City) and reported: "Looking petrified of the crowd, the rapper, wearing long sleeves and surrounding himself with the Funky Bunch, avoided the edges of the stage and didn't take a single thing off (he only dropped his pants for a millisecond. His agency claimed he had a third degree burn on his back. If he's that uptight in future gay engagements, he'll really get burned."

Speaking of being burned, MM told an English magazine that he thought Maddona was great until he actually met her! Now you would have thought that might have been the MEETING of the Century. The headlines alone would tend to turn you on, all those MMM's! But no, Marky was not impressed: "I seen Madonna in person and before that I thought she was kind of cute but she looked like somebody out of 'Beetlejuice,' man! Seriously!" Maddona was not available for comment.

Marky revealed (in an article headlined "Prince of Skivvy" in Vanity Fair magazine) how it all started: "It happened in L.A., at Magic Mountain, right after my first record, 'Good Vibrations' came out. It was just one of those things, man. I was doing something kinda berserk and I just dropped my pants. And I remember I saw 50 million flashes and I was like 'Oh, shit!' I was like 'This might be something.' Then it started getting a little out of hand. Now my fans tend to demand it."

And how did Marky end up in the underwear signing business? "After a while," Marky says, "I was sick of paying $18 for under wear. Then I think somebody from my label who is friends with David Geffen called him up. You know, David and Calvin are cool with each other. So they called me up, and it was like, 'Yo, Calvin wants to hook up with you—he wants to meet you and stuff.' I was like, 'Really?' You know, he's just been so la-arge. I mean, even in the neighborhoods, if you had a pair of Calvin Kleins, you was the man. So I went to his house and I met him, hooked up. We had one set deal. They gave me $100,000 to do the commercials and the photos."

And, just so you know, in the same article, Marky revealed that he lost his virginity over a course of five encounters with the same girl. I mean, this is a stud who takes his sweet time! Heaven! He was 16 and it was the first time for each of them. And just in case you get to meet him and manage to steer him to your bed, be aware his condom of choice is: "Trojans, ribbed, in the gold box." It's good to be prepared. But be forewarned, Marky says he's not bisexual, that he never even "dabbled in homo-ism" during puberty. "You think about everything," he admitted, "but I never did think, Would I like to do him? But a large part of the gay community has shown an interest in Marky Mark. Like I said many a time, it's cool for men to find me interesting, and to show a liking to me. Like I said, I prefer women, and I always have, but if that's what they're into, then great. I work out, I train hard, I'm ha ppy with the shape that I am in. I attracts girls —obviously it also attracts men, which is cool, if it's their thing."

Apparently, Marky's the "thing" for legions of gays; one of the hottest selling books over the holidays was "Marky Mark," a photo book by Lynn Goldsmith that contains some sensational (and revealing) photos of the young star. Appropriately enough, Marky dedicates the book to "his dick."

And consider this: Two men are standing at a light on Third Avenue in Manhattan one recent afternoon, Guy Trebay reported when Marky Mark glides past.

"I'm getting fed up with Marky Mark," Man One gripes, only semi-exasperated. "Every time you turn around, there he is, with his pants down and his arms in the air. I can't take it!"

"I know," says Man Two.

"I was talking to a friend the other day," Man One goes on, "and he was saying he wondered how straight men deal with it, Marky Mark on the bus, 50-foot Marky Mark in Times Square, all these queer images. Does it scare them, or do they find it empowering?"

"Are there any straight men?" Man Two replies, and Trebay says the wisecrack seems to contain a truth central to the Marky Mark ad campaign. The whole country's horny for teen male flesh, and Marky's the proof. What his records can't do for his career, his briefs might. And in the process, decades of cornball homoerotic imagery—from Von Gloeden to Mapplethorpe—have gone mainstream. America is being outed by Calvin Klein.

"So I called X," says a note from Trebay's pal Vince. Vince is a "veryclosefriend" of Calvin and his wife Kelly. Vince contacted X to see if she could get him a copy of the Marky Mark bus shelter poster. "Anyway, she calls me today and says the company has had so many requests they've practically established a desk to deal with them. The bus shelter posters are available at $500 each, she says. She says she might be able to get me smaller ones for free. Where would I put the big one anyway? Under my pillow? On the ceiling over my bed?"

The billboard on Times Square generates much comment, even among the trendy: "The other night, a couple staggered out of the Thierry Mugler opening party at USA, shaking the smoke funk from their clothes. Shivering, they headed toward Broadway and there, high above them, loomed Marky. 'Whoa,' said the woman, a toiler in the fields of journalism. 'I never saw that before.' "'I know,' said her companion, a fellow media slut, 'pretty amazing, right?' "'You know, we tried to get him to pose for the magazine but he blew us off.'

"'Why?'

"'He's too-too.'

"'Too what?'

"'Too big.'

"'But his records are in the toilet.'

"'Yeah, but his pecs are a major event.'"

To say nothing of his dick and balls.

But the stud does have his detractors. Columnist Lisa Jones says that Marky was "way off the mark." "The mantra 'expropriation' is as overused as the act itself, and when you're reading America, it's a muddy term with a muddy payoff. But, as Marky Mark marches on, allow us this: If he ain't the Rocky of the early '90s, let us eat our Vanilla Ice dolls. And does America and New York City in particular, a city that's 60 per cent color, really need another great-white-hope fantasy, imagined by Calvin Klein, oozing down on us from billboards in Times Square?

"Some celebrate Marky Mark, whiter and larger than King Kong, as the mainstreaming of the homoerotic. More obvious is the bite that Marky takes from black male style culture from be-bop to hip hop, from Joe Lewis to Naughty by Nature's Treach. The straddle, the dance moves, the baggy pants, the drawers showing, the jay larger than yours, we've seen it all before. Show a crew-cut Irish-American youth like Marky noodling his jay and it's guilt-free teen fun. Put up a 'Harlem Brown' via Newark, like Treach, and the Times might run an axious editorial on billboards that will promote urban violence.

"More bile-inducing than the Marky spread is sponsor Calvin Klein himself, whose ads do run a whites-only shop. With the Marky campaign, we've caught

Calvin serving up black male panache, but, in keeping with the designer's usual racial codes, doing so by trussing it up in Marky's mediocre white-rap face. Those concerned about images might think of passing on the Klein label until the designer enlarges his camera lens to include a world that ain't just a day at Aryan gym.

"In some version of an ideal world (possibly 'In Living Color's Black World'), chocolate-for-days Treach gets to play Calvin Klein's 40-foot plus Times Square demigod. Ask black girls in the know about hip hop's young gun and they get moist over his classic 'hard' looks. Put Treach up there and you wouldn't have to waste the extra 10 feet to get his jay in the shot. You'd see the brother's face, and quite simply, that's all the information you'd need."

We think you'd have to agree that Lisa has "balls." While every black male we know says he'd rather be loved for his mind that his jay, the obvious cannot be ignored. Seriously, how on earth can you ignore something so big and black and long? And that's just the penis! Add the balls and it's simply overwhelming. Talk about clanging!

Contributors

Listed Alphabetically
(Other Than the Editor, John Patrick)

"Chef's Surprise"
L. Amore

The author is 24 and has been in the book business for over six years. He has lived in upstate New York, Boston and New York City and currently resides in Connecticut with his lover. A frequent contributor to STARbooks anthologies, including the best-selling "Tarnished Angels" and the forthcoming "Seduced," Mr. Amore is currently at work on his first novel.

"The Monster"
William "Bill" Barber

Bill, a frequent contributor to STARbooks' anthologies and author of "Marty" and "Diary of a New York Queen," died shortly after Thanksgiving 1992 of AIDS-related complications. At the time of his death, the author was negotiating with STARbooks to publish his novel, "The Dinner Party."

"Piece Officer"
Mark Canterbury

The mostly-vegetarian Boston Red Sox fan lives with his lover Ken in Miami. Besides being a noted columnist reviewing books, videos, and music, Mark's feature stories have appeared in *The Advocate, Travel America, and Wanderlust.* He is working on a collection of his stories called (what else?) "Canterbury's Tales."

"You Should See My Father's"
Leo Cardini

Author of the best-selling book "Mineshaft Nights," Mr. Cardini's stories and theater-related articles have appeared in a variety of magazines and his two of his stories which were written for "Nights" but did not appear in the final edition graced the anthology "A Natural Beauty." The story herein is an original written especially for this collection. He is the co-author of a musical now being fine-tuned for Broadway.

"The Obelisk"
Leon del Ciervo

A poet and author of "The Colors of Love," published by STARbooks, Leon was born in Havana in 1922; he left Cuba in 1960 for political reasons and now makes his home in Florida.

"Angel in the Flesh"
Alfredo Villanueva-Collado

Born in Puerto Rico, the author holds a Ph.D. in Comparative Literature from SUNY Binghamton and is currently professor of English at a college in the Bronx. He has published literary criticism, poetry and prose. His latest book of poetry, dealing with his lover's death, "Pato salvaje," was recently presented at the Gay Community Center in New York City.

"The Prince's Jewels"
Jamoo

The author is a renowned mulatto writer and artist residing in Texas. Currently a special staff writer for Interrace magazine, he is a frequent contributor to gaymale publications (one of his stories appeared in a special all-black issue of *Advocate Men*). He is presently finishing a novel, "Smooth Talk and Pretty Boy." The story adapted for this anthology was the first one he ever wrote, at the age of 19. Jamoo swears he's a virgin.

"It Had To Be Huge"
Joe Leslie

Author of the best-seller "Randy," a chapter of which was adapted for this anthology, Joe is an educator in the Pacific Northwest. He is currently at work on his next novel.

"What is a Size Queen?"
H. Max

An author of the outrageous limericks, H. Max has multiple literary personalities; he has written and edited more than two dozen very serious books and, as the Wilder-than-Wilde writer H. Max, he is the author of the popular "gay(s)language: a dic(k)tionary," published by Banned Books. He lives in New York City.

"Night Off"
Edmund Miller
Dr. Miller, a professor of English, is author of numerous stories in gaymale magazines and of the legendary poetry book, "Fucking Animals." He is at work on a new collection of his poems.

"The Ceremony"
Kyle Stone
Kyle Stone is the pseudonym of Caro Soles, a Canadian writer, whose novel, "A Mutual Understanding," is being published by Los Hombres Press. One of his stories is appearing in the collection, "Brave Sex." The story in this book was adapted from material that originally appeared in *In Touch* magazine and will appear as part of a novel to be published by Fire Island Press. The author is an active volunteer with The AIDS Committee of Toronto and served on the Board of Directors for several years.

"Billy Couldn't Believe It"
Michael Taylor
The author lives in New York state and is working on a novel, "Matthew: One of Lenny's Boys." This is his first published work.

"Big Top Men" and "Mightier Than the Sword"
Donald Vining
A popular author of gay fiction, Mr. Vining was a contributor to the best-selling anthology, "Gay Nineties." All but the first volume of his four-part "A Gay Diary" is still in print. He resides in New York. The stories in this book have been adapted from ones originally appearing in *Torso* magazine.

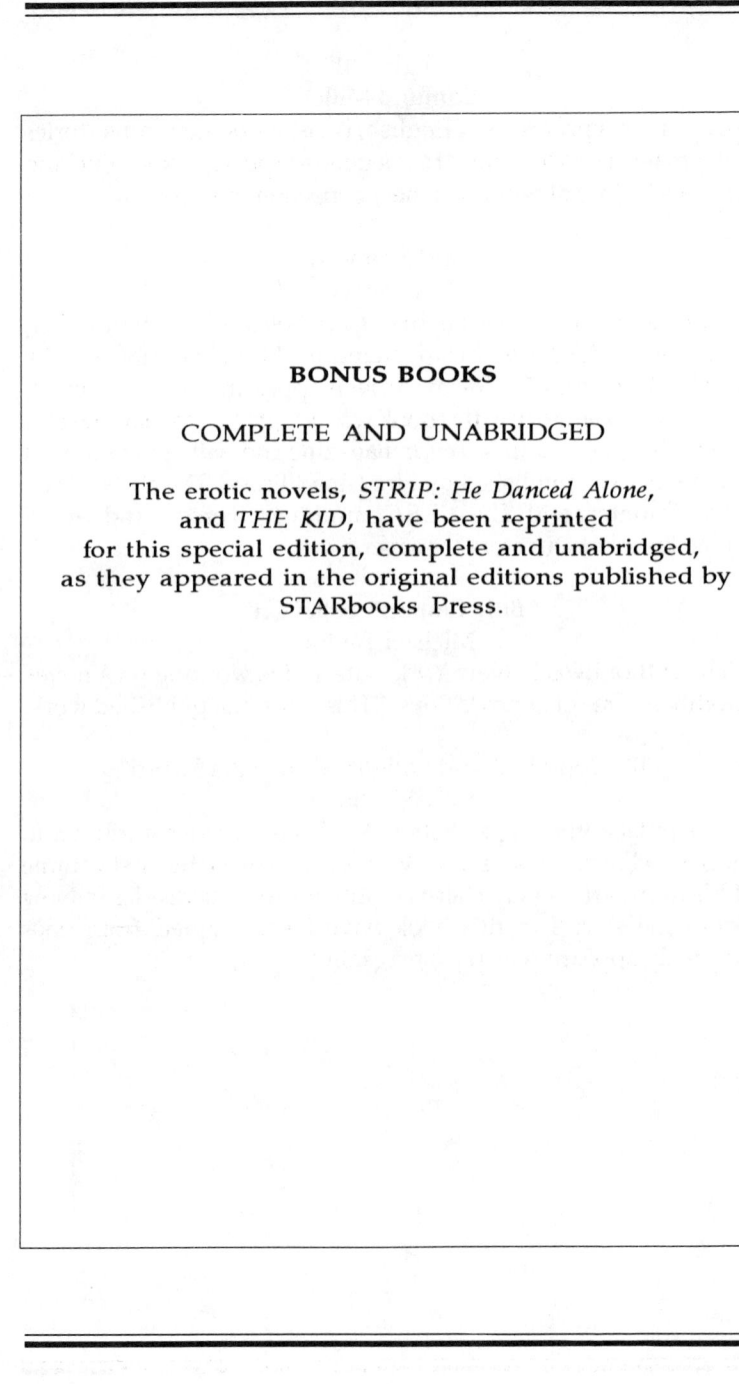

BONUS BOOKS

COMPLETE AND UNABRIDGED

The erotic novels, *STRIP: He Danced Alone*,
and *THE KID*, have been reprinted
for this special edition, complete and unabridged,
as they appeared in the original editions published by
STARbooks Press.

STRIP

He Danced Alone

**An Erotic
Roman á Clef By
JOHN PATRICK**

He Danced Alone

A Queer Romance by

JOHN PATRICK

STARbooks Press
Sarasota, FL

Books by John Patrick

Non-Fiction

The Best of the Superstars 1990
A Charmed Life: Vince Cobretti
Lowe Down: Tim Lowe
The Best of the Superstars 1991
Legends: The World's Sexiest Men, Vol. 1
The Best of the Superstars 1992
What Went Wrong? When Boys Are Bad & Sex Goes Wrong

Fiction

Billy & David: A Deadly Minuet
The Bigger They Are...
The Younger They Are...
The Harder They Are...
Angel: The Complete Trilogy
Angel II: Stacy's Story
Angel: The Complete Quintet
A Natural Beauty (Ed.)
The Kid (with Joe Leslie)
STRIP: He Danced Alone
Huge (Ed.)
The Boys of Spring

Library of Congress Card Catalog No. 91-067529

"Sometimes I think
I've found my hero
But it's a queer romance."

Preface

This is a love story but it's a queer romance. It's the eternal triangle, but with a difference, because boy meets man, more or less, a married man, more or less, and the boy is very young, or so he appears, yet he has many miles on his sinuous body and is ready for this when it happens. And then the boy meets another boy, even younger than himself, and things get a bit wild.

So if you're not into that sort of thing, you'd better bow out now.

On the other hand, if you're like me and you're prone to dream, to fantasize about the perfect lover, here you have all manner of candidates in vulgar abundance, to quite justify the underline, "a queer romance." And, as you will see, it's strange how things work out...in fantasy as well as in life, if indeed there's any difference.

- John Patrick

"O what are you to us,
O radiant dancers
who bring together
all that makes man happy:
Color, lovely movement
and sweet music."

-John Masefield

Prologue.

"They call me Strip."

"I can see why."

"Oh, why do you think?" the boy asked, coming closer, so close Clay could smell his sweat, the sweat of performing, of seducing with his gyrations, every man in the audience.

Clay put his Tanqueray on-the-rocks down on the bar and turned his body on the stool so he could face the boy, the boy he had tipped $50 while he was dancing. He swallowed hard, took off his tinted eyeglasses and smiled. "Because you strip a person bare with those eyes of yours. Your eyes see right through a person. Nobody is safe."

Impetuously, the curly-haired blond slid between Clay's thighs, crushing crotch against crotch, and kissed the older man lightly on the forehead.

"You're safe," the boy whispered in Clay's ear," as long as you're with me."

Clay put his arms around the boy and hugged him, warm in the knowledge that, for a while at least, he had his hands on something beautiful, something wonderful. But something safe, never.

*

Later, after he had brought Clay to orgasm, Strip rose up and leaned over the naked body, gasping as it careened down from an incredible high. Using a light stroke, the dancer started at the top of Clay's head, massaging the deeply-tanned skin, working down across the wrinkled forehead, along the bridge of the aquiline nose, across the pouty lips and down to the hollow under the strong chin. He caressed the jaw and worked his fingers up across the cheeks and temples, finishing with the ears, cupping his palms around them, closing out the rest of the world. He kissed Clay gently on the lips and soon the older man fell asleep. Even in a sleazy motel, with a restless stranger lying beside him, the freshman Congressman from Florida, newly elected to a second term, slept more soundly than he had in years.

1

Item in the "Gulftides" column in the Naples Daily News: "Made in the Shade Dept.: On November 1, Florida Trend Magazine made public its list of the 50 wealthiest people in Florida and, as usual, Hugh Harris, the founder of the former Harris Banking Corporation of Bradenton, Florida, made the list with a net worth valued at $100 million. Hugh, in his eighties, sold Harris Banking to Great Atlantic Bancorp in 1984 for 4 million shares of stock, making him the largest shareholder in the national bank. In 1988, his only grandson, Clay, of Naples, resigned as president of the Southwest Florida Banking Division to run for office as Congressman from the 12th district. He won in a landslide, was reelected last year, and has been one of the Capitol's strongest champions of civil rights issues."

"...There they go again, " Amanda chuckled. "Civil rights? Where do they get this stuff?"

"Public relations, dear," Clay said, sipping his second martini of the evening. "Ninety-eight percent of the black vote. Incredible for a Republican." He was amused when the list came out; Amanda would think she could order another mink. Or a new Mercedes. She never seemed to realize what it cost a family with a net worth of $100 million to maintain their lifestyle in the manner expected of them. But he thought himself blessed she realized so little. And thinking about blessings, he closed his eyes and remembered Tuesday, that night in Washington, the night he met the boy who called himself Strip. Ever since, every time he thought about the dancer, his loins stirred.

"I'm going to Miami tomorrow," he told Amanda matter-of-factly.

She was lost in the columns, relishing the notoriety of being on the magazine's list always gave her. At times, she was so terribly cheap, Clay thought. For the daughter of an ambassador, heir to the

Milwaukee Brewing fortune, she was terribly cheap. But that was all right, too, because gifts were always enough. He could ignore her, treat her shabbily and she would never complain, knowing another diamond something-or-other would be forthcoming.

And she seemed to be sexless; the perfect wife for a man who lived a double life, occasionally seeking the company of other men, especially, now, one special youngster...and his mind wandered again to Strip, who, because he was such a graceful, powerful dancer, had moves like no other boy he had ever seen. After leaving the bar that night with him in tow, Clay rented a motel room and quickly found, once they were naked, there seemed to be no end to the positions Strip could be fucked in. Clay hadn't had a really intense orgasm in weeks and, on that night, he had three. The boy was insatiable. And he seemed to be doing it because he enjoyed it, not because of who Clay was or what favors might be granted. All the youth said was that he liked handsome older men with big dicks, men with obvious breeding. Breeding, Clay thought at the time, laughing out loud. Talk about breeding! Indeed, whoever had bred Strip should have their genes bottled and sold.

The next day, Clay went through the business of government with little interest, eagerly anticipating a return to the bar to watch Strip dance. But when he arrived, he found the young man had gone to Miami. "You know these kids, always on the move," the bar owner said. "Ain't that the truth," Clay muttered, remembering. He tried to push his physical desire for Strip away, to safeguard himself against desiring the unobtainable, but it was futile; the boy was different. He was not a cheap whore; there was no discussion of money. The mystery of why such a beauty should be stripping in a tawdry bar lingered, and Clay's desire heated to lubricity.

On Thursday, while Clay took his usual commercial flight to Florida, at his government rate, he alerted the pilot of the bank's jet he needed to be flown to Miami in time for a very important dinner engagement the following night.

2

Last year's election had sapped the campaign war chest and there were still bills to be paid. Flying to Miami provided the perfect opportunity to solicit more funds from Clay's old friend Paul Taylor, who shared his enthusiasm for young men and was also heir to a great fortune; Paul's father, William, founder of Taylor Container, was also on the *Florida Trend* magazine list, with a net worth of $200 million.

Early Friday evening, Clay rented a Lincoln Towncar at the airport and drove to Paul's penthouse on Key Biscayne and, over cocktails, they joked about being on the latest list.

"The reports are wrong, all wrong," Paul kidded Clay as they settled into the chaise longues on the balcony overlooking the Atlantic Ocean. "As I recall, you have much more than I do. Much more. But I haven't seen it in so long I forget."

"Ha! Yes, if it was just about the size of one's prick, I suppose I'd be a rich man indeed. But it's not what you have, it's what you do with it."

"And you've been doing very little with it lately, I take it."

"Until last Tuesday night."

"You didn't cruise one of those D.C. tearooms?"

"No, no! I went to a bar. Incognito, of course."

"Oh, of course, but still it's terribly dangerous, Clay. Imagine what would happen if you ran into that gay libber who throws drinks in people's faces? Think about that."

Clay nodded. "I know. But I was at a dinner party and got a bit drunk and was passing by - "

"Being a bit drunk is always your excuse and it's no excuse."

"But I had the presence of mind to don my disguise. And it was worth it. The kid's a marvelous dancer."

"He danced for you?"

"And then some. And now he's right here in Miami."

Paul's stare was half quizzical, half defiant, with just the hint of amusement he adopted whenever Clay was around. Although he was only a year older, he considered himself the senior partner in a firm that, if hadn't been for the health crisis, would have put the Marquis de Sade to shame.

"But my dear boy, you don't have to risk everything for an orgasm. I always have something good for you-"

Paul nodded towards Marco, his steward, who was gliding onto the balcony with a pitcher of fresh martinis. Dark, musclebound Marco looked as if he had stepped out of one of Christian Bravura's exotic porno flicks, which in fact he had because Paul was among the young filmmaker's silent backers.

"Yes, we'll take you along on one of those location shoots," Paul laughed.

"Shoots?" Marco joked as he freshened their drinks.

"Not here, not here," Paul giggled. "Later."

Marco nodded and quietly returned to the kitchen.

The penthouse was Paul's hideaway from the demands his father placed on him. He managed to spend three weeks out of four there but the first week of every month he had to travel to Tampa, attending to the family's philanthropies, one of which was to aid needy South American children. He and Marco stayed at the beachhouse Clay's father purchased for him when he was a freshman in college, "So that you won't have to rent hotel rooms," his father joked. Little did his father know what went on there, especially after Clay and Paul became lovers and spent their vacations there.

Marco always traveled with Paul on Foundation business and received $50,000 a year to assist in reviewing the many requests for funds. "And keep me happy," Paul had told Clay.

"He's underpaid, really," Clay joked.

"I give him little bonuses occasionally, but you're what he really wants and you don't want him."

Although Clay could not deny Marco was stunningly attractive he had not accepted Paul's offer because he knew that the Latin was a stud who could "fuck anything" but would not be fucked. Although Clay had once or twice played the bottom role, he preferred to be in control, to use a boy as he did a woman.

Later, over dinner, when Paul agreed to donate $5,000 more to the Harris campaign, Clay said, "Some people appear to be generous, you really are."

"That's why I'm always broke! My father can never understand I'm simply not a manager, I'm only a dreamer, and I love to be needed. I need to relax from life's problems by helping others."

"I know you do - "

"You needed me once, remember?"

"You'll never let me forget it."

"Ha! Every year when that magazine comes out I think that if we had gotten married, why we'd probably make the Forbes 400!"

Clay shook his head in mock disgust. "At least we'd be first on Malcolm's private list."

"God, it's a shame he's gone. You never met him but he had the hunkiest motorcyclists I've ever seen. I don't know where he found them, but they were always there. He said they were his body-guards." He laughed. "That's what you can do, hire this little dancer as your bodyguard."

"Nobody'd believe it."

3

The Tropics bar was appallingly small, about as spacious as some of the halls Clay was so often stuck in, making speeches to lavender-haired ladies about their social security benefits. The stage extended from the bar like an enormous outstretched tongue, tipped at the end by a pole that, as Clay walked in, a scrawny stripper was making love to, writhing and undulating to the music pulsating from the loud-speakers. In an adjacent room, two middle-aged men played pool under bright lights. Music videos flickered from several TV's hung from the ceiling around the room.

Clay gave his business card and a generous tip to the cutest of the young waiters, instructing him to give the card to Strip; it bore only his first name and the number of his private answering service in Tampa, an 800 number. He had given Strip the card before he left the motel in Washington but the boy hadn't called the number. After he married, Clay had taken his sex furtively in tea rooms, baths, bars, at the beaches, even out on the street, but he grew to detest the impersonalness, the ugliness of it. But if he arranged his assignations, there was always the place to be found, then came the name, sometimes a phone call, a desperate cry for help late at night. As his life became more of a public one versus a very private one, Clay invented his alter ego, Clayton Bennett III, and it suited him. He had always been drawn to the theater.

Clay jockeyed for a position near the stage entrance, having to share a table with two other men. He introduced himself and bought them drinks. With his shades over his eyes and his black hair, graying at the temples, slicked back, he appeared to more resemble a sinister drug dealer than a Congressman and the men tried to buy some dope from him. Suddenly, Garth Brooks was singing "I Got Friends in Low Places" and Clay laughed out loud.

After a parade of jaded, sneering bumps-'n'-grinds artists, the Apollonian Strip appeared. As in D.C., heads were raised, drinks spilled, cigarettes smoldered, and conversations halted. He danced enthusiastically to the tune of the O'Jays' "The Backstabbers." How appropriate, Clay thought, but it was not Strip's back he was thinking of stabbing. The pole added a new dimension to the spectacle, with Strip's gyrations bringing on cheers, and Clay was generous with his tips. Stunned at first to see Clay, before he left the stage the boy whispered he would meet the older man at the bar after the show. Clay beamed.

After the last number, an ensemble, Strip kept his word, dressing quickly in scandalously tight shorts and a tank top.

"...My first groupie," Strip kidded Clay as he sipped the Bud the Congressman had bought him. "Nobody's ever followed me around before."

"I'm honored to be the first of something, but I must confess I didn't really follow you. I had some business in Miami and decided to come here and bang, here you are."

"Amazing eh?"

Strip seemed distracted, anxious and Clay put his hand on the youth's thigh. "I really would like some company tonight."

Strip now gave Clay his full attention. He'd never asked men for money; they usually just gave it to him without haggling. But tonight he was desperate. He'd been robbed before he left Washington and was broke. Still, he decided not to ask Clay for anything. His eyes sparkled. "Hmmmmm, so would I," he said, groping the Congressman. "I remember what's in here."

Indeed, Strip was overwhelmed by Clay's cock. He couldn't make up his mind where he wanted it more, in his mouth or up his ass. He had seen a few that were as long but it was the excessive width of it that impressed him. He worked his magic to first get the older man off by sucking it, but he didn't let up, bringing him around again so that a long session of fucking could follow. Even after the Congressman had come again, Strip would not release him. As Clay washed himself in the bathroom, Strip came in and dropped to his knees to take it orally once more. He was disappointed the following day when he awoke around noon to find Clay had vanished, leaving only his business card and two fifty dollar bills on his pillow.

*

22

Clay stopped at the first motel he saw, registered as his alter ego, paid in cash and, when they were at last alone, tried to restrain himself. While Strip went to the bathroom, Clay unpacked his suitcase and poured himself a stiff gin to calm his nerves. The youngster had greeted him warmly, quickly agreed to accompany him, massaged his crotch to near orgasm in the car...it was all too easy, too good. Such adoration always made him suspicious. Still, when Strip came out of the bathroom stark naked, Clay dismissed all of his fears. "You are glorious," he sputtered.

Smiling broadly, Strip glided across the room towards him.

"And where did you learn to dance like that?"

"Shit, I've been doing it all my life, one way or another. I was trained in ballet."

Clay took the youth in his arms and hugged him. "I've always been fond of the ballet. I've never wanted to admit it to Amanda but -"

"Amanda?" Strip pulled back, puzzled yet still smiling. "Married man, eh?"

"I'm afraid so. Does that bother you?" Clay pulled him back into his arms and took the firm buttocks in his hands.

"No. In fact, I've always had the best times with married men. I even had one guy threaten to leave his wife for me, but I stopped that cold. I wouldn't ever want to do that, break up somebody's marriage."

"My wife's very understanding. Of course, diamonds help."

Strip looked away. He suddenly remembered he had left the bar without collecting his $100 salary. All he had were his tips, and that wasn't much. And he had to pay for his own motel room. "We shouldn't have come here. We should have gone to my place." He lowered himself to the edge of the bed. "It's stupid to have you pay for a room when I already have one. I just wasn't thinking when we left. I was too busy-" His hands began kneading Clay's groin again. "And I forget to pick up my pay. See what you do to me, married man?"

Yes, Clay could see the effect he was having on the boy, who now had a splendid erection, and what effect the boy was having on him became obvious as Strip unzipped Clay's trousers and lowered them to his hips. "God, your wife must love this," Strip gushed as he brought Clay's cock to his lips. "Man, it's even bigger than I remembered."

"She's never known anything else."

"She'd never need anything else."

And as his cock slid into Strip's mouth and down his throat, Clay clamped his hands on the boy's head and groaned, thinking that perhaps he just might never need anyone else but Strip.

*

"...Yeah, I guess I have this strange power to make a man happy," Strip chuckled the next morning as he picked up the buttered toast from the stack the waitress brought to their table.

"I'll testify to that. Girls too?" Clay asked, sipping his coffee. He was delighted to have time to spend talking to the boy. The encounter in Washington had been so furtive, desperate almost, he hadn't even bought him breakfast. Amazingly, Strip, Clay now decided, looked even better the morning after, a wondrous figure with a fey expression and lustrous golden hair.

"I don't get into girls, but - " Strip laughed. "I'll tell you one thing, once you start dancing in clubs, shit they're all over you. I've never seen anything like it. I couldn't get a date with 'em just sitting on a bar stool, but once you dance - "

"You began in straight clubs?"

"Yeah, just to see if I could, at a place called the Saints and Sinners in Jersey. They told me if I could handle those women, I could handle anything, and I was ready to try it at that point. It was supposed to be an audition but one of the guys didn't show up so they put me in the line-up. They made me go first for chrissakes. I was shaking. I forced myself to go on that stage. It was worse than any ballet I'd done, believe me. All these women yelling, 'Take it off! Take it off!' I did a little bump and grind and they went wild. Next thing I knew they were grabbing at me, kissing me, sticking dollar bills in my G-string. The owner loved me. He signed me to a contract, five nights a week. And I got offers. Phone numbers, motel room keys, the whole thing. They'd come back to the dressing room and give the guys blowjobs. Blowjobs, always blowjobs. I never knew women got into it like that."

"Neither did I."

"But they do, man! They go nuts. Then I got signed for private parties. Private dancers they called us. Usually it was just a small group of women and they all knew each other. Bachelorette parties, like the last fling before they got hitched or something. They all have a few shots, start talking dirty. Everything. And I thought it was only guys that did that."

"So did I," Clay said, amused.

"And then one night, this'll crack you up, I clicked on my boom box and started taking off my tuxedo and the chicks went crazy. One chick, really wasted, got on all fours and pulled my G-string down. I always get it like semi-hard before I go on and it just came to attention, just like that! They loved it. They couldn't take their eyes off my dick."

"I'll bet not."

"And they shouted at this girl, telling her to suck it. I was standing there, shaking my ass, my cock ticktocking back and forth like a metronome, and these broads were climbing on the furniture, shouting and stomping and I thought the roof was gonna cave it! And she sucked me, right there, in front of all her friends. I couldn't believe it! And what do the rest of 'em do but start counting, One! Two! Three! Four!, like they were watching a game show. And from across the room the bride-to-be comes over and rushes up behind me, grabs my buns and takes a cheek in each hand and squeezes 'em, telling the other girl, Suck him dry! Suck him dry! Thirty! Thirty one! On and on they counted. It was wild. It was as if they'd never seen a dick before. Then she sat up and spun me around so the bride could have some! And she was even better at it. By the time my two hours were up, all seven of 'em had had a go at it. I went back to the bride for the finale -came right in her mouth!"

"Anything like that happen with guys?"

"Hell, no. But no matter where I dance, I'm just a sex object. And I'm tired of being that. I told myself when I started that I'd give it a year, maybe two at the most, being just that, nothing else. It's as if I'm not a human being to them, I don't have any feelings. And the guys that do it, well, they get burned out awfully fast. In the beginning I acted like I was playing a role, that it really wasn't me, but now it's gotten so it's got no meaning whatsoever."

"So what do you really want to do?"

"Go back to ballet. I fucked up in New York. I had it made and then I fucked up. Doesn't matter how — " He paused, his words hovering in the air.

"Drugs?" Clay asked.

"Yeah, and partying all night. I love New York, I really do. Too much maybe. And I was young enough to let it get to me. I didn't have my head screwed on straight."

"But you do now. I know you do."

"I try."

"I'd like to help if I can."

"You would?"

"Of course. I'm sure I can, in some way." Clay sipped his coffee, deep in thought. Then he went on: "My corporation supports several arts organizations. I'm sure I can get you in somewhere, but then it would be up to you."

Strip smiled. "That'd be great. I always wanted to spend a winter in Florida."

When they returned to Clay's motel room, the congressman made several calls, putting on a bit of a show, savoring the moments of doing what he thought he did best, brokering power. He really needed to make only one call, and he saved it for last. The idea had occurred to him early on that he could sequester the boy at the beachhouse in Clearwater, making access easy from Naples, a two-hour drive. The boy would be close, yet far enough away not to arouse suspicion. Besides, that was the reason he had never sold the place, even after Paul had moved to Miami and it sat empty. It had served its purpose as a place where he could entertain a boy he had picked up in a bar or who had advertised his services in the gay newspapers. But lately boys who would bottom for him had become fewer and fewer and he seldom used the place except to visit Paul and Marco when they stayed there once a month. If Strip were staying there, Clay reasoned, he would put Paul and Marco up at the hotel his family owned, the Biltmore.

Clay hung up the phone one last time. "Well, it's all set. You have an interview next week with the New Ballet in Tampa."

"Tampa? But you don't live in Tampa, you said you lived in Naples."

"I do, but I have a place on the beach in Clearwater, near Tampa. You can stay there if you like."

"When would I see you then?"

"As often as I can arrange it."

*

Clay decided they would drive back to Tampa and he would

install Strip at the beachhouse immediately. But before they left the motel, Strip wanted to show his appreciation and Clay could hardly refuse. For the first time, Clay took the boy in the missionary position for the entire time of their interlude and it seemed as if they were making love instead of merely having sex. It had gone beyond sex. It reminded him of his first months with Amanda, after she became accustomed to his size and was able to accommodate him fully. But Clay enjoyed a man more than a woman for reasons he could never fully define. What had appealed to him most about mansex was that he was always able to part from men without repercussions, but now it was he who was initiating a relationship, a relationship that threatened him as none had in many years. It was as if he was out of control, being led by a force stronger than himself.

"Oh, god, fuck me, fuck me," the boy cried over and over, wrapping his legs tightly around Clay. He ran his fingers across the older man's back, massaging the skin, as Clay, his head pressed to Strip's chest, watched his huge cock slide in and out of Strip's ass. And finally, when Clay was close, he withdrew and came onto the boy's hard sex. Then, eagerly, he grabbed the boy's buttocks and brought his crotch to his face and, lapping up his own cum in the process, blew the boy to orgasm.

...They went to Strip's motel and Clay paid the bill while the boy packed and put his suitcases in the Lincoln.

They were ecstatic during the drive to Clearwater. A situation each of them had often dreamed of was about to become reality. Their minds raced with the possibilities. For Clay, it was an arrangement he somehow felt comfortable with. In his position, he could no longer casually frequent public places. He had to be discreet, to carry on with a boy he could trust. He sensed that little by little he could reveal himself to the boy and he would be safe. After all, he remembered, that was one of the first things the boy had said to him: "You're safe as long as you're with me."

For Strip, it was the end of a way of life that had become tedious, often degrading. And, although he knew little about Clayton Bennett III, the older man obviously had a great deal of the two things he lacked: money and power.

Three hours later, as they were finishing the rum cream pie at the place they had stopped for dinner, Chalet Suzanne in Lake Wales, Strip said, "This is almost as good as an orgasm."

Clay beamed.

"Yeah," Strip chuckled, "you're getting better at it."

"I'm getting better at what?"

"Coming. Most people just climax. They don't really get into it. It's all in the breathing. If you let it all out, all the tensions will go too. And I've noticed you're letting yourself go more. Each time you get better."

Clay could scarcely believe his ears. He'd never had anyone complain about him before. But now he was getting better? Where would it all end? He relished the thought.

"Yeah, it's good," Strip said, finishing his pie.

"No, you're good." Clay mumbled, closing his eyes. Loving Strip had quickly become the easiest thing he had ever done.

*

When they arrived at the beach it was after midnight but Strip insisted on taking a swim in the gulf. As Clay watched him wading into the water, the boy's alabaster skin gleaming in the moonlight, he beamed with esthetic joy, the joy of seeing his glorious new young lover in his proper setting of luxury and splendor.

And when Strip returned from his swim, panting, Clay wrapped him in a huge towel and held him tight against his body. They kissed.

After their lips had parted, Clay asked, "Well, do you think you'll like it here?"

"What a question! It's like dying and going to heaven." And Clay began sucking the boy's tongue as if it was something else and they fell to the floor of the living room and made love late into the night.

The next morning, Clay called Naples and told Amanda he was driving back and would be home in time for dinner. She didn't question him, just told him to drive carefully. He gave Strip the keys to the red and white Jeep Renegade he kept at the house and an ATM card. "You'll be able to get cash whenever you need it," Clay told him, offhandedly; he did not consider himself a generous man, he simply wanted the boy to feel comfortable, trusted. And although most people would probably have considered the beachhouse opulent, fearful of the damage hurricanes can do, Clay had never kept anything valuable there. Until now. But then, he knew, hurricane season was over.

"You're so good to me," Strip said, kissing him on the cheek.

"Hey, it works both ways, you know," Clay said, returning his kiss.

"When will I see you again?"

"I'll be back Thursday night. Will you pick me up at the airport?"

"On one condition," Strip said with an elfin smile.

"Oh?"

Strip groped him hard.

"Not again!" Clay laughed, backing away.

"Hey, it's gotta hold me till Thursday for chrissakes!"

And so, again, there on the living room floor, Clay quickly mounted the boy in what had soon become their favorite position, Strip on his back, legs stretching to the ceiling, and the older man screwed him arduously until both of them came again, hugging and kissing each other, to the sound of waves gently, ceaselessly lapping the shore.

4

"Stuart. My name's Stuart Hall." Strip had decided to take back his dignity, use his real name.

Leonard Bachman sat imperiously on a stool in the middle of the dance studio and accepted the boy's resume. While the older man glanced at it, Stuart stood anxiously in front of him. The man's startling resemblance to Bob Fosse was calculated, Stuart thought; this dance master in Florida aspired to Broadway but probably had never even been there.

"I'm familiar with Burgess' work at the Corps. It's a fine company." He looked up and their eyes met at last. Leonard smiled, drew a deep breath, then continued, "I've already called him."

Stuart grimaced.

"Oh," Leonard chuckled, "don't worry. Burgess told me all about you. We would be honored to have you here, but at the moment we only have this weekend tutoring thing available."

"It's a start."

"These are excited children, leaping, having fun. We owe them a chance they can't imagine. That's the basis of the New Ballet. They are just very raw ingredients, but it's important that each has a chance."

"Yes. And for you to want me to teach them, well, it's like being told I'm special."

"Special indeed," Leonard chuckled. "It would be like having a star in our midst. They'd be in the presence of quality. To learn here should be their brush with excellence."

"I agree."

"I like your attitude. Do you think you can instill that attitude in youngsters?"

"I know I can."

"I know you can, too." He slid off his stool and put his arm across Stuart's shoulder. "But there's one problem."

"Oh?" Stuart's eyes held Leonard's.

"You're just too attractive. But you know that."

"It's all in the eyes of the beholder, so they say."

Leonard nodded and brought his hand to Stuart's face. "You have been highly recommended by some important people and I was ready to dislike you intensely, but now I find myself quite taken with you."

Stuart blushed and looked away. "Thank you."

Leonard was familiar at once and Stuart was fearful the dance master would kiss him right there, which, since they were alone on this cloudy afternoon, wouldn't have been scandalous, just forward. But Stuart had lived with such forwardness since he was 13.

It began when the little theater group was presenting "Oliver!" for the Christmas holiday and the director couldn't decide who would play Oliver and who would play the Artful Dodger. He made a competition out of it between a boy named Ned and Stuart. Stuart, being younger, fair and smaller, was finally cast in the lead. Ned, two years older, got the key supporting role. Ned held no animosity against Stuart; indeed, he took a liking to the youthful star and, although Stuart's mother would bring him to rehearsals, the youngster would often hitch a ride home with Ned, who drove his father's van.

One balmy evening in the middle of the rehearsal period, they stopped for burgers and when they left the restaurant Stuart tripped and injured his foot. On the way home, Stuart was obviously in pain and as they passed a park Ned pulled in.

"Where are we going?" Stuart asked.

"I think if we smoke a little something your foot will feel better."

They drove deep into the woods. After they had parked and shared a joint, Stuart felt a hand on his foot and Ned said, "Let me massage it. I'll make it feel better."

The pressure of Ned's hands on his feet went straight to Stuart's head. The older boy rubbed Stuart's calves and thighs, working his way up the body, up his back and he eventually mounted him. Their tender skin touched and Stuart liked what he was feeling; he wasn't sure what it was but he knew he liked Ned a lot. Just as he began wondering what it would be like to kiss him, Ned did just that. Stuart kissed him back enthusiastically.

They rubbed together for a long time and Ned climaxed. As he pulled himself up from Stuart's body, he noticed the boy still had an erection. Gently, he rubbed it with one hand while the other loosened the boy's pants. Ned's expert sucking of him lasted only a minute or two until he came as he never had before and Stuart knew he would never again be content just masturbating by himself.

During the rehearsal period and short run of the play, Ned took Stuart to the park often and taught him precisely how to use his hands and mouth to make another man respond.

On the night of the final performance, they returned to the park and, to celebrate, smoked again. When they were high, Stuart discovered how good it felt to have fingers massaging his anus as he was being blown. It was an experience that whetted his appetite for what he knew would be yet another phase of his education. Ned promised to give Stuart more lessons but shortly thereafter he was arrested on possession charges and sent to a reform school.

"...It's those eyes," Leonard said.

Stuart sighed and, pulling away, asked, "So, when can I start?"

"How about tonight, at dinner?"

Stuart stood close to the door with his hands on his hips. "I can't. I'm sorry, I have a date."

"So do I, but I can cancel it."

Stuart picked up his dance bag. "Sorry, I can't."

"I understand."

"Are you sure you don't want me to audition?"

Leonard let loose with a laugh so earsplitting Stuart crinkled shut his eyes. He could imagine the kind of audition Leonard would like to give him. And perhaps, at another time, in another place...but it didn't seem right, somehow, Clay or no Clay.

"I'll see you Saturday then," Stuart said, easing out the door.

"Yes, come early. We'll go over the roll, I'll introduce you and then you're on your own."

"I'm used to it; I'm always on my own."

Later, as he climbed into the Jeep in the parking lot and turned on the ignition, Stuart wished he'd accepted Leonard's invitation. He was suddenly horny, very horny. It seemed now that he didn't have a worry in the world, he had relaxed and was always horny. And his stud was back in Washington, doing god knows what.

*

On Saturday, it was still unseasonably warm for November, but it was Stuart's favorite weather for dancing. The heat made it easier to warm up without strain. But he knew it would be difficult to convince the youngsters of its benefits. As Leonard was reviewing the names of the students, Stuart turned up the air conditioning, then began playing the tapes Leonard had picked.

Eighteen kids had signed up for the workshop, part of the ballet's community service program. Two were black.

"Okay, it's time to dance," Stuart said after he was introduced as a "guest artist from New York," which, when he thought about it, was true enough.

He gave a rudimentary bar. Then it took ten minutes to teach five basic positions. Plies and tendus took another ten. Half of the students were boys and they kept making fun of each other, making faces, deliberately messing up the combinations. The girls were obviously bored. He had heard one of the black girls say she thought it was going to be like in the movie "Fame," but it wasn't and she was disappointed.

Terrified of losing his class on the first day, Stuart had an inspiration. He tore some pieces of paper from his notebook and made 18 strips.

"Anybody know what an improvisation is?" he asked.

"I know, from my theater class," one of the older boys said smugly. "You just do what you want..."

"What you feel - "

"Yes, like that."

"In dancing, choreography is like a script. A dance is created by the choreographer, a person who has a specific idea of what he wants to create. Sometimes the dance can tell a story or it can just be abstract."

"Abstract?" one boy asked.

"Yeah, you can see in it whatever you want. Everybody'll have a different idea."

And they began the exercise. It was wonderful the ideas the children came up with, Stuart thought, and suddenly he noticed an older boy was sitting off to the side, watching intently. He had been there in the beginning, briefly, and Leonard had introduced him as Terry. Stuart didn't catch the last name, his mind on the class. Now Terry was back, enjoying the little improvisations of the students. When the class was over, Terry lingered.

Wiping the sweat from his face with a towel, Stuart approached the teenager. "How'd I do, coach?"

"Awesome. Better'n I could've done. If you hadn't come here, I'd be teaching it."

"That's what I was told."

"But now I'm glad you got it."

"That's the best compliment I could ever get. Thanks." Stuart's eyes locked on the boy's, big, brown, somehow hurting, Stuart thought. With those baleful eyes, the boy's face vaguely resembled a puppy dog's. And he had the same impulse he did around dogs, he wanted to pet Terry. But he gripped the towel instead. Although the boy had an undeniable sexiness, he couldn't have been more than 17 and Stuart wasn't into chicken, at least he never thought so.

"You're really very good," Terry went on, his eyelashes fluttering uncontrollably.

It was nearly noon and Stuart was starving. "Lunch?"

"Hey, yeah, that'd be great."

As they tumbled into the Jeep and roared out of the parking lot, Stuart was not sure where they would go; he only knew a few roads in this city so new to him.

"Oh, I forgot," Terry said. "I better call my mother and tell her not to pick me up. Will you drop me off at my house after?"

"Sure, man. You can call from wherever it is we're going. Oh, and just where is it we're going?"

"Oh, any place. I could eat anything."

"Me, too," Stuart chuckled, with a sidelong glance at the boy as the bright sunlight streamed into the cab. He was taller than Stuart, the perfect height for a principal dancer, and his skin was flawless. Stuart glanced down at the bulge at his crotch and decided, yes, the kid was good enough to eat.

They headed west on Kennedy Boulevard and made a left on Dale Mabry, listening to the rock music blaring from the speakers, Terry tapping in time on the Jeep's dash. Stuart kept the dial locked on the city's classic rock station.

Over steaks at Bonanza, Terry told Stuart that he liked to dance so much that he had been willing to risk ridicule all his life. "I'm a member of the Tigerettes," he confided. "It's our dancing and flag corps team at school. There's 22 of us and I'm the only boy. They all think I'm gay but I won't tell anybody what I am." He laughed. "I can't, because I don't know myself, but I just wanted to prove a guy could do it. I love the movement and feeling of being in control of my body. And it feels good to do something in sync with other people, even if they are all girls."

"Well, I'm gay and proud of it," Stuart said, and for a moment he couldn't believe he'd said it. He realized he hadn't had the courage to admit that for a long time. But he wanted to impress this kid that it wasn't such a big deal, that a person could live with it. "No matter how much they dish out, it makes you stronger to stand up to it. I've found that. I don't parade it in front of 'em, but I don't deny anything."

"Wasn't it rough in school, though? I mean, you're so pretty - " he hesitated. "I'm sorry, I didn't mean that -"

"Hey, I don't mind. It's better than being ugly I'll tell you that."

For the next hour, they shut out the rest of the world, swapping tales of school, family, dance.

Then with all the boldness and mystery that had fascinated Terry from the start, Stuart suggested they go for a swim in the Gulf. Clay had left that morning for Naples and they would be alone. "The water's still warm," he said.

"Yeah, sixty something," Terry chuckled. Having been born in Florida and used to a heated pool, he never went in the water unless it was at least 80 degrees. But today he said, "I can stand it if you can."

*

"...Wow!" Terry gushed when they entered the beachhouse. "I always wondered what these places looked like on the inside."

"It's my folks' place. They only use it a couple of months in the winter. Hang on a second." Stuart raced upstairs and pulled open a drawer in the bureau. He had used Clay's ATM card to get some cash and bought a dozen Speedos, one in every color the store had. Chuckling, he picked a pink one for Terry and tossed it down the stairs. "You can change in the john down there, right by the front door."

As he stepped out of his sweat pants and peeled off his leotards, his cock rose to attention. He realized having a studly teenager in the house had aroused him uncontrollably. He slipped into his Speedo but his cock would not be denied.

"You ready?" Terry called from the bottom of the stairs.

Stuart chuckled at the thought of just how ready he was.

"In a second," he said, and he grabbed a towel from the bathroom and made his way down the stairs. Even with a towel dangling in front of his crotch, Stuart knew his condition was obvious and Terry stared at it.

"Last one in is queer -" Stuart cried and raced out the back door and down the flight of wooden stairs to the sea. Terry caught up with him and they tousled together on the shore, the waves crashing over them.

5

"I miss you," Stuart told Clay, who was phoning to say he had to stay in Washington until Thanksgiving Eve; he would fly to Naples and drive to the beach on Friday.

"I can't tell you how much I miss you - " Clay responded.

"No, but you'll have fun showing me - "

"You bet I will. Now, tell me what you're wearing, so I can see you perfectly." He had lived for these calls. Stuart recounting every moment of his day, finally to lead Clay into ecstasy as he created a scenario of sex for him. They would, in their minds, be lying side by side in the enormous bed, comforting each other.

"Nothing."

"Absolutely nothing?"

"Absolutely."

"Is it hard?"

"Just thinking about you makes it hard, you know that."

"Are you playing with it?"

"You know I am."

"I wish I were there to suck it."

"I wish you were too. I miss you. I miss your handsome face."

Stuart often pictured Clay's face, smooth and rosy, the face of a man who seems to age more gently than other men. And Stuart loved the way his lover looked nude, not particularly tall, but his broad shoulders filled out a beautiful posture. And the piece de resistance was the cock, oversized even when limp and swaying seductively as he walked. Yes, Stuart thought, if he had conjured up a lover he wouldn't have been as perfect as Clay.

"Is that all, just my face?"

"Hmmm, no. Your hands, your ass - " Stuart paused.

"It's hard as rock right now."

"I'll bet."

"Oh, just stroking it, knowing where it will be in just a couple of days, it's going to shoot."

"Fucker has a mind of it's own."

"Yup, and only one thing on it's mind - Stuart."

Clay listened for the groan, the groan he knew was Stuart at the height of his orgasm. "Oh, Clay, my big - "

"Yes, love, yes?"

"Oh, god -"

And Clay himself came. They would say nothing after this episode, simply hang up their phones.

Stuart laid back on the bed and closed his eyes. He'd never been happier, he was sure of that. He had been homeless much of his life, living in other people's apartments, in motels, hotels, just camping out at a friend's, and the beachhouse had quickly become home. Not only was it the most luxurious place he had ever lived, it was virtually all his. A perfect place for the self-possessed. Yet the nights were difficult; he would watch the moon shimmering on the water, listen to the crashing of the waves, smell the sea; memories of Clay and him making love arousing him. He would masturbate but still the need persisted, sometimes with Clay on the phone, or later, by himself. Drawn to the water, he would go swimming until he was so exhausted he would fall asleep easily. But the next morning, he faced the same dilemma; now he had everything but still he had nothing. The man he loved was hundreds of miles away; the only other person who turned him on was a 17-year-old member of the Tigerettes. He cursed himself that he had begun to think of drugs again.

Then came Terry's call. He said his girlfriend Jodie was going to visit relatives for Thanksgiving and Stuart was welcome to join him for dinner with his parents.

*

Terry introduced Stuart as the tutor at the ballet, visiting from New York, and the older boy relished his new vision of himself as a teacher. Over dinner at their palatial home in Feather Sound, on the bay, Stuart regaled Terry's parents with tales of his days in New York. "If you really want to perform," he told them, "there are always things you can do, whether you get paid for it or not. But if you want to be famous, that's something else again. You can do that and not have any talent."

"What does it really take to succeed in that place?" Terry's father asked.

"Same thing it takes anywhere else, I think: drive. It takes someone who is very focused, strong-willed and not afraid to say what's on his mind. There are so many things going on around you, you just have to assert yourself. But I eventually burned out on it because I have a hard time being assertive 24 hours a day. In the city, you can never let your guard down. If you do, something is going to happen, like you get mugged or run over by a truck. It wears a person out."

Terry broke in: "And you were such a success at any early age. You danced with the Corps."

"I was lucky because I made friends in the city and I lived across the river in Jersey. I could go home at night if I wanted to. I never would have made it if I'd been forced into renting a tiny apartment on the fourth floor some place with no hot water. No, if you're willing to bend -" He caught himself before he admitted he was the type of boy who would never really struggle if he was willing to compromise. "But, eventually if you're not all that driven, you just give up and settle for something less, like a place here at the New Ballet. But I don't think leaving New York means you've given up, it just means that you're evolving. I'm sure I'll be back there one day, doing something."

Terry's parents were so genuinely considerate, warm, real, that it made Stuart envy his new friend's "normal" existence. Terry's father even encouraged his son's dancing and praised Stuart's efforts to make the boy practice more regularly. Stuart saw in Terry the dancer he could never be, the *danseur noble*, elegant long limbs, a regal bearing, the boy who would dance the principal roles, his control in slow movements that display a harmony of line. Terry danced even the most difficult pirouettes and leaps with grace and ease. Stuart, with his compact physique, was destined to be the *demi-caractere*, a quicker dancer, displaying his brilliant footwork, bounding jumps, fast turns. But whichever role they played, each sought to dance with the power and control of a tiger, springing into the air, twisting and turning and landing gently with absolute precision, with no visible trace of effort.

"Terry should continue with his ballet, no matter what the kids at school say," Stuart said. "Men are needed. They were the first dance masters, they wrote the book on technique. For a long time, men didn't dance and that was a sad time."

He stayed, talking, for an hour after dinner. The affection that seemed to flow from them made Stuart's lurid thoughts regarding Terry bothersome to him. When he returned to the beach, he was even more depressed. He became desperate. Having no grass, no coke, no Ecstasy, he opened Clay's liquor cabinet; it was filled and he proceeded to empty it.

The next day, suffering an incredible hangover, Stuart walked the beach and watched the birds and the way they handled things. How industrious they were, yet how patient. Afternoon became evening before Clay arrived. Stuart, watching television in the master bedroom when his lover entered the house, ran down the stairs and flung himself into the older man's arms.

"Oh, I've missed you," Stuart cried.

"Good god," Clay murmured and smothered the boy's face with kisses.

Before long, Stuart's fingers were gently moving across Clay's skin, squeezing here, there, everywhere. Soon Clay was naked, on the king-size bed, letting Stuart work his magic.

"I've missed you too, you know," Clay groaned as Stuart massaged his skin.

"You must have. You're a bundle of nerves. Relax."

But Stuart knew there was only one way Clay could completely relax. He brought his lips to Clay's cock, then deep-throated him. The older man was coming in a few moments. He held Stuart's head, bobbing wildly as the come oozed from his cock. When he squeezed the last drops from it, Clay cried, "Let me hold you. I just want to hold you."

As the boy slid into his arms, Clay realized he had been selfish, he hadn't even permitted him to get completely undressed. He rubbed his hands over the boy's torso, reveling again in the tightly muscled body. "This tutoring job must agree with you. If it's possible, I think you're even more beautiful than the last time I saw you."

"That was too long ago." He hugged him. "Yeah, I may look good but I feel like shit. I drank too much of your gin last night. You shouldn't stay away so long. What do you do up there in Washington anyway?"

"My family's in banking. I guess you could say I'm the liaison in Washington."

"Don't want to tell me, eh?"

"Tell you what?"

"Never mind." Stuart toyed with Clay's cock. "You're just so secretive. But it's okay. You've had to be secretive all your life so there's no changing you now."

"Speaking of being secretive, what have you been up to since I saw you?" It cheered Clay to see how quickly Stuart took on the trappings of wealth. How it became him. Still, Clay wondered what the boy did in his absence. He would call the beach and there would be no answer. When Stuart did answer the phone, there was always the excuse of the beach, running errands, or, occasionally no reason at all, "I was just out."

Whatever the boy was doing, it wasn't costing very much. Clay monitored the bank account and the boy spent very little.

"Oh, I do my exercises every morning. And I swim. Yeah, it's been great, almost like being on vacation."

"You deserve a little vacation."

"So do you. All this banking business has made you so tense I can't believe it."

Stuart pulled away and had Clay lie on his stomach. As the boy continued his massage, a look of assured possession spread across Clay's face.

*

"...Yes, Amanda thought she could take the town by storm, but Washington doesn't work the way she thought it did," Clay said over dinner the next evening. "It's all about power, not money. You don't necessarily need money in Washington to have power. You build up your influence over the years. But after two years of giving parties and nobody showing up, she left. She's never been back."

"Which is good for you - " Stuart interjected.

"Don't — please. I love my wife. I always have. It's just that I don't feel anything for her anymore. I know she knows something's not quite right, she just doesn't want to face it. No woman wants to admit she can't keep her man."

"But at least she's not losing you to another woman."

"Oh, but that's just it. She isn't losing me. You can't lose something you never really had in the first place. I don't know what she'd think if she knew about me. The scandal of it would kill her.

God, it'd kill my grandfather, my sister, my mother, everyone."

"So, we just keep it all a secret, for fear of killing all those people."

"That's what it amounts to. But in Naples, Amanda is happy, the queen of the town. I doubt it would matter to her if I ever came back. I wouldn't except for the children."

"This being with a married man, a married man with children, it just blows my mind."

"Blowing your mind isn't what I have in mind - " Clay said. And they quickly left the restaurant.

...Back in bed at the beachhouse, the older man was now conjuring up ways to please the boy. He had never cared much for sucking cock but he had become enamored of Stuart's cock. It was cut, well-shaped and bent enchantingly to the left.

The boy said he didn't get into fucking but Clay found he loved to straddle him, hands planted firmly on the mattress, and face-fuck him. While Stuart was doing it, Clay ran his hands across the smooth skin of Stuart's legs and thighs, coming to rest on the perfectly shaped buns. And Clay loved the boy's ballsack, he loved to suck it, kiss it, have it rubbed in his face. The boy's natural aroma intoxicated him. And several times, so uncontrollable was Stuart's orgasm that he came in Clay's mouth and Clay found the taste of his come delightful.

"Go for it," Stuart now told Clay. And as Clay went down on him again, Stuart shuddered.

...When Clay returned to the bedroom after washing himself, Stuart reached out and stroked the Congressman's still semi-erect cock. "Yeah, there's something special about a man that can fuck both men and women."

"Ha!" Clay laughed as he slid between the sheets. "I just don't want to limit myself. Oh, I know. I've heard that married guys who are fucking their wives love to get fucked when they get with a guy. I can do it, but I prefer it the other way. I guess because I was never really happy fucking my wife. Never really happy fucking those girls in high school or college. I was never really happy until I began fucking other men."

Stuart nodded but he could not imagine it, living the way Clay had lived, continued to live. And he knew Clay could never understand how it had been for him. How he had never been really happy until he'd been initiated by Ned. Then, it seemed, he could never get enough. But it was seldom more than lust. Now he was confronted with a man he felt he could very well fall in love with, give himself to in every way possible.

Stuart smiled. "You know, I've never really done it. Can you imagine? Oh, I've thought about it, fucking a girl or a boy, dreamed about how it might be, almost gotten there, but I've never done it."

Clay gulped. The thought of the youth on top of him, in control, dominating him, entering him, suddenly seemed a viable variation. He had come to appreciate the quality of the youth's cock, why not take it all the way? Paul had said that as long as a man was well hung and knew what he was doing, getting screwed was a pleasure beyond compare. But Stuart was not huge like Marco or himself. And he had never fucked before. It would be awkward, yet Clay was willing. But by the time he had made up his mind, Stuart was fast asleep next to him.

6

By early December, Stuart was growing restless. His thoughts of unfaithfulness were intensified by going to the dance clubs where teenagers hung out. Girls turned on to him. They would ask him to dance but he was so much better than they were, it was as if he was dancing alone. He became locked in the closed loop with the white noise in an electronic collage of jackhammer beats and bombarding sound effects. He felt the vibrations race through his body, accelerating his muscles, but on the crowded dance floors, he felt somehow cramped, the space extending only as far as his skin; everything beyond was sonic clutter.

Girls would follow him to the juice bar and ask for his phone number. He gave them a fake one, but then wished he hadn't. After dancing for hours he was tired, yet he was horny. By the time he got back to the beach, he wished he had one of his adoring fans with him. He was ready to grab the dildo he had found in the cabinet in the bathroom, which Clay said his friend Paul had left there, and fuck himself with it until he came. His visions during these moments were of some of the girls - and the boys - he had met at the clubs. He imagined himself fucking them. If Clay could do it, he thought, he could, too. And then his mind would wander to the class, to the studio, and finally to Terry. When he was close, he imagined it was Terry inside of him, not the dildo, the taller boy over him, ramming it into him the way Clay did. Other days, he missed Clay terribly, wanted the older man's hands all over him, his colossal sex filling him. Then, at other times, he would see a strange boy walking on the beach and he thought that was what he wanted. He longed to teach the boy what he knew, to put his hands and cock where Clay put his.

But whatever kind of sex it was, he wasn't getting it. He dated none of the girls, Clay seemed to be forever in Washington, and Terry always seemed to be practicing with the Tigerettes or with his girlfriend.

To keep himself occupied during the day, Stuart volunteered to help backstage with the New Ballet's annual presentation of "The Nutcracker." Leonard continued to invite him to dinner but Stuart kept rejecting him, chuckling, "You never give up."

"Part of my charm."

"I think he likes you," Terry said after Leonard had walked away.

"That's his problem."

A few days later, on the first day of Terry's school recess, Stuart took him to Myakka State Park and, after a sightseeing cruise on the Gator Gal, they rented bikes and raced along the road to the nature walk, then by foot down to the river, delighting in the ferns, the birds and the wildflowers. They chased alligators into the dense jungle and, eventually, they came to a clearing. The sky above them was clear and the sun beat down intensely. Stuart slipped off his T-shirt and felt Terry's eyes admiring his definition. He was proud that he seemed to have gotten even more sculpted in the past few weeks and he stared into the boy's face as he wiped his chest with his shirt. "Aren't you hot, man?"

"Yeah," Terry chuckled. Stuart's eyes held his and as if Stuart was somehow ordering him to, Terry lifted his hand and caressed his own groin, looking down into Stuart's eyes, seeing the desire there, a desire he sensed from the beginning was so intense it threatened to explode if it were not vented soon. Stuart longed to kiss the boy but he held back; instead he moved his hand to the boy's navel, then beyond. Feeling the hardness there, he stroked it and his head fell to Terry's naked chest and he kissed one nipple, then the other. Terry began trembling.

Stuart dropped to his knees and pulled the boy's jogging shorts down his thighs. Terry's cock sprang out from the jockstrap and Stuart instantly took it in his mouth, aggressively devouring it. It was a small cock, but thick and perfectly shaped and Stuart engulfed it whole, causing Terry to shudder. The boy came almost immediately. Stuart clamped his strong hands on Terry's buttocks as the come streamed into his mouth and down his throat. Terry gasped and held Stuart's head as the older boy let the cock slide from his mouth. He kissed it one last time and stood, hugging Terry, who was still trembling.

They said nothing to each other, as if speaking would break the strange spell that had come over them. Returning to the path in silence, it was only when they got on their bikes and began pedaling away that Stuart broke the quiet, and then it was just to talk about the weather.

*

Clay was still in Washington when "The Nutcracker" opened. Since Terry had gone to Aspen for a skiing vacation with his family, Stuart worked behind the scenes alone opening night. Stuart was delighted to see how Leonard had updated the classic story, revamping it to appeal to modern children raised on video games. The second act took place in an outer-space world right out of "Star Wars." But the basic story remained and 12 of Stuart's students appeared in the production, their roles small and only in the Act I party scene. They were clearly thrilled to be involved, seeing how a production came together. Stuart laughed when Jesse, his most agile black dancer, counseled another student, "You're supposed to act scared when that Drossmiller guy shows up at the party."

After the performance, Leonard was ecstatic about how well everything had gone. "We must celebrate," he said.

"Okay."

Leonard did a double-take. "You're serious?"

"Sure I'm serious." Stuart's attitude had changed during the course of the staging of the ballet. He had grown to appreciate Leonard's directing talents and admired the fact that Leonard had excelled as a *comique* dancer, stockily built, doing comic parts, and he could have danced well beyond what would be considered his prime, yet he had devoted himself to teaching others. What harm would it do to go to dinner? They agreed sometime between Christmas and New Year's would be ideal.

A few days later, Stuart was teaching his last class before Christmas recess when Leonard came to him accompanied by a youth he introduced as Jamie Parsons, a boy even taller and more powerfully built than Terry. He said he had been active in sports and had become interested in ballet as a form of exercise to tone his body. He was perhaps too tall for ballet, Stuart thought, but he told him, "Well, if you've come for exercise, you've come to the right place." As they shook hands briefly, their eyes met and Stuart chuckled, thinking about the kind of exercise he would like to give the youth.

Jamie joined the class and afterward, as they were leaving the building, Stuart asked him, "Can I give you a ride home?"

"No, Mom's picking me up. See you after New Year's."

Stuart stood still for a few moments, his eyes roaming the boy's muscular body as he rushed toward a waiting car. He thought, Careful, careful. In his loneliness he feared he would make a mistake that he would not be able to undo. The physical ripeness of these youths, Terry and Jamie in particular, coupled with their handsome, boyish faces and seeming openness, had stunned him. As he drove home, their voluptuous images kept recurring, and the combinations and patterns of lovemaking taking many forms until, when he finally drove under the house and turned off the ignition, he merely had to slip his cock free from his jockstrap to climax.

7

For Clay, the holidays began wonderfully. It was good to be with the children again, just enjoying them. Both of the girls possessed their mother's big twinkling eyes, blonde hair and rosy cheeks. They wore red and green full shirtwaist dresses, Christmasy and cheerful. It was a happy occasion.

Earlier, the bank's jet had brought Grandfather Harris to Naples and Clay met him at the airport. On the way to the mansion, they talked about what had happened during the last weeks of Congress. The old man was disturbed that nothing was being done about the economy. He railed on and on about the real estate market and the loss of tax incentives and what should be done and Clay, as always, agreed with every word he said. Like so many financiers of his generation, Grandfather Harris was inclined to be proud of his simple and austere background. The son of a minister, often quoting the King James version of the Bible, he was a lifelong Republican.

As Clay pulled the long white Mercedes sedan into the circular drive, the old man said, "I applaud your concerns about the poor. But that takes money. The easiest way to solve a problem is just to throw money at it, but the money has to come from somewhere. It's up to us to make it and then give it away." He placed an avuncular hand on Clay's and said, "Just keep making those kind of headlines. You confound your friends and confuse the enemy."

The girls were enchanted with their blue and gold macaw, a gift from Grandfather. Amid the sounds of female glee, Clay looked self-conciously at his watch and wondered where Stuart was and what he was doing. Finally, he could stand it no longer and, using the phone by the pool, he called the beachhouse.

While they talked, Stuart opened Clay's present, a set of ten Bolshoi Ballet tapes, and after he hung up, Stuart slipped "Romeo and Juliet" into the VCR. He watched it for a while but grew bored.

He was in an incredible funk. He had grown to detest the holidays. He had lost track of all of his friends from the days in New York. "Once you go into rehab you realize who your friends are," he had told Clay. "I found I didn't have any."

Even Terry's call from Aspen, in the middle of "The Sleeping Beauty," failed to cheer Stuart. He called Leonard but the answering machine was on. So much for fancy dinners, he thought. He took a long shower, got dressed in his best jeans, and went out.

He hadn't been particularly interested in the gay bars but Clay had pointed one out to him as they drove by it and later he went in and picked up a guidebook. Now he knew where all the horny guys hung out. He drove south to Madeira Beach to the Back Room. It was empty. He went further south to Bedrox's and when he arrived he realized he hadn't eaten all day. He took a booth and ordered. At another booth a few yards away, another man was dining alone; he sent Stuart a bottle of wine. Stuart nodded, then decided the least he could do was share it with the man.

"...I couldn't imagine someone like you being alone," the man told him. "I waited for your date to arrive, but when I realized you really were alone - "

"Yeah, everybody's with their families. I should be with mine but I can't."

"Same here. Misery loves company, though."

Stuart nodded. The man was in his fifties, reasonably well preserved, and dressed with obvious care. The more wine Stuart drank, the more Stuart liked the man, who introduced himself as Grayson Darr, author of collections of redneck tales, which Stuart thought was fascinating.

As Grayson spun his tales, Stuart finished the bottle of wine. At one point, he asked, "C'mon, gay rednecks?"

"Ever see that movie 'Deliverance?'"

"Yeah."

"Well, see."

They ordered dinner and another bottle of wine. As they ate, Stuart told his host a bit about himself, not much, just enough to tantalize the man.

"So, you haven't been in town long?"

"No, just two months. And I've been very busy. I guess that's the secret, staying busy. Now I'm not doing anything and everybody's gone and it's so damn boring."

"Well, luckily you decided to come out tonight."

"Yeah, my first night bar hopping. I was just so sick of dancing in those places that I couldn't stomach going in them and I really didn't have any reason to."

"Your lover must be a very happy man."

"Oh?"

"He gave you no reason to go out."

"No, it's not that. I've been busy with school."

"And schoolmates, I'll bet."

Stuart beamed. "Yeah, some."

"Ah, youth," Grayson toasted, and they clinked their glasses.

After turning down Grayson's invitation to spend the night with him, Stuart left Bedrox's and drove towards town, to the park, the one Grayson had said was cruisy. That meant men in cars driving ceaselessly, looking for a quick fix for their sexual hunger.

A few minutes after he entered the park, a late model Toyota began following him, stopped when he stopped, turned when he turned. He became concerned that it might be the police, that they had the license plate number, that he might cause trouble for Clay, and decided to go home. But he couldn't lose the car. It followed him out of the park and up Fourth Street. When he turned at the mall and headed west, the Toyota was on his tail. He pulled into a 7-11 to get gas. The Toyota pulled in across the island of pumps. The driver, a man in his late 20's, got out and started to pump gas into his car. Stuart could sense the man was looking at him; he turned and their eyes met. The young man smiled. Stuart smiled back.

His name was Jack and he lived in a trailer park off Park Boulevard with his mother, who was away for the holidays. He'd had Christmas dinner with his sister and decided to see what was going on at the park. Now he was glad he had.

Stuart said he didn't have much time, that he was expected home. Jack looked Stuart up and down again and chuckled, "Oh, it won't take long, believe me."

After they arrived at the trailer, Jack went to the bathroom and when he returned to the tiny bedroom, he came from behind while Stuart was undressing and began poking at Stuart's ass with his erection. Slowly he slipped a lubed rubber on it and Stuart bent over and let Jack slide it in. Stuart hung on to the back of a chair as Jack slammed into him. Masturbating himself while the man enjoyed himself, Stuart realized how much he had missed mansex. He came quickly and then brought his hands to his asscheeks pulling them wide apart, feeling the hard body as it heaved against him.

"Oh, yeah, fuck it," he cried.

And, as Jack predicted, it didn't take long.

*

After the Christmas meal, which they all had devoured gluttonously, Clay and Grandfather rose from the table and, nestled back in his favorite chair when he visited the mansion, his head propped up, Grandfather mused aloud on the sad state of affairs in the financial world. He sipped a special tea, Clay had a cognac. Clay thought his grandfather's loss of the old animation which had endeared him to his companions was because he had sworn off liquor upon the untimely death of his son, allowing as how abstinence would add years to his own life to make up for the loss. Clay tried to make light of it, reminding him of W.C. Fields' line that when a teetotaler got up in the morning that was as good as he was going to feel all day and the old man always laughed out loud.

Over the holiday, it appeared to Clay that the man was lapsing into senility. The fire, the sparkle were gone, as if he had been paralyzed by the devastating march of events which began with his son's death, then his wife's. And one by one his friends were dying off, with no new ones of much importance appearing. He had survived the bigger and bigger banks gobbling up the small and because, with his vast personal wealth, he continued to play a role, however limited.

But it was Clay that Grandfather fretted about. Earlier, he had tried to get Clay to go to church with the family but Clay had always felt there was nothing there but empty promises and sad faces, even on as joyous an occasion as Christmas. "My grandson doesn't read the Bible," he muttered as he left with Amanda and the girls. "A man who doesn't read the Scriptures will come to no good. No good."

Now he started again: "You're not leading a good life, Clay, I'm worried about you. I can't put my finger on it but you appear to me to be very unhappy."

"I've never been happier, Grandfather. Believe me."

"It's hard to believe when I see you here. I feel your happiness lies beyond these walls, perhaps back in Washington."

"Yes, beyond these walls."

"A man in your position must be prudent."

"I am. More prudent than you'll ever know."

"I pray so."

And, as Grandfather nodded off to sleep in his chair, Clay went out to the pool and placed another call to the beachhouse. The answering machine picked up and Clay did not leave a message.

*

As the holiday progressed, it seemed to Amanda that Clay was becoming edgy, quick to anger. She gave him swift, mothering hugs, placating him, no different than the ones he got when he brought her presents. Finally, he told her he had to rush off to spend a few days at the family's fishing lodge near Tallahassee— to work, he told her, and to have some time alone, to think. Amanda was used to it; she had endured the loneliness, the confusion of loving a man who was there but wasn't there. She knew he thought her frivolous, trivial, and not his physical ideal as a bed-mate. She had inklings, doubts, fears, all of which she shut out eventually, concentrating on the children. But the past four years had been incredibly difficult. The constant campaigning and the failed stint in Washington had taken their toll. And now she knew, as only a wife can know, that her husband was deeply troubled. Many times, she thought, why don't I go into it and settle it once and for all? But she didn't. She loved Clay and felt there were times when you can't, or shouldn't, confront the truth with the people you love.

She opened her arms and crushed him against her, bathed him in maternal affection. She collected her thoughts, then said, "I'm not what you'd call talented but I do make the best of things, don't I, love?"

He pulled out of her arms and got into bed. "Of course, dear."

As she slid into bed next to him, he rolled over onto his side with his back to her and she kissed his naked shoulder. Clay closed his eyes and wondered where Stuart was at that very moment and he wished he were with him.

The next day, Clay called Stuart to say he would be delayed an extra day; Grandfather Harris controlled the plane. But he told him they would be going to the lodge and spending at least three days. Excited by the prospect, Stuart didn't question his lover.

"I'll make it up to you," Clay said.

"You'd better."

An hour later, Leonard called. "What happened to our holiday dinner?"

"I was wondering the same thing myself," Stuart chuckled.

"...We walk the same ground, you and I," Leonard told Stuart over dinner at the Hyatt Regency.

It seemed Stuart had come full circle. Here he was enjoying immensely the company of a Jew and, after Ned, his sex life had bloomed under the tutelage of a Jew, Benny Shapiro. Benny had picked him up and made him feel, if not superior, at least in the running. And by dating him, he was titillated at the prospect of overturning his stepfather's world.

His mother had met his stepfather when he was traveling through. She saw him infrequently but one day he showed up and announced he had gotten a promotion and would be relocating to Manhattan. He would no longer be traveling and he asked Stuart's mother to marry him.

A solid, heavy man, given to drink, he played hard but aimlessly and eventually realized that he wasted his considerable talents and never achieved any happiness. He felt foolish, that corporate take-overs and mergers had left him out in the cold. But it was drink that did it, Stuart reasoned. One day, the old man said: "I had it in the palm of my hand and I simply threw it all away." He pored over maps of the city trying to guess which way the growth would go. Finally, he decided New Jersey was the place and they settled there. Stuart, accompanied by his mother at first, took the train into the City every day to class at the High School for the Performing Arts on Riverside Drive.

Stuart's stepfather felt little responsibility for the boy he considered to be a sissy, a mistake of nature. He paid little attention to him in his childhood and even when Stuart began to achieve success, he found it difficult to imagine that the son of his wife could have been blessed with intelligence.

Before long, Stuart was staying in town with raven-haired Benny, another student in the class, a year older, who could push Stuart into situations that demanded action. Stuart credited Benny with making it possible for him to win parts at auditions.

"Don't let your father stifle your brains with his prejudices," Benny advised; he learned early on that it was impossible to make a grownup change his mind about anything.

Stuart's mother was small and plain and prematurely wrinkled, but she had large, beautiful eyes, which sparkled in a sad, reflective way. She told Stuart he got his dazzling eyes from her and he said that if that was all she ever gave him, he was blessed. His mother's smothering interest continued to intensify and finally he went to New York to live with Benny. His stepfather was disgusted with this turn of events. But by then he could say anything he liked to the boy because Stuart had the confidence, thanks to Benny, to just ignore him. Stuart felt the coarse, selfish man had hate in his heart but he had never really hurt him. He had failed to love him but then he had never loved anyone.

After a stern lecture, his stepfather finally just threw up his hands and said, "You may have brains but I wonder if brains will get you far without judgment. You prefer the advice of a poor Jewish boy to your own family."

"But he's so exquisite for his type," Stuart's mother said in Benny's defense. Stuart had to admit Benny was effeminate. His skin was pale, his brow high, poetic, his hair thick and curly. His chin was square, his nose was more Roman than Jewish, his lips were thin and seemed tightly sealed when closed. Delicacy was one's general impression of him. But it was his eyes that Stuart loved, pale blue flecked with green, and his frequently quizzical expression, faintly amused; it seemed he was always smiling, reassuring, especially when he was getting his cock blown, which was often. It seemed Benny was forever horny and one day, after a long day of dancing, they returned to the apartment to find it deserted. Stuart collapsed on the bed and Benny sat watching him, smiling, brushing his fingers up and down Stuart's thighs. Stuart shivered a little. Benny stood up and pulled down his pants. His cock flopped out, semi-hard. Benny mounted the bed and brought his cock to Stuart's lips. Stuart loved how much the cock would grow when he began sucking it. It would begin to throb and Stuart would moan, muffled because of the now huge piece of flesh invading his mouth. After a few minutes, Benny said, "I'm not gonna come now. I want to work you over first."

Benny began by massaging Stuart's chest. He teased his nipples and ran his warm tongue down his neck and to his ear, darting inside of it, then he returned to the chest, down to the navel, and he could feel a shudder roar through Stuart's youthful body. When his cock sprang to attention, Benny swallowed it. After he had sucked it for several minutes, he had Stuart roll over. He massaged his back, ending up at the beautiful place between the asscheeks. Their previous sessions, Benny felt, were only foreplay for what he considered inevitable: he had to fuck Stuart. However, he had to work Stuart up to it, had to have him begging to be fucked. Benny took some poppers out of a drawer and had Stuart snort them as he worked his fingers in, first one, then two, then three. He greased himself with each probe until Stuart was squirming all over the bed, trying hard to get away but easily captured again.

Benny had proposed anal sex on several occasions but Stuart would have none of it. It terrified him to think of something so large going into something so small. But Benny's fingers felt very good when they found their way to his anus, and when he leaned over and kissed the back of Stuart's neck, saying softly, "This'll hurt just for a second, then you'll love it," Stuart was ready. He closed his eyes and tried to control his trembling but it was impossible.

As the thick column of throbbing flesh began to enter him, he cried out, grabbing the pillow and hanging on. As Benny pushed a little, Stuart's trembling built to a steady shuddering. Benny grabbed the younger boy's hips and held him tightly. His first thrusts were calm, controlled, letting Stuart relax. Finally, Stuart was moaning and Benny stepped up his attack. Once he had Stuart writhing uncontrollably on the bed, Benny screwed him with a frenzy and finally Stuart was lifting himself up to meet each thrust, and, as if he would somehow miss one, he turned and watched over his shoulder. Eventually, Benny had Stuart roll over and, in this position, they both climaxed.

Once Stuart was into the fast lane, Benny could never quite catch him, but he tried; he turned his back on his old Jewish friends, dyed his hair blond, and cultivated the elite gays of the City. As a couple, they moved effortlessly, relentlessly from party to party, bedroom to bedroom. But Stuart never felt a serious attachment to any of the men he slept with. He had became obsessed with being the best dancer in the company, while Benny, ever the comic actor, took an interest in theater, and, before long, they saw little of each other. But Stuart never forgot Benny and sensed that if he ever encountered another Jew, he would get his money's worth, and Stuart chuckled when his stepfather remarked, "Well, if you want a bargain, go where the Jews go."

...Now, almost six years later, here was again, responding to a driving force that could not be denied. Like Benny, Leonard never stopped pushing, but he was not overbearing, permitting Stuart to find his own way, confident that eventually they would crash down together.

Stuart listened intently as Leonard chastised Clay: "I despise everything that man stands for, but I can't help but love someone as good-looking as he is. And he's always seemed a decent sort."

"Yes, he certainly is," Stuart said, licking his lips, "decent."

"Ha! I'll bet! But he's taking a terrible risk with you. I was quite surprised he'd go this far."

"I know, he's a married man."

"Oh, he's more than that. You don't even know do you? How long have you been here?"

"Over two months I guess."

"And you don't even have a clue?"

"Clue to what?"

"Your stud's not only a rich man, he's also in Congress. The United States Congress."

Stuart was stunned. It had all been a lie. A liaison indeed. It had been a snow job of epic proportions. Stuart suddenly felt ineffably stupid.

"Yeah, you really must be something for him to take such a risk for you," Leonard mused. "And he was so good for so long! He told me he had become a confirmed celibate in 1985! I doubted it but who was I to question him? If I had any brains I'd be celibate, too. But my libido keeps acting up. That's what I get for having a Jewish father. A father whose motto seemed to be, 'Every chance you get you should grab.' Anyway, then Clay ran for public office. He'd done nothing but hold appointed positions but with that name recognition, well, he was a shoo-in. That kind of money can buy you anything."

"And how much money is that, really?"

"You don't even know that?" he chortled. "Well, you wouldn't, I suppose. Here in Florida they say what the Harrises don't own isn't worth having. They even own this restaurant, one way or another. And Clay is the heir to all of it. And the wife, I understand she's old beer money but still it's nothing to sneeze at. And god, he isn't even a goddamn Jew!"

"I thought Jews were proud of being Jews."

"Some are. But I'm not. It seems everybody has freedom of religion except Jews. They always have to be Jewish."

Stuart chuckled nervously. "One of my best friends is Jewish," he mumbled. Thoughts of Benny between his thighs, his sweat dropping onto his face as he plowed into him, smiling broadly with ecstasy, flashed in his mind briefly. He could only think of how cheaply Clay really regarded him, that he could not be trusted with the truth, for fear that he would be what, blackmailed? He paid little attention to Leonard, who, on a roll, continued blasting Clay. "But as a candidate, and now as an elected official, he's like Tennyson: mellifluous, sonorous, high sounding, with no thought content."

Stuart came back to earth only briefly, half listening as Leonard went on about how Clay had sold out his gay supporters. He poured himself another glass of wine and became desolate. Leonard tried to cheer him with his jokes and after dinner the dance master ordered brandies. As he was signing the charge, Leonard suggested a nightcap at his apartment and Stuart, feeling tipsy, simply nodded his ascent and Leonard roared with laughter as they went out into the night.

Once at the apartment, Stuart decided since he was nearly drunk he would get completely so and poured his own brandy. Leonard watched him with amusement, then took the boy in his arms, joking that it seemed fitting that they be together, two people who had been conned by Clay. Leonard tried to kiss the boy but he pulled free and poured another stiff brandy, which quickly took its toll.

When Stuart became incoherent, Leonard put his arm around him and led him to the bedroom. Tossing him onto the bed, he slid Stuart's shoes off of him. Stuart moaned as Leonard unzipped his trousers and pulled them from his body.

After Leonard had removed his own trousers and lowered his briefs, his erection was exposed and he stopped and let Stuart feel him with his eyes. Having left the bathroom light on, he could see Stuart studying him.

Leonard slipped his briefs completely off and spread Stuart's legs. He stared between them, his look grave and hungry. He saw that the boy's sex lay limp but he did not touch it, or try to arouse him. Instead, he unbuttoned Stuart's shirt and lifted it. His eyes feasted on every marvelous inch of him, unhurriedly, as if he was an explorer about to descend to uncharted terrain.

Stuart felt more heat than if Leonard's fingers were tracing him and he groaned, rolling over onto his stomach, his shirt bunched up around his pecs. Now Leonard's fingers touched the boy's smooth skin and slid between the asscrack. He kissed the ass cheeks, first one, then the other, until finally he brought his tongue to Stuart's skin, first nuzzling the fuzz-covered balls, then flickering and dancing over the puckered hole, darting inside, plunging in as deep as he could go. Stuart crooned.

After moistening the hole for a few minutes, Leonard slid a lubricated condom over his cock and mounted the boy. He lifted and spread the muscular legs and, after the first jolt, his thickness glided into him inch by inch, gently, slowly. He closed his eyes, reveling in the splendid tightness. He had waited for this assignation for so long and, since it was entirely possible he would never capture this moment again, he saw no reason to rush it. And Stuart didn't fight him. As Leonard stuffed his prick all the way in, he envied Clay, Terry and the ones he knew nothing about, for he knew there had to be others, many others; no one with a body as magnificent as Stuart's could spend very many nights alone.

But fucking a drunken Stuart was like fucking a corpse. The boy didn't move a muscle. And after he had come, Leonard was revolted because the boy had passed out before his climax, had not even seen the luscious stream of jism that he made across the perfect white buttocks when he slipped off the condom.

The next day, as he took the boy back to the hotel to pick up his Jeep, they rode the entire distance in silence.

*

By the time he returned to the beach, Stuart was beside himself. He recalled little of the previous evening except his lover's deceit. He vaguely remembered being fucked but it was of little consequence compared to the hurt he felt being distrusted by his lover.

He soaked in the hot tub and, after pouring himself a strong gin and tonic, laid in the sun on the deck. He dozed fitfully for a couple of hours. When he awoke, he felt even more depressed and decided to run on the beach. One mile, perhaps two, later, as he returned to the house, a boy he had seen jogging earlier passed him again.

The youth's dark hair flopped in his face as he ran by and briefly their eyes met. Stuart stopped in front of the house watching the youth run a few yards further, then turn around. The boy was attractive to Stuart as a jock type, not particularly good-looking, just muscled, active.

Stuart stayed his ground, hands on his hips. "Hi," he said as the youth slowed in front of him.

Catching his breath, the youth managed to say, "What's happenin'?"

As the youth's eyes drifted to Stuart's basket in the bright pink Speedo, Stuart knew he was home free. "You're gonna wear yourself out," he said.

"Naw, it's good for me."

Stuart nodded. "What would really be good for you is to relax, get out of this sun. Have a drink." He motioned towards the wooden stairs.

"Sounds cool, man," the boy said, following him.

As Stuart fixed drinks, the boy, who introduced himself as Doug, plopped his sweaty body onto one of the bar stools and wiped his brow. "Yeah, feels good in here."

"Thought it would," Stuart mumbled. "Before I add the gin, are you old enough to drink?"

"Hell, no."

"At least you're honest." He held the gin bottle over the tonic in the tall tumbler. "Should I?"

"Shit, why not?"

Stuart nodded and splashed gin into the glass, then handed it to the boy.

Doug gulped the drink. "Boy, you make 'em strong."

"Stronger the better."

"I'll say," Doug said, glancing at Stuart's basket again as the older boy came around the end of the bar and slid down on a stool. It had become a basket to behold because he had become aroused just thinking about what he wanted to do to his visitor with the smooth olive skin and a shock of unruly brown hair that drooped sexily over his dark brown eyes. But it was the mystery hidden in the boy's crotch that fascinated him. He showed nothing in the jogging shorts.

"We hardly ever get any joggers this far up the beach."

"I like it up here, easier to run. And it's real private."

"Yeah, it's private all right, especially up here, above everybody."

"Nice place," Doug said, looking around. Then he finished his drink in one swig.

"Whoa!" Stuart cried.

"I was thirsty."

"It'll go to your head."

"So?"

As the youth turned, Stuart noticed he had pulled up his shorts and a good bit of pale scrotum skin peeked out from the left side of his crotch. Doug brought the fingers of both of his hands to a growing column outlined in his shorts.

Stuart felt a surge of excitement; sex was a constant, round-the-clock need and now, more than ever, it needed to be satisfied. He began to secretly hope that Clay would come roaring through the door; it would serve him right.

Doug said nothing, just stared at Stuart and continued rubbing.

"Booze gone to your head?"

"Yeah, both of 'em." Doug chuckled, pushing the head of his now erect cock out from the fabric and onto his thigh.

Stuart stared at the head of it, large and quite dark, then pushed the bar stool between them aside and dropped to his knees next to Doug. He brought his lips to the head of Doug's cock and slid the fabric back, exposing more of the impressive shaft. He began nibbling, then sucking the head, tugging at the shorts all the while. Doug raised up enough for Stuart to draw the shorts down his thighs and onto his ankles. Stuart tantalized the boy by caressing the lightly furred thighs, his eyes fixed on the cock bobbing uncontrollably before him.

Doug leaned back, his elbows on the bar, and watched intently as Stuart brought his hands up the gleaming torso, then leaned forward, taking the cock deep. His fingers stroked muscles and tweaked the nipples, then moved down the torso again as he freed the cock. Stuart's tongue traced the heavy vein on the underside of the penis and then his mouth clamped over the head of it again. Stuart was relentless in his assault on the prick, savoring every inch of it, playing with the heavy, sweaty ballsack.

"Oh, yeah," Doug groaned, "nobody sucks dick like a queer."

Stuart tormented the youth, pulling back just when he knew release was imminent, until suddenly, Doug had Stuart's head in his hands, forcing it down into his crotch. Stuart took the cock down to the pubes in one deft movement, then let Doug control the action. He pulled his own erection from the Speedo and jacked himself off while he sucked.

Soon Doug was moaning, "Oh, yeah, suck it, suck it. Damn, that's good." He refused to release Stuart and came in his mouth. As Stuart came, Doug freed him.

"Yeah, nothin' like a queer to suck dick," Doug said, standing and pulling up his shorts.

Stuart struggled to his feet and muttered, "No, nothin'."

Doug began making his way across the room to the deck. "Hey, thanks man; I gotta meet my girlfriend. She'll be wonderin' where the hell I went off to."

Eyes downcast, Stuart said, "Yeah, you wouldn't want to worry her."

Doug nodded and rushed down the stairs to the beach. Stuart stood on the deck and, as he watched the jock run south, he wiped the stickiness from his chin.

...A couple of hours later, Clay called from the St. Petersburg/ Clearwater airport where the private jets land and asked Stuart to pick him up. The boy decided to wait until they were home to tell him about his dinner with Leonard and the fact that he was now aware his lover was in Congress. The matinee with the jock had taken the edge off and Stuart was now thinking much more clearly. He was able to almost casually mention that Leonard had told him what he really did in Washington.

"I'm sorry - "

"I understand why you have to lie. I don't blame you."

"I tried to tell you a hundred times - "

Stuart interrupted by kissing him. They held each other, hands moving aggressively over each other's bodies. Stuart pleaded, "After dinner, okay? I'm starving."

"I'll bet," Clay chuckled.

"It's been so long."

"Too long."

"...Well, who cares what a smart-ass Jewish dance instructor says?" Clay responded at dinner when Stuart told him some of Leonard's venomous remarks.

"But I care," Stuart said. "He's upset with you, that you haven't come across for the gays like you promised."

"I never promised anything." He finished his drink and summoned the waiter to bring him another. "These days, all you can say is that you'll think about it. I'm still thinking about it."

Seeing that Clay did not wish to discuss the gay issue any further, Stuart bowed to his wishes, for now. Besides, all Stuart wanted was to feel Clay inside him, to be reassured that he loved him as he loved no one else. But fortified with two martinis, Clay had become angry that he had been rebuked by Leonard, someone he had trusted. Clay had been instrumental in securing Leonard his position and this was how he was being repaid?

Later, when they were in bed, Clay took out his aggression on Stuart's asshole, showing no care. Stuart screamed but Clay held him down and although he dismissed the notion that Stuart would have permitted Leonard to take liberties with him, still he was fancying it as he orgasmed, pleased to be able to put a face on the indiscretions he imagined his young lover was guilty of.

The next morning, Stuart was up early, doing his arabesques and other exercises in the living room in front of the mirrors. Clay came down the stairs and stopped on the last step, watching him. There was no more splendid figure in the world, Clay thought, and tears came to his eyes. He wished to make amends for the harsh sex. He wrapped his robe tightly around him and strode across the room, took the boy in his arms and crushed him with a kiss so violent, Stuart shook from it.

When their lips parted, Clay said, "I do trust you. Now, I do. In the beginning, I couldn't be sure. I was so used to playing - "

"But we aren't playing any more, are we? This is for keeps, isn't it?"

Clay blanched. What had he done? Everything was now out in the open, the boy knew who he was, but damage control would have to be performed. He had never wanted anyone as much as he wanted Stuart. Last night was as good, perhaps even better than first night they were together. He recalled the three orgasms, the lingering lust that made him pursue the boy to Miami. He had dissolved into the eroticism Stuart spun; the boy had ceased to be the archetypical young stripper or the gifted ballet dancer and instead had become a complete and overwhelming presence as Clay's one true love. The boy may even have other ones on a string, may even have let Leonard fuck him, but it did not lessen his passion. If only he had met the boy in 1985, he thought. Even 1986. Before it was too late. Now the die had been cast. He had even won reelection. The Governorship might be next, then the Senate, then, who knows? But a politician's life was an all-consuming life, a life into which he had stumbled, pushed along by the momentum of it, and now it seemed a hollow victory at best if it meant giving up his private life, giving up the moments like this with what he considered heaven in his arms.

He held Stuart tightly against his chest, his hands fondling the boy's crotch and, finding Stuart's cock hardening with his touch, he whispered, "Yes, my love, this time we're both playing for keeps."

8

The long shadows of approaching twilight streaked the lake as Clay tacked against the last steady breeze, hiking out slightly as Stuart shifted sides. They grinned happily, the wind streaking their faces, rippling their hair, spraying them with freshness, until he whipped the tiller in, cutting windward head-on, braking the boat deftly against the dock. The boy hopped ashore as Clay lowered the mainsail and secured the bow. Walking across the wide, green swath that lead to the cabin, Clay watched as his lover walked before him, his buns glorious in the little Speedo. He came up behind him and caressed the asscheeks. Stuart turned and took his lover in his arms. "Thank you for understanding," Clay said. Then, his hands clutching the boy's buttocks, he whispered, "I love you so."

Stuart hugged him, then kissed his cheek. They walked hand-in-hand to the lodge. Inside, they built a fire in the fireplace and ate a hearty supper. Afterward, they lay beside the fire, entwined, joyous in the profound quietness that comes after a long struggle. It was a heady sense of unreality.

"It's so peaceful here," the boy said, closing his eyes.

"It's our own world, here."

"Why must we hide from the world? Why can't we be free to love each other? Why does the real world have to be so dirty, so horrible?"

"Power. People want to grasp power however they can. And then there's greed. Nothing but simple greed."

"And you have so much money, yet you want more."

"Oh, not me. I'm hardly greedy, except when it comes to you." Clay gave his lover a smoldering glance.

"I feel pretty greedy myself - "

They clung happily to each other, luxuriating in the closeness for several minutes until the boy could stand it no more, he had to have

Clay inside him. And, their shadows dancing crazily with the leaping flames, they kissed and moved in unison, one atop the other, and they became one, obliterating the world, at least for the night.

*

During the nearly two-hour drive to the lodge in the Jeep, Clay was glad he was finally free to talk to Stuart about his work. He talked mostly about the environment, about which he was well versed as a member of the House Republican Environmental Round table.

"We need to make permanent the moratorium on offshore oil drilling on the Gulf Coast. We need to allow the states to enforce their own environmental protection laws. We need a comprehensive long-term strategy that moves us away from our dependence on oil."

Finally, Stuart grabbed his arm. "Okay, okay! I'll vote for you!"

"Good. I need to make young voters understand that this is a long tough haul. I've dropped a pebble, maybe it's the wrong pebble, but over time, people will talk about it. My solution to our economic woes is pro-business, but I'm a liberal when it comes to health issues. But first and foremost is the economy. It's like Grandfather says, 'No goose, no golden eggs.'"

After serving on two state blue ribbon committees dealing with coastal zone management and environmental regulation, Clay was appointed by a Democratic governor to fill a vacancy on the scandal-ridden Collier County Commission. When the incumbent congressman Porter Anderson suffered a heart attack and said he would not run for reelection, Clay became the front-runner. On the campaign trail, Clay amazed his aides by jotting down names of those he met so he could write little thank-you notes. He instructed staffers to handle any constituent problem. "No potential voter is to be ignored," he told them.

After listening to Clay endlessly recycle his campaign speeches, Stuart giggled, "God, you're always running-"

"Look, anyone who's running for office and feels comfortable is on the verge of being unemployed." Clay sighed. "And I could be out so quickly. I'm not at ease with it anymore. I guess I've become too controlled. I labor over every remark and decision while others settle issues. And in Washington, deliberation can be interpreted as indecision."

"You're just cautious. If anybody's seen that it's me."

Clay slipped his hand between Stuart's thighs. "It's not important when you make a decision as long as you make the right one."

*

The next day, the boy did not ask to help Clay with the sails; he was too competent even to pretend that he could be assisted. Stuart sat on the fantail and watched him, a towering figure of sublime masculinity.

Finally, the boy took up the tiller as Clay pulled up the sails, but once they were settled on a course along the shoreline, with a mild breeze behind them, Clay slipped into the seat beside him and relieved him of his task. Stuart leaned back and basked in the sun. "This is what I want. To be here, with you, always," he murmured, and Clay dropped his hand to the boy's thigh and left it there.

At the pier, when he had taken down the sails, expertly, speedily, Clay said: "I'm so horny I can't stand it."

Stuart smiled. "So am I." It was not simply sex appeal. It was the intriguing sense of having no further decisions to make, of being folded up and packed into what each imagined as a cocoon fashioned just for him. All they had to do was accept each others' love. But each of them seemed to be asking, Was that going to be like everything else, impossible?

By the time they reached the lodge, Stuart was in an extraordinary state of arousal. Clay was astonished to find his lover going down on him as soon as he closed the front door. Faster and faster Stuart moved his fingers, probing Clay's asshole, rubbing his loins with his damp lips and the muscular column grew hard.

Clay began wriggling his full buttocks. "Oh, I've been bad, haven't I, not trusting you."

Stuart looked up from his labors and sighed, "You're a terrible man. Just terrible."

"I didn't trust you. But I do now." He caressed the boy's cheeks. "Believe me, I do."

Stuart took Clay's cock from his mouth and asked, "Do you trust me completely?" His fingers dug into Clay's asshole.

"Completely."

It began as a slow fuck. Clay lay on his side and Stuart slid next to him, letting his erection find its own way. Stuart was surprised to find how easily his cock slid into his lover. Clay went into a slow rolling motion and Stuart's cock dragged in and out of his anus, milling it. Clay groaned and hunched his ass up to meet Stuart's jabs. Soon Stuart stepped up his tempo, giving it to his lover the way he loved to get it, every inch of him inside Clay, slapping his ass until he came.

Exhausted, they collapsed next to each other. Then Clay rolled his lover over and licked the stickiness from the boy's belly, his navel, his cock. He began running his tongue up and down the boy's torso, licking the sweat, kissing the nipples, working his way back down.

"I love this cock," he said, finally. "In any orifice I can get it."

"And it loves you."

"Was it okay?"

Stuart nodded. "But there's things I like better."

"Me, too." Clay said, and he returned to the cock, sucking it for several minutes, rejoicing in the sweetness, the smell of youth. They had now taken each other every way possible. He truly possessed the boy and was possessed by him. He kissed the tight skin of Stuart's belly, then returned to the fine pubic hair and the cock that now lay pointing towards the navel, throbbing toward his mouth, so eager to be serviced again.

"You're a beautiful man, Clay."

A whore's line to be sure, but Clay loved it nonetheless. As they fell into a sweaty embrace, Clay regretted he had doubted the boy but now he was susceptible to his every whim. Men had desired Clay and pursued him so often in the past and, with some, their irresponsibility enchanted him. He adored artists, bought them clothes, sent them plane tickets, paid their rent, adding up the sexual favors with each stroke of his pen across the checks. But Stuart had asked for nothing. Just how different Stuart was was never more evident than here at the lodge.

Years before, when Clay took Shannon to the lodge it rained the entire weekend but they didn't care. He had met him, a struggling artist, at one of Amanda's parties, and his dark eyes struck him as those of a bear, momentarily friendly but ultimately dangerous, because he too was married.

He found the young man vaguely attractive: The long, thin, bony face under a high wide brow was extraordinarily rejuvenated by the curly blond hair that was almost boyish. But what turned him on was how he could vary from a delicate, romantic, poetic figure of the deepest sensitivity, to one of crudity of the vilest sort. He loved to get fisted, loved Clay orgasming all over his face, and he loved to eat Clay's ass out, and Clay reveled in it.

After they had sex for the third time that Saturday, Shannon said: "I'm known around town as a terrible slut. I'm surprised you'd have anything to do with me, you being a paragon of virtue."

Clay chuckled and turned from Shannon's steady stare to gaze past the table and out the big window to the lake. There was a strange completeness in their silent communication. He was tired of the mundanity of Naples; the lake was the perfect getaway. And this isolated but charming cabin, decorated with white wicker furniture and hung with Picasso prints, was the scene of six grandly squalid fuckings that weekend.

They drove back in silence. Clay tried to keep in mind the fact that the man was as married he was, that this affair was never going anywhere, yet he wanted it to continue. He was ecstatically happy and at the same time achingly miserable.

But Clay was quick to get over it; Troy Lassiter came into his life, the first actor with whom he was to carry on an affair of any duration. It began with polite little smiles at a bar in Tampa. When Clay bought the young man a drink, something clutched at his heart and he stared into the boy's glinting eyes.

The next night, over dinner at a swank restaurant, they discussed the Elizabethan theater and the Renaissance, which Troy characterized as "a period of hope."

"But the fine hope of the Elizabethans," he said, "was lost in the corruption of the court, the divine right of kings. Man was back in chains." Clay recalled it as a prophetic way to end the discussion because, less than a week later, at the lodge, he was being tied to the bed, not by chains but by his own neckties.

Sputtering with rage, Troy told him that he saw the banker as a symbol of corruption and he would have to pay for his sins.

"At the top of the heap there is such hypocrisy!" Troy snarled.

"Just as much at the bottom - "

And the bottom became a top as the older man marveled at the inventiveness of the youngster as he proceeded to take him to the depths and then make him rise again with a pleasure that he would recall with great fondness years later. It was the first time Clay had played bottom and his ready capitulation to the role stunned him.

"Please don't punish me any more," he begged. "I can't take this."

"I want you to."

"Are you sure?"

Troy leaned over him and shoved his cock to the hilt one last time. "Yes."

Troy continued his assault on the older man's asshole, jacking Clay off as he did.

"Yes, yes," Clay cried as he came.

The next night, with a cool glare of hostility that overwhelmed Clay, Troy said, "I detest contradiction and you are the most contradictory of men. You're more terrified of someone finding out about you than anybody I know."

"I rather enjoy it. You're an actor, you can understand."

"No, I don't understand."   Troy began slapping him.

"No, please, don't - "

He had dragged him by his cock, wrapped with the necktie, and pushed him onto the bed. Exposed, vulnerable, Clay's balls ached for it, but Troy teased him, kissing, licking, toying with the head of his cock. Suddenly, Clay came. Still, Troy kept on, sucking the balls and then, finally, the cock, taking it all the way down to the pubic hairs. Clay became hard again and Troy lowered himself over the mammoth sex and began to fuck himself with it, his back to Clay, making the man suffer, for he knew how much his mentor enjoyed watching him getting off on it. Clay struggled to get free and the harder he struggled, the harder Troy fucked himself. Clay was still struggling, still hard, when Troy came, so when Troy pulled himself off the cock, he curled up between Clay's outstretched thighs and went back to sucking it again. He drifted off to asleep with the cock he had become obsessed with, now semi-flaccid, in his mouth.

Weeks later, on another visit, while sailing, his voice high and shrill, Troy ranted on and on about Clay's obligations to him. When they got back to the lodge, a person of tact would have absented himself but Troy saw an important scene in the making so he made them each a drink. Clay left his drink on the coffee table, leaned back and closed his eyes.

"I'm not one of your empty-headed hustlers," Troy began.

"I never said you were."

"But you treat me like one."

"I don't treat you any way at all."

"That's just it, you ignore me."

Clay opened his eyes, unzipped his pants and let his erection pop out, enormous as ever. "Now, does that look like I'm ignoring you?"

Troy began slapping it, sucking it, playing with it. He had Clay close to coming twice, then he slipped his own trousers to his knees and backed over it, ramming it in him. As Troy jacked himself off, Clay did nothing except to hold firm. When Troy was finished, he turned around and sought to relieve Clay but the older man begged off until after dinner. With wine in him, Troy became contrite once again. He began to cry and Clay thought the whole scene disgusting. When the boy went down on his knees and began pleading with him to leave his wife, Clay promptly left the lodge and took the sailboat out on the lake alone.

"...I live for days like this," Clay said to Stuart over dinner at a small seafood restaurant down the road from the lodge. He had gotten what he bargained for, three days of incomparable beauty.

Stuart was at peace, in a reflective mood. "I feel like I've come to the end of a long trip."

"I'm glad."

"You have no idea what it means to me. I guess you could say my life began last year, in the spring, when I decided I was going to live. I decided I would live my own life, not somebody else's."

Stuart had come to know Michael as a dealer but mostly as an actor. The swarthy Italian had been a member of a community theater and at one time had studied mime and jazz dance. To make ends meet, he became a street performer. Stripped to the waist, in Turkish pantaloons and yarmulke, he would dance to strange tempos emitting from his boom box. Stuart was walking through the theater district one day when he saw him. He was instantly smitten.

Michael's specialty was mutation. He could turn himself into anyone he pleased. The key to his trick was his anonymity. His face was like a slate upon which he could draw anyone he fancied. All he had to do was study someone for a few moments to master their postures, expressions, gestures. Stuart became hooked on the act.

In his rented room, Michael stood before the mirror, admiring himself, fondling himself. Stuart thought he was the only person in the world who loved himself that much. It was as if he was looking in a mirror at a fun house. They stood there, admiring themselves, each other. They were the mirror images of each other, one dark, the other fair. They held their cocks together; they were the same shape, the same length, with Stuart's bending more to the left. Stuart panted. They jacked each other off, then Michael turned him around so that his back was against his chest and he pumped Stuart's cock, then fucked him with his fingers. It wasn't long before Stuart was begging for it and they were sprawled on the bed on top of the covers, Michael on his knees, climbing between Stuart's thighs. He lifted his legs over his shoulders and, smiling as broadly as Benny ever did, he lubricated his cock. Soon, the entire length of it was roaring through Stuart and Stuart came quickly. Michael kissed him on the forehead and continued to fuck him relentlessly. Stuart moved in the next day. It was a decent place; the towels were changed every week and even though their room was nothing more than a cell, ten feet by eight with a naked overhead bulb, the wallpaper had pretty big pink roses on it and when they were in bed, which was most of the time, they could see themselves in the large mirror that Michael had hung on the back of the door.

At night, with only the street lights illuminating their room, Michael appeared monstrous, as if he was going to ravage Stuart, as if Stuart's body drove him into a frenzy. They would drink Night Train and Michael would pour it all over Stuart and lick it off. And, often high on crack, their love would burn as a raw, intensely sexual flame. Michael said, "You're the purest person I've ever known. You get fucked as if it was the first time, every time."

"In a way, that's the way it seems."

"But I'll break your fucking heart. I don't want to, but I know I will."

And he did. Stuart grew accustomed to the sexuality at its darkest and to the hangovers, but less so to the long absences. One cold night, he received a phone call at the pay phone down the hall from their room. He agreed to come to police headquarters.

He dragged himself out into the freezing cold and made his way to the police station. The whip of the wind sent him staggering, nearly spun him around. He was exhausted by the time he reached the building. He thought Michael had been picked up and needed to be bailed out, but a lieutenant was asking him to identify him. At first, Stuart thought it was a line-up. He followed the officer down some stairs and could tell by the smell that something terrible had happened. The officer pulled out one of the drawers. Stuart nodded.

"Somebody must've hated him," the officer said. "They went at it a long time after he was dead."

Stuart's answers to their questions seemed to satisfy them. He admitted he knew Michael was dealing.

"But it was smalltime, nothing that would make somebody - "

"When somebody's high, there's nothing smalltime, you know that."

Stuart nodded.

They didn't give him a drug test, just let him go. He went back to the room and finished the bottle of Night Train. He began to feel guilty, rotten deep inside. He cried himself to sleep.

The next morning, with vague surprise, he came to the realization that, quite simply, a world that had been expiring slowly, gradually over many years had finally died. Too much in love with himself to notice, he had gradually let it all slip away. He had lost his place with the company, he would be evicted from Michael's little room, and he had nowhere to go but home.

He resolutely refused to leave the room. Finally, the landlord called the police. Two tall, strong officers arrived. They had been through it before and were patient and kind, insisting Stuart go with them to the hospital. Once inside the patrol car, his energy faded, his anger receded. He sat quietly until he saw the entrance to the hospital. Then he started to weep. "Please," he cried, "don't do this to me. I'm not crazy. Don't lock me up. I didn't do anything wrong."

As at any hospital, Stuart spent the first few minutes filling out forms. Finally, they called his mother. He hated the thought of crawling home. His mother said he wouldn't be. He could stay there, in a private room, until he was well. They had carried insurance for him for years, now it would pay for itself, and what it didn't cover, she would pay out of her savings. And she promised to visit him every day.

Life in the unit was well-structured. After years of dance training, the discipline came easily to Stuart. His doctor asked him to continually work to identify his problems, understand his feelings, regain his ability to function. "You have a predisposition to perfectionism," the doctor counseled. "This means you have trouble dealing with failure and rejection. You're not alone. We are living in a culture where you take a pill for pain and frustration, you don't deal with it."

Part of Stuart's "dealing with it" was taking part in all of the therapies: group, art, and recreational. Before he left, he had taught several of the patients how to dance.

At night, he would play a game of Trivial Pursuit or watch TV, then take his medication and go to bed. His room was just like a prison cell but he began to think of it as a beautiful place. Once alone in the dark, he would masturbate and the reverie of the past would return to him again and again. The cocks, all shapes, sizes, colors, and how they responded to his ass, to his mouth, to the ways he had of arousing them: the sighs, the groans, the shaking, the bucking, the fucking. And, he kept reminding himself, the fields of paradise were still there, on the other side of the wall.

He had been in the unit two months when his mother came to visit and told him of a club in New Jersey advertising for male dancers.

"I can do that," Stuart said, undulating his hips as he began dancing around his mother.

She laughed. It was the first time she had laughed in a long time and she knew her son was on his way to recovery.

...After dinner, when they returned to the lodge, Clay stoked the fire as Stuart stripped. When Clay stood and turned, the sight of the boy lying on his stomach on the couch at the far end of the living room stunned him. The orange of the fire fell across the tightly muscled young body and the ringlets of hair held a golden glow. Clay's gasp was audible.

Stuart lifted his buttocks. "I need it." He reached behind him and his fingers slid into the crevasse. The shadows of the flames played across the buns as his legs parted like solid branches of a tree bearing a fruitful treasure in the center. As he usually did, Stuart had prepared himself before they left for dinner so Clay's cock slid in easily, all the way. Squashing his lover beneath him, Clay braced himself on the arm of the sofa and began an intercourse that was surprisingly gentle, with the older man taking his time, each of them cherishing the splendorous moments.

9

Clay went back to Naples for Amanda's New Year Eve bash at the mansion, then flew to Washington for the opening session of Congress, promising Stuart he would stay only two days. But two days dragged into four, then six.

It took the phone call from Terry to bring Stuart out of his funk. Terry asked Stuart to pick him up at school: "I got something I want to share with you." Stuart hoped that meant what he thought it did. But it was pot, not his body, that Terry wanted to share, weed he had gotten from another youth at Aspen.

It was too cold for swimming but they sunbathed on the deck, unobserved by anyone walking by on the beach below.

"Great weed," Stuart said, savoring it.

"Yeah. It was an awesome time."

"Dancing down the slopes?"

"Unreal. But there was something missing."

"What, no sex?"

"You got it." He shook his head sadly. "The guy was this super-jock and the girls, well-"

"I know what you mean."

"And now Jodie's on the rag again."

"Messy business. Doesn't she give head?"

"You kiddin' me?"

Stuart noticed the bulge in the Speedo he had given Terry to wear was beginning so show some promising definition. "Looks like you're horny all right."

Terry grinned and gently stroked the bulge. "I'm just remembering what happened that day at the park."

"I'm sorry about that; I guess I got out-of-control."

"I'm not sorry. Not a bit."

"I'm glad," Stuart said, leaving his chaise longue and dropping down on his stomach between Terry's legs. Slowly he pulled the fabric away from the boy's engorged sex and delicately began to play with the fine pubic hairs at the base of the cock. He teased Terry unmercifully, nibbling at the head of it, licking it, adoring it, until finally he slid it all the way down his throat with one gulp. Terry leaned back and, high on the reefer but no longer discombobulated, caressed by the dazzling late afternoon sun, he sighed deeply and closed his eyes. Stuart licked the moist skin all the way up to the navel and then back down again, sliding his tongue along the throbbing rigidity. A trickle of semen seeped out and Stuart lapped it up, then deep-throated Terry again. Terry's spasms of delight grew steadily stronger until finally he was gasping, his body heaving in heady convulsions. Come gushed into Stuart's mouth and he swallowed it all and kept sucking, unable to give up the prize.

"Oh, god, oh, god -" Terry kept crying.

Stuart, close to coming himself, drew his own sex from his Speedo. As Stuart began to come, he let Terry's cock slide from his mouth. Terry opened his eyes to see Stuart lift himself up and shoot the white loops of his jism onto the cushion of the chaise. Stuart opened his eyes and saw that Terry was watching him.

"You've got a gorgeous cock," Terry said. "Hell, you're a gorgeous man."

"A man?" Stuart thought. It was the first time he could recall being called that. He leaned down and kissed the boy on the forehead, but as Stuart closed his eyes and prepared to bring his lips to Terry's, the younger boy turned his face and Stuart kissed his cheek instead.

Rising from the chaise, they said nothing to each other. Stuart picked up a towel and began to wipe Terry's sex. "Can I take a quick shower?" Terry asked, slipping the Speedo from his body.

"Sure."

Stuart followed the boy to the downstairs bath. "No sense wasting water," he said, slipping off his own Speedo and following Terry into the glassed-in enclosure. Stuart soaped Terry all over and tried to take him into his arms, but Terry backed away.

Stuart smiled. "You can touch me, I won't break."

"I know. I'm sorry, it's just that this is all so strange - "

"You've never made it with a guy before?" Stuart asked, fondling the boy's ballsack.

"Only once. I was twelve. He was a neighbor, before we moved to Feather Sound."

"He blew you?" Stuart stroked Terry's hardening cock.

"Yeah, that was all. But he wasn't as good at it as you are."

Stuart dropped to his knees and took the slick cock back into his mouth and, holding Terry's firm buns in his hands, proceeded to demonstrate once again just how good he was.

During the long ride across the peninsula to the bayou and Feather Sound, they talked little, just listened to music, and when Terry leaped from the Jeep, Stuart asked, "Can I see you tomorrow?"

"Maybe Saturday, after dance class," Terry responded, not looking at him.

Stuart nodded. "It's a date."

But by Saturday, Clay was back at the beach. Over lunch, Stuart explained the situation: "My folks are visiting. I can't take you back to the beach."

"It's okay."

"No, it's not. I never know when they're coming down. It's driving me crazy."

10

At the end of January, Clay went to Washington for the State of the Union address and stayed a few more days to confer with his aides and consultants over the issues his Merchant Marine and Fisheries Committee would address in the new session. When he returned to Florida, he landed at Tampa International and Paul was waiting for him.

"...I hope you don't mind staying at the hotel," Clay said as they were headed across the causeway after having lunch at the revolving restaurant at the airport.

"Oh, not at all. Marco loves it. Better than the beachhouse, as a matter of fact. His chances of scoring are multiplied a hundredfold. Yes, if you stop to think about it, Marco and I make a wonderful team: My social graces, his charisma, my honesty, his dishonesty, my ability to manage finance, his ability to steal, my degrees, his sexual prowess."

"You've saved the best for last: sexual prowess. A mundane life becoming an ecstatic life."

"Precisely. And that's what you are experiencing now, a state of perpetual ecstasy?"

Clay nodded. "And it just keeps getting better and better."

"I'm happy to see you bewitched. It's the first time in a long time I've seen you so addled."

Paul, although deeply attracted to the material pleasures of the world, had thrown away much of his inheritance to heed the call of the carnal. Clay thought it was stupid to live one's life nearly on the edge of what he considered poverty, a slave to something that everyone considered an abomination. No, he thought himself clever enough to find a way to have his cake and eat it too.

"You know how it's been for me lately. I'd given up finding anyone." His dreams were of unabashed sexuality, to lie down with strangers, men who were vivid while they fucked or sucked but whose images faded as the next day progressed until, a few days later, they seemed to have vanished completely.

"I know. It's all the drugs these days. Everything pretty is into it. I have to watch Marco like a hawk."

"Stuart was into it but he pulled himself out of it. I admire that."

"I had one like that, but he was a backslider. But he was fun when he was sober."

"Stuart is more sober than I am. He's so together now it's scary. But I don't demand a lot of truth from him."

"Still, how you can be so trusting is beyond me."

"Trusting means allowing him an area of privacy. Amanda has allowed me that, I have to allow Stuart that. If I don't, I could lose him."

As Paul pulled his Jaguar into the drive at the beachhouse, Clay asked, "You are coming for dinner tonight aren't you? Nothing fancy."

Paul chuckled, "Come now, if young Stuart's there, it'll be fancy. I just know it."

*

As the opening titles rolled, first Marco's face appeared, then his entire body. Bravura had seldom featured a performer as prominently. Most of the videos were ensemble pieces, but in four successive ones, Marco had built up a following. Stuart had found the large stentorian voiced man an imposing presence. He could imagine him on a movie set, a beautiful, graceful animal, a king of the forest, everyone paying him homage.

Clay slid down next to Paul on the sofa and, as the video flickered the younger men grew bored, excusing themselves to finish cleaning up in the kitchen.

A few minutes later, Paul fast-forwarded the film to a certain spot. "Ha, this is the scene I remember the most. How 'bout you Marco?" Paul turned and saw that Stuart and Marco had pushed the dining table aside and were dancing to the beat of the soundtrack. "Well, look at that," Paul laughed.

As Stuart and Marco cavorted, Clay and Paul moved closer, brandies in hand, watching them. It was a strange dance whose rhythm, though hard to follow, was intriguing, the music startlingly punctuated by the moans and groans of the actors.

"You know," Paul laughed, "for all their seeming desire to be loved, make no mistake, these boys are so much alike, they are one-man shows. All they need is an audience."

They seemed to be swaying to a music half heard, half imagined, in rhythm with its mood rather than its beat. Soon Clay became caught up in the gentle undulation, a dance more within than with the body. He began dancing with them. Paul joined in and they finally ended up in their lovers' arms as the actors in the video were shooting their copious loads.

After their guests had gone, Clay and Stuart went to bed and, as they had sex, the boy couldn't get the startling image of Marco out of his mind. It was the first time he had met a video performer and, as he was being fucked, it was Marco's rich dark, absurdly thick cock he imagined was impaling him, as it had the dozens of men in the video, and when he came it was with such an intensity that, after all of the wine, almost caused him to black out.

Three days later, alone in Washington, Clay recalled the evening and, as he masturbated, he fantasized that it had gone beyond harmless dancing. He had visions of watching Stuart and Marco together. In his mind, their attraction to each other was so strong that he soon realized he had erred in bringing them together, but he had always thought it was better to err in the direction of risk than to shut out experience; he had made the reprehensible plausible.

He fantasized that they all descended into a whirlpool of lust with increasing urgency. Stuart was afraid, sensing that if he touched the live wire that was Marco's humungous bulge an explosion would blow them all up. Clay made the first move, showing for the first time an interest in Marco, fondling him as they danced. Paul joined in, dancing closely with Stuart. Then they switched partners, each of them swaying with the tempo in unison. Stuart seemed to melt in Marco's strong arms. In his presence, Stuart's breathing became hard. He could not look directly into Clay's eyes. Marco's body scent intoxicated him and his longing made him lose his senses. He let Marco pull him down and roll on top of him. Soon Stuart reversed their positions, expressing a new found freedom and happiness by covering the hard muscles of the stud's magnificent body with hungry kisses and loving caresses, sliding Marco's flimsy shorts down as he proceeded. Slowly his lips parted and he took the impressive uncut shaft, aroused by

Clay, in his mouth, moving further and further down its length and forcing himself not to choke on it. Soon he had reached the base and was burrowing his nose in the dark pubic hairs. Eagerly he continued to move up and down on the throbbing prick, longing to feel the cum gushing from it. Marco writhed and gasped with Stuart's ministrations, his legs soon clenching the boy's head, his body arching as he began undulating his hips until finally he rolled over and impaled Stuart on the floor. Paul, who had been masturbating beside them, got between Stuart's legs and began fellating him. As Marco was cumming, so did Stuart begin, and then Paul, in a fiery stream.

But Marco was not finished. He had desired the blond's ass since he had entered the house and he was not to be denied. Marco had Stuart get on his knees and bend at the waist.

Clay stood in front of his lover, his cock dangling in his face. Clay imagined he would feel a tightening in his belly as Marco entered the blond and began pummeling the upturned buttocks with a boldness that would cause the boy to grab his lover's legs and, as he cried out, Clay would shove his prick into his mouth. Stuart, Clay fancied, would become delirious being screwed at both ends for several minutes, and Paul would add to his pleasure by insinuating himself beneath the dancer's body and taking his cock into his mouth.

They would remain in a state of beatific dazedness for several minutes until Marco, grunting with passion and from exertion, pulled himself from the blond and began fucking his lover. Clay imagined he would withdraw his cock from Stuart's mouth and shove it into his moist hole, down to the base without stopping. But it seemed that the wonderful tightness was gone. The cock kept sliding down, deeper and deeper, until his balls followed, and he reached down to halt the descent and his hands became submitted as well and he cried out in abject horror...

Clay awoke from the dream feeling suffocated. As he opened his eyes and came to his senses, he wanted nothing more than to have Stuart beside him. He reached for the phone and realized he had called him earlier.

Every night he called Clearwater. But lately, he would get no answer. By Tuesday, even the answering machine had been turned off. He could stand it no longer and instead of his normal Thursday evening flight, he left Washington on Wednesday afternoon, arriving in Tampa at dusk. He rented a Lincoln at the airport and by the time he got to the beachhouse it was nearly five. He parked south of the house, across the palm-lined boulevard, in a condominium complex's parking lot, watching the house as the sun was setting. The Jeep was in the drive. There were no signs of activity. His heart sank. He should not have questioned Stuart, should not have left Washington early. Now he would have to explain why he was not on the Thursday flight. But he could stay overnight at the Marriott at the airport and act as if nothing were amiss, just come down to the baggage claim area and join Stuart, standing waiting for him, beaming, happy to have his lover back.

What Clay did not know was that little more than two hours earlier, Stuart had picked Terry up at school. The younger boy said he wanted to finish the pot he had stashed at the beach. Stuart readily agreed.

When they entered the house, it began to rain and they sat in the living room and finished the joints Stuart had rolled from the fine sinsemlia Terry had gotten in Aspen. When Terry's deep brown eyes became glazed with a light pink tone, Stuart led him to the bedroom. After closing the curtains and slipping off his jeans, Stuart lay on the bed and watched the boy undress. When Terry turned, now naked, his cock erect, he stood staring at Stuart. Stuart thought he was a striking combination of vulnerable shyness and direct boldness. Stuart rose up and extended his hand. Terry took it and Stuart pulled him down onto the bed.

At first, Terry was still wary; his trembling told Stuart the youth was not free of the fear he held about expressing his innermost desires. Stuart massaged his tender skin until the tension left his muscles and his cock was throbbing.

Their skins moist and shimmering in the darkened room, their breathing rapid and eager, they started simply, gently, almost awkwardly, until finally, urgently, hastily, Stuart lowered himself onto Terry's prick and soon the youth was responding to Stuart's rhythm and they began moving together, the tempo of their bodies building to a faster and faster beat, their breathing becoming audibly heavy. At the final, mighty thrust, his orgasm shaking his entire body, Terry cried out and clung to Stuart's shoulders, his fingers digging into his flesh. Feeling Terry explode within him, Stuart climaxed.

They dozed for a time, then Terry got up and went to the bathroom. When he returned, Stuart had pulled the curtains open and was standing by the window. They stood side by side and looked out onto the Gulf, saying nothing. The rain continued to pelt the windows. Stuart kissed Terry's cheek, then knelt beside him and guided him to the rug. Pressing him firmly down, he placed the length of his naked body on top of Terry. His very weight made Terry short of breath and the heat of his flesh against Terry's caused him to begin to perspire. Stuart rolled him over on top of him and lifted his own legs. Once again, the muscles of his ass completely enveloped the firmness of Terry's cock and the younger boy began thrusting into him with all the force he could muster.

Finally, Stuart brought Terry's throbbing phallus under steady control, never stopping until Terry flooded Stuart's ass a second time with his come.

The rain had stopped and Clay was about to put the car in gear when he saw them: Stuart and Terry came bounding down the stairs, jumped in the Jeep, and drove off, heading north on the boulevard.

Even from a distance, Clay could tell Terry was young. He was taller than Stuart but he could easily have been younger, and he moved with same fluidity Stuart did. Perhaps he was another dancer. A friend. Someone from the ballet. Was Stuart not to have friends? What had happened to the trust he had in his lover?

Slowly, he drove the car across the road and parked in front of the house. He would be waiting for his lover -and his lover's new friend - when they returned.

But an hour later, Stuart entered the house alone. "Clay?" he hollered. "What's wrong?"

"Nothing." Clay was sitting in the living room, on the sofa, rolling the remains of a joint between his fingers. He had finished two martinis while he was waiting.

Stuart ignored the evidence in the ashtray. He dropped to the sofa and hugged Clay, then pulled him to his chest. The older man said, "I had an emergency crop up so I grabbed the first flight I could."

"So you took care of the emergency?" Stuart's hand found Clay's crotch and he rubbed it.

Clay pulled away angrily. "I think the emergency has only begun." He held out the evidence. "You know I don't want any drugs here."

Stuart stared at the floor, saying nothing. Clay had once re-marked how much he admired Nixon's penchant for stonewalling. If there was ever a time for that, Stuart thought, it was now.

"And the bedroom's a mess. You must have had a goddamn orgy up there."

Still Stuart did not respond, struggling with how to deal with the worst of scenarios.

"Speak to me!" Clay hollered, holding back tears as well as his fists.

"I don't like martinis so we just had some pot, that's all."

"Before you took him off to our bedroom, right? It is our bedroom, remember."

Stuart glared at his lover with no trace of emotion.

Clay got up and stood at the windows, his fists clinched. "It's over then?"

It was a question, not a statement, Stuart sensed, and he rose and stood behind his lover. Tentatively, he began stroking the older man's neck, then worked his way to the shoulders and soon he was massaging Clay's back as vigorously as he could.

"I guess it's up to you," Stuart said. "I can explain everything but I don't know that it'll do any good. You'll believe only what you want to believe."

Clay wanted to believe that his lover was faithful, that the demolished bedroom was only due to carelessness on Stuart's part. After all, the boy was not a good housekeeper. Clay wanted to beat on the windows, to beat on anything, rather than beat Stuart, but soon he was moaning as the nimble fingers worked their magic. He closed his eyes. Stuart had become the perfect mistress: discreet, cooperative, unpossessive. Yet one can't have fire and passion without jealously and anger, and the potential of his young lover's unfaithfulness aroused Clay. He knew the boy was hypersexed and that was what had endeared him to him; what did he expect him to do, sit around waiting for him to show up?

Besides, the boy he saw was hardly a threat, a youth who would undoubtedly go off to college, marry and live happily ever after. He recalled for the first time in some years the only boy in college he ever wanted that he couldn't have. The youth spurned him saying, "You're trying too hard." After that, he had resolved to take things in stride, to roll with the punches, but now the punch was one that struck him in the gut, unbalancing him, he was fighting something out of his control. The sudden robust vision of the two of them in bed together, invading each other, robbed him of the desire to protest. He turned around and took Stuart in his arms. Now he saw the boy as a statue, glowing, shining, unveiled. His beauty remained astonishing; he had, if it was possible, become even more ravishing living at the beach. As he looked into Stuart's hypnotic eyes, Clay's own eyes flickered, as if a flame was consuming him. He held the boy in awe. Yet the doubts continued to nag him. Hugging the boy tightly so as not to have to look at him, Clay asked, a bitterness to his tone, "How old is he?"

"Seventeen."

Clay blanched. "From the ballet?"

"Yes. He's sorta the assistant tutor on Saturdays."

"And on the other days?"

"He goes to school."

"Unless he's here?"

Stuart didn't answer; the less said the better. Clay closed his eyes. He had developed a raging erection just thinking of the two of them in the bed one floor above them. From the looks of the bedroom it must have been wild. Stuart with someone younger, more innocent than himself. Stuart fucking instead of getting fucked. Stuart the stud. Perversely, he wished he'd been there. "When can I meet him?" he blurted.

"I don't think that'd be a good idea."

"No, you're right." He held the boy away from him, looking deep into the eyes that had captivated him, continued to enthrall him. "You deserve to have friends. But no drugs in this house, please. If something should happen, it's my house and I'd be held responsible."

"But you've rented it to me, on paper, and if anything happened you could say - "

"I don't want to have to say anything."

Stuart nodded resignedly and then proceeded to lavish Clay's face with kisses which didn't stop, even as Clay slipped the boy's shorts from his waist and got behind him, his cock banging against the zipper of his trousers. Finally, Stuart reached behind him and relieved the organ of its agony, then, bending over, backed onto it. A quick probe by his fingers indicated to Clay that someone had been there before him, and suddenly different scenarios tormented him as his prick invaded his lover. He began screwing Stuart with a vengeance that soon reduced the boy to his knees and eventually flat on his stomach on the carpet. There, in front of the windows, the stars blinking in the western sky, Clay's thighs flanked Stuart's upturned ass and it seemed he couldn't screw the boy hard enough. Stuart groaned and reached behind him to steady the older man but the assault was unrelenting. Despite the drinks he had consumed, Clay found incredible strength, as if he were an ineluctable glacier, moving relentlessly on, as if to screw from his lover all memory of another boy's cock.

The next morning, Stuart lay in bed, naked, on his stomach, thinking. His asshole burned with the vigor of Clay's assault coming so soon after Terry's spirited thrusting. Clay apologized at one point, but the fucking continued, even as they moved to the bed. After Terry, Stuart needed a rest, not another assignation, yet he did not want to refuse Clay. No matter how painful the man's lust was, he had to endure it; his future depended on it. He didn't know anymore what he really wanted but one thing was certain, he couldn't lose Clay's love, not now anyway.

Clay entered the bedroom still damp from his shower. He'd already spent an hour on the phone. One of his calls had been to Amanda. For reasons he could not explain, he wanted to go to Naples, remove himself from the beachhouse, from Stuart, for a time. He stood over the bed, drying his crotch. He was contrite. "I have to go home for the weekend. Will you forgive me?"

Stuart grinned. "Only on one condition."

"What's that?"

"That you fuck my mouth with it."

Clay smiled and climbed on the bed, straddling Stuart's head. He slipped the towel away and his semi-hard cock flopped in Stuart's face. Without saying another word, Stuart worked it over until it was fully erect, then Clay planted his hands on the bed and facefucked the boy until he orgasmed. As soon as Clay had come, Stuart came himself. They cuddled and Clay whispered, "Nothing like breakfast in bed."

He now wanted to stay but he had already committed himself. Perhaps it was best, he reasoned, to give the boy some room.

Stuart smiled but his mind was elsewhere. As much as he loved Clay, it was Terry who was on his mind. And Clay was going to Naples, to be with his wife.

11

When Stuart saw Terry at the dance class Saturday, he was chagrined but hardly surprised the boy pretended as if nothing of consequence had occurred between them. Even over lunch, Terry talked only about Jodie, what he was studying at school, the Tigerettes, everything but fucking Stuart.

The charade continued after lunch, with Terry telling Stuart he had to get home, Jodie was waiting for him, and when they arrived, he invited Stuart to come in and meet her.

Stuart shook his head. "Some other time."

By the time he reached the beachhouse, Stuart was in a state of high anxiety. His two loves, so different, yet so similar, possessed more problems than he was capable of dealing with sober. As much as he hated the taste of it, he drank some of Clay's expensive gin and fell asleep in the sun.

In his dreams, his fantasies were lewd. He awoke with an erection and, stroking himself, he replayed in his mind what he had dreamt. Clay had taken Terry and him sailing on the little boat at the lake. As Clay sat at the tiller watching them as they joked around, the bulge in his blue swim trunks became a heavenly vision and before long his arousal was evident. The shaft thickened as the base surged downward until the ridge of his cockhead pressed out below the fabric, then slid down against the thigh, pinned by the tight cotton. Terry's eyes would have popped, Stuart was sure, and he would have begged him to do something about Clay's condition. Clay tossed out the anchor and as it splashed into the water, Stuart got down to it, as only he could. Terry soon would give Clay something to do, presenting his own perfect phallus to him. Clay would have begun by fondling the ballsack and examining the quality of the entire youthful package as if it was a gem he was thinking of buying and then, there, in the middle of the tranquil lake, with the beastly sun beating down on them, Stuart would take turns sucking both of them and when they came, almost in unison, they would shoot streams of lovely white juice into his face, congealing into teeming mass that he would spread with his fingers to his lips and mouth and then he would dive into the icy water to cleanse himself...

After he had come, he fell asleep again as the sun was setting.

12

Before Clay returned to Washington from Naples, he stopped in Miami to see Paul for lunch.

"Thank you for sharing him with us," Paul told him after they had ordered their drinks. "I always said if I was going to live vicariously, it would be with a vengeance."

"Showing that tape was a scandalous idea."

"Yes, I admit I did it as an idea starter."

"Maybe someday. But I doubt it."

"Oh, I know. I've always believed in share and share alike, but you are a product of puritans. I don't recall that you've ever shared anything."

"No, I've never had to," Clay muttered, thinking of the boy he suspected of being his lover's lover.

"Well, I can't blame you. He's divine."

"And it terrifies me."

"Me, too."

"No, you don't understand. I suspect I am sharing him."

"Oh, no."

"Yes, with a boy even younger than he is."

"No competition."

The waiter brought their drinks and Paul went on: "We're all dealt difficult hands to play, Clay. If we're going to be judged, it'll be on how we play 'em and it's no big deal to make a grand slam if you hold all the high honors. Now you've probably been thinking that your hand is too poor to even bid on, but you're wrong. He'll be over this fling before you know it. You just go about your business. Stay on the stomp, go back to Washington. Leave the boys to me. God, if I had your looks and your talent - "

"Some talent." For the second time in his life, Clay was beginning to wonder how such ineffable joy and atrocious agony could be simultaneous.

On their way back to the airport, Clay said, "I come here to hear the truth."

"But truth can be whatever you want it to be. You identify truth with what's good for you."

"No, what's good for my constituents."

"You are your constituents. You own all that swamp, all that farm land, all those apartments; you own all their cars, they buy their food at stores you own. No, the Harris name isn't on the buildings anymore, which is very convenient, but it's still you. You have to tell them what to believe."

Clay shook his head in dismay. "I preferred the anonymity of the bank to this."

"Now you know. But you have the chance to do something for humanity, in the showy way you've always wanted. You wouldn't be content working anonymously like your wife and I do. You couldn't handle it. I hated it too, in the beginning, before I saw the possibilities of it." He chuckled. "I'll never forget my father saying, 'It hurts me to do this, but the board says - ' What a father!"

"What a son!"

"Best fuck you ever had."

"Second best."

"Ah, but you remember the race between the tortoise and the hare?"

Clay laughed; he couldn't be mad at his oldest and best friend. The sad thought flickered for a second in Clay's brain that Paul was living his life through him and it was more important to him than anything that he not throw this away, yet what did he want him to have - his career or his happiness?

"You love this boy because he's of a world of paint and pasteboard. You've always wanted to be in theater. But, after all, now you are, in a way. The greatest play-acting of all: politics."

"No, staying married, that's the best acting I've ever done."

After his marriage, Clay's double life began in earnest. As an officer of the main bank when it was headquartered in Bradenton, he lived at the beachhouse, commuting every day in a limousine so he could work on the way; he went to Naples on the weekend. His long absences didn't seem to bother his bride. Sensitive souls tend to admire qualities they lack themselves and Clay saw in her an innate goodness. Never a man who could have been content with a mere debutante, he found other girls of similar background appalling. Her voice was high, affected, cultivated, sweet, and at times absurdly affectionate, the word "love" seemed always at her lips. She had had a brief marriage to the scion of another wealthy Milwaukee family but he was irresponsible and drank to excess and she got an annulment. She had never suffered poverty, filth, repression and was hardly a frustrated social climber. She detested shouting and bad manners and shared Clay's inner compulsion to improve the world. Not pretty in a conventional sense, Amanda's mother said her smile could catch a husband. She was blonde, blue eyed, tall, willowy and had exquisite taste in clothes, her Givenchy gowns seemed to pour over her thin figure.

They met at a charity event sponsored by the bank and she was attracted to Clay's polished, formidable exterior. He would own a woman, and she didn't mind. From her seeming whirlwind of unhappiness she suddenly reached out and made a grab for the gold.

Clay had always admired Amanda's ability to make the best of things and when she embarked on making her parents' old mansion on Gordon Drive one of the city's showplaces; he never objected to a single bill.

During those first years, Amanda made a house that was a jewel of style and precision, a charming mix of period and contemporary. Clay raved about her decorating skill and encouraged her, even suggesting she open a store and decorate others' homes. But she felt her real talent lay in choosing the right art to adorn the walls and she devoted herself to it. Clay would chuckle when she would applaud an artist he knew to be gay. As Naples grew, galleries thrived and artists jockeyed for times to show their work; Amanda hosted grand parties for them at the mansion. Clay would often find the place filled with people when he arrived Friday evening. It seemed all of the elite of Naples were enchanted with the couple, envying his masculine beauty, charm, quick wit, and vivid imagination; her manners and exquisite good taste. And Clay and Amanda were invited to every event during season.

But Amanda soon found she was in love with a stranger, perhaps not even a very nice one, a man who was seldom at home. He blamed her for their lack of time together. It was her decision to make their residence her parents' old winter home in Naples, far from the headquarters for the Harris bank. While they were dating, she thought that he would be better off to be young and free the way his friend Paul was, but no, he seemed to want to be tied down, to take on responsibility. There would be no illicit relationship; they had to be married, so they were. They went to Paris on their honeymoon, took a motor tour of the cathedrals of France, and it was a charming interlude. Amid the soaring spires and blue glass of Chartes, craggy magnificence of Amiens, and lacelike delicacy of Rheims, it hardly seemed appropriate that the holy sacraments would ever be violated. Yet, upon returning to Paris, Clay would only have to see a boy in the street and his mind would wander. Several times, he felt, she would catch where his eyes had strayed. When they returned to their hotel suite and he was fucking her, visions of the street urchins were what aroused him. He felt guilty for a time but then decided that he had to live in his own time, and his own morality, although he realized it wouldn't be easy.

Occasionally, when Clay was in Naples, he was short with her and their sex, if they had it at all, was perfunctory. She was helpless, shaking herself angrily for dreaming of marrying a man as handsome as Clay. Eventually, she became antagonistic to him. Her decorating and her interest in art became a defense behind which she hid her bewilderment at what she imagined went on behind her back.

When her parents were visiting from Milwaukee, she asked her father what she should do about her crumbling marriage. "You ask what you should do, Mandy? Why do anything? I've learned that people get into worse trouble when they talk of having to do things."

"I can't go on living with a man whose private conduct is so abominable."

"And what is his conduct?"

She stopped short. She had no evidence of misconduct of any sort; just her lewd suspicions. She threw her arms around him and wept. He shuddered. The unspoken word can be thunderous.

As the years passed, Clay's imagined misconduct somehow seemed less abominable to Amanda than if he had another woman stashed away somewhere, another woman who might actually be a threat to her marriage. No man could ever be a threat, she decided, and made a pact with herself never to feel sorry for herself again, a pact which she frequently broke when, she would go out onto a party veranda to see Clay and some handsome young man deep in conversation. He gave her proper credit for the wonderful party and a knack for assembling a delightful group of guests. And there was always one that would catch his eye.

She began to cultivate these young men, as if offering them up to him, challenging him. And it seemed he always came away a winner, at least in her mind. When he would return from errands or from the beach in a jubilant mood, she assumed he had spent a lovely time with his latest conquest. And it fed on itself, it seemed. He would not discourage her advances. In fact, he would welcome them. But eventually she grew bored with the effort, deciding the sex was not worth the bother, the humiliation.

From time to time, there were women who fancied her husband and she found it less agreeable to deal with them. Clay was especially attracted to Marjorie Keenan, with her luminous eyes, a speculating black. Her face was oval and very pale, her chin round, her lips small, thick, crimson, her nose small and turned up. She affected long gowns and very high heels, and seemed to be against the society she dominated. She had a habit of twitching her shoulders and jangling heavy gold bracelets and he found her very amusing.

"He's the most wonderful man in the world," she would swoon to Amanda.

"Isn't he?"

Amid much rattling of jewelry, Marjorie approached Clay and spoke with a frankness that gave Clay the impression that they were the only ones at the party. Later, he discovered that she was this way with everyone, but that only made this virtue even more remarkable, the secret of her charm. Even when she was talking about herself, she seemed to be talking about him. She was so soft and smiling and fragrant, with such faintly fading beauty that she made one think of a fine old Chinese shawl. Yet it was draped, Clay always felt, over a hard substance. She would yield temporarily but always snap back. Her husband was brisk, tweedy, loud. They maintained grand establishments in Beverly Hills, in New York City, on Long Island and in Naples. Amanda summed it up to another guest: "She lives in too many places and spends too much money." And soon she was interrupting to herd them to the buffet. After they filled their plates, they sat together at the far end of the garden. A waitress passed wine goblets and Clay gulped his nervously.

Marjorie had busy hands, her lips fixed in a half smile that preceded her invariably intelligent qualification to every uttered generality. He saw that her concern for humanity had almost obliterated her interest in the things most women cared about.

As taken with her as he was, his attention was soon drawn to the late arriving guest of honor, a young artist named Steven, who thought he might be too obscure to warrant Amanda's attention. He never forgot her kindness and, when he went to bed with her husband, he did it only with Clay's assurance that she knew of his proclivities. Afterwards, the young man was so enchanted with Clay that it did not really matter whether it was true. The young artist knew full well a perfect work of art had to have validity in itself.

They began their first secret rendezvous at the gallery where his paintings were on display. "Representational painting no longer has a valid function in our society," Steven explained.

Clay never cared for modern art, especially abstract, but he kept an open mind, especially as far as the artists were concerned. Intensely dedicated and quick to admire that dedication in others, Clay stood before one of the canvases and asked, "What should I be seeing here?"

"Don't bring your preconceptions to it. Just absorb it."

"I can't help but think I've seen it before. It reminds me of the sea, when we're out on the Amanda II, anchored, just the waves lolling us." At first he had thought there was something pathetic about it, all the blues, greens, even a rusty red slipped over the canvas in cascades, but, as with Steven, the more he looked at it the more he liked it.

"It sounds wonderful," Steven gushed, "all that lolling about."

"I'll take you out some time."

"I'd love it."

And Steven did love it. They began by discussing art again, with Steven telling Clay that he had to learn to "feel, without constantly objectivizing everything," And while it was Clay who did the feeling, it was Steven who did the objectivizing, on his knees in the main cabin, choking on Clay's cock as the older man slammed into him.

It seemed that whenever Clay needed to work out his irritations he could find a mouth that could deal with it. His affair with Steven lasted several months before the young man moved to California.

They enjoyed one last cruise on the yacht and Steven sent Clay a card every Christmas. Clay bought four of his canvases and Amanda had them put into storage.

Shortly after the birth of the twins, Amanda held a christening party and one of her friends brought along another young artist named David Rolfe, from Pittsburgh, whose work was being shown for several weeks at a gallery on Fifth Avenue. The first thing Clay noticed about David was his eyes. The eyes were, Clay always felt, the windows to the soul, and he could tell David was a fire-brand. It wasn't long after they had been introduced that they were at a far corner of the garden talking.

"...Bankers are the very apostles of greed," David said, chuckling.

"Quite so," Clay said, sipping his martini. "But one must learn these things first hand in order to fight them."

"You never condemn anything unless you've tried it?"

"No."

"Very noble."

"Hardly noble, just interesting."

"I think you're interesting...very interesting for a banker."

"Rest assured I do not intend to be a banker all of my life."

Clay smiled, but out of the corner of his eye he could see Amanda watching him. Them. It was his own fear of exposure that caused him to cut conversations off, cancel dates, feel ugly afterwards. But this boy was too attractive to pass up. He hit upon an idea. "You know, I hate to look at paintings without the artist to explain to me what the hell it's all about."

"Sounds reasonable."

"Tomorrow afternoon then?"

"Yes, around three."

Clay nodded and moved off to join Amanda at the bar.

...The Leitner Gallery was empty when Clay arrived. Mrs. Leitner, a small gray woman, was sitting at a charming reproduction of a Louis XVII desk in the main room, talking on the phone.

Clay nodded as he passed her, proceeding to a smaller room on the left, which led to successively smaller rooms with larger and larger canvases until he arrived at the very back where one canvas alone occupied an entire wall. He stood before it questioningly.

"Do you like it?" David asked, sidling up next to the banker.

Clay nodded. "Quite impressive. Almost as impressive as the artist."

"Now that you've seen the paintings, how 'bout a drink?"

"I just got here. I really haven't seen anything."

"No, the best is yet to come."

Clay left first, going to the bar at the Regency where David was staying. David followed a half an hour later. By then, Clay had drunk two martinis. While Clay seemed to need such fortifications, David was only thirsty for one thing and Clay hastily paid his bill and followed the young man to the elevator. As the car ascended to the 15th floor, they were alone and David's hands roamed the older man's torso. When it ground to a halt, they both had erections.

By the time David closed the door to his room, Clay had unzipped his trousers and was sliding his cock between his fingers. David knelt before him and worshiped it. Clay held the younger man's head as it bobbed in front of him, devouring his sex with a fervor that he would remember vividly later that evening as he had sex with his wife.

A month later, on a vacation in Paris, at Maxim's, sitting very straight beside him on the banquette after they had ordered, Amanda stared across the room. "Have you ever considered what it would have been like if we hadn't gotten married?"

"I can't imagine not being married," Clay answered.

"But why would a man who wanted to be free want a woman shackled to him?" It was said with all the tension and conflict of premature menopause. It had begun to bother him that, even then, Amanda was beginning to show signs of the terrible depression and disorientation that were to plague her later.

"I'm not shackled, we aren't shackled." Then, with absolute conviction, he added, "We live the perfect existence."

He could not imagine a life without her. He seemed quite replete with life as it was, finding he needed to feel desire more than have sex, feel the juices flowing, to be restless with appetite. But he was beginning to realize the best pleasures in life were managed, structured, carefully sculptured.

13

A week later, Clay made good on his promise to spend the entire weekend at the beach.

Shortly after he arrived and had fixed his martini, he began leafing through the drawings littering the dining table. Carrying them into the living room where Stuart was watching television, he asked, "What's this?"

"Oh, just some doodling I've been doing."

"Doodling? It looks pretty professional to me. What are these anyway, dance movements?"

"Yes, I really want to choreograph. Shit, I have choreographed. I have everything at my folks' place but I've been trying to reconstruct it."

"Why bother? Why don't you send for your sketches?"

"Well, I'm never sure how long I'm going to be staying in one place - "

Clay sipped his martini, then put it on the coffee table.

"Hell, you've been here for three months now, I guess that almost makes it permanent, doesn't it?"

"I guess." Stuart smiled shyly.

"Don't keep guessing. Know. You know."

"I know," Stuart said empathetically, while he unzipped his lover's trousers. "As sure as I know this is the biggest cock I've ever seen."

As Stuart began, Clay leaned back and closed his eyes. As the boy set about arousing him as no one else ever had, he thought there is no ecstasy greater than creation and as he was discovering new, surprising depths to Stuart's creativity, he wanted more than anything to be a part of it.

*

Over dinner, Stuart told Clay about the dances he had choreographed. One work, 25 minutes long, was called "Love Stratagem." It had been performed at a workshop before he was fired from the company for his drug-taking.

"There was so much pressure being in that company. I thought if I could do this, create dances, it'd be happier. There's always someone stronger, someone thinner, someone younger, someone who could turn quicker and lift higher, waiting in the wings."

He told Clay about the *pas de deux*, set to portions of Mozart's "Requiem." It was about the ill-fated love affair of a two drug addicts. "I have men touching men in ways that were wild at the time. I suppose they'd be even more wild now."

"Just thinking about it gets me excited. Let's go home and get wild - "

Back at the beachhouse, Clay came up behind Stuart and his arms circled him. He swayed his pelvis against the boy's ass and his hands went up under his sweatshirt and caressed his nipples. They hardened to the touch. Stuart pushed back against Clay with his ass. His hands reached down and unbuttoned the top of his jeans. For a while Clay sucked on the boy's tongue as if it were something else, then whispered in his ear, "I know you want to put it behind you, go on to other things, but will you strip for me one last time?"

Stuart smirked and backed away. As Clay sat across the room, the boy stepped over to the stereo. He loved the music of the '70s and put on "Lean on Me" by Bill Withers.

"I can be an erotic dancer and not take my clothes off," he had told Clay and proceeded to prove it, by moving in small, insinuating movements, touching myself a lot, as if his hands were the audience's hands.

By the end of the first chorus, "...It won't be long before I'm gonna need someone to lean on..." His hands were caressing his buttocks. Clay smiled.

On the second chorus, "...I might just have a problem that you understand..." Stuart's hands moved to his crotch. He kneaded it lewdly, playing to the mirrors. He loved the bronzed mirrors of the living room. He had said, "I like mirrors, to watch myself dancing, jacking off. It's not exactly narcissistic, but I suppose it is." Because dancers work in total isolation from the audience, never seeing what they do, always giving, Stuart had told Clay that at one point he had become obsessed with watching himself, picking out his imperfections, overlooking his attributes. But Benny's beguiling influence had cured him of that, teaching him to make eye contact, really look at his partner.

With the dazzling images of his lover exploding before him in every direction, Clay could stand it no longer. He stood and fondled the bulbous crotch and dropped to his knees. As Clay slid Stuart's hardening sex from its captivity, the boy could feel the hot breath on his cock, tormenting him until Clay finally took the boy fully in his mouth. After several minutes, Stuart reached down and pulled his lover back up into his arms. "Lean on Me" repeated as, hungrily, they kissed. Stuart moved to kiss Clay's hairy chest and stroke his stomach, working his way to the Congressman's erection. As he began his sucking, Stuart tried every tempting, teasing trick he knew to delay Clay's orgasm but he had been without it for so long it was no use. When Clay came, Stuart swallowed it all.

They moved to the bedroom and as Clay sunk his prick into Stuart, he stopped in mid-stroke. He could hold off now, and he withdrew, tantalizing the boy with just the large head of it. Stuart pressed in closer, arching against his lover, his fingers lacing through the shiny hair. He wrapped his legs around Clay's body and moaned, "Oh, come in my ass." And Clay obliged.

Clay's shriveled cock slid out of Stuart's ass with a pop and he rolled over onto his back. Stuart mounted his head and shoved his cock towards Clay's mouth, pressing it to the older man's lips. Before long, the Congressman, his hands firmly planted on the boy's buns, was swallowing his lover's heavy load.

*

The next night, at dinner, the discussion returned to Stuart's dances. Clay said, "The best thing about performance art is that it's so ambiguous. It includes just about everything you might want to do."

"Does that include 'Unspeakable Acts?'"

"Eh?"

Stuart had first encountered Laurie Anderson's album "O Superman" in New York and used her song "Strange Angels" as the background for one section of his ballet, "Unspeakable Acts." He sang it for Clay: "Strange Angels. / Singin' just for me. / Old stories, they're hauntin' me. / This is nothing / Like I thought it would be."

Clay smiled. "How apropos."

"I suppose once things that we take for granted are gone then we realize we're just making all this up and we can make up a new story altogether, but it'd better be good."

"That's what we do in Washington all day."

"You know, I always thought politicians were the bad guys but now that I'm fucking one I've lost my bad guy. Maybe nobody's the bad guy, eh?"

"Ha! There are plenty of bad guys in Washington. I just don't happen to be one of them and that's probably why I really don't belong there."

"I really never thought about the government controlling things until just a few years ago when they decided they were going to tell people what to paint and what to write and I resented it. I guess that's what this piece is all about, about shoving it up their ass. Laurie Anderson does a song about Mapplethorpe called 'Big Black Dick,' and it's sticking out of a gray business suit." He recited the lyrics: "So he made a law that said / We're not going to look at this / And you're not going to look at it, either."

Chuckling, Clay asked, "Ever have one?"

"One what?"

"Big black one?"

"Not that I remember, and I'm sure I would have remembered! Of course, there's a lot of stuff I did in New York I don't have the faintest memory of. That's what the drugs will do to you."

"I've never asked this before and I should have I suppose. I mean, during that time -"

"Oh, I've been tested. I was tested when I went into rehab. I don't know how or why I was spared but I was."

"I know why, why you were spared, why we both were spared."

"Oh?"

"So we could be together, don't you see?"

"Nice thought, isn't it?"

It was a statement, not a question, and Clay saluted the boy with his glass of wine.

Back at the beach, Clay fucked the boy's face hard, deep, never permitting more than half of the ten inches of his cock out of Stuart's mouth. Trickles of spittle ran down Stuart's cheeks as Clay pumped his flesh into him. The boy never gasped for air until Clay grasped Stuart's curls and held his head as he came. As Clay pulled away, Stuart's lips, slathered with come, glistened in the moonlight and Clay bent down and licked him clean.

*

As he returned to the beach after taking Clay to the airport early Monday morning, Stuart recalled what he had said to Michael, that if he ever had a lover he wanted it to always be as if they were on a holiday...and that's what it seemed like now, being with Clay.

14

DeWitt Clinton met Clay at the Palm Beach airport in his new red Ferrari. "What do you think, stud?" Like a stork, DeWitt turned his small, still pretty head on a long pale neck and smiled at his old friend.

His knees pressed against the dashboard, Clay laughed. "I could never drive one of these. I can't get my legs in here."

"No, no, there's lots more room on the driver's side. It's the passengers that have to be short."

"So you don't date anyone taller than five foot five."

"As long as they carry a wallop between their legs, I couldn't care less how tall they are."

"You're obsessed with it, that's what you are. Obsessed."

"Once you've had the best - "

"Thanks."

"Oh, I didn't mean you, Clay."

"Bullshit."

"I love you."

"I know," Clay chuckled, patting his friend's knee.

DeWitt lived in grandeur in his parents' great gray Renaissance chateau on the beach, dark and gloomy but bright within, with illuminated canvases, large and small, which seemed to cover every inch of the walls. He favored David Hockney and collected his swimming-pool paintings and Polaroid photo collages.

As they sat with their drinks, Clay's martini, DeWitt's apple juice, Dewitt's body, now wrapped in blue silk, was still, the long, emaciated arms folded on his chest. He seemed to be just another curious piece of delicate, ancient art that adorned every table in the mansion.

Finally, he spoke: "I want to die yet the prospect of it terrifies me, like the nigger in 'Showboat,' I'm 'tired of livin' and feared of dyin'."

A frown of concentration coming to his face, Clay said, "You're allowed to say it scares you but no more talk of dying." Despite his words, Clay's compassion for his old friend was so great he wanted everything to be over for him and the spectacle of this slow, sure decay angered him. Yet DeWitt had always been frail and sickly, bothered by a heart condition, on constant medication. Because of his health problems, he had always been excluded from athlete's heaven, a place he considered voluptuous, a place where sweat and strain had a magic all their own. His collection of jockstraps, suitably stained, most not only with perspiration but semen as well, was legendary.

He followed polo avidly, more for the players than the game, Clay always kidded him, yet curiosity seemed to glow most intensely in his eyes whenever he discussed art or literature with Clay. They could argue about it for hours.

"So it's still art any at price?" DeWitt joked. "And nothing matters but beauty?"

"Nothing. And, yes, to answer your question before you ask it, the new one is beautiful."

"I would expect nothing less, but is he as beautiful as Jake?"

"Different type altogether."

DeWitt looked out to sea and said, wistfully, "For me, it will always be Jake. People think just because a guy is a jock means he doesn't care for beautiful things. But Jake always had a natural good taste, he disdained the vulgar."

"He was the Polo God, wasn't he?"

"Yes. Well, the god of sport, I liked to think. Jake the Jock you called him, remember?" DeWitt chuckled. "But of course you remember, how could you forget?"

No, Clay could hardly forget Jake. When he met him, he appeared to be tense, hesitant, but with a hint in his eyes that he could be fun. He was a big, raw-boned blond with large reproachful eyes who cared a good deal about animals, his polo ponies in particular, and less for people, impatient with those whose values were not his own. And Clay was to discover his energy was limitless, even after hours and hours of making love. His only prediliction appeared to be for 69-ing and Clay found him to be an expert fellatist.

"Yes, Jake wanted to start by learning all kinds of things from me. 'Wonderful things that you know and I don't,' he used to say. It was if he was saying, 'I want to profit from this. Someone should.' But it was me who profited."

Clay nodded as DeWitt went on, deifying his dead lover and if he wanted to touch up the past a bit, Clay saw no harm in it. Jake was an antidote to the misery of life, someone who could be counted on to keep him going when things seemed so pointless.

"Yes," Clay murmured. "How well I remember."

What Clay remembered most was the last time he and Jake were together. The young man had been just been diagnosed as HIV-positive, something he had been expecting, yet he was unprepared to deal with the consequences. It was one thing to have a lover who was dying, but to get a death sentence oneself was quite another matter. While once Jake was bursting with the life DeWitt lacked, now he became cold, distant, hateful.

There were many ways of having sex, Clay assured him, yet Jake began shrieking obscenities at him. Clay wanted to wear a rubber while Jake blew him, but Jake saw no point in it, telling him if it hadn't mattered the week before, why would it matter now? To Clay's utter dismay, their argument escalated to quixotic violence that shocked him. Indignantly, Clay left the hotel room where they had shared many stolen moments.

"But you knew how wonderful he was, didn't you?" DeWitt asked softly.

The coldness of Clay's reaction was the mirror of DeWitt's stare.

"Oh," DeWitt went on, "I knew, but I never minded it, not a bit. He was such an athlete, at least he was giving it to a friend, not some pickup in a tearoom."

Clay was silent, sipping his martini.

"You've always been the great cocksman in our crowd, Clay. We all talk a good game but you, you live it." Suddenly DeWitt became animated, relishing every jab as if it were a rapier. "You know, I think Paul and I have been wrong all these years. I think you people who live in a closet have a lot more fun than we do, out in the open, with nothing to hide. What do you say?"

"No comment."

"Oh, god, honey, I'm not a reporter for the Palm Beach Post or CNN, I'm Clint. You can tell me. How is it in that closet of yours?"

After a deep abdominal chuckle, Clay said, "Cozy. It's very cozy."

DeWitt chortled. It was his first good belly laugh in a long time.

Composing himself, he asked, "So when can I meet this little fairy prince of yours? Paul hasn't stopped raving about him."

"If I have anything to do with it, you'll never meet him."

"Don't sulk, junior. So you can't stand a little competition?"

Clay finished his martini. "You're an old man, he'd never go for you."

"Only two years older than you, Clay, but I'll admit I do look much older these days. It's this terrible business." The face that once radiated energy and sexual mischief had become a mask of desperation and pain.

"I know. That's why I'm here, to see if I can cheer you up."

"Seeing you always cheers me up, you know that. But there's times when I feel so low I think I might just do it. Pop, and that's the end of it."

"Don't start that again. They're finding new things every day. Look at all those drugs you're taking. They're working wonders."

"I know, and the destruction of my precious T-cells has been slowed. But what about the people who can't afford it? What happens to them?"

"That's what's so wonderful. I'm seeing more and more support groups spring up. I gives me hope."

"Well, you and Paul and Marco are my support group. Paul calls every day. Marco is a doll, and absolute doll. He comes up once a week and gives me the most marvelous massage."

"I'll bet."

"Oh, he has no fear of me. I don't do anything that will contaminate him, believe me. I wouldn't hurt him for anything. But he isn't Jake, after all. Jake brought more happiness to my life than anyone else. Maybe there's just one person in your life and that's all."

"Could be," Clay sighed, thinking of Stuart.

"But now happiness doesn't mean a thing. It gives you a certain freedom, this business. Now I'm ready for anything because I've got nothing."

"Clint, you've got plenty," Clay said, pouring himself another martini.

"Ha! But speaking of having plenty, tell me all about him."

Clay knew he would have to, sooner or later, let DeWitt know about Stuart, so he resumed his place on the sofa and regaled DeWitt with the tale of how they met, the second meeting, and the subsequent weeks of adventure. "He's the strangest boy I've ever met. He has such discipline. He doesn't need people around to make him happy, he's very much into his dancing, his dreams, his fantasies, himself."

"And into you."

Clay beamed. "Each of us into the other."

"Ah, sounds like the perfect match."

"Perhaps too perfect." His sipped his martini. "But I do need your help - "

"Me? You want my help with this little boy?"

Clay nodded. "I want the New Ballet to get a grant of some kind to produce experimental works. Stuart's choreographed some things and I'd like to see them get produced. Do you think your foundation could handle it, surreptitiously, of course?"

"I'd love to. On one condition."

"Name it."

"I want to see him, ah," he paused, then, smirking, went on, "perform."

"Of course."

"If I feel up to it." He smoothed the silk of his robe, then added, "Oh, but I will. I have to. I simply have to."

15

After Stuart's boxes from New Jersey arrived at the beachhouse, he spent two days going through them. When he finally found all of his original notes on the choreography for his version of "Love Stratagem," he took them to Leonard, who promised to look them over and let him know in a day or two if he would produce it.

"But," Leonard told him, "I want you to dance in the spring festival."

"I'm not ready for it."

"You are. You're back in shape. You've been doing your exercises and you are more splendid than ever. Just do a solo."

"I'll think about it."

*

A couple of days later, Leonard called Stuart. "You aren't going to believe this but we just got a grant from some foundation over in Palm Beach to put on experimental works."

"Oh?"

"And I haven't any other works in the house but yours. Strange isn't it?"

"Not so strange."

"What?"

"Nothing."

"We'll start to work right after the festival is over. I've looked them over. You've got some good things there."

"Thanks, boss."

Stuart had taken to calling Leonard "boss" and now he found himself agreeing to dance in the festival, as part of the "Fact and Fancy" ensemble, in which some dancers "rehearse," some watch, and a lot of different things go on at the same time; Leonard had adapted it from the original for the New Ballet by spotlighting the performers. It was agreed Stuart would have his moments in the spotlight, but they would be brief.

The grueling rehearsal schedule meant that when Clay was at the beachhouse, Stuart would be absent most of the day, but the Congressman seemed perfectly content to sit on the deck in the sun, his cellular phone at his side, poring over the briefing books his aides had prepared for him.

When Stuart returned, he seemed to be so energized by the dancing, and he would insist they go to bed, with him on top, riding Clay for all he was worth. Then, after dinner, he would want Clay on top of him, making love to him until they would fall asleep in each other's arms. To Clay, this was the most blissful existence he could imagine and soon his trips to Naples were becoming infrequent, so infrequent that Stuart found himself agonizing over his lack of sex with Terry. He decided he would have to make his own opportunities.

After the Saturday class and lunch, on his way to Terry's house, Stuart turned the Jeep into the entrance to the mall.

"Are we going shopping?" Terry asked, bewildered.

"Sort of."

It had begun to rain very hard and Stuart drove to the far end of the lot at the mall and parked under the only tree he saw.

"What's happening?" Terry asked.

Stuart turned off the ignition. "I told you, it's driving me crazy. If I don't have it again soon I - "

"Here?"

"Why not?"

Before Terry could stop him, Stuart had unzipped the younger boy's pants and was going down on him.

The next Saturday, it was bright and sunny. Stuart suggested they rent a motel room.

"Ugh! Too sleazy," Terry said. "And no more parking lots. It makes me too nervous."

"Didn't stop you from cumming."

"No, but it's too dangerous." He paused, then, smiling, suggested, "Let's take a day off and go to the park again."

But with the rehearsals and Clay always around for the weekends, Stuart didn't see how.

On the way home, Stuart told Terry, "I want you to be in the show we're doing right after the spring festival."

"I have school and the Tigerettes. I just couldn't."

"Please -"

"Okay. But just for you."

"I want Jamie in it, too."

"You like Jamie, don't you? I'm beginning to think you like him more than me."

"Hey, why not? He's younger than you and I'm tired of these old guys that never have time for me."

"You'd better be careful, that's all I gotta say."

As he drove toward the beach, Stuart was anxious. He had been hoping Terry would agree to the idea of a motel. He had planned it, had picked one out, the Royal Palm on Route 60, equally distant from the beachhouse and Feather Sound. He had even packed a bag. As he passed the motel, the vacancy sign was up and that made him even more anxious. It was spring break and he had stopped at Clearwater Beach earlier in the week on his way home to see the sights, and such sights they were. Now he saw that the pool in front of the motel was crowded with young people. Stuart hung a left and pulled in. After he rented a room, he slipped into a Speedo and went to the pool. He dove into the water and swam a few laps, then rested on the lip of the pool, observing the crowd. Everyone was matched up. He regretted having been so impetuous to have carried through with his plan. Without Terry, this was a zero.

He pulled himself from the water and grabbed a towel. After drying off, he wrapped the towel around his waist and made his way to his room. As he crossed the parking lot, a boy passed him carrying a tool box. Their eyes met.

"You a guest here?" the boy asked.

"Yes, why?"

"You must've just checked in."

"Yes, why?" Stuart persisted.

The boy grinned. "No reason. Everything okay in your room?"

"I guess so, why?" Stuart was growing impatient.

"Oh, we've been havin' trouble with the faucets. I've spent all morning fixin' them."

"I'll let you know," Stuart said, stepping away towards his room.

"Yeah, just call the front desk. They'll send me."

Stuart closed the door to his room and went to the window. The boy stood at the fence around the pool watching the sunbathers. He was cute in a rough sort of way, Stuart thought, and he certainly was young; he couldn't have been more than 17, probably a high school drop-out. He was almost as tall as Terry and the longer Stuart looked at him, the better he looked. Stuart began to wonder what the muscles were like hidden under the ugly brown uniform. He picked up the phone and told the woman at the front desk he couldn't get his hot water to stop running.

Moments later, as he stepped into the room swinging his toolbox, the boy chuckled, "Yeah, we've been havin' this problem lately. The fixtures in this place must be a hundred years old."

As Stuart closed the door and pulled the curtain shut, the boy dropped his tool box on the floor and stood before the bed with his hands on his hips.

"Must keep you busy," Stuart said, sitting on the bed.

"Yeah, man, never any time to have any fun." He stepped over to Stuart until his crotch was in Stuart's face. "I'm horny as hell."

Stuart leaned forward and ran his fingers up and down the bulge in the boy's trousers. "I guess so." Then he began lowering the zipper.

"I haven't got much time," the kid said.

"Neither do I," Stuart said, undoing the belt and then the button.

The pants fell away and the boy wore no underwear. The lean, cut cock was warm and damp and it quickly bobbed its way out of the pubic hair. Once it was in Stuart's mouth, it grew to about seven inches. The kid held Stuart's head as he was being sucked and his body soon began quivering and Stuart tried to pull back, to make it last, but it was no use, the boy began to pump Stuart's mouth. Stuart gulped for air and the come slid right down his throat.

"I get off at five," the kid said, zipping up his pants.

"I thought you just did, get off I mean."

"Hell, that's just for starters. I bet I know what you like."

Stuart stood up and the kid's hands clutched his asscheeks.

"Yeah, it'd be fun, but -" He gulped. "Well, if I can -"

The kid picked up his tool box. "Do that."

After he had gone, in the shower, Stuart gargled, savoring the lingering taste of the stud puppy, and, even though he stroked himself, he didn't come. For some reason, he wanted to save it until he got home, where Clay was waiting. Where now, it seemed, Clay was always waiting.

*

The next Saturday, Leonard would tell the athletes, "Dance class legalizes being creative with your body."

Stuart whispered to Jamie, "See, everything's legal here."

Jamie blushed.

Stuart got the class doing acrobatic dancing, each movement a kind of kinetic sculpture with human forms lifted, hung, cantilevered, balanced in surprising ways. When the class was over he invited them to join him for lunch. Jamie refused.

"You're getting as bad as Leonard," Terry teased as Jamie raced out of the building.

Stuart stared at Jamie's bluntly muscular body. "Hey, man, wouldn't you like to get a piece of that?"

Terry shook his head. "You'd better be careful, that's all I gotta say."

The night before, the members of the company who were part of the festival were rehearsing, still exercising at the bar but doing extensions and turn-outs by the wayside.

"Technique is no longer important," Leonard stressed. "The goal is survival, just to get off the stage alive!"

And, to electronic music, performed only in dance belts, they began choreographic pulsations, joining to form breathtaking and novel configurations.

When they were finished, Stuart, exhausted, had Clay drive over from the beach and pick him up. They had dinner and on the way home Stuart fell asleep.

"You're working too hard," Clay told him when they were in bed.

"It's just that I'm not only dancing in the corps, I'm also doing a solo. I don't want to disappoint the others."

"You won't. You'll be marvelous, I know it."

And he slid between the sheets and hugged his lover. For the first time in their relationship, they were going to spend a day without having sex.

On Saturday, Clay took Stuart to Tampa and when they pulled into the parking lot, Terry was emerging from his mother's car.

"Shit," Stuart mumbled.

"What?"

"Nothing."

The two boys waved at each other and Clay swallowed hard.

Seeing Terry close-up for the first time, he realized how extravagantly blessed the boy was, his every move beautiful, his face boyishly handsome, his eyes deep and dark. Jealousy raged within him once again. "I'll be back in time for dinner," Stuart said, slamming the car door.

Clay sat still in the car, breathing heavily, watching them greet each other and rush into the theater. Together they were fluency and grace personified. Quite possibly, Clay thought, too much of a good thing. It occurred to him to follow them, to watch them dance together, but he knew that was wrong. All he could do was wait at the beach and continue to love Stuart the only way he knew how.

"Who's that," Terry asked, "your dad?"

"Yeah." Stuart opened the door and let Terry go ahead of him.

"Nice lookin' man, but so different from you. You must look like your mom."

"Yeah."

"Some day you'll have to introduce me to your folks."

"Yeah, I'll have to do that," Stuart said, letting the door slam shut behind him.

16

Easter had always been a disappointment to Stuart. There was always a hunt for eggs and when it was all over, it was hardly worth it. Christmas it wasn't.

But this Easter promised to be special. Congress had recessed for two weeks and Clay called to say he would be sailing the yacht up and mooring it at Tarpon Springs. Amanda would rent a car, take the children sightseeing and then return to Naples. He and Stuart would go sailing, just the two of them and the crew. Stuart felt like telling him he didn't care about sailing, he just wanted Clay to come to the beachhouse and make love to him but he didn't. "Whatever you want to do is fine," he told him.

Then Terry called; he would be going to church with his family and Jodie, having breakfast with them, but he would borrow his mother's car and drive to the beach that afternoon. "Whatever you want to do is fine," Stuart said, chuckling.

On Easter, when Terry arrived, his dark hair was neatly combed, he was wearing a white shirt and tie and Stuart thought he was a curious mix of the angelic and the devilish.

"Why don't you go upstairs and change?"

"I'm afraid," Terry smiled. "I remember what happened the last time you got me up there."

He took the boy's hands in his. "You're safe with me."

After closing the curtains and slipping off his Speedo, Stuart lay on the bed and watched the boy undress. This time, Terry put a little show into it, dancing to the music coming from the MTV on the television downstairs. Stuart had told him a little about his past, about dancing in straight clubs, and Terry said, "What do you think, Teach, could I get a job?"

"When you're 21 maybe. Not now. Now you've got a job, finishing school."

"Is that my only job?" Terry teased, stroking his erection.

Stuart didn't answer, simply rolled over onto his stomach and stuck his ass up in the air. His face pushed to the pillow, he looked back over his shoulder and said, "Been missin' it, eh?"

"Yeah, it's that time of the month."

"I wondered why you called," Stuart sighed as Terry climbed onto the bed. "Yeah, my door's always open."

As Terry anxiously shoved his hard cock between Stuart's asscheeks, he said, "Yeah, it sure is."

Stuart groaned. "Not so fast."

"Sorry." Terry spread the cheeks even further apart and his cock went in to the hilt. Stuart rose up, leaned back, pressed his back tightly against Terry's firm chest, and, with Terry slamming into him mightily, stroked himself to orgasm. Terry stayed with Stuart as the older boy sunk to the mattress, hardly missing a beat, and soon he too was coming.

They lay together quietly. Toying idly with Terry's now limp cock, Stuart was solemn; he realized that their love possessed problems that could never be solved. He knew he would be alone again but for now he seemed to have the best of both worlds, a new lover and an old one, a younger one and an older one, both so different yet so much alike: they were both promised to someone else, yet they adored him as much as he adored them.

*

In a light wind, a lone windsurfer cut across the surface of the water alongside the yacht. The red and yellow and green striped sail brilliant against the cloudless sky, the teenaged surfer waved. Just as Stuart waved back, Clay stepped onto the deck carrying beers.

"Cute, eh?"

"Yeah, but I bet he isn't hung like my man." Stuart reached over and stroked the considerable bulge in Clay's trunks.

"Don't," Clay said, pulling away. "The crew."

"Fuck the crew."

"They'd love it."

"Ha!" There was just the skipper and another man, even older and even uglier, Stuart thought, and what their opinion was hardly mattered to him, but to Clay, appearances were everything. "Let's go to your cabin," Stuart whispered.

It was a quick fuck but a joyous one, Clay roaring into Stuart as swiftly as the boat was slicing the water, and soon they were back on the deck enjoying the sun.

"I like it better at the lodge," Stuart said, closing his eyes.

"Then that's where we'll go. Tomorrow."

"Promise?" Stuart's eyes opened brightly.

"Promise."

As the yacht was being anchored dockside, the people on the quay were staring at them as if they were pastries in a shop window. It was like a reverse zoo, with the caged animals those gaping at what they imagined to be total freedom: the people on the yachts. Stuart could hardly wait to jump from the boat. The truth was, he reasoned, nobody should envy anybody, because everybody is where they are supposed to be all the time, and not really missing anything. But he knew it was hard to understand that until you got to the place you thought you wanted to be and then discovered you were happier where you were. "Freedom my ass," he muttered as Clay joined him on the dock.

"What?"

"Nothing," Stuart said, rushing through the crowd to where he had parked the Jeep earlier in the day.

*

"If this isn't heaven, it at least has the same ZIP code," Clay joked as they lay in each other's arms in the largest of the bedrooms of the lodge.

"Yeah, this is the way I like it, just the two of us."

Stuart brought his ass up next to Clay's satiated prick. Clay closed his eyes. He didn't think he'd be able to get it up again, they'd fucked three times that day, the last time just moments before. As he ran his hands across Stuart's sweat-varnished skin and squeezed the nipples, Stuart moved even closer, and Clay's prick responded, the head honing in on the boy's sphincter, as if guided by radar. And as Clay began again, pushing it in, then drawing it out until it nearly popped from the anal lips, then thrusting forward again, Stuart breathed a long, shuddering sigh.

17

As blissful as it had been at the lodge, Clay was forced to cut short his vacation to go on the defensive when Marlene Johnson, the Palm Beach County president of the Human Rights Commission, was quoted in the *Miami Herald* that he had never publicly said the words gay or lesbian and every time she approached the Congressman's office they had been immediately rebuffed. Later, she went on TV to comment that two of Clay's Georgetown University classmates, known to be heavy campaign contributors, were openly gay, millionaire philanthropist Paul Taylor and prominent Palm Beach attorney DeWitt Clinton. Clay told his aides to set up a meeting, giving them thirty minutes and asking that only 12 people be permitted to attend because of the small office he maintained in Palm Beach, then he flew directly to West Palm Beach and spent the night at DeWitt's.

"One of my least favorite things is clarifying something I said," Clay said on their way to the chateau from the airport. Trying to cheer him up, DeWitt let Clay drive the Ferrari. It didn't help.

"I know. But they want someone who gives them more than ambiguity."

"I will not be reduced to Bushspeak - "

"But you are, all the time. You're as bad as he is, if not worse."

"Thank you, but all of us, you, Paul, Grandfather, even Amanda, we all made the decision I would seek elected office, figuring out my specific stands on issues as an afterthought."

"You've always had hindsight, I've gotta give you that," DeWitt chuckled. "Pretty hindquarters always turn your head."

"C'mon, get serious. I'm sorry your name had to be dragged into this."

"So am I, but when you've got nothing to lose, it doesn't matter any more does it? But I'm more worried about this meeting tomorrow. You just stubbornly cling to the notion that you can't whittle down your ideas to sound bites."

"I know my ideas don't always connect. It's just that there has to be fundamental change in this country and it's a fairly complicated message and the more complicated it is the more vague it sounds. When you're talking about fundamental change rather than reeling out 10 or 12 snappy programs, then it gets more difficult."

"What will you tell these people tomorrow?"

"That I believe we can achieve a lot by uniting," Clay said loftily. "The sense of being an outsider is at the core of most people's misery. Sometimes their exclusion is obvious, the Jews, the blacks, the gays. But, actually, the sense of not being part of something is universal, it's a state of mind." He gulped, seeming to be surprised at his own words, as if he had not known they were stored inside of him, aching to get out.

*

Marlene began the press conference by stating, "We need people who are willing to stand up publicly with us, whether it's politically popular or not."

The group cheered.

"You must understand - " Clay said. He was booed. He vowed he would not let them get to him. He sipped some cold water, then smiled. What did they know about it anyway? he wondered. Everyone has their own agenda. He had to answer to over half a million voters. He had to be the candidate for all of the people of the district. Did they stop to think about that?

Someone said, "In September the state ran out of federal money for HIV testing and emergency funding had to come from the state. What are you doing about it? And have you ever met anybody with AIDS?"

"Yes," Clay responded. "And I pray that we find a cure for AIDS and cancer and hunger."

"Praying isn't enough!" someone cried.

Marlene smirked and continued the questioning, asking why Clay had spoken out so little about gay issues.

"Actions speak louder than words," Clay said. "Most gay issues are based on the AIDS situation. I have embraced the findings of the two separate National Commission on AIDS reports and I have a good record on public health issues. But it's out of my hands. If I were president, I'd gladly sign an executive order repealing the ban on lesbians and gays serving in the military and in the State Department for foreign service. I think everyone should have the right to serve their country. When the Pentagon study was published, I felt sorry for the Secretary because if you listen to what he said, it appeared that he wanted to lift the ban but they wouldn't let him. And of course his PR guy is gay."

"What about the federal bill for gay and lesbian civil rights?" someone asked.

"I'm basically open on it. It seems they have been introducing this bill every year for the past ten years or so. I can't understand what's fundamentally wrong with it. I've studied it and think we need a wide range of privacy rights and some mutual forbearance so that we can define our common values and come together. I think we're moving towards an open rights position in this country. I've always had people involved in my campaign who are gay, not because they are gay but because they are competent in a particular field, such as fund-raising or foreign affairs. But we've never wanted to hold a press conference to announce that.

"Most people who have problems on these issues are people who have a lack of experience and exposure, a lack of human contact. Most people have or have had gay or lesbian friends, they just didn't or don't know it."

Someone else said, "The problem is that so many people are so deep in the closet that when they are prevented from getting promotions and jobs, they cannot reveal it because there is no law to protect them from experiencing more discrimination."

"I have great empathy with these people," Clay said with a slight smile.

Another reporter noted, "None of your literature contains any mention of gay and lesbian rights, nor do you ever use the term sexual orientation."

Clay smiled benignly. "I promise I'll take another look at that."

*

Paul and Marco drove to Palm Beach in the Jaguar and met DeWitt and Clay for dinner after the conference. It was a grand reunion; they loved to reminisce about their glorious days in

Georgetown, a place where the rich, the appointed, and the diplomatic congregated, representing the last bastion of the aristocracy in a capital dedicated to democracy.

In a simple, three-story, oblong brick house with only two windows on the street, the trio lived during their college years. The house had been purchased by DeWitt's father, whose own father made his fortune in New York publishing. When he was appointed in the 1950s as a roving ambassador to discuss nuclear treaties, he and his wife Elsie used the house to entertain while in Washington, but spent most of their time when not traveling at their estates on Long Island or Palm Beach.

When DeWitt enrolled at Georgetown, he took the place over and renovated it to his specifications. A year later, Paul joined him. Their fathers had both served on the boards of several major corporations and introduced the boys one summer weekend on Long Island. It was a liaison which began on an intimate level but, after it cooled, they remained fast friends. "Paul seems to have the uncanny ability to turn his lovers into friends. I admire that more than any other quality I can think of," Clay told DeWitt early on, and then proceeded to follow his mentor's example by seducing DeWitt.

But it was more a menage a' trois of the mind rather than the bed and Clay, being the youngest and the most aggressive, was always the most in demand. Having him around made life easier for DeWitt and Paul. "We just wait to get his castoffs," Paul often joked. They maintained a special supremacy in the gay world in those years and their parties became legendary.

The charming parlor in Georgetown had been Frenchified by DeWitt and it was often joked that Clay had become its principal ornament. If Clay was at home, it was in the parlor he could be found, drink in hand, reading or entertaining another student. DeWitt enjoyed it when he brought women into the mix, adding a measure of "respectability" to the place. He enjoyed keeping the neighbors guessing and his parents as well. The men responded to the smooth sailing of their existence and the college years sped by. Although an excellent student, Clay's grades were nothing extraordinary but he did excel in amateur theatricals, appearing in a play every season. His favorite role was as Jack Worthington in "The Importance of Being Earnest." The play, Clay thought, mirrored the lives of the trio during this period, leisure-besotted young upper crusters who spent their days visiting, taking tea, and dashing about, sometimes inventing different identities to abet their convenience.

The difficulties of the outside world hardly penetrated the house on Q Street. And they were never sucked into the vortex of the whole whirling crazy life of Washington. After the tradition and discipline of prep school, they felt free to do things their own way. DeWitt began to favor brilliant vests, bow ties and striking gold and jeweled cuff links.

They did a minimum of homework but listened intently to the lectures and with their remarkable memories were able to recite every word of the professors. "They were in love with their own words, their own thoughts, ideas," Clay was to recall later. "You didn't have to crack a book, just toss the garbage back to them."

Grandfather was always attempting to interest Clay in matters of importance and one such occasion was an arranged lunch at the Pentagon with Dudley Jenkins, an old friend now stuck in a desk job with the Navy. Sitting at a corner table in the officers' dining room, his glum stare was that of a teacher wondering if there would ever come to an end to student intransigence.

They discussed the slaughter of civilians in Vietnam. "There is no difference between that and the shooting in the heat of battle," Jenkins told the young Clay. "A difference only in degree. And principle is what you should care about. No regular officer would have been guilty of either the massacre or the assentation. Those are things that happen in modern war when you use civilians. They are unfortunate irrelevancies."

"But it seems to me they would happen more in a war that isn't supported by the public. Evil in war can corrupt even the bravest of soldiers. The people were behind our other wars. Here, it's missing, there's nothing."

"Only a moral cause can justify a war. And no cause has been more moral than this one. We are fighting for no conceivable material gain."

"Yes, and it's costing us a fortune," Clay scoffed.

"My advice to you, young man, is to never be distracted from the main point, distracted by things that don't matter. Keep your eye on the prize."

"I'll do that," Clay mused, watching a particularly attractive officer walk by, his ass fetching.

As he was returning to the house, he passed a group of protesters and was inspired that there were so many young people so resolutely challenging hypocrisy and greed. He suggested to DeWitt they attend a peace rally. Once they were in a packed gymnasium, large and smelling of varnish, they did not get close to the platform until two ragged young students made short, inane speeches and then returned to their seats in the front row. Something in the ballistic steps of the two told DeWitt and Clay that if they could get them into a discussion, invite them for drinks, they might have their way with them. Although they disdained pot, they kept it on hand for such occasions. And that night, the one Clay fancied, a hirsute young man named Wolf, got to talking very animatedly about the War.

"It's worse than a crime, it's a blunder," Clay agreed.

"It is immoral to ask men to die for idiotic reasons. Or to kill."

Both Wolf and the other young man, Frank, were amiably articulated and they enjoyed their debate. In high school, Clay was on the debate team and found he had the politicians' gift to argue either side of an issue convincingly, to suit his mood, and that night his mood was to agree with everything the boys said. DeWitt just absorbed it all, sitting placidly, basking in the glow Clay always brought to a gathering. Clay's wonderful words, the crisp and pungent phrases, the sharp staccato sentences interspersed with longer, subtler mellifluous ones, swarmed in the dazzled minds of the students to overwhelm their criticism of their hosts' obvious wealth. Clay seemed to delight in the bedraggled nature of the young men, finding it suited what he hoped would be the filthiness of their sex.

When they finally went to the bedroom, once his cock was exposed, it was Clay who again dominated the proceedings. Wolf fell to his knees and began sucking the massive, glistening penis that Clay held out to him.

"That big dick will cost you," DeWitt joked to his two guests. "You have to fuck me first. All of you."

They took turns sucking Clay, then fucking DeWitt, who whimpered softly from time to time as the two protesters took turns ramming his anus with their stiff pricks until he seemed to disappear into a drug-induced, anticlimactic fog. It was only when Clay slid his saliva-coated cock into DeWitt that his own cock was rejuvenated and he could masturbate himself to orgasm. Then Clay pulled his pulsating muscle from DeWitt and jammed it into Wolf's ass from behind with an angry force that sent the young student flat to the floor. Suddenly Clay felt Frank's rough beard against the skin of his ass, finally to probe Clay's sphincter with his tongue, driving Clay to new heights of ecstasy. Engrossed in their heavy labors, all of their bodies became drenched in sweat. Clay pulled out of Wolf in time for the young man to turn and catch the load on his face. Frank moved from Clay's ass to his ballsack and then to the slippery cock, licking it clean of come and applying lubricant so that he could be fucked by it. Clay was able to respond to the young man's need; his cock was only half-hard but once inside Frank's ass, it grew to full strength and he pummeled him from behind until he orgasmed, this time with DeWitt, reviving enough to enter the scene, catching the load in his mouth.

The next day, when Paul returned from visiting his parents, they had lunch and Clay made filth of the ideals and aspirations of the boys he had fucked the night before. He was especially hard on the psychopathology of protesters, small groups, pockets of dissent that were enormously influential, their anarchic philosophies encouraging free use of drugs and sex spread like wildfire through the young and up into the middle aged and middle class. "This has meant a mass disenchantment with government."

"And what can we do about it?"

"One of these days I'm going to figure that out," Clay replied. "But they are right about one thing, the poor and the wretched. We have to do something to contain them or they'll revolt."

"Keep the lid on them."

"Containment. That's the game these days. Containment."

"Contain yourself, Clay. That's the name of the game."

Paul had used the expression frequently once Clay discovered the joys of D.C.'s infamous tearooms, often joking about the law in the Capitol that any sexual activity aside from the penile penetration of the vagina between married couples being a felony. "Can get you ten years and a fine!"

"From what I've seen here, they'd have to put the whole city behind bars!"

Paul sniffed, "The secret is, always, don't get caught."

It was during this period that Clay developed a preference for blonds. He grew especially fond of an amiable, feckless lad named David, who had long blond hair parted in the middle and had come to a rally from his college at Chapel Hill. They saw each other occasionally for several months and Clay showered him with gifts as well as ravaging him as no other man had. But when it seemed the youth wanted to possess not only his body but his very soul, Clay stopped seeing him. He felt threatened by a gay love. He became unhinged.

"You're drinking too much, dear friend," Paul said, in a gravely warning tone.

Shocked, angered, with sudden tears in his eyes, "I know it. And I hate myself for it."

Finally Paul put his arm around Clay's shoulder. "If you really love that boy, take it. What's all your money for if you can't be happy?"

"But I don't know if it's what I want. If I lived with him he might reject me, then where would I be?"

"And then again, he might not. You're his knight in shining armor, seems to me. And you can afford to indulge his every whim. But you'll have to let him be him, you can't own him."

Clay shook his head sadly. "I wish I could have my cake and eat it, too."

Paul smiled. "You'll figure it out, Clay, you always have. But follow your heart, not your hard-on."

18

On his way from Palm Beach to Clearwater, Clay stopped to visit his mother. In the past few months, since the affair with Stuart began, because he had so often driven to Naples from Clearwater, he found himself stopping and having lunch with her more frequently than he ever had, quite of his own accord, and their conversation was always cheerful.

To Virginia, marrying Clay's father was as if a fairy godmother had waved her wand and removed her from her tiresome parents, her ludicrous social career, and changed the scene to a land where it was always sunny and beauty and youth were revered beyond all else. On the edge of a cliff overlooking the Gulf, they built a modern house of craggy gray brick where it was not glass. It was there that Clay's father lived out the last of his days and his mother remained, devoting herself to her church work, making frequent trips to California to visit her other child, a daughter, much older than Clay, who had married a millionaire land developer in San Diego.

Virginia remained an old maid in marriage, sweet, unruffled, affectionate. But she was disappointing in the way she failed to respond to the deeper love that she always invoked in him. It was not that she rejected her son. She was always happy to run a hand gently through his hair or lightly touch her cheek to his, but she was remote. It seemed to him that she could never comprehend that the pleasures of sex would be much of a loss. She never wanted to discuss his "condition," always passing everything off with, "all in due time."

Now alone, she seemed to have come to terms with long repressed esthetic side of her nature. She was painting watercolors again and he always praised her latest work.

Clay was relieved to find her particularly sympathetic about what he regarded as a tangled mess.

"God will take care of it," his mother said. "You do believe in God, don't you son? I've never asked you that."

"I don't know about God, but I believe in evil. I believe that man was basically rotten, mean, and that the universe was made out of bad things but I believe you can hold it back and do things. To live, be happy."

"But you aren't happy now, are you? I've seen it. Lately, this job has gotten you down terribly."

"It's not the job, Mother. It's a combination of things. But I've realized I'm really not cut out for it. I'm approaching forty and I'm tired. I'm tired of the struggle. Winning the election was a challenge. I ran unopposed last time. There was no thrill to it."

"You achieved great success very young, Clay. You deserve to retire if you want to."

Clay remembered another lunch, three years before, after he had been elected to Congress, when she said: "From the very beginning I could see that you were always struggling with yourself. I was always afraid that you were struggling with something bad in yourself. That was the puritan in me. Good and evil, wrestling with each other. What I couldn't see and your grandfather could never see was that a child might be simply struggling to be himself, to be his real self, to be free. Your father understood, though. He always had to be hurrying in the moral reinforcements to help the good side of your nature win out. And I threw in with your father to keep you on the straight and narrow. But he never wanted to interfere with you as Grandfather had with him -"

"And still tries with me, even now."

"And so all your father wanted to do was love and keep his hands off. He was so proud of you doing what you wanted to do. Grandfather would howl about it and your father would always shrug and say, 'What can I do?' Then we'd laugh all the way home. The biggest surprise was when you decided you wanted to go work at the bank."

"I did it for him. He wanted me to do it."

"And he never could figure out how you did it but you did the job better than he ever could. And now look at you."

"Yes, look at me," Clay grumbled. "But I wouldn't retire, Mother. It's just that I think I can work behind the scenes more effectively than I can in Washington."

"And Amanda, what does she think?" She caught his hand in

both of hers.

"She'll support me, whatever it is I want to do, you know that."

"Yes, she's a true partner in your work, Clay. Never forget that. And she's been a wonderful daughter to me. And I sense there's something going on in your private life you don't want to share with me and that's all right, you've never shared much of anything with me. But all I ask is, don't hurt Amanda."

Clay's father often said, "Men of great wealth are not generous, simply expiating their guilt." And it was abominating that Clay should ever be like him, weary, deflated, exasperated at having a mischievous young son running about. He cursed the boy, calling him an "afterthought." But Clay did not understand his father was ill with the cancer of the lymphatic system. He told no one, the symptoms not detectable to the lay observer to almost the end. Clay now felt as if he was suffering in the same way, with a illness, indeed a madness that he could share with no one. He realized after his father's death that the man loved him, rarely showing it, and he labored under a constant sense of disappointing him.

Grandfather Harris had admired Clay's quality of political enthusiasm, his vibrant faith in a better world. But he argued with him that progress was accelerating at such a rate that a violent upheaval might not be required to make the forces of greed give way to benign and universal socialism. He believed that if the way were made clear, the world might find a solution short of outright socialism. He was all for help from the private sector but felt that too often trusts were set up to evade taxation mostly, not help anyone. He often said, "They are like keepers at a zoo who are brave about going in and out of the cages and sometimes even cuffing the big cats but the moment the cat snarls, they jump out of the way."

Virginia Harris shared all of the prejudices of her husband and father-in-law but did not hesitate to make exceptions when it was convenient to do so and as they drank a bottle of soft wine with lunch, then lingered with coffee on the deck overlooking the gulf, Clay felt again the serenity he could now experience when he came to see his mother. He relished the feeling that no one knew where he was, that he and his mother were strange allies, and even though they said goodbye in the same way that they had always done, he took comfort in the fact that knew she knew, for him, after this affair, whatever it was, nothing would ever be the same again.

*

When Clay arrived at the beachhouse, he found a note from Stuart saying he was rehearsing the ballet and would be home in time for dinner, around eight.

Clay fixed a shaker of martinis and, as he sipped his first one, he noticed the house was a mess and set about picking things up. He ended up in the bedroom and, as he always did, he wondered what had gone on there in his absence. Was Stuart still bringing the boy home with him? Was he entertaining other, unknown men in his bed? He pulled back the coverlets and examined the sheets. They were obviously stained with come but Stuart, he knew, was a chronic masturbator. He smelled the sheets, the pillowcases. Nothing but the lingering scent of the Obsession cologne he had bought Stuart.

He noticed a bottle of beer sitting on the nightstand. He fantasized that it had been drunk by Stuart's teenaged lover. He imagined how the boy would have swigged from it with gusto, and how he would have sucked Stuart's cock with equal vigor. He lifted the bottle and saluted youth. He sucked the lip of the bottle one last time and put it down. He looked about the room for more clues to the scenes that had been played out there. In the pile of clothes heaped into the corner he found several of Stuart's colorful Speedos, some still damp and salty from the sea. A pair of jeans, a T-shirt, sweats, finally a jockstrap. He brought the strap to his nose and inhaled Stuart's sweat. He shivered as he fingered the jockstrap, knowing the beauty, the abundance that it held. He brought it to his own groin and rubbed it across his skin. His cock sprang to life and he crawled into the bed and lay there luxuriating in what he imagined to be a bed of sin.

He closed his eyes as if to bring back more vividly the scene he fantasized. Just as a play can be more than reality, clearly he saw it all, directed their movements, their speech, interpreting for them what, because of their youth, they could not interpret for themselves. Every detail stood out in a scorching light. He watched Stuart's lips closely, his mouth soft and promising, his tongue seeming to caress each word as if it were flesh. His smile, like the sun coming out after a summer shower, dissolved any doubts the other youth may have had. Never having seen Terry's cock made the thrill even greater. He could imagine it was divine, to keep Stuart's interest, it had to be divine. And when Terry fucked, it was awkward, unpracticed, yet that was its charm, and even to Terry's last heated thrusts, Clay had it down.

And he masturbated with Stuart's jockstrap, leaving his heavy load in the basket of it.

He dozed off, only to be awakened by the sound of footsteps on the stairs. Suddenly, looming in the doorway was Stuart.

"Couldn't wait for me, eh?" he cried, bouncing on the bed and shaking his lover.

Clay didn't answer, just grabbed the boy in his arms and kissed him furiously.

"What a sight for these eyes you are," Clay said when their lips finally parted.

"Hmmmm," Stuart murmured, quickly finding Clay's sex and going down on it. Clay tried to stop him but Stuart would not be denied. After licking it, Stuart smacked his lips with the taste of the come coating the cockhead and the shaft. Squeezing it, as if to pull more juice from it, Stuart looked up. "You really couldn't wait for me."

"There's more where that came from."

"There'd better be," Stuart smiled, bringing his tongue back to the head of the enormous cock once again. He quickly brought Clay to another roaring orgasm and as he watched it gush into his hand, he cried, "After dinner, I want mine."

Clay ran his hand through the blond curls and sighed, "That's guaranteed," and drew his lover's head toward his and kissed him deeply.

*

Clay had a knack for finding little restaurants off the beaten path where he could eat and not be recognized. He always dressed as if he were a fisherman, wearing a floppy hat with a fishing lure pinned to it. Stuart delighted in the disguise, calling himself "bait," which Clay quickly amended to "jailbait."

"Don't you wish!" Stuart said.

"Speaking of that, how is that young protege of yours working out?"

Stuart blanched, but, recovering quickly, said, "Great. You'll really enjoy his dancing when you see it. He's so good."

Clay bit his tongue, then mumbled, "I'll bet he is. He's had a wonderful teacher." He sipped his wine. "Oh, I haven't told you this but I've invited everyone to the show and I'm throwing a party for you at the City Club afterward."

"The City Club?"

"It's the restaurant on the top of our bank's building in Tampa."

"You don't have to do all that, just come to the performance, that's all. Just you."

"No, you deserve something grand."

"Can Terry come?"

Clay chuckled, thinking about how many times Terry must have come if Stuart had anything to do with it. "He's one of the stars of the show, isn't he?"

"Yeah."

"Well, of course, he can come. I want everyone there."

"Even Leonard?"

"Hell, I might even be able to put up with Leonard in your honor."

Stuart chuckled. "Shit, I wouldn't miss that party for anything!"

Clay was pleased to see Stuart so radiantly happy, working so hard, realizing a long-held dream. That he could be part of it excited him more than all of the seemingly futile things he had to do in Washington.

As they went to bed, Stuart passionately threw himself into the fuck and after the boy had come, although exhausted and slightly drunk, Clay enjoyed a third orgasm. As his cock slid out of the boy's ass, he closed his eyes, ready for sleep, content that such exuberance on the boy's part after over six months of being together meant something; he wasn't sure exactly what it meant, but it had to mean something.

19

"...Who are these gay people working for you?" Amanda asked when Clay finally returned to Naples. The news conference had not been covered in the *Naples Daily News* so she knew nothing about it, but someone had sent a copy of an article from Florida's weekly gay newspaper directly to the mansion. Amanda opened it and read it. She was in a nervous state when Clay finally arrived.

"Oh, I guess Langley was," Clay answering her, avoiding her stare. He began fixing a pitcher of martinis. "But you knew him. What did you think?"

"Oh, yes, Langley. But no one since?"

"No, no one since. That I know of."

Clay had not thought of Langley in some time. Although he was not attracted to him physically, he had admired the young man immensely. His being gay had nothing to do with his being hired. He was a staffer for a senator who had passed away and his qualifications were excellent and Clay never expected Langley would push him into a position where he had to fire him. The boy seemed to be a mild-mannered individual, slow to anger, and relatively harmless, but once involved in the campaign, he became a nuisance to Clay, dropping hints that he knew what Clay liked. Clay blamed himself for the turnaround. He had invited Paul to a fund-raiser in Palm Beach and his old roommate immediately gravitated to Langley. Whenever Clay and Paul were together, it seemed, there was something electric in the air and when Langley was added to the mix it became explosive. Paul took Langley home with him and reported to Clay the next day that the boy was "a marvelous fellatist." Clay was amused at the time but Langley soon became tiresome to him and, finally, Clay was able to secure the young man a position at a public relations firm in Washington at a great increase in salary. Still, Clay now recalled, Langley sends him a Christmas card every year. Thinking back on it, he wished he'd let him blow him. At least he'd have something pleasant about him to remember.

Clay slumped in his favorite armchair and sipped his martini, faintly amused at Amanda's visible agitation about the articles sent to them by what she termed as "the Gay Liberation Front." "The envelope was addressed to Mr. and Mrs.," she exclaimed a few moments later, exasperatedly tossing the articles onto the coffee table in front of him. After she rose from the sofa and came over to him, she ran her hand across his shoulders, saying, "You look terribly tired."

"I am."

"I thought you were through with the bank's business."

"I am."

"Well, all these trips into Tampa - "

"There are still matters to tend to and, besides, it's more convenient. They've got the flight schedules so screwed up these days. And then if I pick up a car, I can drive down and see mother." He sipped his martini, then changed the subject. "How are the girls?"

"Fine."

"I'll look in on them," he said, getting to his feet, martini in hand.

Amanda pulled him towards her. They kissed. It was a sweet, pleasant kiss, the type of kiss a brother might give his sister, and as her husband left the room, Amanda shrugged.

*

From his upstairs bedroom, Clay placed a call to the beachhouse. The machine picked up. This time, he left word that he missed the boy terribly and he would be there Thursday night, in plenty of time for the ballet. He added that it would be longest two weeks of his life. When he hung up the phone, he finished his martini and checked his watch again. The boy should be home, he thought. Perhaps the reason he wasn't answering the phone was because Terry was there, fucking him. He closed his eyes, took his erection in his hand, imagined them in bed together, and stroked himself to orgasm.

*

That night, being fucked by Terry would have been heaven to

what he was having to endure. Susan Epstein had been a volunteer fund-raiser but was becoming more involved with the company. She had attended several of the rehearsals of the show and while Leonard had encouraged Stuart, she was critical, severely so, Stuart thought. He incanted, railed and sought her approval and, by taking her out to dinner, he hoped to smooth things between them.

"What am I doing wrong?" he asked after they had ordered.

"Wrong? You aren't doing anything wrong exactly, it's just that you could be so much better than you are." She found his references to bygone eras of beauty and careless fun quite good, but the lack of cohesiveness pointed to opportunities missed, to a talent that hadn't quite found the equable weather in which to blossom as it promised.

She went on to say that, aside from having the ramshackle air of a work still in progress, which she rather enjoyed, most of Stuart's dances were weak only in that the scripts were more entertaining than the choreography. In one *duex*, the bodies of the boy and girl were fused in combat or succor, or is it an erotic embrace? She wasn't sure and Stuart didn't seem to be either. Not being sure was what irritated her the most.

She found his ballets were outer-directed to excess and one of them approached the realm of poster art where manner substitutes for matter. The choreography seemed to have been formulated for effect rather than emerging from necessity.

"There's no way to get into this!" Susan cried at one point.

Stuart, though angry, had to laugh, as if Susan was speaking about her cunt. He thought a good fuck might work wonders but she was too ugly for him to even consider it. Although she had a reasonably fine figure for a woman in her mid-30's, she wore little make-up and had no flair for clothes and looked dowdy. Trying to better understand her motivations, he got her talking about herself. She had been a dancer in New York but had retired to Florida, gotten a real estate license and sold condos. With the decline of the market, she had time to devote to her first love, ballet. She criticized the awkward and difficult lifts for the boys to perform that would exhaust them and had the potential of embarrassing them. Stuart listened intently because, if nothing else, he admired the fact that she had been taught by Lucia Chase at the Ballet Theater, but left when Misha came in.

"I've heard all kinds of stories," Stuart said.

"And all of them are true. Misha had some strange visions and the company became a parody of its former self, a travelling circus of fear, petty vanities, chaos. I'm glad I wasn't involved."

"Now he has his own perfume."

"And smelling all the way to the bank. Jane Hermann took over but she's just a bean counter. The future of dance is little companies like ours. You were smart to come here."

"I really just stumbled into it - "

"I doubt you ever stumble."

For the first time, Stuart saw something besides criticism in her eyes. He smiled brightly. "When I do, it's all the way. I worked on these dances as therapy. I had to work things out somehow."

"And you have, obviously."

"Not completely, but I've made a start."

As they were leaving, pleased with his progress, he walked her to her car. The wine had gone to his head and he took her hand in his. She squeezed it. "Why do all the nice men have to be gay?"

Stuart smiled. "They don't have to be one way or another, they just are."

Despite his attempts to cajole her, the next day Susan was still relentless in her criticism of him.

"You've reduced the dancers to the status of children, even dolls! This is not kindergarten," she cried. "Dancers represent gods and goddesses, a high, full life. But with your work there are elements of nastiness and sadness just beneath."

Stuart fought back. "What I am trying to say is that people should have a right to do what they want with their bodies. That includes death, abortion, homosexuality."

Leonard defended his protege: "He doesn't mean to say anything but express much. Dancers don't talk, they move. And he likes leaving things unsaid."

While they argued, Leonard kept toying with the program. To Stuart, it was like watching an experienced locksmith fit different skeleton keys into a lock until it clicked open.

Finally, it was agreed Stuart would open and end the program and two of his ballets would be presented, interspersed with works of other fledgling choreographers. Leonard ended up calling it "Variations on a Well Known Theme."

*

Clay flew in a day early to attend the final rehearsal, along with family members, and he sat discreetly in the last row of the theater. He found the show a blend of childlike glee and fun and games with no trace of sadness.

Stuart had strung a strip of fabric horizontally between two pillars, 18 inches above the floor. The dancers sat in a row behind the curtain, favoring the audience with a view of anonymous backs stretching idly and buttocks settling in. Stuart's face appeared in front of the curtain on the closed-circuit TV. The camera wobbled. He let the dancers introduce themselves comfortably. While only eight feet away from the audience in the front row, the process of electronic metamorphosis provided an illusory distance. Matching the slipping-out-of-frame faces with the colorfully attired buns got Clay laughing. Stuart kept things informal by passing a microphone down the line. Some of the dancers looked embarrassed, blurting out only their names and essentials, while others thought themselves very good and told a little about their life. The camera returned to Stuart, looking radiant, wanting the audience to know he loved all the dancers and owed a lot to them.

Introductions out of the way, an array of short dances began. Clay was especially affected by "Bruises," the ballet Stuart had talked the most about. First a lone derelict appeared: Stuart, homeless, crazed or both, who is eventually joined by wraiths, Jamie and Terry, desperate, abandoned. The boys danced sensuously in close proximity to each other, their gestures ripped from a context only Stuart could know. Clay interpreted it in his own way, sexually, and the thought of the three of them together caused a terrible stirring in his loins.

A comic ballet followed featuring acrobatic dancing and Clay chortled when the dancers crossed the stage to inspect the musicians' scores and, at the end, seized, crumpled, and tossed them away.

This was followed by "Trio," Stuart's personal favorite because it was filled with chain formations, jumps, whirling motions and solemn processions. It brought back Terry and Jamie with Stuart, bare-chested boys, in whirling long white skirts, dancing to Bach's canatas. Stuart, carried aloft by the younger boys, suggested a diety enthroned by his disciples, or perhaps, Clay wondered, a human sacrifice. And their soaring leaps suggested to Clay a flight of angels and he smiled, contemplating all of the fantasies the dance would fuel when he was alone in Washington.

The final number, to the melody of Bizet's "Les Pecheurs de Perles," returned the entire company to the stage with Stuart as the star, insistent in his slide towards the audience as if on wheels, then gathering up the applause, as if he was picking it out of space.

Stuart had begged Clay to come to the show without a bunch of preconceptions. "Oh, don't worry," he laughed, "if there's one thing I've learned, it's how to approach art."

"And artists," Stuart said.

Clay slipped out of the theater and returned to the beach alone. When Stuart arrived, exhausted but exhilerated, he found Clay already in bed.

After stripping off his clothes, Stuart showered and when he returned to the bedroom, Clay was sitting up, eyes sparkling. "If the function of ballet is to tell a story completely through the body then you did that, in spades," Clay said, arm outstretched.

Stuart took his hand and fell into him. Intensely excited by the idea that his daydreaming was not, after all, only that, that there was a reality waiting to be taken up, he melted as Clay enveloped him with his arms and began kissing him, first on his bare shoulders, then, lowering him across the mattress, on his lips.

Stuart sighed, "I love you."

And when Clay entered him, his young lover wrapped his legs around him and pulled his lover's head towards his. Their lips didn't part until after Clay had come.

20

Holding DeWitt by his elbow, Clay entered the City Club dining room and seated him at a special table where a microphone had been installed. He had a waiter bring his friend a glass of apple juice, then went to greet the arriving guests.

Stuart found his way to DeWitt and introduced himself and thanked him for underwriting the program.

"It's been a pleasure," DeWitt beamed, holding Stuart's hand. "You were wonderful."

Stuart slid down into the chair beside DeWitt. "What's Palm Beach like? I've heard so much about it."

DeWitt squeezed Stuart's hand and smiled. "I live there quite comfortably. It's so irreverent. People are above it all. They have no need to worry. Today, it's said that it's a place where the people have Campari on their breath, mousse in their hair and love on their minds."

"Sounds like my kind of place."

DeWitt let go of Stuart's hand and ran his fingers up the boy's arm, caressing the satiny white shirt Clay had bought him for the occasion. "Yes, it is." Eyes twinkling, he sighed, "You are lovely. I'm so happy for you - and Clay."

"Thanks. I don't think I've ever been happier in my life."

"I can see that; you absolutely glow."

Just then, Paul and Marco joined them at the table. "Well, look at who came to the party," Paul said.

DeWitt smiled. "Oh, I'm like the palm trees in Florida, they've withstood storms but they're still standing."

Stuart saw Leonard come in the door and Clay stepping up to him. It appeared to him that they were greeting each other as old friends. Clay did greet Leonard jovially, congratulating him on the performance and thanking him for giving Stuart a chance, but it was a brief truce; peering over Leonard's shoulder, Clay said, "Oh,

I must attend to the other guests," and he abruptly moved on.

Leonard quickly found the bar and ordered a double Johnnie Walker Black; after all, Clay was paying for it.

A half hour later, with the tinkle of spoons on glasses, Clay approached the microphone, which became more of a hindrance than a help. At first it sent Clay's voice booming off the back wall. Then it screeched feedback, then it shut off altogether. But he blithely played through the technical glitches.

He thanked the guests for coming and then praised the company: "Tonight we've seen another milestone in the history of the New Ballet. I have a hunch one day this company will be famous, not only in Florida but throughout the country, perhaps the world. I know we're all proud to have been a part of it."

How smooth he was, Stuart thought. It seemed everyone in the room gravitated to him. In any crowd, Clay was the star, Stuart realized, and he loved him even more, in ways that he couldn't describe, in ways that he might never be able to adequately describe.

"I don't want to single out any one member of the company," Clay went on, "that wouldn't be fair because the evening was an ensemble affair, but I would like you to join me in a warm round of applause for the representative of the Clinton Foundation here this evening, my old friend, Clint Clinton."

DeWitt rose slightly from his seat and waved his hand, acknowledging the applause, then promptly sat down again. He suffered from the notion, almost at times the obsession, that he was of no real use to anybody any more, but tonight, thanks to Clay, he had been part of something grand and he found the strength to last throughout the party. "I'll stay until Stuart leaves," he told Clay at one point. "I wouldn't miss riding back in the limo with him for anything."

Clay beamed.

Stuart saw Susan Epstein at the bar and started to make his way to her when Leonard drew him aside.

"I was watching you while Clay was speaking. I'm terribly jealous."

"Why?"

"I can read it very well. You really are in love with him."

"Yes, I really am."

"But what business do you have being in love with a married man?" His remarks were not accusatory, merely declarative, but Stuart took offense.

"I guess I just don't know any better, boss. Excuse me."

"...Thanks," Stuart told Susan, extending his hand.

She met his eyes and in an even tone said, "You're welcome."

Patting him on the shoulder, she added, "Keep it up," and began making her way through the crowd to Leonard.

"I do that better than anybody," he chuckled after her.

After he ordered a glass of wine, he noticed Terry and Jodie standing at the end of the bar, chatting happily. He had noticed them before, when he was seated at the table with DeWitt, and chose to ignore them. The moment he saw her, he decided the girl was ugly. Maybe ugly was too strong. Perhaps plain. Certainly not good enough for Terry. But there was only one person who could be good enough for Terry, Stuart chuckled to himself. Now Terry was bringing her over to meet him.

Stuart was polite, shaking her hand, thanking her for attending the party.

"I have to see you for a second, alone," Terry interjected, with a hint of urgency.

"Excuse us, Jodie," Stuart said, following Terry to the men's room. They stood at the sinks, washing their hands, until they were alone. Then, Terry said, "You lied to me."

"What?"

"That man wasn't your father. That man was - is - Congressman Harris."

"Yeah, so?"

"So, shit! Why did you have to lie to me?"

"I didn't think you'd understand, that's all."

"I don't, but I don't care either. What I care about is that you lied to me." He began pacing, fists clinched, trying to control himself.

Stuart started to leave. "Look, let's not talk about this tonight. Let's talk about it tomorrow."

Terry stood still. "Fuck you, creep."

Stuart glared at him, shook his head sadly and went back to the party.

*

In the limo, speeding to the beachhouse, DeWitt sighed, "It's so good to be away from all those acronyms for a while."

"The what?" Stuart, wedged between Clay and DeWitt in the back seat, asked.

"The AZT, the FDA, the ddI and the NIH." DeWitt patted Stuart's knee and left his hand there. Stuart put his hand over DeWitt's and stroked it.

"Clint's new vocabulary," Clay said, sipping the champagne he had uncorked earlier as they were leaving the bank's tower.

"All this jargon one has to learn just to cope. Like discordant; I love that, discordant. We're a discordant menage a' trois you know, only one of us is sick."

"Everybody's sick, one way or another," Stuart said, sipping champagne, thinking of Terry and how sick the situation had suddenly become.

"Speaking of being sick," Clay chuckled, "Leonard seemed quite pleased with my performance as well as yours."

"No, he's not sick, he's just jealous," Stuart said.

DeWitt interjected: "Yes, just promise to come out of the closet and you'll get Leonard's vote — "

"And lose the election."

"Here's to the election," Stuart said, raising his glass.

"God help us. God help us all," DeWitt muttered.

After Clay made DeWitt comfortable in the guest bedroom, he joined Stuart in their bedroom.

"He adores you," Clay said, undressing. "I knew he would."

Stuart, lying flat on his stomach, nude, gathered up a pillow under his head. "I like him, too. All your friends have been so nice to me."

"It's easy to be nice to you," Clay said, sliding between the sheets. He kissed Stuart on the shoulder and held him for a moment.

"Somehow it isn't right," Stuart said.

"What?"

"Oh, a lot of things. But right now I'm thinking of us in here and him in there."

"Let's just go to sleep," Clay said, bussing him on the top of his head.

Stuart rolled into the crook of his arm and they fell fast asleep. It was the second since they had been together they didn't have sex.

*

On their way to the airport the following morning, DeWitt told Clay, "Being here has reaffirmed my conviction in survival. I keep saying, 'This can't be it.' You've been so kind to me, everybody's been so kind to me—"

"You've never done anything to deserve otherwise."

"Oh, not that I'd admit to. But the longer this goes on, the more I believe in the kindness of people. It's funny isn't it?"

"No, I'm just beginning to believe in that, too. Everything that's happened, your disease, Paul's love affair, meeting Stuart, it's all made me see things differently."

"He adores you, Clay. I'm jealous."

"Don't envy me, please. I'm sick about this. I never thought this would ever happen to me."

DeWitt smiled mischievously. "Great isn't it?"

After taking DeWitt to the airport, Clay went to the Biltmore to have lunch with Paul. They had just sat down with their martinis when, freshly showered, Marco came into the room. His sleek body, hardened by barbells, glistened. Every time Clay saw him, he remembered the video, that happy night they showed it to Stuart, and the fantasies that helped him make it through many lonely nights in Washington.

Marco kissed Paul on the forehead and made his way to the tiny kitchen in the suite.

"I admire you, being able to live with Marco like this."

"All I ever wanted from him was to be what Madame de Pompadour was to Louis XV when their affair was over."

"What was that?"

"A marvelous companion, procuring other women for him."

Clay shook his head. "I don't know that's what I want from Stuart."

"You don't know what you want. You never have. But it's not your fault. It's everyone's fault. If people would just leave well enough alone - but they won't. Being gay is like having leprosy, an unmentionable, dreadful thing."

"Yes, today we have all these mad, querulous people trying to convert us to their brand of Christianity by denying our freedom."

"I'd love to hear you condemn them on CNN!"

"I wish I could. God, it takes us back to the days when the State had the Church do its dirty work for them, punishing the dissenters."

"But you, Clay Harris, are the State! You've become their spokesman, carrying their spears for them, now that you've been elected. You even got reelected because you never spoke out. Some might say you're a hypocrite of the worst sort."

"I know I am. But what choice do I have?"

"Oh, I suppose you could work behind the scenes, as I do." Paul's left-wing good works had discredited him in conservative circles, with his father especially, but his agenda was far more impressive than Clay's, who had to be elected to do good things while Paul simply had to volunteer.

"But you didn't want me to do that."

"No, I thought you could change things, I really did. But now I understand. Even you can't make a difference against them, they're too powerful."

"But I hate the thought of quitting. I feel I owe something to my constituents. They voted for me."

"They never would have voted for you if they'd known what your true feelings are. You've become like every politician there ever was."

"At least I didn't write any bad checks! I told them that was a time bomb waiting to explode."

"No, you were lucky, you have your own bank! But I've always felt only millionaires should be elected - "

"Mark my words, from now on that's all we're going to have. You take way those perks and what's left?"

Paul nodded. "Well, you're proof that Americans actually like being told what to do by rich patricians." He took a long swig from his drink. "But I'm not going to let it pass, Clay. You have become more like them than you realize. You talk all around something so as not to offend anyone and you end up offending everyone. Your worse than Qualye for godsakes!"

Clay finished his martini. "That'll be the day."

Chuckling, Paul went on: "You remember when Qualye was campaigning in Philadelphia, the time what the *Times* reported as 'a slight youth' came up to him and said, 'You are such a weenie?'"

Clay shook his head in mock sadness.

"Oh, I loved it!" Paul chortled, "How Danforth's smile instantly vanished and he snapped, 'Only someone who likes Dukakis would say something like that!' Now, I would hope that you wouldn't be so insecure. I can see you saying, 'You should see my weenie, you'd love it!'"

"Never met anyone who didn't, including you."

"See, you can joke about it but when it comes right down to it"

"Okay, okay. You've made your point." Clay got up to pour another martini.

"A lot of good it does."

Clay didn't answer.

"Do you realize you're going to have to start campaigning again?"

"I'm always campaigning. But now, with the redistricting coming in, it's going to be a nightmare. I don't think I can face it. I'm just as fed up with me as you are. I may not run again."

"See, you cave in."

"No, just admitting a mistake. It's been a great experience and maybe I've done some good - "

"For beach nourishment?"

"That's one thing -"

"And the farmers! Don't forget the farmers! Oh, I'm sorry but it's become such a joke, this whole country and the way it's run. I wish there were some other place to go but there isn't. We just have to do the best we can with this, fight it as best we can."

Clay sipped his martini, then mused, "I think I'll offer my services to the ACLU."

"That ought to make headlines!" He draped his arm across Clay's broad shoulders. "I can't solve this for you, Clay, but I think you've let this kid take over your life and Amanda is bound to become suspicious. When was the last time you were down there?"

"You're right, as much as I want to stay for the weekend, I'd better go down. Damage control," he said.

"We'll keep Stuart busy."

Clay did a double-take. "On second thought, I think I'd better stay."

And they shared the laugh as they prepared to make their way to the table to eat the meal Marco had prepared.

*

Over the weekend, the air was still cool in the evening but the sun was hot enough to burn. Clay coated the girls' skin with sunscreen. Amanda didn't go to the beach anymore for fear of skin cancer; she preferred a tanning salon and stayed behind puttering in her garden.

When they returned from the beach, sandy and sweaty, the girls jumped into the pool, laughing and acting silly. Amanda grilled hamburgers, Clay opened a bottle of wine.

After the girls were in bed, Clay and Amanda sat on the veranda with brandies. She had just finished reading "The Candidate's Wife" and was now becoming agitated over a report that there were a dozen reporters in Arkansas searching for dirt about Bill Clinton and his wife. "Hillary Clinton managed to diffuse that situation with the Flowers woman but now she's in trouble because she's an attorney."

Clay looked up from his briefing books. "Nasty business."

"I worry about what they might dig up about us."

Clay returned to his reading. "We have nothing to hide."

A look of incomprehension spreading across her face, Amanda stared at her husband. "Sometimes I wish you weren't running."

Not looking up, Clay said, "So do I."

21

"She's been here."

"Who?"

"Your wife."

They had attempted to shut out the rest of the world but, like King Canuto trying to hold back the waves, they could not.

Saying nothing more, Clay stepped across the room to the bar and poured himself a strong gin. He gulped it, then poured another and took it into the living room.

"Okay. Tell me about it." He sat on the edge of the sofa.

Stuart sat next to him, afraid to touch him. "I had just gotten back from the theater and the door bell rang. I opened it and she said, 'I'm Mrs. Harris, who are you?'"

"Oh, God."

"I told her I was a student of Leonard's, just renting the house, that I'd be leaving very soon. Then she came right into the living room and stood there, as if she was staking claim on the place or something."

"And then what?"

"She looked around a bit and then said, 'I'm sorry I disturbed you. I wasn't aware my husband had rented the place and when I drove by and saw you pulling into the drive...'"

Clay interrupted. "Damn, I'm sorry, Stuart. Really I am."

"I'm the one who's sorry. Sorry for you. This is going to be bad for you, isn't it?"

"Oh, I don't know. There's a term in politics, damage control. I guess that's the mode now. I'll go down tonight. She's not a spiteful woman. She's very protective of her position. She'll do nothing to jeopardize it."

"But she'll make it hell for you." He held his hand. "I'm afraid."

"Don't be. I'll handle it. I better go down right away."

Clay walked to the window and stood with his back to Stuart. He recalled how he felt when he found out about Terry, how one can't have fire and passion without jealously and anger. Now there was both on both sides and Clay was growing aroused.

Stuart rose and put an arm briefly about the older man's shoulders.

"It's been coming a long time," Clay said. "Perhaps it's just as well. Maybe now I won't be concerned about what she's thinking every minute. She's developed this obsession over the years that I am torturing her with my affairs. But I've never let her know about anything."

"Maybe not knowing is the worst torture of all."

"Yes, I agree. I know it was for me. But now that I know about you and Terry-"

"What about us?" Stuart cried, stepping away from him.

"Oh, not the details, of course, but the general fact that there's been something going on."

Stuart gulped. "I really admire his talent - "

Clay smiled and took the boy's hands in his. "I'll bet."

"No, he's a wonderful dancer. You saw that."

Clay shook his head.

"And once there might've been something but now, now there's nothing."

"I would never ask you to give him up."

Stuart hugged Clay. "I would never ask you to give your wife up."

"I know. But what if I wanted to give her up? What if I wanted to live here with you?"

Stuart was silent. He didn't know how to respond. He'd never wanted to actually live with someone day after day. He always kidded his lovers, "I dance alone." No, it could well be disaster.

Clay drew the boy into his arms. His cheeks were a vivid red. Stuart could not recall such a color on his complexion before. Clay was flush from the excitement of the moment and his erection pressed mightily against the boy's crotch; they kissed but only briefly. Clay was agitated over the thought of Amanda in this house, his private domain, a place she had never violated in all the years of their marriage, and now confronting Stuart, grew more painful with every second. And with this knowledge, Stuart, luscious Stuart, never looked more ravishing, more desirable. Her eyes had feasted on him. She now knew what she was up against. Clay took the boy's head in his hands and held it before him. How often he had looked at this face, this adorable face, kissing every smooth, unblemished inch of it. Stuart closed his eyes and dropped to the floor, bringing Clay with him and they kissed again.

Stuart struggled to bring his legs around Clay and hold him. Before long, Clay was parting them, lifting them, pulling the shorts off Stuart's nimble body, exposing his hard sex, then he unzipped his own pants and exposed himself. Stuart was quick to bring Clay's cock to his mouth, but Clay did not want that. He simply wanted to hold Stuart, roll across him, crotch against crotch, and after a few minutes they went to the bedroom so that Clay could have what he had grown so fond of, taking Stuart in the missionary position.

Stuart lay on the bed, greased Clay's cock and lifted his buttocks to meet the older man's erection. And when Clay fucked the boy it was as if it was the first night all over again, pulsating with the fervor of their ultimate intimacy.

Yet Stuart had a nagging doubt, if he gave himself completely to one man would he cease to exist at all?

*

"I'm disgusted with myself," Clay said to Paul. He had stopped at a pay phone on his way to Naples; he had to talk to his old friend.

"Well, join the club. The most powerful current today is disgust with politicians. It's all this negative advertising. It's poisoned everybody's view of politicians. Remember poor Goldwater and the H-bombs falling on the heads of blond little girls?"

"So?"

"I can imagine the commercial they could run about you, with your prick sliding into that little blond boy!"

"Thanks, but I don't need that now." He went on to tell Paul about Amanda's journey to the beachhouse.

Paul listened intently and when Clay was finished, he said, "Now I'm terribly frightened for you. Once you let that woman know -"

"That woman knew about you."

"Hardly the same, dear boy. Hardly the same. We were just a college fling, we both grew up. But this - this is unforgivable. How could you let this happen?"

"I didn't let it happen, dammit, it just did. I had no idea she'd go to the beach, that she'd spy on me."

"You know very well about a woman scorned and lately you've frustrated Amanda terribly."

"But what can I do?"

"I guess it boils down to what I told you a long time ago about following your heart...?"

"I know, follow my heart, not my hard-on," Clay interjected. "But both of them are in the same place."

"Well, there you are, Clay. There you are."

*

For Amanda, a terrible image had slowly formed, a gradual recognition of something she didn't want to think about. She suspected her husband and Paul had been close, perhaps too close. And the artists. There were always the artists. She suspected anyone as good-looking and charismatic as Clay would not be happy taking just one person to bed all of the time, that perhaps an occasional interlude would do him good. As long as the liaison did not threaten what they had, she was secure.

But now it seemed this little dalliance of her husband's had gone on far too long. She felt compelled to do something about it. She began spending hours examining the telephone bills, charge card receipts, and checking Clay's itinerary. It had become clear to her that he was keeping someone at the beachhouse. She made up her mind: although fearful of discovering the truth and incurring his wrath, she would have to go there and see for herself. Her father told her that the worst thing you can do to a man is humiliate him, but she felt she had been humiliated and she wanted an eye for an eye. Yet, after she had seen this person, this little blond youngster, what did it all mean? This wasn't another woman, but not another man either, not what she considered a real man. This was someone in between, even more puzzling to her than Paul was. She knew very well what Paul was, although nothing was ever spoken about it. She had always felt she had actually snared her husband from under Paul's thumb and, whatever Clay's attraction was to this mere boy, she was confident of working the same wonders again. Suddenly it seemed her enervating mood swings disappeared and she felt the first real surge of sexual energy since the girls had been born. She had seen the object of her husband's affection and it was of such a nature that she could overwhelm it by virtue of everything else in her life, the children, their position, their wealth. No, she would not be denied her victory. She took a leisurely bath, dressed in a new nightgown, put on Mozart and waited.

When Clay came into the bedroom looking disheveled and exhausted, his tie askew, his hair rumpled, circles under his eyes, a strong drink in his hand, she realized she was not the only one suffering.

"I can explain everything," he said, setting down his drink.

"No need. I understand." She rose from the bed and came to him, helping take off his jacket. Even though he tried to turn away, she managed to get to his zipper and undo it, grabbing him and pulling his cock out, as though she would lose him if she didn't have him inside her immediately. They fell to the floor and she wound her arms around his neck. As he slammed into her, she gasped and wrapped her legs around him. He continued to fuck her as hard as he could, eyes closed, thinking about the contradictions inherent in making love to Stuart: the tightness and the looseness, the smoothness and the coarseness, the hardness and the softness. He would, he feared, in order to achieve climax, always think of his beautiful young lover now every time he did this.

After he was finished, he got up and went to the bathroom and when he returned, they laid on opposite sides of the bed, not touching, not speaking. Soon Amanda began to cry. It was only a whimpering; she was no longer hysterical. Now she only felt sorry for herself, but she knew, like everything else, this would pass in time.

The next day, in the shower, she saw her reflection in the mirror, her stretch marks and sagging bosom, and felt ravaged by time. She pictured the young blond at the beachhouse and felt terribly old, terribly alone, and began to feel sorry for herself all over again. She cried so hard she doubled over and finally ended up on her knees. Clay came to her, cutting off the water and wrapping her in a huge towel. He carried her to the bed. The only way to calm her was to enter her, which he did, cruelly, but she loved it, biting his skin, gnawing at him until he came, then he rolled away from her.

It was not Amanda's fault that she was still attracted to him. Indeed she had been a good sport about the original cessation of sexual relations, bravely putting the blame on the burden of the campaign. She was willing to settle for what the French call a "white marriage," rather than losing him. She looked the other way, assuring him the guaranty of his reputation. By keeping the beachhouse, he could satisfy his passion without disturbing his family. The setup seemed foolproof. But now, although she had betrayed his hideaway, after he had fucked her twice in twelve hours, Clay felt he had subdued her and felt more physically fit than he had in years. It seemed he had pulled it off, that he had silenced her with his charm, with the enormity of his cock. He was able to do it even after his intense sex with Stuart just hours earlier. It seemed that every talent with which he had been endowed was being utilized and he felt god-like, able to work it out to the satisfaction of everyone.

He took Amanda to lunch at the Ritz-Carlton and after the waiter brought them their martinis, he said, "I was hoping we could face this thing without recriminations."

"That's what I've been doing for years, not recriminating. Where the hell has it gotten me?"

Startled, he said, "You want me to give him up?"

"Oh, it's not just him. He's only a detail. I mean your whole attitude toward me, the children, well, the whole world, has become abominable."

"I'm sorry."

"But if it's necessary to tolerate your absences, I will. I can be quiet as a mouse."

He nodded. Hurting her was unthinkable. Yet the real weakness, the real cowardice, was to turn his back on a life that offered the finest fruition of heart and mind. But he had the invariable habit of retreating, like a squid, into a cloud of blackness.

22

After the incident in the men's room at the party, Terry had absented himself from the Saturday classes. Stuart called his home and left messages but Terry didn't return them. It was painful for Stuart to think about losing the dancer but he accepted it.

But now Terry was calling. "We're going to the mountains for the summer," he said matter-of-factly.

He had told Stuart about the cabin his parents owned in the mountains of North Carolina, how they went there every summer and this year he had hoped they would permit Jodie to spend some time with him there. They finally consented.

"When do you leave?" Stuart asked.

"Mom and I are driving up on Memorial Day weekend. Jodie will drive up with Dad later. I'm staying for my prom, of course."

"Of course." Stuart swallowed hard. "Do you think you could squeeze me in before you leave?"

There was a moment of silence. "Why should I?"

Stuart sighed. "I can't think of any good reason. None at all."

Terry giggled. "Oh, I can."

Clay said he would be arriving shortly before Memorial Day but he wasn't sure exactly when. Fearful he would turn up at any moment, Stuart decided to rent a room at the Sundial Resort hoping, now that he knew the circumstances of his home life, Terry wouldn't think it was sleazy, simply expedient.

Over dinner at the resort's restaurant, Terry admitted, "Yeah, I've been thinking a lot about what you did and why you had to do it. I understand, really I do."

"I'm glad."

"I guess that's why I wanted to see you before I left -"

"Oh?"

"Yeah. To let you know that, I, well," he stammered, having trouble finding the words. Finally, he blurted, "Shit, I didn't realize just how much I - "   He paused again.

"Yeah?" Stuart beamed.

"Shit, when I saw you with Congressman Harris, well, it just did something to me."

"Oh?"

"I was happy for you, I guess. I was jealous, but happy for you. No matter what you say, I really hate the idea of being gay. I told you I don't care what people think but I do. I'd rather keep them guessing."

Stuart nodded resignedly and summoned the waitress.

The boys had fun during dinner, Stuart slipping wine into Terry's water glass when the waitress wasn't looking and they became giddy. When Terry climbed out of the Jeep in front of their room at the resort, he laughed, "Hey, this is great - our own place."

"I was hoping you'd like it."

After they entered the room and Stuart had closed the door, he grabbed Terry by the arm and pushed him against the wall.

"I know why you wanted to see me before you left," he laughed, groping the boy hard.

"Yeah, but, trouble is, you aren't a girl. I'm supposed to like girls. And just girls."

"I know," Stuart said, stroking the swelling flesh.

"I love Jodie, I really do."

"I know." Stuart unzipped Terry's chinos.

"I want to marry her and have kids."

"I know."

Stuart realized when Terry would be home from college, Jodie would be his first priority. A boy could only be carved up in so many pieces.

"You'll make a great daddy," Stuart said, finally pulling out Terry's erection, shaking it.

"So would you - " Terry said, touching Stuart intimately for the first time.

Terry's familiarity stunned Stuart and he held him, one arm wrapped around his waist, as he stroked his erection. Terry squeezed the shaft of Stuart's cock and sighed, "Let's go to bed."

When they were undressed, Terry was the first to lie on the bed and Stuart positioned himself so that their erect cocks were in each other's faces. As Stuart began to suck on Terry's cock, Terry took Stuart's in his hand and held it, examining it. "You have a beautiful cock."

"You've said that before."

"But I mean it. I really do. I think you've got the most beautiful damn cock I've ever seen."

Stuart paid him no mind, so intent was he on sucking the boy.

Then Terry said, "I bet the congressman's big, isn't he? I mean, he just looks like he'd have a big dick."

Stuart pulled Terry's cock from his mouth and, begged, angrily, "Please, I don't want to discuss him."

"Hey, don't get mad about it! I just can't help but think about him being with you, what he does to you —" His hand squeezed Stuart's asscheek.

"For chrissakes, shut the fuck up!" Stuart screamed, jumping from the bed.

"Hey, look, I didn't invent him, you know. He is your lover."

"Hey, you look!" Stuart screamed. "Do I ask you about Jodie? Do I want to know about Jodie's fucking cunt?"

"Hey, look - "

"You look! You spoil everything! You always spoil everything!" Stuart rushed off to the bathroom and slammed the door.

Pursuing him, Terry nearly pulled the door off its hinges opening it. "You should talk! You're the one that fuckin' spoils everything! You act like I'm the only one that can get you off and here you're being fucked all the time - "

"All the time, shit!"

"Yeah, all the time - by some big-dicked zillionaire and god knows who- "

"You're the only one who gets me off, who really gets me off."

Terry seemed to tower over Stuart at this moment. Stuart backed up until his ass hit the vanity. "Oh, so you like it when I do it, eh?" Terry said, stroking his erection.

"Shit, you know I do. How much I do."

"You get a big ole hard-on just thinkin' about me, don't you?"

Across Stuart's face spread a broad smile. He sat on the edge of the vanity as Terry slid between his outstretched thighs. Terry's cock slid under him, pointing towards his ass. Terry lifted Stuart's legs over his shoulders and entered him in one gut-wrenching stab. Stuart cried out, his head snapping back against the mirror and he grabbed Terry's biceps as the younger boy began fucking him. They stayed there for a few minutes, Terry pummeling him with his usual gusto. Finally, keeping his cock inside Stuart, Terry lifted the smaller boy up and took him to the bed, where he continued his assault on him. After Terry came, he lay between Stuart's thighs, running his hand up and down Stuart's still rigid prick. "I want to make you feel as good as you make me feel."

Stuart moaned. "You don't have to do anything."

"But I want to. I don't think I'll ever have a chance like this again, with a cock as beautiful as this one is and a man as beautiful as you."

Stuart closed his eyes and started to say, "I love you" but stopped himself. Things were complicated enough. Then he sighed when he felt the tongue touch the head of his cock. Terry nibbled on it, apprehensively, working himself up to it. Finally, he just let it slide into his mouth. Stuart rose up from the bed and climbed over Terry's body, bringing his crotch over Terry's head.

"It'll be easier this way," he said, and slowly, delicately he began to fuck Terry's mouth with it.

Terry gagged but bravely kept the cock in his mouth. "Don't cum in my mouth," he mumbled at one point.

"I won't." And Stuart didn't. He pulled it away just in time, his heavy load soaking the comforter on the bed, his jerks and moans matching Terry's in their intensity.

Terry was sorry he couldn't spend the night but they didn't leave the room until after three, Stuart not wanting to give the boy up. He made him come two more times, once more in his ass and then in his mouth as they showered together.

Before they left the room, Stuart took the younger boy in his arms and when he brought his lips to Terry's, for once, Terry didn't turn away; he let Stuart kiss him and he kissed him back. It wasn't a French kiss or a very long one, but for Stuart it was enough after all that had gone before.

By the time Stuart returned to the beachhouse, Clay's rented Lincoln was parked in the drive. When Clay heard the ignition of the Jeep being turned off, he staggered to the front door. His flight had landed around eight and hadn't eaten but he had managed to finish a shaker of very dry martinis. "Well?" he asked Stuart as the boy entered the house.

"Well what?" Stuart brushed past him, stopped and stared at him. "You're drunk."

"No, I'm just insane with jealousy, that's all. I've never cared for anyone the way I do you."

"I can't live with someone who's insane. Hell, I can't live with anybody!" He stepped to the stairs. "I'll move out tonight. Right this minute."

When Stuart began racing up the stairs, Clay was fast behind him. The older man grabbed the boy's leg, pulling him down onto the stairs. They tousled, Stuart not fighting, Clay pressing his heavy weight on top of him, sucking the wind from him, his gin breath insulting to Stuart.

"Don't do this," Clay cried. "Don't do this to us." Clay had been able to objectify his jealousy in the body of Terry. This had gone on for months but Stuart said it was over. Now Stuart was out till the wee hours and with whom?

Stuart bit his lip and clinched his fists. "Don't do what?"

"Keep on with this boy. All these boys. Leonard called me. He says you could get into serious trouble - "

"Sonofabitch!" Stuart now started to struggle.

"He says you've been putting the moves on these kids -"

"Fuck him!" He tried to free himself but Clay had him pinned.

"He's worried about you. You're in a position of trust there."

"I've never touched any of 'em!"

Clay pressed down on him. "Terry? You haven't touched Terry?"

"No."

"You keep on with this you'll lose everything. You're jeopardizing everything for this boy!" Stunned, Clay loosened his grip and stood up. What had he said? His own situation was now mirrored in that of his lover and he was desperately angry with him, with himself; he wanted to collapse, at least he thought he would collapse. It was only the anger that kept him erect, anger at the ghastly thought that he had even considered simply flinging away his life for this boy, who was all the while preparing himself for his own life with another, someone underage. He began moving up the stairs.

"I haven't done anything I'm ashamed of," Stuart spat. "Nothing."

Clay stopped and turned back to look at his lover, disgust in his eyes. "Then where were you tonight?"

"I wasn't with him."

Clay shook his head sadly and continued moving up the stairs. Stuart leapt to his feet and came after him. "Okay, no more lies. I was with him, but for the last time. He's going away." Stuart clutched at Clay's arm. Clay stopped.

"Not far enough, I'm sure." Clay took the boy's head in his hands and held it. He stared into his lover's eyes. "Oh, God, forgive me but I love you."

Clay embraced him, ran his hands through the golden curls, and ground his crotch into Stuart's. Even though the boy had washed himself at the resort, to Clay he still smelled of sex, hot, illicit sex.

Stuart began to cry. "You can forgive me? Please, can you forgive me?"

Clay hugged the boy.

"Promise you'll stop this foolishness?"

"Yes, it's over, I promise." He hugged Clay back, fiercely. "Oh, Clay, fuck me, fuck me as only you can."

That was all Clay needed to hear. Saying nothing further to each other, they quickly undressed and got into bed. Before Clay entered him, he felt the grease already inside his young lover, or perhaps it was cum. Terry's cum. Whatever, it no longer mattered.

Stuart wrapped his legs around Clay as the older man entered him, slowly, gently.

And as he began fucking the boy, Clay fantasized once more about Terry and Stuart together, the two beauties. Then he remembered the ballet, the three of them, stripped to the waist, the two younger ones holding the prize, Stuart, aloft.

Clay couldn't help himself; he whispered, "Is he bigger than I am?"

"Nobody's bigger than you."

"Then why? What's he got?"

Stuart pushed his hands against Clay's chest. "Please, I don't want to talk about it. After tonight, it's history."

"Thank god," Clay muttered, sliding his fingers through Stuart's hair and kissing him.

Still, when Clay thought about Terry he had to admit his own ass quivered; he imagined what it would have been like if things had worked out the way he had so often fantasized, that the tall, studly dancer would fuck the both of them until they became delirious. Terry must have something, something unique, Clay thought, and he pressed himself in to the hilt, thinking somehow, in the confusion of his drunkenness, that if he went in deep enough he could somehow obliterate Terry's presence, and he began his orgasm.

As Clay labored over him, even if he was still a bit drunk and only half-hard, to Stuart he was still a tower of strength, the only kind of man he could really love. What did it matter that he was so much older? What did it matter that he loved Terry? Terry didn't love him; Clay did. And, feeling the onslaught charge up the monstrous shaft as Clay's orgasm began to fill him, he realized he loved Clay in a very special way, and perhaps, all things considered, it was the best way.

23

On an afternoon's sail on the yacht as far north as Captiva Island, Clay left the tiller to his skipper and sat on the divan on the fantail, contemplating the blue-green of the shoreline. The girls were up forward, playing games. But even as the white yacht was breasting the billows he was not safe. Paul, visiting for the weekend without Marco, had Clay cornered. He leaned over and whispered, "A reliable source has informed me -"

"Oh, stop it!"

"Washington's the meanest town in the world, Clay."

"I know. There's poison in the air, you've told me a thousand times."

"Oh, but nothing can match the poison of a jilted wife. No, nothing can make up for withdrawn love, but a diamond necklace can make all the difference."

Frivolity aside, Paul could feel his friend's sense of futility. "I've never seen you this upset. What in god's name does this boy represent to you?"

"Everything, dammit! Charm in living, beauty in life. Life as an art. When we're together, life becomes something to wonder at. And all this goddamn toil and struggling, rescuing the downtrodden, it's gotten to me."

Paul looked out to sea. "I can see that. It's odd but this kid seems to have this x-ray vision that's scary. He sees right through you, you can't get away with anything with him. He scares me, I'll tell you that. I felt he could have tied me around his finger if he'd taken a mind to. I think he's always known what he wants and how to get it, and what scares people is that they feel stripped naked by him. Nobody's safe."

His eyes wide with surprise, Clay had to laugh. "Nobody's safe," he repeated. His mind was a tumult but what kept bobbing up was the inescapably fine, fresh, wonderful idea of Stuart and that first night, coming to him when Clay had grown tired of people who wanted things from him. First they wanted his money. Then they wanted his parties and good times. Then they wanted his powerful body and his big dick. And they grew greedier yet. They wanted him to run things for them. And he began dreaming of a boy who would give him all and ask for nothing. Then he went to a gay bar and in that most unexpected place, there he was, stripped down to a G-string. Making love to him was a symphony of sighs and groans. Their affair had made real the exquisite possibility of complete sexual fulfillment.

Over the past several years, he'd thought of leaving Amanda several times, knowing that he could never tell her the real reasons, which were complicated and certain to hurt her deeply. Instead, quite clumsily, he cut himself off from her, deliberately setting himself adrift. After he had met Stuart, a simple, unimaginative lie would have made things easier on them both. He could have told her he had fallen in love with someone else. It happens all the time. He could see the luminous tears in her lovely eyes, but she would get over it. No, he would tell her, nothing extraordinary had happened, not really. But now she knew the truth. The whole truth. She didn't create a terrible scene, even with the knowledge that the person her husband was in love with was a boy almost half his age. An extraordinary boy. He would have to be extraordinary, but she would never accept that he was. She had simply dismissed him as a detail.

"Sometimes I wonder," Clay went on, "how is it all going to end? Sometimes I think I'm going to explode into a million pieces. That would be a solution."

Shaking his head, Paul said, in a careful, lawyerly cadence, "Oh, I know you won't fumble. When you move it will be with absolute assurance."

Clay rose without comment and went back to the tiller. Even as a younger man, reveling in the poetry of Byron and Shelley, he had never imagined he would associate another person with acute pain, but now the mere idea that he might have to give up Stuart was like a drill on a tender tooth.

24

In the Capitol, Clay often walked from the townhouse to Morton's. On the first of June, it was warm and he strolled peacefully, in no rush to meet Congressman John Dunby, head of the House Energy and Commerce Committee, who had called him just as he was leaving his office. He would dine alone and then have a cognac as Dunby railed on about the banking industry, as if Clay had something to do with it, which, if one considered the size of the blind trust, he certainly did.

This night, Clay greeted Morton, a former executive with *Playboy*, and joked with him about the latest covergirl, then made his way to his usual cream-colored leather booth in the back of the cozy main room. His favorite waiter, the blond with close-cropped hair named Jimmy, presented his martini. Clay waved aside the menu, telling Jimmy he was in the mood for a crabmeat cocktail, "In honor of the crabby fellow who's joining me later."

Clay relaxed with his martini and admired again the LeRoy Neiman sports prints that adorned the wainscotted stucco walls, then began reading the briefing books his aides had prepared for him.

Dunby arrived as Clay was finishing his souffle Grand Marnier. After ordering a cognac, the rotund Congressman from Michigan settled into his side of the booth and lit a cigarette. "...I've admired you for a long time, Clay. I admire any man who can charm the rattles off a snake."

"Is that what you came to tell me, that I'm charming?"

Dunby chuckled. "Oh, it just helps to start off with a compliment. I came here to let you know that it's my responsibility to tell people that the majority of the banking industry, your grandfather for one, are playing craps with the safety and soundness of the system. The voodoo's going to hit the fan, I'll promise you that."

Nodding bemusedly, Clay sipped his cognac.

"You know as well as I do that the bank insurance fund is broke," Dunby went on. "The cost to the taxpayers'll hit $140 billion in cash up-front."

"That's the same factoid you gave on 'Nightline,'" Clay smirked.

"Joke if you want to but it was some program. I love that Koppel. Get on there every chance I get." He blew smoke into the shaded lamp on the table.

"You would," Clay muttered. He had slept uncomfortably after watching the telecast. Dunby had revealed that the top ten banks had given one-third of all gifts given to Congressmen. The reason for this generosity was to secure so-called reforms enabling banks to create Japanese-style behemoths that could sell insurance, underwrite securities, develop real estate, drill for oil, even manufacture automobiles. "It's a conflict of interest," Dunby told millions of viewers. "The banks would have access to funds in the worst of times under the most favorable terms. They'll reduce competition and increase their fees."

Now Dunby was telling Clay: "That's the power of TV. I'm just beginning to see how we can use the media to change things, build them up, not tear them down."

"I take it you're all for the *Globe* and the *Star* and the *National Enquirer* - "

"Oh, they can serve a purpose. Look what they did to that bastard Bill Clinton. We don't need another Kennedy in the White House. Those rags bring out things the Post would be ashamed to."

"I wonder who paid that Flowers woman to come forward."

Dunby chuckled. "You bankers are all the same. It always gets down to a matter of money, doesn't it?"

Clay shook his head. He knew the secret of negotiation was to break the deal into smaller, tradable parts and he wondered what Dunby was really after, how much it was going to cost him.

"You people are making a slow-motion run on the nation's banks and it's going to be the S&L scandal all over again."

"Look, John, for godsakes stop saying 'you people.' I am a Congressman now, not a banker."

"A leopard doesn't change its spots. You might as well be one of your own lobbyists."

"I don't think this is going anywhere," Clay said firmly.

"What, you're having flashes of conscience?"

Flushed, Clay started to rise from the booth.

"Wait." Dunby held up his hand. "Don't go just yet. I think this could go very far indeed." He tossed three photographs across the table and Clay picked them up. They had been taken with a telephoto lens and were blurred but the images were distinct: the dock at the Harris fishing lodge was in the background. In the foreground, on a path leading down to the dock, were Clay and Stuart. In one photo, Clay had his hands clamped on Stuart's Speedo-clad buns. In another, Stuart was holding Clay's hand, walking back to the lodge. And in the last, Stuart and Clay were kissing, Clay's hands still firmly planted on the boy's buttocks. Clay remembered what he had told Stuart, "I live for days like this."

Dunby took a long drag on his cigarette, then said: "You can keep those prints if you like. I have the negatives locked away."

Without comment, Clay slipped the photographs into his breast pocket, signed the check, and strode from the restaurant, his head held high.

Epilogue

Clay could hardly imagine a more idyllic place. From their bedroom terrace, and from the bed itself, in Room 108 of the Hotel Splendido, the shape of the skyline bell tower of the Church of San Giorgio was echoed by a single rounded cypress. Other cypress trees, more slender and pointed, punctuated the dense, subtropical vegetation as if they were exclamation marks, as did the masts of the yachts at anchor in the harbor.

In the morning, the birdsong that awakened Clay was magical, almost as magical as his lover's exclamations, the sighs, the groans, as they made love the night before.

With the arrival of the waiter bringing in the breakfast cart, Stuart stirred in the bed, evoking Clay's image of him in the gilded light of evening, nude, as they made love for the third time that day, their second full day in Portofino. Clay preferred the fishing village turned resort to Saint-Tropez and Capri, mainly because of the hotel, grand in the classic continental tradition, set amid peach, orange, and lemon trees, accented by trailing jasmine. Clay enjoyed the cosmopolitan clientele of beautiful people, Germans, Belgians, Dutchmen, French, and English and many who arrived by limousines with Swiss and Milanese license plates.

As Stuart rose from the bed, Clay was beginning his breakfast on the terrace. After relieving himself, the boy pulled on his robe and joined his lover. "I love you," he said, kissing Clay on top of his head as he slid into his chair.

Clay beamed.

As they planned their day, with a speedboat ride over the clear green waters of the gulf to Santa Margerita Ligure, Clay knew he had never been happier in his life. And after breakfast, they went back to bed and made love for over an hour. It remained a source of amazement to Clay how Stuart relished sex. A prosaic listing of their acts could in no way approximate the mysterious bliss of their lovemaking. But no matter what form their sex took, Stuart always wanted to end up in the same position, facing Clay, in his arms, surrendering to him. He would let Clay come first and then finish himself while Clay remained inside of him.

On this glorious morning, after they both had come and were lying back recovering, Clay was content that everything he had been through had been worth it. Amanda would not agree to a divorce, so they merely separated. She stood firm in her conviction that the affair between her husband and the person she called "that beach bum" would die of its own accord.

Redistricting had indeed changed the electoral shape of the state and it became a graceful time for Clay to bow out. He took over the Harris Foundation and moved it into a suite of offices at the bank's virtually empty office tower in Tampa. Like Paul, he vowed to spend only a week a month at the office. He would work out of the beachhouse, his cellular phone never far from his hand. And to give DeWitt one more thing to do, one more reason to live, Clay appointed him a director. "I'll accept, provided I get free tickets to the New Ballet."

"I'll ask Stuart," Clay chuckled. "But they'll have to be season tickets. You'll have to attend every show."

"It'll be worth it."

With the success of his show, Stuart signed a contract with the New Ballet as assistant director and choreographer and agreed to continue tutoring on Saturdays. He begged Clay to rent him a small apartment in Tampa so that he could be nearer the theater. "And besides, I want you to miss me," Stuart told him. At first, Clay was cool to the idea of his lover being in town while he was at the beach but he was willing to give Stuart the benefit of the doubt.

"You have to give him his space," Paul counseled. "And you need your space, too. You know how long a leash I give Marco."

Clay sighed. "I guess I'm finally eating my cake and having it, too."

"Yes, now you've got it," Paul chuckled.

And even if Amanda was right, that the affair couldn't last, at least he had seized the moment.

For his part, Stuart still had nagging doubts he could pull off a *pas de deux* in real life but, when he was in bed with Clay, the older man on top of him, taking him, he felt they were somehow one and, perhaps, they could go on dancing alone, together.

Photography for STARbooks furnished courtesy of the
Brown Bag Company. For information on available Brown
Bag products, send a self-addressed, stamped envelope
(with over 21 signature) to
Brown Bag Co., P. 0. Box 1067,
Los Angeles CA 90078.

The KiD

The Confessions of a Rock Star's
Secret Young Lover

A Shocking Love Story by
JOHN PATRICK

The KiD

The Confessions of a Rock Star's Secret Young Lover

A Shocking Love Story by
JOHN PATRICK

With Joe Leslie

STARbooks Press
Sarasota, FL

Books by John Patrick
Non-Fiction
The Best of the Superstars 1990
A Charmed Life: Vince Cobretti
Lowe Down: Tim Lowe
The Best of the Superstars 1991
Legends: The World's Sexiest Men, Vol. 1
The Best of the Superstars 1992
What Went Wrong? When Boys Are Bad & Sex Goes Wrong

Fiction
Billy & David: A Deadly Minuet
The Bigger They Are...
The Younger They Are...
The Harder They Are...
Angel: The Complete Trilogy
Angel II: Stacy's Story
Angel: The Complete Quintet
A Natural Beauty (Ed.)
The Kid (with Joe Leslie)
STRIP: He Danced Alone
Huge (Ed.)

Library of Congress Card Catalogue No. 91-067530
ISBN No. 1 877978-27-2

I Knew This Kid

I knew this skinny little kid
   Who never wanted to play tackle football at all
But thought he'd better if he wanted
   His daddy to love him and to prove his courage
And things like that.
   I remember him holding his breath
And closing his eyes
   And throwing a block into a guy twice his size
Proving he was brave enough to be loved, and crying softly
   Because his tailbone hurt
And his shoes were so big they made him stumble.

I knew this skinny little kid
   With sky-blue eyes and soft brown hair
Who liked cattails and pussy willows,
   Sumac huts and sassafras.
Who liked chestnuts and pine cones and oily walnuts,
   Lurking foxes and rabbits munching lilies,
Secret caves and moss around the roots of oaks,
   Beavers and muskrats and gawking herons.
And I wonder what he would have been
   If someone had loved him for
Just following the fawns and building waterfalls
   And watching the white rats have babies.
I wonder what he would have been
   If he hadn't played tackle football at all.

- James Kavanaugh
"Will You Be My Friend?"
Published by
Steven J. Nash

JOE SKINNER
Sings Songs of Love

I REMEMBER YOU

"I love comebacks. Of course, the best way to make a comeback is not leave in the first place."

- Joe Skinner

Prologue

"I'll show ya how, kid," Kenny said.

And, as simple as that, a new way of life started for me. "Most of the older dudes wanta blow ya or want your prick up their ass. They like to get fucked by a young, good lookin' stud. Some of 'em'll wanta screw ya, too, and if they do, charge 'em more. Lots more." I nodded. That'll be the day, I thought, when I let anybody stick anything up my ass.

When we arrived at his little furnished room up three flights of stairs, I told him I felt like I needed a shower and he said he wanted to bathe me. Well, okay, I thought, I can act like a baby if that's what turns him on. He soaped me all over very carefully in a kind of neutral way, not lingering anywhere except maybe to massage my nipples and then he dried me with a big towel as if he were my mother. After he had rubbed me dry, he found some oil and had me lie on my stomach on the bed and he went over me very slowly, deliberately, starting at my shoulders and then moving on, down my spine, over my hips and ass, then sliding his hand in, down between my legs until I squirmed. I couldn't believe it but I had an erection. As he was massaging the soles of my feet, I was ready to come.

I reached down and stroked my cock. "Hey, wait," he said. "Wait for me."

He rolled me over and climbed onto the bed, his knees between my legs, pushing them apart to make a V. Then he put his hand down, rubbing my prick and balls. "Yeah, ya got a helluva nice big one. Make it work for ya, never settle for less'n twenty."

His lips rested gently on mine. It wasn't really a kiss, just lips touching lips. Then his tongue moved to the right side of my chest, then the left, then down, finally coming to rest on the head of my cock. I ran my fingers through his hair. He flicked his tongue around the head of my cock and then swallowed the whole thing, down to the pubic hairs. "Oh, shit," I cried, moving my hips upward.

He slid his hands under my raised ass and a finger began to probe my asshole. He kept sucking, expertly, until I was ready again; then he pulled away. "Never rush the guy. Ya never know who might become your sugar daddy." He climbed off the bed and started to undress.

I watched intently as his shorts dropped to the floor. I sighed when I saw his cock. It was smaller than mine but it seemed much more elegant, perfectly shaped, standing out like a rose in full bloom. I'd never seen a prettier one.

"Now, you try it," he said, stroking it.

Seconds before, I was hornier than I'd ever been in my life, but my cock went soft. I shook.

"Just lick it," he instructed. I tried it. It tasted good. I made out like I wasn't in any hurry but I was. He groaned a little. It was not so much from pleasure as impatience. He nudged me and I began to suck him the way he had sucked me. The more of it I took in, the more I wanted. But I let it slide from my mouth so I could lick the wiry hair on his balls and feel the weight of them as they lolled against my tongue. Then I moved up to the crease between his balls and thigh to the very root of his sweet dick. I toyed with the hair at the base of his cock, then moved a few inches where his belly began, soft, hairy. I found his navel and nuzzled my nose in it. He groaned again. I could feel him tense with excitement as I lowered my head and took the shaft between my lips.

He began thrusting it into me and I held on. "Oh, yeah. But hold it. Take it easy. We ain't even halfway through the lesson."

And he pulled away again and lit a cigarette. I lay there, silent, stroking myself, watching him pushing smoke rings to the ceiling. "Yeah, you're a pretty one all right. You'll do good. Nice cock, decent bod. Yeah, you'll make it."

When he finished his cigarette, he took some lube from the drawer and applied it on my cock. "Shit, man, guys are really gonna love this - " It crossed my mind maybe he was speaking for himself more than anyone else, so anxious was he to lower himself over it, have it in him. He tilted his head back and closed his eyes. I just lay there, letting him guide it in. As he bounced up and down on it for a while, I enjoyed the sensations of the energy that hovered over me, taking me in, then out. "Oh, yeah!" he cried.

Soon he was lifting himself off, away from me and lying back down on the bed. He spread his legs wide and I got between them.

He took my slick cock in his hand and guided it in again. When it was all the way in, he grabbed my ass and held me tightly.

I began. It seemed like every part of my body was singing. I could see my prick, then I couldn't. His hard stomach muscles rippled as he worked his ass in a fury beneath me. The hair of his legs, now resting on my shoulders, caressed each side of my face.

The way I look at it, when your meat's up and pressing, straining, does it matter where it goes? I'd fucked a couple of cunts back in Ohio but this, this was different. He knew how to touch, how to stroke, to get a guy so horny there'd be a real show. After all, he said, it was his business. He saw me getting off the bus and offered to carry my suitcase. It was as if he was expecting me. In a way, he was. "I like to get 'em when they're fresh," he told me after buying me dinner. "I was fresh once myself."

The sensations I was feeling were so new, so foreign. The tightness sort of hurt at first, then, as the whole length of my cock settled into him, it was warm, moist, and it seemed it was inviting me to linger there. But I didn't. I withdrew, but quickly plunged back in. Dazed, I just kept on, calmly, almost mechanically. When I opened my eyes, I saw him smiling, watching me as I worked over him. Gently he moved his hands up and down my arms, then massaged my neck and left his hands there, still watching, enjoying the view, moaning low. I took his cock in my hand and stroked it. It wasn't long before he was coming and I realized I was coming, too. But even after I shot my load, I was still hard and not ready to stop. He just groaned, closed his eyes and held me as I kept on.

It was a long night, perhaps the longest of my young life.

From the LP "I Remember You"/Sung by Joe Skinner/Side 1, Cut 1, "I
Remember You:" "...You're the one who made my dreams come true / A
few kisses ago / I remember you / You're the one who said / I love you, too
/ I do, didn't you know? / Oh, I remember, too / A distant bell / And stars
that fell / Like rain / Out of the blue / When my life is through / And the
angels ask me to recall / That thrill of them all / Then I shall tell them /
I remember you."

"Ya gotta advertise, man. Kid like you could get killed on the
street." That was Kenny's advice. So he helped me run an ad. And
got me a beeper. I was in business.

"Photo. Ya gotta run a fuckin' photo," Kenny told me later when
I bitched because we got only two calls. "Kid like you, shit, it's all
in the photo. Let 'em see some of what they're gonna get."

I didn't have a fucking photo; nothing but a couple of Polaroids
a guy took of me once. But a guy who picked me up on the street
one time told me if I ever needed some photos, he'd even pay me
to pose. I searched for the business card for three days and finally
found it. "John D. Strange, Master Photographer." That's all it said,
with the phone number in tiny type. I called.

Strange said he didn't remember me but if he'd given me his card,
I had to be a hot number so he agreed to see me. I took a cab to the
address on Sunset, way out, almost to the ocean.

"...Oh, yes, how could I forget?" he laughed when he saw me,
then he groped me.

"I just need a shot to put with my ad," I said, pulling away. If he
wanted it, he was going to have to pay.

"A whole layout or nothing."

"I dunno." I started to get the hell outta there.

"I'll tell you what," he said, moving close again, touching my
shoulder. "I'm a fair man. I don't take advantage of boys. I'll be
able to get several hundred dollars for a layout on you. 'In Touch,'
'Advocate Men,' one of 'em'll eat it up. So, you spend the night and
I'll give you the photo you need, with a negative, and I'll throw in

a hundred-dollar tip. How's that sound?"

I took his hand and placed it on my groin. "Like fuckin' music to my ears."

And fucking, not music, was certainly what he had in mind. "That blow job I gave you in my car, parked on that side street, that was just for starters," he said, finally remembering.

He took me to his house, a comfortable little place in Malibu. He decided I would look best in a bed and he had the perfect one for it, a round one with pink silk sheets and funny pillows with lace on them. He said he wanted to soften my "stud" look and I said, "Sure." I was used to being whatever the john wanted. Kenny had taught me that. He had me playing every role, even dressing in drag. He got off eating my asshole out when I had black lace nylons on and a nightie. It blew my mind.

Strange wanted me to be a sissy, too, I knew that right off. It began with the make-up. There had to be make-up. He said, "No imperfections in my pictures."

It took him an hour to get it all right. The lip gloss was the crowning touch.

But it was more than just for the pictures. He wanted to have a real sissy fuck him. I couldn't figure it. Pose, pose, then jab, jab. It got to be boring as hell but I played along.

We stopped for dinner. He wanted to take me out. "I want to show you off to my friends," he said.

When we were seated at a cozy table at the Sandbar, he ordered drinks and then toasted me. "To my next star."

"Me, a star? You gotta be crazy!"

"Oh, it won't be the first time a photo layout of mine has led to a kid becoming a movie star."

"Yeah, who?"

"Jeff Bailey, for one."

"Never heard of 'im."

"How many gay videos do you watch in a week? In a month?"

"None."

"Well, see. How would you know him? But he's big, I'll tell you that. He posed for me two years ago and now he's made ten videos. When we get back to the house I'll show you one."

Looking at Jeff Bailey I couldn't believe anybody would want to fuck him much less take a picture of him or put him in a video. Strange went on and on about him, though, and I just couldn't figure it. Maybe he gave great head but you couldn't tell it by the video. Then Strange told me what must have been Bailey's secret. "He can get it up just like that," he said, snapping his fingers. "Never fails. They call him 'ever ready.'"

I can do that, I thought. Kenny taught me. When I'm with a trick I don't like, all I have to do is close my eyes and think of Kenny and I get hard. Just the thought of fucking him and bang! It's unreal but it works every time. But then, after a while, I have to open my eyes and reality kicks in and it's a struggle, especially when they get greedy, even after you've come and they've come, they want more. Always more. More and more these days, I have to think of Kenny. And not just fucking Kenny, either. Sometimes, suckin' him. That cock that could only be described as elegant. They go on and on about my cock, but Kenny's cock, that's the prize.

Strange had some silk panties that matched the sheets and he had me slip them on. He liked sucking me through the fabric until I was hard, then bent over at the waist. He watched in the mirror as I slid my cock and balls across his ass. He moaned, loving the feel of the silk against his skin, "Oh, honey. Honey, honey, honey."

I slipped the silk down and shoved my cock between his cheeks. As I entered him, he cried, "Oh, baby. God, it's so big - I can't take it. I can't! I...Oh, it feels so good."

Jacking off as I slammed into him, he screamed, "You're such a little queen, but you have such a big dick! Oh, fuck me, fuck me raw, baby, I love it."

When he came, he said, "Oh, you little fairies know how to fuck." I couldn't fuckin' figure it but I wasn't being paid to figure it.

After dinner, we started the whole routine over again, only with lighting, lighting all over the place. I'd pose, then he'd suck me and get it up, then shoot some more, then bend over. I'd do it for awhile, then it was back to shooting again until he decided he'd had plenty of poses.

I'd agreed to stay the night but I was so anxious to see the photos that I begged him to take the film to the studio and develop them. He had shot a roll of black and white just for me so that was what he processed, first as a proof sheet. There were 36 pictures, each one better than the other. He really was good, I had to admit it. I didn't know which one to pick so he suggested three. He said the magazine wouldn't run a full nude anyway so he decided to make a print just for them. Trimming me right below my belly button, he laughed, "I'm cropping out your best feature but that's the way it is. They'll have to pay to see it."

*

And pay they did. I had ten calls the first day and it kept getting busier. It was so busy, I was glad that just after I had gotten here I'd done all the stuff I'd always wanted to do if I ever visited L.A., like go to the Walk of Fame and the Chinese Theater and see some TV shows being filmed. I even went downtown on the bus to see them film a scene for a movie at the Park Plaza hotel. But the reality of it didn't impress me. Somebody working the lights told me that they were spending an entire day on a scene that would take less than two minutes in the actual movie, just Dudley Moore running into the hotel and into an elevator. I figured I had better things to do, like watch the movies on my TV.

Then I got a call from a guy who said his name was Van and he said he ran "the best damn escort service in the country, the Beverly Hills All-Stars." He said Kenny had told him all about me and he knew I was one of "his kind" of boys. I made an appointment for the next day.

*From the LP "I Remember You" /Sung by Joe Skinner/Side One, Cut Two,
"I Won't Send Roses:" "My heart is too much in control / The lack of
romance in my soul / Will turn you gray, kid / So stay away, kid / Forget
my shoulder / When you're in need / Forgetting birthdays is guaranteed
/ And should I love you / You would be the last to know / I won't send roses
/ And roses suit you so."*

"Gorgeous ass," Van said as I turned around, displaying myself
for him. "My clients'll love plugging that."

"I don't get fucked."

"Everybody says that at first."

"No. I just don't. Never will."

"Well, it's a pity. Ass like that could go for two hundred easy.
Maybe more."

"Gettin' fucked is for queers."

He brought his pudgy fingers to his lips. "I'm sure you've heard
the expression, 'Yesterday's trade-'"

"Yeah, but I ain't trade. I know trade. It's just that, well, the idea
of gettin' fucked is such a turn-off for me. I've had guys try it and
I just couldn't handle it."

"I would have loved to have been there," he murmured.

"Yeah, I guess you would've had to have been there all right."

"I meant, I've been around a long time. Seen everything." He ran
his hand across his bald head. "You were just scared. Maybe I
could have helped the situation."

"Nobody could've helped that situation, believe me."

"Well, in today's world, you can get by very easily never even
pulling your pants down. It's a whole different scene than it was
when I started in this business back in the '70s."

He went on and on and I tuned out, looking about the room, a
shabby place with funny little cats running all around. Beverly
Hills my ass.

"Yeah, well," I said, finally, remembering an old movie I saw
once, "Hell's Angels," "my philosophy is like Jean Harlow's."

"Oh?"

"Yeah, she said, 'Life's short and I want to live while I'm alive.'"

"I hope you do. The more living you do, the more money I'll make."

He'd hold one cat, pet it for awhile, then it'd leave and another one would jump on his lap. I knew I would be calling him Catman before long. "Van the Catman," I giggled.

"What?"

"Oh, nothin'. You sure love your cats."

"Only kind of lovin' I can get any more. Sad, isn't it?"

I understood him completely. On the farm, the animals were my lovers. I had a cat once, too, before the girl down the road dropped it over the back staircase so that his skull cracked. And we'd been told cats always landed on their feet.

"Shit, what you talkin' about? I mean, you got all these boys."

"Oh, my no! After the first interview, I never see my boys again. They pick up their money from the box downstairs. They hardly ever make it back up here. You, on the other hand, you could come up any time."

"How do you know? You ain't even seen the best part of me."

"Kenny told me but, okay, if you're so proud of it, show me. But slowly, so I can enjoy it. I won't touch. I don't touch any more. Sad, isn't it?"

I didn't answer. By my silence I was agreeing with him about how sad everything was for him and that's why I wanted to give him some pleasure right at this moment, so I loosened the zipper and lowered it slowly, like he told me to, moving closer to where he was sitting on the couch. As I pushed the jeans down my hips my cock slipped out, then my balls. I stood there, not moving.

"Oh, god, it is pretty. How big does it get?"

I closed my eyes and thought about Kenny. My cock sprang to full attention.

"Wow!" He swallowed hard. "Step just a bit closer."

His hand left the cat's spine and stroked my cock, as if he was petting it, too.

"My oh my, what I would have done with that in the old days. Hmmm." He gently squeezed my balls. "Such a stud. Such a stud." His hand returned to his cat, who was purring loudly. "Oh, I've heard about you, you know. I was curious how long it would take Kenny to start advertising you. Well, you can forget Kenny, forget all of that now. You're working exclusively for me. You go where

I say and do as I say and we'll be fine. There's not many that can get it up no matter what."

"Yeah, no matter what."

"Okay, you can put it away."

I was suddenly glad he didn't want me to perform for him. I'd had fatter, uglier johns before, but there was something about him that was beginning to turn my stomach, even if he did like animals.

"For a kid like you, there's films, too, you know. There's one shooting right now just down the street. All you'd have to do is go onto the set, pull it out and let three guys give you head. Want me to book you?"

"How much?" I asked, stuffing myself back into my jeans.

"Two fifty. But only if you come for the camera."

I didn't hesitate a second. "I'll take it."

From the LP "I Remember You" / Sung by Joe Skinner / Side 1, Cut 3, "Easy to Love:" "...You'd be so easy to love / So easy to idolize all others above...We'd be so grand at the game / So carefree together / That it does seem a shame / That you can't see your future with me / Because you'd be, oh, so easy to love."

The Catman was right. It was the easiest thing I'd ever done. I just walked onto what they called a set, something out of one of those movies that they're always saying are the worst ones ever made, like "Plan Nine from Outer Space." I walked right up to the man with the camera, an ugly man in his mid 30's with fuzzy hair. "I've been a movie fan all my life," I told him, and he just stared at me as if I wasn't there.

"Just take your clothes off, kid and put this on," the director yelled at me.

"And be quick about it, we ain't got all day, you know."

So much for learning about movie-making, if you could call that movie-making.

He handed me a little silver bikini and after I was ready, I was told to walk through this dry ice as if I was from outer space, visiting these three guys on a spaceship. There were no preliminaries. They were all over me, yanking my bikini off and sliding down on their knees around me and going at it. I was more interested in what was happening alongside us, the taping of it, than I was the action.

It took less than an hour for them to shoot me having my cock blown. The fuzzy haired man must have taken it from every angle six times. When I came, they went nuts. The guys kept kissing me all over while they jacked off. When everybody had come, the director talked about another movie the following week. "You're good, kid," he said.

I signed a release and got my fee in cash. "Hey," the assistant, a skinny guy named Jerry, yelled as I was leaving, "what name do you wanta go by?"

I was startled. I didn't think I'd have my name in the credits or anything.

He laughed, "Not that it makes any fuckin' difference because they'll probably change it anyway, but we always ask."

"My name's William, William Kidd. But they've always just called me 'kid.' Like in, 'Hey, you kid' or Billy the Kid. Yeah, that's it, just call me 'The Kid.'"

*

Three days later, the Catman got me another job. He asked me if I could fuck a woman as well as I fucked a man. "Sure," I said.

...Brandy came to the set in a little black tube of a skirt and high black boots and a tank top held to the skirt by teeny suspenders, creating the impression that her whole body was in a garter belt. It was an outfit that backhome would have the local boys hanging out of their car windows and howling at her. The director got her topless right off.

The first scene had me on my back and her doing what they called a backwards cowgirl. Brandy didn't want to do it. "Yuck! It's so unnatural. His dick goes one way, my body goes the other. And with a cock that big, it'll hurt." But the director said that's what they wanted and she had to do it. "Great view of the action," he said as he prepared to film it. She blew me a while and then did her thing. They said I didn't have to come until the next scene but she went through all sorts of gyrations making believe she had six or seven orgasms.

"...This ain't the job I dreamed about in college," she told me matter-of-factly while we are waiting for the other guy to arrive to film the next scene. "Can you imagine what it's like to tell people you just made a movie called 'The Slut?'"

"No, I can't imagine." I wanted to tell her about the movie I made last week but I didn't. I didn't want her to think I was carrying some kind of virus.

"...I told my daddy; I says, look, Pa, nobody pays me to sit at home. First I was in a John Robert Powers Modelling School but there was this ugly bitch with five facelifts tellin' ya how to walk with an umbrella and how to get in and outta a car. I mean, let's get real."

"Not what you planned, eh?"

"Honey, I never make a plan, " she winked. "I kinda think whatever happens, happens; you know what I mean?"

"Yeah, I sure do."

She went on talking. She said she loved to shop in thrift stores. I told her that's the only place I ever shopped and we sort of hit it off right then. And she was crushed that the pair of huge dangling clock earrings she wanted were $25, out of her price range. "Will yah git 'em for me, kid, soon as this is over?"

"Sure, we'll run right over."

The guy, a stocky, smelly Cuban who said his name was Juan and who everybody called "Don Juan," entered from the right. Brandy made a face but she went right ahead and made herself comfortable on the mattress that had been laid out on the floor of the gas station. The action started with a close-up of her running her hand across Juan's naked ass. They were shooting it from two angles because, they said, they needed one version for soft core, like for cable TV, the other for video cassettes.

As she opened her mouth to take Juan's still limp prick, she turned to me and whispered, "You know, I came out here more to be warm than to act."

"Hey, bitch, you're gonna be real warm in a minute," the director yelled at her. "Now cut the crap 'n suck that dick."

She seemed so much like me, so plain, so stupid, so honest, I suddenly felt sorry for her. I even felt sorry for Don Juan, not being able to get it up, and then I even began to feel sorry for myself. I liked fucking in private better than this. This was somehow taking being a whore too far. I decided I didn't want to do any more movies but that I would give them their money's worth.

"Okay, kid, let her suck both of yah."

I knelt down next to Don Juan and she struggled trying to get both of our cocks in her mouth at the same time, my hard one and Don's limp one. She worked one, then the other, then finally took them both. I had been told not to touch Don Juan, that this was a strictly straight video and men don't touch each other. I was glad about that because Juan was sweaty and too hairy for my taste. I looked up at the ceiling while Brandy went at it. One cameraman was shooting from the rear, the other aiming right at our dicks, getting every stroke as she went back and forth, then together. I wasn't getting off on this at all. I closed my eyes and thought about Kenny.

"...Okay, Juan you first."

Shit, I thought, I wanted to go first. Why didn't they let me fuck her pussy first, then it would have been over with and I could have collected my $200 and gone home. I straddled her head and began plowing into her mouth while Don fucked her cunt. I kept thinking about Kenny.

This scene seemed to go on for hours. My cock was really beginning to hurt. She tried her best but Juan was throwing it into her so hard, trying to get it hard, she'd slip and bite me. The cameramen were all over us. I began to really sweat and I hate to sweat. Then I felt myself going soft. I couldn't lose my hardon, not now. I kept thinking about Kenny and stroked it and suddenly I started to come. She gagged, tried to pull away, I grabbed for it, held it high, and came all over her face. One camera was on it and they were all cheering me.

"Great shot, kid. What a fuckin' load!"

After I climbed off of her and headed for the john, Juan just kept on. Poor Brandy just lay there with my juice all over her face. When I walked back into the garage, somebody had given her a towel and she was wiping her face. Her makeup was getting smeared all over and she looked like the slut I suppose she was. Juan just kept on. I couldn't believe it. Finally, the director yelled cut and we took a break.

"...You ready?" he asked me.

"Ready? I came. What more do you want?"

"You gotta fuck her, kid."

"No, man. Not for a million dollars." I didn't care if it ended my porn career.

I'd already made up my mind that wasn't something I wanted to do.

*

"I can't believe you did that!" Kenny screamed when I met him at the coffee shop off Sunset near Vine and told him I'd signed with Van and made a video, all in one day.

"When you're hot you're hot."

"Look, kid, porno's no good. And Van's dangerous. He'll book you into the worst scenes. A kid like you, you'll get the worst fuckin' scenes he can come up with."

"But you told him about me."

"Sure I did. But I didn't think you'd go for it. I get a finder's fee for every kid I send up there. But you didn't have to agree to workin' for him, much less a porno! Shit!" He shook his head angrily. "Look, I thought you'd just go up there and then run like crazy. Once he's into you, he wouldn't budge. No, Van's gotta have it all. And now he's got it."

"I can quit any time I want. I walked off the set. I don't want to do any more porno."

"Now that you're with Van you'd better not pull any more shit like that. You wouldn't be able to get shit in this town if you fucked him over. No, you're on your way, all right. Where to, I fuckin' don't know, but you're on your way."

I wanted Kenny to be jealous. Not mad about Van, just jealous that I was having sex all the time with everybody but him. Instead, he was mad at not getting a piece of the action. And, damn him, he looked better than I'd seen him in a long time. He'd dried out and was just sipping black coffee. Still, I knew it was only a matter of time before he'd start with the coke again. That's why I never started, because I knew I wouldn't be able to stop. "Just a joint now and then," I would tell everybody. But now it was Kenny's joint I was thinking about. When I was with him, it was hard to think about the business, about anything else. It had been so long. I could almost taste it.

"...You want to come back to my place?" I asked him as we left the coffee shop.

"Nah, kid, I gotta meet a bus. You know how it is."

Nodding, I stood there feeling like an idiot, not knowing what to say.

From the LP "I Remember You"/Sung by Joe Skinner/Side 1, Cut 4, "Unforgettable:" "Unforgettable | That's what you are | Unforgettable | Though near or far | Like a song of love that clings to me | How thoughts of you do things to me | Never before has someone been more | Unforgettable."

"Now that you're a porn star..." Van said over the phone.

"What?" I interrupted.

"Well, you did a couple of 'em and even if you never make any more - "

"I won't." He was still smarting from my walk-out. He hadn't called me in four days. I was getting desperate. I missed the business Kenny threw my way.

"Well, even if you don't, now you're a star, at least as far as the Star Fucker's concerned."

"The who?"

"I call him the Star Fucker. He's somebody in the music business I think. I don't know much about him really, 'cept he only wants guys that have been in pornos. And real studs. No sissies. Guys with big dicks that can always get it up. Guys with a history. Makes 'im feel safe, he says. Like, 'I got the goods on you, kid.'"

He was silent for a minute, waiting for me to say something but I didn't have anything to say.

"Yeah, the guy pays big bucks to have a porn stud fuck him."

"A stud? Me, a stud?"

"Well, you've the dick for it, kid."

"Yeah, and I sure don't have any trouble gettin' it up, unlike others I've seen that say they're studs, but I'm just a kid."

Just a kid but I learn quickly. Since I'd been in L.A., I learned a lot can depend on a little. After not having had much sex except with myself, suddenly sex was all there was. I just had to stand on the street corner and in a few minutes it would start again. In the beginning, it was a high more incredible, I was sure, than any fuckin' drug. I didn't need drugs. I'd seen so many kids hung up on drugs, I didn't want that. Me, I'd been set free by sex. The men became faceless. I just remembered cocks. And I learned what turned their little peckers on. I wasn't like the rest of the boys, in a hurry to get it over with so they could buy more crack. I even played hard to get, willing yet not so willing. I teased 'em. Teased 'em into wanting more. Yeah, a lot can depend on a little.

"Well, shit, where do I have to go?" I finally asked him.

"Way out almost to the beach. And allow youself plenty of time. Shit, I wish you had a fuckin' car."

"So do I. But hell, even if I could afford it, I couldn't drive it worth shit -"

"What?"

"Oh, never mind. I can handle a tractor on a field but I'm trouble behind the wheel of a car, man, that's all."

"Well, whatever," he said. I could hear the second line cutting in. He was busy all right, just not booking me. Till now. "Well, just give yourself plenty of time."

*

I didn't follow the Catman's advice. Sometimes I lose track of time and when I finally got my shit together and caught a cab we got stuck in a jam on the freeway. The driver swore we'd make better time on the freeway than just going out Sunset and we ended up waiting for 45 minutes, with the driver going on and on about his addiction to Ex-lax. Finally, I got out of the cab, walked down to the street and hitched a ride. I was at least an hour late. It was a place called the Lonely Sands Motel. I found the room right away. Just like Van said it would be, a sea green 1967 Chevy Malibu convertible was parked in front of the door. I knocked but there was no answer. I tried the door, it opened. It was late afternoon on a Sunday and the smog hadn't lifted all day so it was dull and gray, and I stepped into a dull, gray room. The spread had been pulled off the double bed and lying on the white sheets was a dude, on his stomach, nude. I stepped into the room and closed the door behind me. What struck me right off was the guy's back. I've seen naked backs but this was right out of the magazines. Like he was modelling for Calvin Klein. And then the ass. Absolutely perfect. More muscular looking than mine and very white against the deeply tanned rest of him. His left arm stretched across the bed and hung over the side. A bottle of Jack Daniels lay on the floor, nearly empty. He looked for all the world like he was dead but I figured he just passed out from drinking. It was my fault. If I'd been on time, he wouldn't have drunk so much and we'd be finished by now. I cleared my throat over and over, louder and louder, stepping closer and closer.

"Hey, man," I said finally, shaking his shoulder. He didn't come to. I looked around the room. There was a pair of tattered button-fly jeans hanging over a chair. I checked 'em out. No wallet, just a roll of cash, maybe $200, and car keys on a silver skull 'n' crossbones ring. I stuffed all of it back into the pockets of the jeans. There was a pair of black cowboy boots, very expensive ones, socks, and a smooth black silk shirt just thrown on the floor. Another bottle of bourbon and a liter of Coke sat on the bureau with a bucket of ice and some glasses, next to a pair of gold-rimmed Ray-Ban aviator sunglasses. I poured myself a Coke and sat on the edge of the bed. I waited.

I finally turned on the TV, real low, and watched a couple of movies. The end of one and the beginning of another. I'd seen them both before but I enjoyed 'em again coming up with the dialogue before the actors even got it out of their mouths.

Finally, the Star Fucker groaned and rolled over. The front view was even better than the back. His face reminded me of my hero, Randy Travis. And so did his torso. His legs were thin, a bit hairy, but his stomach was smooth, with a nice tuft of dark pubic hair. The cock, thick with a small head, hung to the left, with nice pink hairy balls. I leaned back between his legs and took his cock in my hand. I stroked it several times until he began groaning. Slowly he opened his eyes, then began blinking wildly. "What the?" he said, lifting himself up on his elbows.

I didn't say anything, just took the head of his cock between my lips and began sucking.

He looked at his watch. "How long you been here?"

"Coupla hours I guess. I'm not good with time."

He collapsed back on the bed. "Shit, shit, shit," he said, over and over.

Finally, he pushed me away. "Hey, I gotta get goin', kid. I'm late already."

"I'm the one who was late. I'm really sorry but the cab got stuck in traffic."

"Cab?"

"Yeah. I don't have a car."

"No fuckin' car in L.A.? What are you, nuts?" he asked, standing up.

When he stood up he was enough to take your breath away but I was able to mumble, "Yeah, I guess I am nuts." I wanted him in the worst way.

Suddenly he lurched forward, then dropped right back down on the bed again. "My head! Shit!"

I leaned against his body. I smelled an expensive cologne I couldn't place. I wanted to start licking his body and never stop. "I'm sorry I was late. It's all my fault." I kissed his shoulder.

"Yeah, yeah, it's all your fuckin' fault." He looked me in the eyes for the first time. "Hey, you're a beautiful little kid, ya know that?"

I blushed.

"Yeah, let me look at you." He took me by the shoulders and held me out as if he was judging me for a contest. "Yeah, you're hot."

"Thanks."

"But I can't believe Van sent you. You're just a fuckin' kid. I bet you're not even 18."

"I am. I've always looked young for my age."

"Well, if Van sent you you must have somethin'. What is it?" He chuckled. "I bet I can guess." His hand dropped to my crotch. He groped me hard. "God, would I love that! But," he said, rising from the bed again, "no time now. I've gotta get back."

He tried to walk but dropped back down on the bed, holding his head. "Christ, my head's killin' me."

"You'll feel better if you take a shower. I'll help you."

...He stayed in the bathroom for ten minutes. Finally he came out drying his hair with a towel. I was watching TV again. "You still here?" he asked with a chuckle.

His cock was semi-hard and I wanted to reach up and suck it again but I just sat there on the edge of the bed, waiting for him. He saw where my eyes were and brought the towel to it, stretching it, then drying the balls. It was a beauty, all right. Just as good as Kenny's. It was my fault, I was late.

He dropped the towel on the floor and picked up his jeans. After he tugged them on, he reached in the pocket and found his money roll. "You know, I can't figure it - "

"Figure what?"

"You find me in a drunken stupor and you don't steal my money or my car. No, you just wait for me to wake up! And then all you want to do is play. You can't have been in Hollywood very long - or the world for that matter!"

"No, I'm just a country boy."

"Oh, which country?"

"Ohio."

He laughed. "Ohio, shit! I'm from Alabama. Now that's country!"

...He said he'd drop me off on Melrose about a block from my little efficiency. He was a fast driver. Lots of weaving. The green buttons glowed on the Alpine car phone but it wasn't ringing. Supertramp was blarring on the stereo: "It's just a heart breaking / I should have known that it would let me down / It's just a mind aching / I used to dream about this town."

"Like that song?"

"No. I like Randy Travis, if you got any of his, like '8 X 10'."

He chuckled. "No, sorry, no country. How 'bout this," he said, pulling out Supertramp and slipping in another cassette. "It's brand new."

The song "Unforgettable" came on. "Nat King Cole," I said.

"Shit, no. One of the newer guys. White guy."

"But he's got soul," I said. "He almost sounds black."

I listened for a few minutes and then said, "Yeah, you can tell he's got soul. Randy Travis has soul, too. That's why I like him."

He chuckled again and turned up the volume.

*

"...What the fuck did you do to the Star Fucker?" Van yelled into the phone.

"I was late."

"Late, shit! You should be late every time! He's never wanted to see anybody more than once, but he wants to see you again. You! I can't fuckin' believe it."

"I can't either."

"Look, it's for tomorrow night. And get this, he'll pick you up at the corner of Melrose and La Brea at 10 sharp. He says, 'Tell him not to be late.'"

"I won't. I'm never gonna be late again."

*

I was early. I pretended like I was waiting for the bus in case the cops drove by. Guys cruised me but I paid no attention. I could've made a hundred just waiting for my date.

"...Glad you could make it," he said. He had a baseball cap with "Sox" on it and his Ray-Bans. Sunglasses in the dark, I thought.

"Glad you invited me." "Unforgettable" was playing on the stereo again. "I'm beginning to like that song."

"Me, too," he said, his hand dropping to my thigh. "Come over here."

I edged closer and leaned against him.

"You're a strange one, you know," he said.

"So are you."

...He didn't waste any time. He turned on Vine and went a block and a half, pulling in at the Econo Lodge. He handed me a fifty. "Rent us a room, okay?"

I got the key and walked to the room while he followed in the car.

I opened the door to the room and held it open for him. He looked both ways before he got out of the Chevy, then came in. Closing the door behind him, he held out his arms. "I'll bet you're a good kisser."

"Not usually." I suddenly realized I'd never kissed a trick. I'd never even kissed Kenny. But I wanted to kiss this guy, whoever he was. I wanted to kiss every part of him.

It was a movie star kiss all right. Like Monty Clift and Liz Taylor in "A Place in the Sun." I didn't care who he was, I wanted to eat him up.

"...Wait, wait," he pleaded when I dropped to my knees in front of him and started to unzip his pants. He pulled me up by the shoulders like he did the last time and held me, staring at me. "Shit, you are a pretty one."

And then he kissed me again. His hands were all over my body, pressing me against him. I ran my hands up and down his back, remembering how gorgeous it was. I smelled the liquor on his breath but I didn't mind. In fact, I was practically getting high from it as he shoved his tongue between my teeth, then started eating my chin, my cheeks, my ears, then my nose. All I wanted to do was eat him up but he was eating me. "Hmmm, you taste so good," he cried and kept at it, pulling my shirt out of my jeans and unbuttoning it, then lowering it off of me. His mouth slid down my neck and onto my shoulders, sucking, biting, kissing, licking. I got a fierce hard-on and rubbed it against him. "Oh, yeah," he cried.

I fell to my knees again, to escape him but also to work on his crotch. I had left the zipper undone and I reached in and grabbed it. He let me this time and I took it all in one gulp, then pulled it out and worked on the balls. He was hard in no time and I blew him like that, on my knees in the fuckin' Econo Lodge on Vine Street. When he was close, I stood up and led him to the bed. Suddenly, he was putty in my hands. If he wanted a porno stud then he was gonna get a porno stud. I undressed him completely and then worked on his cock some more, bringing it back up and ready to pop. I rolled him over on his stomach. The buns, gleaming in the dim light, were as beautiful as I'd remembered. I couldn't imagine anybody having a nicer ass than that. My cock was so hard it jumped out of my pants as I pulled them down.

He looked behind him as I undressed. All he did was groan.

Sliding a lubed rubber on my dick, I mounted him and started sliding back and forth across his ass. He reached around and took my dick in his hand. "You're from a farm all right, a stud farm."

"You get what ya pay for," I chuckled, and let him guide it in.

...He couldn't get enough of it. He had to have it in every position he could think of, but it ended up with us sitting on the bed facing each other, his thighs over mine, my cock in him, holding each other. He moved it the way he wanted it and started kissing me again. I had no idea what it meant to be in love but at that moment I knew I'd gone into a different orbit. He came but kept on, going crazy with it. Finally, he had me pull out and he took the rubber off and sighed, "I hardly ever suck cock but this is somethin' else." He kissed it and then began sucking. He wasn't good at it but he was enjoying himself so I just closed my eyes and held onto his shoulders. When I came he was so happy he kissed me again.

After I took a shower and came back into the bedroom, he was still lying there, still nude, his eyes shut. I dropped down on the bed and kissed his navel.

"I've been thinking," he said, slowly, deliberately.

"Yeah.?"

"I want you to come back to the house with me."

"You do?"

"I know I shouldn't but I just have these great vibes. I can't explain it. I've only felt like this once or twice before and it was always somewhere else, like Mexico or Rio." He stroked my hair. "It's like I know I'm gonna want you tomorrow morning before I go to the studio and you won't be there and -"

"The studio?"

"Yeah, I'm working at Disney and I've gotta get up at six every morning. They spend an hour every day on my makeup and all I do is sit around all day. It's boring as hell, but it's almost over."

Disney? I thought Van had said this guy was in the music business. Now I find he's a Mickey Mouse. I started to chuckle.

"What's so funny?"

"Nothin'. Just me and Mickey Mouse! I never thought I'd be going to bed with Mickey Mouse!"

"Hey," he said, chuckling, "they make more than cartoons there now, you know. This thing we're doing is a sci-fi piece of shit. I play an alien for chrissakes!"

"Best looking alien I've ever seen," I said, hugging him.

"I'll call Van and tell him you're on special assignment and can't be reached."

And he picked up the phone and did just that. I would have loved to have seen the look on Van's fat face while he was listening to it.

It was two in the morning when we got in the old Chevy and soon he was speeding up into the foothills, on Mulholland Drive. We stopped at a gate almost hidden by the trees and he slipped a card into a slot and suddenly we were passing through the brick walled entrance, past a tiled fountain and into a double garage. From what I could see in the darkness, this was something right out of the movies.

"It's an old house," he said. "Built in 1928. I bought it a couple of years ago but this is the first time I've actually lived here for any length of time. But it's lonely, just me and the maid."

I realized I still didn't have a clue as to who this guy was. Here I was in a hilltop house with somebody who was playing an alien in a Disney movie and as many movies as I'd watched in my life I couldn't place him. "Have you been in any other movies?"

"Only one. It bombed. But it's become what they call a cult

classic."

No help there. We went into the house. Every room was on a different level and the view from every room was out of this world. From the living room I could see the flats, from downtown to the Ocean.

"This is the loggia," he said, leading me out onto a wooden balcony. I got dizzy looking out over what he called Cahuenga Pass. I felt I was suspended in space. He led me down the stairs to where the master bedroom was, then the guest bedroom below it, all hanging on to the side of the cliff. More steps down led to a tiny garden and when he flicked on more lights I could see it was full of spine-covered prickly pears and there was a hottub almost hidden in all the greenery. "Wanna soak?" he asked.

Struck dumb by all of it, I didn't even answer, I just started taking off my clothes.

Soon we were in the tub and he was kissing me again like before and I never wanted the night to end.

From the LP "I Remember You"/Sung by Joe Skinner/Side 1, Cut 5, "I Could Get Used to This:" "...Imagine my surprise when I found you / Darling, I have nursed this lonely heart so long / It's hard to let go and trust that we belong / I could get used to this / Having you to hold me through the night / I could get used to this..."

"It's my housekeeper Matty's day off," he whispered, "so you'll be alone all day. I'll be back by seven. If you need anything, the number in my trailer at the studio's written next to the phone in the kitchen."

I rubbed my eyes and looked at the clock on his nightstand. It wasn't even seven a.m. He kissed the top of my head and was gone. For a long while I lay there in the huge bed trying to fit all the pieces together. The afternoon at the beach, last night. Now.

I looked around the room. It was an ordinary bedroom, I decided, in an extraordinary house. Everything was beige, the walls, the rug, the draperies, the satin sheets on the bed. But it was the mirrors that fascinated me. He loved watching us together. He liked it best on his knees, his elbows digging into the bed, watching the action in the mirror that filled the entire wall alongside the bed. "Better than any video, eh, kid?" he said several times. Since my only experience with sex videos was being in two of them, I didn't even try to answer.

I hugged the pillows and began to fuck them the way I had fucked him, after we'd blown each other in the hot tub. I was getting off on how I fucked him in his bed until he couldn't take it any more and how I fell asleep holding onto his arm, afraid he might disappear if I didn't.

After I came, I tried to go back to sleep but I couldn't. I was too excited to sleep.

My first day on the hilltop was one of discovery. It was an even more marvelous place in the daytime than it had been at night. As I stepped out the front door, I smelled the flowers and felt the tingle of the mix of dew and warm sunshine. What a day, I thought. Then I remembered that it was like this every day in California but I was feeling it as if it were the first time. I prowled around the house like a burglar, one room to the next until I found what I was looking for, just by accident. It was a record album, one of many stacked by the wall in the living room that had a TV and every kind of electronic gadget you could imagine. "The Skins, 1976" was the name of it and on the back cover was a picture of the group. In the middle of the line of four guys with no shirts on and close-cropped hair was the man I'd just spent the night with. Only now he had long hair almost down to his shoulders and a little mustache. He was Joe Skinner. I said the name over and over again. I didn't know much about rock 'n' roll, being a country fan, but I had heard of the group. They were big in the late '70s and early '80s. Two of the guys eventually OD'd and they stopped recording. That was all I knew. I sifted through the records and the tapes. There were maybe five of the Skins, each with a year after their name, and then I found the tape I was looking for. Joe was alone on the cover, wearing his "Sox" baseball cap and he had his legs stretched out real sexily. "Joe Skinner Sings Songs of Love, I Remember You," it said on the cover. I wanted to kiss that fucking cover, he was so adorable. I bet millions of girls did kiss the fucking cover. I turned the box over and read the song titles. "Unforgettable" was there, all right. It was Joe singing that afternoon in the Chevy. I pulled the tape out of the box and slipped it into the player. I was prepared to like it. What happened was, I loved it. Right from the first song, I knew this guy had a voice that was almost as good as Randy Travis'. I couldn't believe it.

I had come to Hollywood because somebody on TV said Randy Travis was here and then somebody told me that he lived in Nashville with an older woman who was his manager. I began saving up to go to Nashville.

But now I was on a hilltop in Hollywood in Joe Skinner's house. It was like my grandpa used to say, "Ya take what God gives ya, kid."

As the music followed me from room to room I went back to Joe Skinner's bedroom. I pulled the drapes open and the room was filled with sunshine. I looked into the mirror again. I ran my hands over my body. All I knew was that I suddenly really loved looking at myself. Incredible as it seemed, a handsome rock star loved the way I made him feel. He was somebody that could order up anybody he wanted but he'd ask me to stay. But I didn't look like my own idea of what a stud was. Oh, I had a thick, long dick all right but I was just a kid. A short little kid. But then I remembered how Joe got off on it and how great it felt being up his ass and deep down his throat. I must be able to do something right. What I saw in the mirror was a different person than I knew me to be. And last night I had seen a different man than the public, especially the screaming teenage girls who were his fans, knew to be Joe Skinner. Or maybe mirrors have a way of distorting things, that we are nothing more than reflections, reflections of a crazy, mixed up world where so many people think what we were doing is bad, so bad that they're always trying to take away the mirrors and shatter them.

And now, listening to Joe singing, I started to sway back and forth with the melody. And the music worked its magic. The song was "I Could Get Used to This." I jacked off again to my own reflection and could hardly wait until seven o'clock.

*

The limo pulled up the drive a few minutes after seven. I watched from the window as he stepped from the car, said something to the driver, and crossed the patio. Seeing him again after 12 hours alone, I fell in love with him all over again. He was so cool. I shivered just thinking he was coming home to me. I was glad I'd taken a shower, splashed on his cologne and put on a pair of shorts I'd found in his closet that, if I pulled 'em tight enough, sort of fit me.

"Hi, Joe," I said as he was coming through the door.

He smiled. "Now you know, eh?"

"Hell, I've had all day to find out."

"Okay," he said and he held me in his arms. "Unforgettable" started playing again on the stereo. It seemed so incredible to have the man who was singing actually holding me in his arms.

"I've been listening to it all day."

"God, you must be bored out of your mind with it."

"No, it's all I ever want to hear."

He kissed me on the tip of my nose. "You always know the right thing to say. How do you do it?"

"Just honest, I guess."

"That's what I like about you, kid." He kissed me hard on the mouth and then we went to the hot tub and took turns blowing each other. Eventually, we made it to the bedroom.

He liked to watch me coming toward him naked. I would start at the bathroom and work my way across the room and to the bed, taking the long way, stopping in front of the big mirror and doing a little posing into it, my erection growing stronger by the minute. I would step over to the bed and he'd be lying there on his stomach, propped up with his elbows and I'd stand in front of him with my hands on my hips, my cock swaying before his eyes. I'd step closer and closer, my cock caressing his cheeks, his lips, his eyes. He'd run his hands up and down my thighs and try to catch the tip of my cock with his lips. Eventually, he'd have it in his mouth and I'd start shoving it, gently, deep into his throat. He'd look to the side so he could watch in the other mirror behind the headboard.

"...Do you want to stay?" he asked after three hours of sex, with a break for some beer and pizza that he'd had delivered from the Pizza Kitchen on La Cienega ("Best in town," he said, and he ordered it with Peking duck topping).

"Sure. Who wouldn't," I said, rubbing his chest.

"Okay. I want to hire you -"

"Hire me?"

"You are in business, as I recall."

"Oh, yeah. I guess so. Well, now I guess I'm retired."

"Oh, really?"

"Yeah, retired at the ripe old age of 18." I laid back and closed my eyes.

"So, what kind of pension is suitable for an 18-year-old?" He had his hand on my cock again.

"I dunno. Just leave a little something on the nightstand when you leave in the morning. I'll get by."

*

Earlier, he'd noticed I was wearing his shorts, before he peeled them off as we got in the hot tub, and he asked me if I wanted to go back to my little room and get my things. I said yes. So the next day after the limo took him to the studio he had the driver, Harold, come back and take me to the apartment. Joe had left two hundred dollar bills on the nightstand that morning so I paid the landlady what I owed and Harold helped me lug my things to the car. The old woman stood at the door to her apartment watching us put my suitcases in the trunk. I don't think she could believe this little kid was moving from her crappy old efficiency to a white stretch Lincoln limo; so after everything was packed I went up to her and said, "You should see the house!" Then I winked. She shook her head and slammed the door in my face.

Joe called Matty "Old Pruneface" behind her back but he said he loved her. She had been his maid ever since he bought the house and he could trust her. He told her I was his nephew from Ohio and would be staying in the guest room for a week or two. So when I came into the house with my old suitcases with Ohio State stickers on them and my little TV, she must have assumed that was the truth. I didn't tell her they were my father's old suitcases. (I had always wondered about it; why my father had to go to college to become a farmer. All I ever did on the farm was shovel shit and mend fences. He said, "You gotta go to college in order to learn to do anything these days." I wondered if I had to go to college to have sex correctly, that maybe going to college would have made my fantasies of having sex with another boy go away and I would think about girls from then on.)

"You Mr. Skinner's sister's boy?"

"Yeah, I guess you could say that," I replied, figuring Joe must have had a sister or a brother somewhere since I was his nephew.

"From Ohio?"

"Well, no that's where I go to school. We're all from Alabama, though, you know." I tried a Southern drawl but I don't think she bought it.

She nodded. "You flunk out?"

"I guess you could say that."

She just shook her head and went on making the apple pie we were going to have for dessert that night. ("Apple's Mr. Skinner's favorite," she said. "Mine, too," I answered. I felt very all-American right then, almost collegiate.)

When Joe came home, he looked at my belongings and shook his head. "I think you could use some new things."

"What for, I never go anywhere?"

"Well, you might and this stuff looks like you got it at a rummage sale."

"I did. My dad never bought anything new if he could help it. Even my mother had been divorced twice. It was like the song from

'Funny Girl,' 'Second Hand Rose.'"

It was decided. The next day, Harold took me shopping. We went to Ralph Lauren on Rodeo Drive. Joe had said I could buy anything I wanted but when I got to the store the clerk said that Joe had phoned and given him a list. All I had to do was pick out which colors I wanted and try everything on.

When Joe got home, I modelled every outfit. I discovered that clothes can be very sexual. That they can do more than just reveal a big basket. Good clothes, expensive clothes, tailored ones, made me look like Joe wanted me to look. I looked in the mirror and didn't even know the person. It didn't look like me but it was somebody Joe liked. A lot.

"These are great," I said. "Like I told you, I've never worn anything that hadn't been damaged before I put it on."

"You'll never wear damaged goods again."

I collapsed on the bed next to him. "But I'm damaged goods, Joe. That's the way I feel, like I shouldn't be here with you. I don't belong."

He kissed me. "Look, kid, anything you've done, well, it was practice. Practice for now. If you hadn't done all that, well, you wouldn't be here now."

And I knew he was right. And I dug him all the more.

Later that night, after we had the dinner Matty left, he poured us brandies. He swirled it around in the big glass and then drank some of it. I tried it but didn't care for it. I decided I'd like it better if it were on his cock, so I poured some of it there so I could lick it off. "Whoa," he said, as I dribbled some on his crotch. I licked and sucked him, now loving the taste of brandy and sweat and precum, until he was going wild, pushing my head down into it, forcing it deep inside my throat, thrusting it deeper and deeper, then waiting for me, then again and again until he came. It was the first time he'd come in my mouth. It was warm and sticky and just kept coming. He usually came while I was fucking him, but he said he couldn't help himself.

Cum oozing from the sides of my mouth and onto my chin, he pulled me on top of him and licked my face clean. His hand found my cock and knew I was ready. He took his own snifter and poured brandy all over my cock and started in, but I knew what he wanted. I pulled away, got a rubber and when I walked back to the bed he asked for it. As he began sliding it on, he kissed my balls. When he had rolled it all the way on, he held it in his hand, looked up into my eyes and sighed, "Hmmm, I could get used to this."

And I was sure the smile on my face was the biggest one I'd ever had in my whole life.

*From the LP "I Remember You"/Sung by Joe Skinner/Side 2, Cut 1,
"What a Difference A Day Makes:" "...Twenty four little hours...My
yesterdays used to be blue, dear / Today I'm a part of you, dear / Lord, what
a difference a day makes / There's a rainbow before me / Skies above me can
be stormy / Since that moment of bliss / That thrilling kiss / It's heaven
when you find romance on your menu / What a difference a day makes /
And the difference is you."*

I made it a point to get up in the morning, slip into my new silk
robe, and fix a pot of coffee and put out some of Matty's homemade
cinnamon rolls for him. I also put "I Remember You" on the stereo,
filling the house with his husky voice. He hated it. "I can't stand
it!" he'd scream. "Turn that fuckin' thing off!"

"But I love it," I'd say, ignoring him as one of my favorites, "Easy
to Love," came on while he was finishing his first cup of coffee.
"That song sounds so familiar," I said.

"It should. It's by Cole Porter."

"It's odd. Certain things I can remember now but don't know
why. As if it happened in some other life."

"That was another life. Whatever went before, it was another life.
This is your life now."

I wanted to believe him but something told me, taking everything into account, I was only passing through. But I was determined to make the most of it. When Harold drove up the drive and
tooted the horn, Joe jumped up and was gone, but not before he
kissed me. He always kissed me goodbye.

*

That night when he came home he was furious. He threw the
National Enquirer across the room and poured himself a strong Jack
Daniels. He hadn't drunk anything stronger than beer or wine since
I had moved in. He gulped it down like my grandpa and my pa
used to, then poured another. It was as if he was slowly turning into
a wild animal, like that movie "Dr. Jekyll and Mr. Hyde."
I went to him, tried to stop him, but it was like he'd gone insane.

He shoved the newspaper in my face. I stared at it. His picture was on the front page and I tried to read the headline as best I could.

"Read it!" he screamed. "Fuckers!"

I stood there scanning the type of the article on the inside. I started to mumble.

"Well?"

"I can't make much out of it."

"Shit, man, you mean you fuckin' can't read?"

"I can read, it's just that it gets mixed up sometimes. Backwards sometimes. I can't explain it."

"Oh my God! Just what I need, a fuckin' mental cripple! My sister was a mental cripple. Shit-" Suddenly he stopped. It was as if a light went on in his head. "What am I saying? What am I saying to you?"

He took me in his arms and shook me. I was afraid of him for the first time. His eyes were like fire, staring right into mine. He started to cry. But he kept shaking me. Harder and harder. I couldn't lift my arms to defend myself. All I could do was finally pull myself free. I ran out of the living room, down the steps to my room. I sat on the bed, terrified of what might come next. I had let him down. He'd found out my secret. They always found out my secret. In the end, everyone knew. I wanted to hide, to run away but I couldn't. I knew the front gate was locked and the only way out would have been off the balcony and down the rocks. I didn't move. I just sat on the edge of the bed the way I did back home when my father would start in after my mother died when I was nine: "They say you're sick in the head," he'd yell. "They're not tellin' me anything's wrong with my kid. No, sir!" And he would smash the dishes and then slam the door behind him. When I'd hear him get in the pick-up to drive into town, I knew it was safe to turn on the TV and watch my movies. Later, when I saved up, I bought my own TV, a little black and white one, and then I didn't ever have to go downstairs.

I could hear Joe on the steps, then he stood in the doorway. The sun was setting behind him and it made him look like Christ rising from the grave. "I'm sorry," he mumbled.

This wasn't my father. This wasn't anybody I'd ever known. Nobody'd ever said they were sorry before.

I started to cry. Joe came into the room, put his arms around me and hugged me. I must have sobbed for a good five minutes.

"You know," he said, finally, "now my sister can read better than I can. She teaches school in Alabama, for chrissakes! My father got the best people in the country working on it and I learned all about it. You can be cured." He kissed the top of my head. "I shouldn't have said what I did."

I didn't say anything, I just hugged him harder than I had ever hugged anybody in my entire life.

They say you can get used to anything but I never did. I never got used to being made a fool of.

I stood up in class.

"It's your turn," the teacher, Mrs. Snodgrass, said.

"But I can't."

"It's time you did."

"I can't."

"You really should try harder."

"But sometimes I see things backwards."

And as the kids howled with laughter, I sat down again and wanted to die.

When I got home, I told my father, "I hate school."

"But the teachers say you're smart. I just don't understand it."

"I don't either."

"I had one of those teachers tell me it's sometimes caused by a head injury, then I got to thinking, you used to bang your head against the wall. We couldn't stop you. Just bang bang bang."

"Oh, please, pa."

"Shit, boy, if you can't read you're no better than apes in a zoo."

And the last thing he ever said to me was when he dropped me off at the bus station: "I won't be writing you. No point, is there?"

He pulled our pants away and had me slide between his thighs and he guided it into his ass. He just wanted me to be in him, and to hold him, and so did I. He gently wiped away my tears and we kissed each other. As I slowly fucked his ass, he told me he was tired so I jacked him off. "Please, don't cum inside of me," he moaned, and I didn't. I let my cock slide out and then I came on his chest.

Later, after we'd returned to the living room, I asked, "...What was it that got you so upset?"

"They've dug up some cunt that says she was with Paul and me the night he died. I'm convinced they can find somebody that'll say anything for a price."

"Do you know her?"

"Hardly! Shit, if I could remember a tenth of the cunts I fucked on the road it'd be amazing. They get thrown at you every night. It's just a matter of which one gets there first." He took the paper and shoved it in my face again. "Now, would you remember somebody that looked like that?"

"No, but that's not a fair question. I'm not into cunts."

"Oh, yeah," he chuckled. "Well, I was into 'em for a long time and where did it get me?"

"All over the 'Enquirer' it looks like. But it's a great shot of you." They had used a picture of him on stage, at the height of their popularity. I decided he looked even better now, especially reflected in the mirrors of his bedroom, bouncing up and down on my cock.

"I'm gonna sue, that's what I'm gonna do." He took up the paper and read the article out loud. The bitch claimed that five years ago, when they were appearing in Indianapolis, she had met Paul and was in his hotel room after a show. Her story was that Joe came to the room, gave them drugs and partied with them, then left around 3 a.m. Before dawn, Paul was dead from an overdose. The girl left the hotel room and never reported her participation in the incident. Until now.

"Why now?" I asked when he was finished.

"Fuck, how should I know! Maybe with the album out it occurred to her that I'd want her story, whatever bullshit it is, stopped. That I'd pay to have it stopped. But I won't pay blackmail. Benny told me somebody had called but I told him there was nothing to it."

"Benny?"

"Benny Kaplan discovered us when we were in school in Athens over ten years ago. He was like a father to us. He still handles all my business." He looked at me calculatedly. "Benny doesn't approve, you know."

"Approve of what?"

"When I called him today about this trash in the paper, I told him I had a house guest. He said he wanted to meet you."

"Okay."

"Haha! Wait'll he does, man. Wait'll be does! But I'm not rushing it. He thinks I've gone crazy again. I told him you were helping me with my memoirs. I told him I needed somebody to help me get everything down so I could go public with the whole thing. If they're still interested, shit, they should know the truth."

"So that's why I'm here, to help you with your book?" I rubbed his crotch.

"Insane, isn't it? You haven't known me a week but you're helping me with the story of my life!" He took me in his arms again and hugged me. "Well, you're a part of it now, you might as well help with it."

"Shit, I can't even read. What good am I?"

"Your mind, it's like a fuckin' tape recorder. I've heard you, everything you ever heard on TV or the radio you've got memorized. "

Not quite. I'd memorized bits of dialogue. Words came at me like riddles, most of the time. People were like concrete to me, their faces, gestures, clothing, eyes, odors, voices. I didn't remember their names most of the time, unless I worked at it. Stars names were easiest. I heard them, knew them. I didn't have to read them.

"You can just listen while I talk and then you can put it all down. We'll teach you to put it all down."

"Like in 'Auntie Mame' when Mame tells Patrick to write down every word he doesn't know - "

"See, there you go again!"

"But how can I put it down? If you can't read, you can't write."

"If my sister can do it, you can do it. Trust me."

"I do." And I reached down to find he had a hardon again. At least there was something I could do for him.

*

It seemed he suddenly had a cause besides going to the studio every day at seven and getting fucked every night. He remembered things best after he'd had a drink, "just one, to help with the tongue," he'd say. And I knew he meant that in more ways than one.

Once he said, "I got this feeling I don't have long, you know? Like, we're all dying, all the time. Every day." He seemed to be preoccupied by death. Always dying. He was dying of thirst.

Dying for a joint. Dying for my cock. He was always dying and it seemed like I had just started to live. I gave him my line from "Hell's Angels." He just shook his head.

"Yeah, life," he said once, "it teaches you to be cautious. You'll also learn to be more careful how you judge the rest of us."

"I don't judge you, Joe."

"That's what I love about you. You don't. I tell you I did all these things that might blow some people's minds or that I fucked a thousand cunts or whatever and you don't say anything. And you don't do anything, you're just here." He took me in his arms. "Just for me."

I kissed him. "Why you want me I don't know but as long as you do, I'm here."

"I want you because you're different. There's something special about you. And I don't mean just that big cock. I must have had a dozen guys come to that motel. They were zeros, every one of them. Most of 'em couldn't even keep it up." He groped my crotch. "Hmmm, you're different all right. And I know if I got into trouble you'd be the one who'd help me out of it. I can feel that."

"Like a mother?"

"God, no. Not a mother. More like a brother. You know, I never had a brother, just a sister. I always wanted a brother. But you're better than a brother."

"Yeah, I'm legal. A brother'd be incest." I slipped out of my bikini and stroked my dick for him. It was hard again. Every time he looked at it, it got hard.

From the LP "I Remember You"/Sung by Joe Skinner/Side 2, Cut 2,
"Impossible:" "...If they had ever told me / How sweet a kiss could be / I
would have said, impossible / Impossible for me / And if they said I'd find
you / Beyond the rainbow's end / I would have said, impossible /
Impossible, my friend / To dream about what might have been is strange
enough for me / But now it seems I'm living in a dream too beautiful to
be / ...Now it seems nothing is impossible..."

The evening was our time for remembrances. When Matty didn't
come to the house and leave dinner, Joe would order Peking duck
from Mr. Chow or New York steak from Trumps sent in. "Don't
eat so fast. And little bites. Chew slowly," he'd say. It made him
happy to see me polishing the manners my mother had taught me
long ago. It seemed with Joe it was natural to be perfect, to do
everything just like rich people do in the movies. It was as if we
were in the movies.

If he didn't go to the studio, the morning was our time for new
ideas. He'd wake up fresh, ready to work. I'd always look forward
to the mornings, hoping that on days he had to go to the studio, he'd
get really inspired and want to finish a story, then he'd let me ride
along in the limo. We'd arrive at the lot, the big Disney lot in
Burbank, where the white water tower has Mickey Mouse on it and
all the bushes are made into little mouse sculptures. And we'd tool
right through the gates, everybody tipping their hat to him, to the
car, to Harold. Joe would get out and tell Harold to take me right
home and put me to work.

On the way home, I would sit in the limo listening to one of his
tapes, usually my favorite, "I Remember You," trying to figure out
what made him so irresistible.

I couldn't put my finger on it but it was like someone on TV had
said: "You can't describe what Joe Skinner has but he has it. He's
like pornography, you can't describe it but you know it when you
see it. It's that thing they've come to call charisma. His voice is
charismatic. We know he can be that way in person, when he wants
to, but his voice, always." Little did he know how much like

pornography Joe was.

*

Joe arranged to have the "Professor" come every other day. That's what I called him. He was a tutor to people like me and Joe was paying him to give his nephew private lessons.

He started with the lyrics to Joe's songs on the new LP. "Uncomplicate the words," he said, but it was difficult for me. And it was boring; sometimes I wanted to throw up my hands and quit, but the Professor was very patient and when Joe arrived he'd give me a good report. I always suspected other men, always searched for clues, but the Professor was so dead-ahead straight he was comfortable. I could relax and concentrate. I was required to read the lyrics five times without a mistake before we went on to another song. "You must learn to pay attention," he kept saying.

"Why is it you can watch TV or mess around with that tractor for hours and hours, yet you can't read?" my pa used to ask.

I had no answer. What I considered real, teachers considered fantasy. What I considered fantasy, they considered real. Words came at me like a riddle, uninvited, boring.

My mother, before she died, went to the counselor at the school and said, "He can't be disabled. He's so well coordinated. Has been since he could walk. His problem is the teachers. They don't have time to spend with the kids anymore."

"Mom," I said, "it's not their fault."

"Well, it's not your fault and it's not my fault. I don't know whose fault it is, but it has to be somebody's fault."

"Can't something just happen without it being someone's fault? Mom, it's the way I am. Nobody's to blame."

"No. You're not the way you are. And somebody's to blame."

"I'm just slow."

"If you say that again I'll hit you right here. Somebody's got to knock some sense into you. If your father can't - "

"Here we go again," I said, standing up.

"Keep your mouth shut and sit down," she said.

"Look," the counselor said, "let's try to forget the past. William is bright enough. We'll see if we can find a teacher who can help."

"It's hopeless," I said, racing out of the room.

They never found a teacher who could help.

The Professor said he was going to use what he called the melody technique. "Melody is the ease at being what we are and doing what we do. It is the center of wholeness in a frog that makes it jump, in a lizard that makes it skitter, in a dog that makes it fetch. In humans, it makes them communicate with spoken and written symbols. Without melody, we move without direction. It unites reception and expression. When the body and the mind dance to melody there are no wallflowers."

"You mean flowerwalls."

"That's what you used to say. But no more."

"No more."

"If melody is involved, the eyes, ears and the rest of the body have to join in, and you block out the rest of the senses to bring everything in balance. You are marvelously coordinated so what we are doing is transferring your body-mind-brain melody to perceptual, semantic melody, your physical coordination for sensory coordination. It's the best kind of transfer."

Symbols were the hardest. "Look at those symbols, examine them from every angle, write them so you get to know them up close from every angle, build their 'melody of movement' in your body, then your mind. You'll seldom confuse them again." I began to feel comfortable with them. I would make guesses, "with strong clues woven by melody," the Professor said, and it would almost always equal certainty. "Almost equal" became the words we used as he kept making me practice. After I would write a sentence a few times, he would require me to write it again with my eyes closed. I continued to write it, one time eyes open, one time closed, until the rhythm of it took over. If I made a mistake, I would correct it in the next writing. If a sound or word showed up alone and lonely it began repeating itself as if it was looking for company. We put the music on and I wrote the lyrics down, dancing with them, getting them right more often than I got them wrong. My handwriting had always been terrible and it improved, improved so much that Joe could actually read the lyrics. The pages became love letters to him that I stuck everywhere so he could find them.

Joe had a computer delivered and put in his den. The Professor convinced him it was the perfect thing for me: "I've had boys that have had the same difficulty William has and they've gone on to be computer programmers. Their persistence, accuracy and speed at visual tasks such as keyboard work make them ideal."

"See," Joe said to me, "and you thought you were disabled, for chrissakes."

He started me on the games and finally I was actually writing sentences on the computer. The Professor would check my work when he visited. It was easy to correct the mistakes on the computer. Sometimes I'd have the TV on and type the dialogue from the movies as they were saying it. I had memorized bits of dialogue so that I could say them and feel important. Now I was doing the whole script. "You've learned to type in the bargain," the Professor teased me. "I want a bonus."

Before I met Joe the only bonus I could give him was between my legs, but now I found myself saying, "I'll have Joe take care of it." The Professor laughed.

Matty would have to bring my lunch into me; Joe would come home and have to drag me away from the computer. "I'm so proud of you," he'd say. And then I'd fuck him silly. He'd scream for me to stop and when I did, he'd beg me to continue. He was so happy I always had a hardon. "I guess if you're gonna have a stud around, get one who's 18," he'd say.

I started to say, If you're gonna have a sugar daddy, get one who's under thirty and a movie star, but I didn't.

*

"...That must have been wild," I told Benny. (Joe had said: "We had our attorneys, our agents and our manager. But Benny was like the fifth member of the group. His vote counted the same.")

"Yeah," he went on, lighting another cigarette. "I couldn't imagine a life when you didn't have to check the exits! Check security! Oh, but, it was a time when there were no reservations, no checking thoughts before you went to bed, you could just live. We'll never see those days again."

"No."

"But if I hadn't done that I would've been involved in entertainment, somehow. I love the idea of promoting, hustling, hyping. I like that kind of vaudeville, snake oil, extravaganza thing. Not only selling things but convincing 'em they need it. And when you've convinced them, they're just amazed that they ever lived without it."

I thought of saying, "Sorta like living with Joe Skinner," but I didn't.

"Yeah, the boys loved that life for a long time. All the booze, all the drugs, all the sex they could ever want. They were living everybody's fantasy about what it was supposed to be. But the truth is, they were just covering up; they weren't the Stones or Van Halen; they were just ordinary guys, really."

"Yeah, sure."

He smiled. "So what does Joe want to know?"

"Things you wouldn't tell him to his face."

"There's nothing I wouldn't tell Joe Skinner to his face."

"Well - "

"He can tell you all about it. I suppose he has. Those were long nights. I never thought he'd make it. He really wasn't cut out for it. He was just singing in the choir at school when we asked him to front the group. You see, in the old days, there was the orchestra or band or whatever and they had a singer. Sometimes a woman, sometimes a man. Sometimes both. You had to have a pretty face upfront. Same today. Joe made the group complete. We changed the name and went on the road. He wasn't much of a singer in those days, but good enough. Today, he's a great singer but he wants to do all these old things. That new album is a mistake."

"It's wonderful."

"You think so? See, I don't understand kids today. You can't even be 18 and you like it."

"I am 18, but I'm not your usual kid."

He laughed. "I can see that. But, still, you like the songs."

"The way he sings 'em, I like 'em. I like country music and the way he sings them, well, it's like that. Lots of feeling. It's different than rock 'n' roll."

"I'll give it that. It's different all right. I wish him well with it. I didn't like the contract we got with those Disney people. Their label's never had a hit. After two years, not a hit. You know what Pearson, he's the honcho over there, you know what he told me? 'So we lose $20 million, we've got $700 million!' That's the kind of people you're dealing with! Look, they've got Queen, right? Imagine, Joe Skinner and Queen! Paulie would have had a heart attack! Anyhow, we went to the party they threw for Queen's new album. They held it on the Queen Mary, for chrissakes! Anyhow, me and Joe go to this thing and there's Michael Eisner, who runs the whole damn studio, sitting between two loudspeakers blaring this Queen shit! Joe got a drink and all I got was a headache! And now he's making a movie for them besides!" He shook his head. "Did ya see the billboard on Sunset, kid?"

I shook my head; I hadn't.

"When you go back, take a look. Bigger than anyone else's. He looks great."

I made a note to tell Harold to drive by it.

"Yeah, Joe's coming back. I'm happy for him."

"Do you think he should come out?"

"Should what?"

"Come out, you know, tell everybody he likes men?"

"Why?"

"Why not?"

"Look, I know Joe. He used to say he likes to watch the wheels go round. Now, I interpret that as anything from watching peple have sex to looking at people walking down the street. But whatever he's into is nobody's business. It makes no difference what anybody does in the dark as long as they are consenting adults. I'll never change my philosophy on that. Never. And you'll never change Joe's. Look what happened in this town when Rock got it. A whole new wave of homophobia set in. No, you'll never convince us anybody should know what we do between the sheets."

I went to his small office in downtown L.A. because Joe decided I should meet him on his own ground. Pictures of The Skins were all over the walls, but there was one of Joe by himself that dwarfed them all. It was a poster, in fact, the size of a door, in color, of Joe at the beach. He'd grown all his hair back by then and had just come from the gym. Bennny caught me staring at the poster.

"He's a beauty, isn't he?"

"Yeah, he really is." (Little did he know, I thought. But then, maybe after all these years, he knew Joe as well as I did. I couldn't figure all that Joe was into, or all who may have been into Joe. I decided it would be fun to find out, for the memoirs.)

"So what do you really want to know?" he asked, snuffing out one cigarette and lighting another.

"About Paul."

He sighed, blew smoke in the air. "You would have loved him. Sweet kid. Real sweet kid. But it all started with Johnny. Johnny was our drummer and he'd OD'd once before and they just saved his ass. Then he went through counseling and stuff but then one night he was out alone and -well, he had to go to jail, no amount of money would get him out of it. It was just for driving while under the influence but he would have had to do three weeks, just three weeks. He couldn't live with that! He was willing to die to avoid that! His death was a serious setback-not just in the sense of losing a friend and all that but it was all of a sudden - boom! We found a new drummer but it wasn't the same. It wasn't his fault. It was just that it was hard being a new person around us."

"And Paul."

"When Paulie died Joe's whole world collapsed. It was the truly final blow." He looked away, out the window. "His love for Paulie had entered his soul. Now he has it forever. It's the one certainty in life that can be never taken away from him. Paul loved him till the day he died. And Joe loved Paul but he could never express it, physically or any other way than just be his friend."

He finished his cigarette, looking me up and down, then hard in the eyes. "I'm glad you came up here today. I feel better about it now." He moved from behind his desk for the first time and stood in front of me. His smile was nice, but there was desperation there, too, like he wanted me but knew it was impossible.

He seemed so desperate in his desire that it reminded of me when I was little and a rat got caught in a sticky open roach trap. The racket dragged me from my sleep and into the kitchen. When I turned the light on his scream was so loud I held my hands over my ears. I realized that he may have been a rat but he was as afraid of dying as we humans are. And, as he pressed himself deeper and deeper into the gluey trap, I went outside and got a shovel and was able to end his misery. In my dreams, animals would never die.

Benny leaned against his desk and ran his hand down his thigh. "You know, you remind me of Paul back in the beginning, except you're prettier. When I saw you, I thought, maybe now Joe's doing what he should've done ten years ago with Paul."

"At least he's not dying any more."

"What?"

"When I met him, he had this thing about dying."

"Oh, I know. He's been preoccupied with that for years. When he was on all the little girls' lunch boxes and the poster was the best-selling one of the year and all that -"

"That poster?" I asked, pointing to the one on the wall.

"Yeah."

"I'd love one. Do you have another one?"

He laughed. "Hell no. I wish I did. They say collectors' are getting fifty bucks for one these days. Anyhow, he had this thing about rock stars dying young. You know, Morrison, Joplin, all the rest. I'd kid him, 'Rock 'n' roll will never die, but when those who play it do, it's good for business,' and he'd laugh like hell but I know he thought I was just waiting for him to die. And then Johnny went and then Paulie. It was a nightmare for him. It was as if the public was waiting to see which one would go next. Everybody had Joe marked and, you know, there's a certain charisma about a guy that everybody thinks is about to drop dead. It's like when Daffy Duck blows up onstage and then you see him as an angel in heaven saying, 'Yeah, folks, it's a great show, but you can only do it once.'"

"Well, I'm happy he's not dying any more."

"You must be something," he said, his hand coming to rest on his crotch.

"No, it's not me," I said, preparing to leave. "It's Joe that's somethin'. Somethin' else."

"You don't know the half of it, kid. But I have a hunch you'll find out."

*

"I have an appointment to see Mrs. Skinner," I said.

"I'll see if she's free," the funny little receptionist said, giving me the once-over. Just as she began to open the left door of the big double doors, a tall, slender woman came out.

"You have a visitor," the receptionist said.

"Oh," Luisa said, her eyes drinking me in. "You must be little William."

Nodding, I gulped.

"Right this way," she said, pushing the double doors open.

"Take my calls. I may be a while," she said to the receptionist, closing the doors behind her.

"...What's going on?" she asked after we were seated, me on the couch, she across from me in a big chair.

"I'm working on a story about Joe. Well, it's by Joe actually. I'm just taking notes."

"You are?" She was suprised I had no notebook.

"Yeah. I have a good memory."

I couldn't imagine Joe being married to this lady. She was like the woman in a movie I saw once, "The Fountainhead." Patricia Neal played her. She drove Gary Cooper crazy. I could see that's what this woman must have done to Joe. Joe said she was into women now. I bet that she fucked her women with the biggest dildo she could find. She told me about how she was working for CBS Records when they met at a charity thing and how she pursued him trying to get him to sign with her company but instead, she got Joe to marry her. It only lasted a few months. "The divorce took longer to get than the marriage lasted, thanks to Benny. Have you met Benny?"

I nodded.

"I'll bet old Benny liked you."

I nodded again.

"Well, you are a nice little kid. I didn't expect that."

"Thanks."

She lit a cigarette, then clear out of the blue she said, "Joe's nuts about you."

"You think so?"

"Oh, yes," she said, taking a long drag. "When he called me and told me he wanted me to see you, I knew. I knew there was something good happening with him. It was in his voice. He's happy. I knew when he loved me and when he stopped. First he was happy, then he was unhappy. It didn't happen overnight but it didn't take long. Joe needs simplicity in his life. Everything's so hectic around him, he needs to come home to something simple." She sighed. "Yeah, I guess I know Joe better than anybody and I always knew, eventually, it would be a boy. 'Girls are too complicated,' he'd say. Yeah, a boy. A boy with a nice, squeezable ass. No, I'm never wrong about these things." She took another drag of her cigarette then asked me, "What more do you want to know?"

"I was just told I should meet you. That you might be able to give me a few quotes about Joe that would help the book."

"A few quotes? Look, kid, I could write a whole book all by myself, and I might some day. But what is it that he wants me to say? What couldn't he ask me himself?"

"It's about Paul. He said he never knew how you felt and he was afraid to ask you."

"I know he'd never do anything to hurt Paul. Whatever happened, it was an accident. Joe had nothing to do with it. Paul loved him. Joe had to live with that. Every day he had to live with that. And he lived with it very well. Nobody wanted Paul in the band but Joe stuck up for him. He wouldn't listen to the other guys. Paul was so mixed up. When Johnny died, Paul went bananas, saying he'd go the same way, and sure enough he did. But Joe had nothing to do with it. With either of them. Joe was at a party with me the night it happened. I told all that to the police, at the inquest, to the newspapers. What more could I do?"

I shrugged. "You couldn't have done any more."

"No. And Joe's never forgotten that, either. I have my business because of Joe. He set me up, paid for my condo." She chuckled. "Joe's a better ex-husband than he was a husband."

I smiled.

"You're lucky. You won't have to go through a marriage and then a divorce. You can just leave when the bed grows cold."

I frowned.

"Oh, it will, you know. He's restless. He bores easily. He must have had more roadies than any performer in history. And they can eat you alive. He never thought about it, it was just part of it. Now he's regretting it when some of them come out of the woodwork like that woman now, what's her name?"

"Brenda. Brenda Bartholomew."

"Yeah. What a joke. She's probably got Joe confused with somebody else. Maybe Jeffrey. Now he's the one you oughta talk to."

"Oh?"

"He's the one that hated Paul. Wanted him gone. I think they were all stuck on Joe, if you want to know the truth. Joe had this macho thing and they all wanted to challenge it but none of 'em would dare and then when Paul went to Germany and came out, well, that was it! They thought it would look bad, that it would make all of them look like they were sissies so that's why they wanted him to leave. When Joe wouldn't hear of it, well, then they started to wonder what was really going on between the two of them. It was all so incestuous! If they hadn't been so homophobic and all slept together, none of it would have happened. That's my opinion." She laughed. "And now Joe's a star again, all by himself, and he's got a cute little boy besides! Jeffrey would die!"

"Where is Jeffrey?"

"New York. He owns his own theater there, putting on little musicals, strictly off off Broadway, but it keeps him off the streets and out of the clubs. Benny invested his royalties for him and he can afford to do anything he wants. You know, they were making twenty million a year in old days." She looked me up and down again. "And from what I hear, Jeffrey's into lots of weird stuff himself now. But I doubt he could top what Joe has. That was the trouble, he never could top what Joe had."

*

"Squeezable," she said. "Squeezable ass." I kept repeating it in the limo as Harold was taking me back to the house. Joe had never asked me to roll over and I wondered why.

As we slowed in a traffic jam, I ran the tapes back in my mind. I saw how it happened. She was a woman who wouldn't take no for an answer. She strangled Joe. He wanted what he had been taught to want, a wife, but then he didn't. Damned if I could figure what he wanted, but I was determined just to give him what I knew he liked as often as he wanted it.

"Harold, you know where Joe's billboard is?"

"Yes, sir."

"Let's drive by it, and then let's go back down Santa Monica."

"Yes, sir."

I chuckled. Good old Harold.

Benny was right. They used the picture from the album cover. How jock can you get? Benny had told me, "They're gonna spend a million on promotion and a million on the video." "He's worth it," I said.

We took the long way home and went down Santa Monica. I didn't recognize a soul on the street. It was as if the cast had changed completely. Same old show, though. The little waves we got from guys trying to flag us down as we cruised by were so outrageous I laughed like hell but as we turned onto Mulholland and began our climb into the hills, I got real quiet, thinking about Kenny, wondering what had happened to him, thinking about how far away all of that seemed to me now in just a few days. Harold asked me what was wrong.

"Oh, nothing really. I'm just happy."

"You don't look happy." He was sneaking looks at me in the rearview mirror. I'd been noticing him noticing me more and more. I had begun to think he knew the score but shit with him I didn't need.

"Oh, I'll be happy when Joe gets home."

"He's quite something, isn't he?"

"Yeah, incredible."

"You're a lucky boy."

"Yeah, that's why I'm so happy."

He looked in the mirror again, longer this time. "Yes, now you look happy. Just talking about him makes you happy, doesn't it?"

"Well, he's my uncle, you know, and I'm glad to be here and I'm glad he's making a movie." I figured I'd better stick to the story. I wasn't sure about Harold. When I got out of the car and closed the door, he slid down the window and asked, "Will you be needing me tomorrow?"

"You'll have to ask Joe," I replied, with a big shit-eatin' grin on my face.

*

"...How was Luisa?" Joe asked me when he got home.

"Fine. But, you know, I was beginnin' to wonder that myself, while I was talking to her."

"Wonder what?"

"How she was."

He laughed. "A ball buster, that's what she was. Never stopped moving. I'd have to pin her down."

I slipped between his thighs. "You'll never have to pin me down."

"No, it's the other way around, isn't it?"

"You like it that way, with me pinning you down."

"Yeah, that's the way I like it." He locked his thighs around me and kissed me.

"...When did it start, your liking it that way?" I asked after I'd fucked him.

"In Mexico, after Paul died. I went on a long vacation. I'd read about Spanish men and I wanted to find out."

"What about 'em?"

"They're macho, they fuck and that's all they do. There's no kissing, caressing, they're just there to get their rocks off. That's what I wanted. I don't know why, just to find out what it was like. When I was in high school, it had been a fantasy of mine. A couple of guys I knew on the football team I would have taken to bed, believe me. But I didn't understand why. It was against everything I'd ever been taught. And then when I found out Paul was really into it I couldn't believe it."

"Paul wanted you, didn't he?"

"I suppose." He hugged me tighter. "I could have, hundreds of times, but it just wasn't right. We were always with other people, never alone. I guess I made sure that was the way it was, once I knew for sure that's what he was into." He sipped his Jack Daniels and thought a while. Then he went on: "I'm going to tell your tape recorder things I wouldn't tell you."

"Okay." I wanted to tell him I really wanted to know, that knowing would turn me on like crazy but I didn't. I just listened.

"Well, I've always been into watching. I sometimes think I'd rather watch than anything else."

"So I've noticed, in the mirrors."

"Yeah, I've gotta have a mirror. Now that you're here maybe I'll get one for the ceiling, too. Anyhow, sometimes it would be the three of us, Jeffrey, Paul and me, and these girls, sometimes four or five of them, all in the room, running from one of us to the other. We were so high it was hard to tell which one was which but it didn't matter."

"You were really into the drugs then, eh?"

"Yeah. But now, well, I don't know. I've been round and round with the drug thing. People are always wanting me to take a stand on drugs. I can't. To me, it's so relative, so personal. A person's relationship to drugs is like their relationship to sex. I mean, who's so all high and mighty that they can say, 'This guy's cool, this guy's not?'"

"George Bush."

"Yeah, sure. And Jesse Helms. But for me, all kinds of drugs have been both useful and a hindrance to me. But cocaine and heroin, those are the dead-enders. If someone could figure out how to do them without getting strung out, or without having them take over, then fine, but they haven't. I don't want to be a slave to any drug. I'm hopeful they'll come up with some good drugs, drugs that'll make you feel good and make you smarter."

"Smart drugs?"

"Yeah, if somebody said a drug would make me smarter, I'd say, 'No shit? Give me that.'"

"No shit."

"But now I got sex, that's the best drug of all," he said, climbing over me. He got into position and backed down on my prick. "Oh, God, you make me feel so fuckin' good."

I started moving my hips, sending my cock into him as far as it would go. "Best drug in the world, right?"

"...So," I said, coming out of the bathroom after washing up. He was still in bed, catching his breath. "You were on drugs with all these girls in the room and you - "

"Yeah, and I noticed that what Paul liked best was watching me ball some chick. He gave me the creeps at first having him watching but I decided it was better than other things that I didn't want to think about at the time. We were all so afraid of each other, afraid of coming out to each other, of what we really wanted. We believed our own publicity, I guess. And Benny saw to it that there were always plenty of girls. The boys he kept for himself. That was really hysterical. The boys would come and Benny would promise to introduce them and they'd spend the night with him and we'd be gone before they woke up. It was cruel but it was about the only way Benny could score."

He got up and poured himself another one, a short one, and I got a beer. "Oh," he chuckled, "I need to soak my ass." And we moved to the hot tub.

"...Yeah, I wanted to understand Paulie's pain. To feel his pain. Believe me, I found pain in Mexico. I enjoyed it there. I could walk around freely, nobody knew who I was. I didn't have to wear shades. I could let my hair grow really long. In Mexico City I met a guy who worked in a bank. He was what they call a loca, that's Spanish for queer, and he told me that he only wanted a man with a big cock who was masculine because he loved to have it inside of him. But he was upset because all they did was get off and leave. 'What am I supposed to do?' he asked. All he wanted was a fuck and I didn't want that. So he introduced me to one of his boyfriends, a man who was engaged to be married. He said he was going to love being married but he didn't know if he could ever give up boys because there was something different about having sex with them. 'But I know I'm not one of those locas because I only like to coger,' which is their word for fuck. 'I tried it once,' he told me, 'to take it, but it hurt too much. And, besides, I no woman!'

"He told me that in the town where he came from all the men have sex with boys at one time or another. But the boys always paid them, just a little something. It worked the opposite way in Mexico City, where the whores, the chichifos, always get paid for letting men fuck them. He said where he came from, men would hunt the boys up so they could get money to buy booze. They have a saying, 'Any hole is good, even if it's a man's.'"

"And so you had your first with this man?"

"Yes. Cortez. He was very gentle with me and we spent many nights together. He introduced me to many other men, but always with him in the room. I sometimes took on two or three in a night, altogether, one after the other, but after a while he said we were becoming enculado, which is to be joined by the anus, and he broke it off. But I came back to the States a happier man. And now look at me."

He rose from the steamy water and damned if his cock wasn't rigid again, pointing heavenward at the damndest angle I'd ever seen. It was a strange looking cock, very white, very thick but with a small head. It wasn't as long as mine, but it was as thick and as I slipped it into my mouth, I wondered what it would be like to take it up my ass. Suddenly, I was jealous of all the girls. For the first time, I was willing to admit I desired a guy that way. And I wanted it to be Joe. To become *enculado* with Joe.

From the LP "I Remember You"/Sung by Joe Skinner/Side 2, Cut 3, "Fairy Tales:" "...I can remember stories, those things my mother said / She told me fairy tales, before I went to bed / She spoke of happy endings, then tucked me in real tight / She turned my night light on, and kissed my face good night / My mind would fill with visions of perfect paradise..."

It seemed time passed so quickly I hardly noticed there were only two weeks to go on the filming of Disney's alien epic, the title of which had been changed three times during the shooting of it. Joe shook his head, "They told me I could sing the title song, but they don't even have a title let alone a song!" I thought about all the movies I'd seen and wondered what had gone on behind the scenes; I guess it's a wonder they got made at all.

There was some talk of going on a tour to promote the new LP. I didn't want to think about the tour. I didn't want to ask about it, for fear Joe would tell me I couldn't go. Then, out of the blue, he says, "We're going to New York tomorrow."

As usual, I didn't know what to say so I didn't say anything.

"I've agreed to make an appearance at the New York Film Festival. They're showing my first movie, can you believe it?"

I hadn't even seen his first movie, which ended up being released as "Private People." He didn't even own a copy of it he hated it so much and we're going to New York to celebrate it? "No, I can't believe it," I replied.

"Oh, you'll love New York. Benny said he'd go with us. My folks are in Europe so I'm going to have the company plane come out and get us and fly us to New York."

It was the first time he'd mentioned his parents. I had to know more: "The company plane?"

"Paper. Daddy's big in paper, didn't I tell you?"

"In Alabama?"

"Tuscaloosa. The only place to be big in paper. The only place. But you gotta have your own plane, so you can leave."

It had begun to dawn on me that he'd always had everything he wanted and, although it had been hard work being a singer and being on the road, he put up with it because he loved the spotlight. He said: "After the first album hit and the teen magazines started on us, it was wild. Just walking out on stage they screamed for us. I could hear them screaming my name, not paying attention to what I was singing, nothing but me. I wanted them to like me but I realized they loved me. And it was great. They didn't even know me and they loved me. If they had known me, they would have hated me, but as long as I was my image, they loved me."

He never really suffered to become a star the way others did, and because things came easily for him, he could discard them easily. With each new day I wondered how long it would go on, this dream I was in, how long before he'd trade me in on a new model. But now he was actually saying I was going to New York with him. He'd never taken me out, other than to drive out Sunset to the Pacific Coast Highway and then up to Malibu on a Sunday to watch the sun setting over the sea. And with his eyes hidden behind his shades and baggy clothes hiding his brawn, we were just like any other couple. But now he was taking me to New York. In his parents' plane. It wasn't happening, yet it was.

*

It was a small white jet with a big red S on the tail of it. The two pilots paid me no mind at all and treated Joe like he was a member of the family, which I guess he was.

As we were taking off, it began to rain but soon we were flying above the rainclouds. Sunshine streamed into the cabin. A few raindrops clung on the windows and they sparkled when the sunlight caught them.

Joe gave me a beer and when I gulped it, he and Benny laughed. "You're not nervous, are you, kid?" Benny asked, patting my knee.

"Who me?" And I laughed harder than either of them.

Still, I was terrified. Only a few months before, I had never even been to the bus terminal. So many places I'd never been. When I told Pa I was going to take a bus to Hollywood he said, "You can't be serious. Now, no more nonsense. You're always talkin' nonsense." I chuckled to think what kind of nonsense he'd think this was, flying across the Grand Canyon in the Skinner Industries' jet, with the guy I thought to be handsomest man in the world sitting across from me, pouring me another beer.

Suddenly, I felt very comfortable. Benny and I sat facing Joe. There was a table between us where we put our drinks and Joe was reading the latest issue of *The New Yorker* while Benny and I talked.

After Joe told the pilot to "buzz the Canyon," Joe began reading us an article about a new club that had opened in New York and Benny broke in: "...Celebrities go to places like that now. We could never do that in the old days. But still, there's such a stigma attached to being gay and it's worse today, with AIDS. I hate that. I can live with being a Jew but being gay is something I could never deal with. It doesn't mean a thing, it's just an aspect of my life, that's all. I hate ghettos, making tiny islands in the middle of humanity. Jews do that, gays do that. And like the Jews, most of the gays today have lost touch, they don't try to communicate, to tell people that they are not a threat to society. They're as uptight about straights as straights are about them. Us, we're in-between, aren't we Joe?"

Joe chuckled. "If you say so."

"Yeah, in-between. Hey, what's that word they used to describe you guys in the beginning?"

"Androgynous."

"Yeah, that's what they always called the boys, androgynous."

"We could go either way," Joe said, closing his magazine, shifting slightly in his seat and then winking at me.

"But it was Paulie who went every which way. Yeah, he and Johnny, they were always into excess. If you said jump two feet, they'd jump ten."

"Paulie taught me the big rule, though," Joe said, taking another magazine up from the seat next to him.

"Yeah?"

Joe looked up, his eyes sparkling. "Yeah, that there are no rules. Every rule can be broken." And he winked at me again.

*

Joe had the pilot "buzz the City" and as we came down through the mist it was like a Polaroid picture, printing before my eyes. The City was exposing itself to me, glittering and showy and everything I'd ever imagined it would be from seeing it for years on TV. Joe identified all the biggest buildings and the Park. "Our hotel's right there, on the edge of it," he said, pointing to the Plaza.

"We'll have to stop staying there, Joe. Trump's going to turn it into condos."

"So buy one of 'em."

"I'll make a note of it."

Benny was always making a note of everything Joe said, although he never wrote anything down.

"You'll feel at home in Manhattan. Most of the people have dyslexia," Joe said. "But they aren't like you. They never get any help. You've risen above 'em. They're all still stuck on their rock."

"On the brink of nervous breakdown," Benny chimed in. "Still, it's a fun place to visit."

Joe smiled. "Like Johnny used to say, in New York you've gotta just 'let it ride.'"

I knew Joe'd be doing a lot of riding in New York, riding my prick for all it was worth. I wondered if they had any mirrors at the Plaza, then I decided they must have or Joe wouldn't stay there.

*

In the glare of the klieg lights, I saw a different Joe Skinner. He was transformed into the star I saw in the music videos from the late '70s and early '80s he kept at the house, the star I imagined on stage. He waved to the crowd, smiling, loving every minute of it. I walked silently behind Benny. Joe had a "date" for the night, a starlet named Dorianne Dempsey, who accompanied him onstage while he answered questions from the audience.

At one point he said: "I'll never forget this film because Alec Guinness has a cameo bit as a homeless man in London right at the beginning...He was great, wonderful to work with, so many jokes. And he gave me a lot of confidence because he told me he's always very nervous, very unsure of himself. He told me it never goes away, that insecurity."

"Lack of confidence doesn't seem to have been a problem with you," someone said.

"Oh, yes, from the beginning. Appearing on stage, in front of a bunch of screaming girls, is terrible. But being in a movie, with real actors, people who have been doing it for years, is even spookier. Every time I see this movie I wonder why I did this or that in it. Luckily, I didn't have many lines to learn. You know, the truly perfect movie has no dialogue. That's what they were trying for...Yeah, this is an action picture like no other. All in bed or in the shower or on the balcony!"

I thought, like me and Joe at the house on the cliff, and I closed my eyes, remembering, wishing I was back there. Now, seeing him make love to some girl on the big screen, even if it was make-believe, was not my idea of fun.

Joe and the girl sat together at the beginning of the movie, then left. I started to follow them but Benny said we had to stay. "It's cool," he said. I believed everything Benny said because he was so final about it. You never argued with Benny. If Benny had forced it, I figured, I might have been history.

"It was pretty bad, kid, " Benny said on our way out. "I don't remember it being that bad, Alec Guinness or no Alec Guinness. Joe really can't act worth shit, you know?"

"He was beautiful, though," I said. "Especially when he was naked."

Benny smiled. "Yes, he was."

"I meant, Mr. Kaplan, that Joe is beautiful." (I always called him Mr. Kaplan. He loved it, I could tell. "Kid's got respect," he told Joe once.)

"Yes," he said, grinning, "he certainly is, kid. He certainly is."

We found Joe and the girl at the little bar in the lobby, laughing and joking like a couple of lovebirds. I would have been insane with jealousy but I knew who Joe was going to take back to the suite at the Plaza, who he would be sleeping with that night and it wouldn't be her.

I stood next to a man in a tuxedo who was gabbing on a cellular phone while Joe posed for photographs with the starlet and with some of the girls who came to the showing. I asked one of them what she saw in Joe and she just groaned, unable to put it into words. Another said, "Oh, he's got such a cute butt."

That really made my day. If she had known what I was doing to that cute little butt every night she would've had a heart attack. But, of course, that was the point of the whole deal. We were like characters on the screen only we were off the screen...but not very far.

Joe politely signed autographs and then said to Benny, "Give me air." Benny nodded and we began our move toward the door. Benny had many years of experience getting Joe in and out of a crowd and we just kept moving, steadily toward the door, slicing through the crowd, and in moments we were back in the limo.

Benny and I sat in the jump seats and Joe and the girl sat across from us. They were still laughing and joking. I decided Joe was a better actor than anybody gave him credit for. Benny fixed everybody a cocktail and by the time we got to what Joe called "Cafe Lux," actually Cafe Luxembourg on 70th Street, the girl was falling all over Joe. But he told the driver to take her back to "wherever she came from" and then call for us in an hour or so. "Give me air," Joe sighed as we were going into the restaurant.

While one problem was disposed of, another awaited us at the Lux. I wasn't told that Joe had invited his old partner Jeffrey for a reunion. After I was introduced and we were seated in a deep red booth in the back of the room, Benny and Jeffrey were head-to-head talking and I whispered to Joe that I thought it would be better if I left. He just shook his head and, under the table, took my hand and held it. I guided it to my crotch and he left it there for a few moments and I grew stiff under his magic touch. Everything was going to be fine, he was saying. From the looks I was getting from Jeffrey, I wasn't so sure. Finally, Jeffrey acknowledged my presence by asking, "So, how long have you been in Hollywood?"

"Just a couple of months."

"Not long enough to have acquired any bad habits, eh?"

"Well, maybe a couple." I smiled, looking at Joe. I thought it best to smile. Joe quickly changed the subject, talking about the festival.

Jeffrey's date was an Italian actress named Carmen, a tall woman in her 30's with brown hair streaked blond. She wore a man's dinner jacket. I never caught the last name but if I ever see her in a movie I'll recognize her and be able to say I had dinner with her.

When we first arrived, she was in the rest room so we all had a chance to get acquainted before she re-appeared. Everybody in the place watched her as she moved through the room to where we were sitting and when she sat down, Jeffrey said, "Joe's always wanted to meet you."

Joe laughed. Not five minutes earlier he'd said he'd never heard of her.

"Oh?" she asked, squeezing into the booth next to Jeffrey.

"Yeah, he read you like men with power," Jeffrey said.

"Oh, no, that's not true at all. I don't like powerful people. Oh, I've liked some, but, generally, no. But I do have to admit I like to wield my own power over others."

"Does she ever -" Jeffrey laughed.

"Yes, I'm a monstrous individualist. I can't work up interest in others and I can't be influenced by the men I'm with. I am curious about their life but then I grow bored."

"Does she ever," Jeffrey kidded. "She's bored with me already and she's only been in town three days."

"I have to come to New York once a year. I love it. You meet such interesting people here. Jeffrey knows such interesting people."

"Thanks. I think," Jeffrey laughed.

"No, I love artists," she said, smiling at Jeffrey. "Their work is immortal."

"Are you staying at Jeffrey's?" Joe asked.

"Oh no, heavens no. At the Palace. I love hotels. If I had enough money, I'd live in hotels all the time. And I always sleep alone."

"Really?" Jeffrey asked.

"Oh, you know what I mean. I hate to sleep with someone. In the morning, if I've slept with someone, I feel unclean."

"Nothing worse," Joe muttered.

"What's your favorite hotel?" I asked. She seemed shocked I was even entering into the conversation but I was fascinated.

"Oh, I suppose the Mamounia in Marrakesh."

I nodded as if I knew all about it. I wasn't even sure I knew where Marrakesh was. "Yes, I've heard it's nice," I said.

Joe chuckled. "When in Rome - "

"Oh, the Cavalieri Hilton on Monte Mario," she gushed. "I love the pool."

While they chatted away, I watched Jeffrey in the mirrors all around. He caught my eye several times and smiled. I just sat there as if I belonged, nibbling on the crunchy sourdough rolls and listening, committing what they said to the tapes in my mind, nodding at times as if I really understood. And maybe I understood more than they thought I did.

I remembered what Joe had said about Jeffrey, and especially what Luisa had said, that he was weird. And then that Jeffrey had invited Luisa and Joe to a place in the mountains for a weekend and how they got high and at some point they switched partners and when Joe saw Jeffrey fucking his wife he freaked. He got up and said, "That's it, we're leaving." Joe put it this way: "Nobody fucks Luisa but me. Her doing it with another girl I could live with, but not another guy, especially my best friend." He didn't speak to

Jeffrey for a couple of weeks and then he didn't blame Jeffrey, he blamed Luisa.

Finally, Carmen said she was hungry and Jeffrey called the waiter. She ordered salmon and more champagne and we all had the same. After the waiter left, she said, out-of-the-blue, "You can live without sex, you just can. You absolutely can sustain life without sex."

"Yeah, you can, but who would want to?" Jeffrey laughed.

"Oh, sexual tension's everywhere. I feel it?"

"Yeah," Joe snickered. I beamed.

"Oh, and I support it. But I don't partake of it all the time."

"Only when in New York - " Jeffrey chuckled.

"Well, you know, when you go out maybe seven times out of ten a situation occurs because somebody was giving off this wonderful energy that somebody else was picking up on. And you just seize the moment."

"Yeah, that's what I do all the time, seize the moment," Joe chuckled, squeezing my crotch.

I drank some more champagne. Things were finally getting interesting.

"You've all read the papers and know what I've done and what I haven't done. It's so bizarre! Why the fuck would anybody care? And when they completely fabricate something it really blows your mind."

"Yes," Joe said. "I've seen years of my life summed up in five sentences. It sounds like it all took place over this wild weekend."

"Was all a blur to me," Jeffrey laughed.

Carmen chuckled. "I've read flat-out lies so hideous but I stopped reading it because I wasn't going to let them get to me. Give me a fucking break."

"You've had some great romances, though, Carmen. Marcello and even David Bowie!"

"Oh, God! I spend twenty hours a day on a set with this person for three months out of my life and I know him, right? I sure as hell know him better than somebody I tried to make time to see maybe three times in those three months.

"I think a complete relationship can last a week if you walk away with something that you don't forget or something that moved you or something that altered you. "

"It makes for interesting conversation at lunch in Hollywood, though. Like, 'Well, I just saw Joe Skinner and he was drunk again.' 'And what did he do this time?' They get seven minutes of glory and I look like shit."

Carmen nodded. "It's all part of this mass insanity. It's a mass sickness, this interest people have in us, their jealousy, their envy."

"It's like a kind of disease," Joe said. "I don't have an entirely objective view of what that is, but I do have pretty good idea of what people think of me now - that I was this teen idol and then I became a drunk and now I'm a two-bit actor making cameo appearances in other people's movies." He laughed. "Once I was trying to make a call on a house phone in a hotel and this guy comes up to me and asks, 'Hey, man, are you as big a drunk as they say?' And I said, 'Yeah.' It takes longer if you try to defend yourself."

"They're cowards," Jeffrey said. "They don't look at the truth."

"It's as if they realized that the wolves needed some food so they said, 'Hey, here's this kid, name's Joe Skinner. Have a feast.'"

I looked at him and chuckled to myself, realizing how few people really knew what a fucking feast he was.

"Well, with this new album and this new movie, you'll have the last laugh, Joe."

"Yeah. You know, I dearly love rock music when it's good, but it really wasn't me. I'm pop rock, for chrissakes, really an old-fashioned, sentimental piece of shit. Sure, you can say what the hell is this shit in the new album, but I think these songs are talking about the kind of love everybody wants."

"I love it," I chimed in.

Joe smiled. "Yeah, it's like Dylan has written songs that touch into places people have never sung about before and I admire that. But I can't write 'em, I can only sing 'em."

"And dance. You sure could dance. Yeah, we had it all then," Benny said, "Jeffrey on keyboard, best in the business. Johnny on drums. And Paulie on guitar, unreal. And Joe, he was on stage only half the time, singing and dancing, carrying on."

"Well, I can't just stand on stage. I feel like an idiot most of the time. It was like getting up in front of the senior class when I was elected president and making my little speech. I need these songs, these powerful kind of songs, as an armor I can hide behind."

"Yeah, when we went out onstage and started the music, it was as if we were transformed, from these ordinary guys into something like forces of a larger consciousness. The audience wants that, they don't want reality, they want fantasy, and we gave 'em that. They never knew what to expect next."

"And we all got along."

"Yeah, because, the thing was, we treated each other like equals."

"Sure we did," Jeffrey laughed. "The thing was, I learned to always get out of the van first because once Joe got out, all hell broke loose."

"Really? I thought all the commotion was for Paulie."

"Paulie, shit."

"I seem to have problems wherever I go," Joe said. "But now I kinda miss it, I really do, but it's scary being on your own. But I just couldn't go on after Paulie died. I just couldn't. All I needed was people yelling, 'Sit down, man, you're a fuckin' disgrace.' So now I'm taking more heat for doing something ambitious than other people get for just cashing it in. The truth is I did this because I wanted to, not to get anybody's approval."

"And it's great, it really is. Shit, man, I wish I'd been on keyboard for you."

"You weren't available, remember?"

"Yeah, yeah."

"But that's why I wanted to come to New York, to see if I could convince you to do this little tour with me, just twelve cities in a month. No big deal. Just play the piano. As if we were in a saloon."

"I'll think about it."

After dinner, Jeffrey invited us to a party. "You oughta expose the kid to some theatrical types," Jeffrey chuckled.

"Sure, why not," Joe said. And we were off in the limo.

It was a small apartment, beautifully furnished, and the host, a balding queeny type, Eddie, was thrilled Joe could make it. "You must sing for us," he gushed.

"Only if I get paid," Joe laughed, brushing past him. "Where's the bar?"

The host pointed into the dining room, introduced Benny to a guy bulging out of his Gold's Gym tank top, and then turned his attention to me. I thought I looked pretty good in my dark blue Ralph Lauren blazer and tight chinos but this guy really got off on it, saying how things had really changed since he went to college. "They really wear clothes like that at Ohio State?"

"Sure," I said. "Every day."

He led me from room to room introducing me as Joe's nephew

from Ohio State.

"He's too little to be a football player," one guy said.

"Maybe, but boy, does he know how to ball!" Eddie kidded.

Finally, Jeffrey left Carmen with some "artists" and rescued me. We sat on the little terrace looking out at the skyline, drinking champagne cocktails. I kept checking on Joe in the living room but eventually he disappeared. "What's wrong?" Jeffrey asked.

"Joe. He's had too much to drink again."

"Hey, you can't keep him on the wagon for long."

"So I've found out."

"Just like you can take the boy out of the country but you can't take the country out of the boy."

"Is it so obvious?"

"Yes, but you're not obvious. That's what appealed to Joe, I know. Shit, you look straighter than he does. You're so fresh, so honest, so trusting, you really look out of place here. It's almost as if you'd be out of place anywhere but the farm you came from."

"Is that bad?"

"No. I think when you've been to college and done everything Joe and I've done, well, you get old and tired and maybe even sick and things stop being new and exciting. To see you enjoying everything, to be so crazy about Joe, well, it's nice."

"Thanks." It was a surprise, his being nice. I suddenly liked him, liked him a lot. He wasn't as handsome as Joe but he had a certain quality about him, decidedly macho yet something I could work on. If Joe hadn't been there, I don't know what I would have done. But as it was, I got up and went to find my man. He was where I knew he would be, at the bar, pouring another Jack Daniels.

"I'm really tired -" I said.

"I'll bet," he said, "After Jeffrey now are you?" And when he turned to face me I saw the coldness was back in his eyes and I wanted to run again. I did just that, out the door without saying goodbye, looking for Benny, without stopping for anything. I took the stairs rather than wait for an elevator and instead of the limo I took a cab. When I got back to the Plaza they didn't want to give me a key to the room but I caused such a commotion they decided I must be with the Skinner party.

Less than an hour later, Joe threw open the door to the bedroom. I hadn't been sleeping, just lying there in bed wondering what would happen when he finally showed. He swayed back and forth as he came to the bed. He yanked the sheet away and saw that I was nude.

"You liked Jeffrey, didn't ya?"

"Jeffrey?"

"I saw you, smiling at him, turning it on for him. What can he do that I can't?"

"Hey, Joe, this is crazy! We were just talkin'."

"What can he do?" he insisted.

"Nothin'. He can't do anythin'."

"No, you're wrong. You're fucking wrong! He fucks! That's what he does best. He fucks! He fucks people over, he fucks around with the music, he fucks everything in sight. The girls love him because he's the best goddam fucker there ever was!"

I felt like saying, "If you say so," but I didn't. I just rolled over, ignoring him.

"Yeah, turn your pretty ass to me why don't ya? That's what you want, isn't it? You're just a little fairy, just a goddam little fairy, like all the rest. All ya want is to get fucked. You just live to get fucked."

I wanted to say, no, Joe, you're the one that lives to get fucked, but I didn't. I kept ignoring him. I heard him undressing. I hoped he'd pass out before he got naked but he didn't. He climbed on the bed and grabbed my ass, one cheek in each hand and spit between them. I tried to roll over. "No, Joe, not like this."

"The only way for you, fairy. The only way."

At first I squirmed, attempting to get away, but I knew he could easily   overpower me. He wanted it this way, I decided. And whatever he thought of me in the morning I would just have to deal with. It was as if we had created new characters just for the night. If I could live with that, it was okay. The room had a big, gilded mirror that Joe had taken off the wall earlier and propped up against some chairs so that he could watch me fuck him. Now with the dim light coming from the living room. I watched our reflections as he slapped my ass and fingered me. It was turning me on.

"Yeah, Jeffrey knows a good piece of ass when he sees it. But this one's mine. Shit, I've fuckin' paid for it a thousand times."

It always got down to that. He'd paid for it. That's all I was. A whore. I wanted to cry, "Yes, yes, only for you," but I didn't. I didn't say anything because I didn't know what to say. My father had taught me that.

I lifted myself up to meet Joe's fingers but he slammed me down.

He kept spitting, then took a bottle of champagne, left over from the afternoon, and poured it all over my ass, then began licking it off. He split my cheeks and poured it into me, followed by his fingers. He was rough and I cried out in pain. I kept squirming and the more I did, the more force he applied. He had shoved me up on the bed and pinned me against the headboard. Soon he was lying on top of me, sliding over me. His cock was semi-hard; he would get the head of it in my ass and but when he tried to stick more of it in, it slid out. I cringed with the pain a couple of times and that turned him on, but not enough to get a full erection. The champagne was gone and he threw the bottle into a corner. He continued to lick my skin, my shoulders, my back, then my ass again. Finally, I came when his tongue went into my ass. I couldn't help it; the pressure on my cock between the mattress and my abdomen was overwhelming. It wasn't a very intense orgasm, just a relief, but he felt my shuddering. He reached under me and ran his fingers along my prick, feeling the wetness.

"Yeah," he snarled, "this is what you've wanted all along isn't it?"

I didn't say anything.

"Isn't it?" He yelled in my ear, shaking me again.

"Yes, yes!"

"Yeah, that's right, sissy," he moaned and it seemed to satisfy him because he rolled across my back a few more times and then slid off of me onto the bed, finally passing out.

I staggered out of the bed and went to close the door to the bedroom. As I was shutting it, I looked into the living room of the suite and saw Benny was sitting on the couch. He had seen it all. I just stood there in the open doorway and made no attempt to hide my nakedness.

He shook his head. "I don't know how anybody can be so mean to someone as beautiful as you are."

I stepped into the room and dropped down into the big overstuffed chair across from him. I didn't know what to say so I didn't say anything.

"I know how tough it is being with these guys," he went on. "It wore me out. But you're young, you can handle it."

"Not many more scenes like that I can't. I just don't understand."

"I never did either. There's this terrible war going on in their minds and they try to make you a part of it. They succeed most of the time and then it's you that has to pay, not them."

I really looked at him for the first time. He had done so much for them and continued to do it, yet he took whatever was dealt him, and I knew he was trapped. What else could he do? He was over 40, ugly, with a terrible toupee, and he was willing to live his life through his band. But I had a choice. I could leave.

He stood up and began walking towards his bedroom. "Get some sleep. We'll have some fun tomorrow. There's some things I haven't seen here in years and I want to take you along."

"Okay," I said, closing my eyes.

*

When the cute room service boy rolled in the cart with a gold linen tablecloth on it, then very efficiently began laying the breakfast out, Benny took the newspaper off the cart. "Three places?" the kid asked, his eyes moving from me to Benny and back again.

I shrugged.

"Yes, three," Benny said, picking up the check from a silver tray and signing it. As he dropped the check back on the tray, he gave the boy a once over again, then looked at me and winked.

"Thank you," the boy said, "thank you very much," and then left with the little tray in his hand.

"Adorable ass," Benny said after he was gone.

Nodding, I drank my orange juice in one gulp then started in on the eggs and toast.

As he promised, Benny took me sightseeing while Joe slept it off. It was a gray day and the tops of the buildings were lost in a fog and he said, "The mist is the veil between this world and the other."

It started to rain and the people scurried along, the patterns of their umbrellas shifting like a weird video. The cars swished in the pothole puddles and the traffic lights blinked. As the rain started coming down sideways, Benny and I ducked into a coffee shop.

"This place is just too much, " I said. "It's everything I ever imagined and more."

"Are you?"

"Am I what?"

"More than anyone imagines?"

"Hardly."

"God, from what I saw last night, you're more than I'd ever

imagined. Talk about hung!"

He was looking at me in a new way, a greedy way. I avoided his eyes. "Let's not talk about last night."

When the rain stopped, we decided to take the ferry to the Statue of Liberty. Looking back at Manhattan I realized it really was an island and that all the people on it were trapped, forced to somehow get along with each other. There may have been bridges and airports so you could escape but, when you got right down to it, all those different races and sexual orientations had to get along. Looking at the island as it came and went in the mist I felt a rush of excitement that I didn't ever get in L.A.

When we returned, Joe was on the phone. Wrapped in his silk robe that matched my new one, he waved to us and went on talking. I took a beer from the refrigerator and sat down beside him on the couch. His eyes were bloodshot and his hair was damp from a shower but he still looked good enough to eat. I set my hand on his thigh. He picked it up and held it to his lips and nibbled my fingers as he listened.

"We'll see you tonight, after the concert. It'll be fun. Maybe I can even talk Diana into coming. Haha!"

He hung up the phone.

"Concert?"

"Diana Ross's opening at Radio City tonight. Jeffrey got us seats and then we're meeting him at his place after for a little buffet. He's become a gourmet cook. Can you believe it?"

He put his arm around me and drew me into him. As we were about to kiss, Benny said, "Excuse me. I'm going to take a nap."

"Benny doesn't like to watch," Joe said after he'd gone.

"Oh? News to me."

He did a doubletake, then said, "Yeah, Benny's very private. He goes off and does his own thing. Like tonight, he'll go to the concert but he'll beg off dinner."

He held me and looked out the window. "It's sad about Benny. He gets into dangerous scenes. I hope he buys something tonight that won't kill him." His eyes returned to mine and he reached down and took my cock in his hand. "God," he chuckled, "I bet this could kill Benny."

He was stroking it, admiring it, like he always did. It was as if the night before had never happened.
*

"...Don't ever let me get stale like that," Joe said to Benny after the concert. Benny was leading us backstage and there was a security guard behind us. No one recognized Joe, his face hidden behind his dark glasses.

Joe'd complained all during the performance about Miss Ross. "You should've seen her in the '70s," he said at intermission. "Now, that was a show. I saw her in Atlanta when I was a teenager. She was over-the-top, man, just unbelievable. This is shit. She doesn't even have a band, for chrissakes, just the synthesizers. She acts as if she's sleepwalking. Going, going, gone."

In the second half, with long black hair that flowed past his shoulders, a guy impersonating her tried to get onto the stage. The guards stopped him but Diana had him brought on. "Who are you?" she asked. "I'm Diana Ross," the guy said.

"No, you aren't me!" She wagged her finger at him. "Not with straight hair you're not!" Then she asked us which hair we liked better. I voted for the drag queen; Joe voted for Diana. Benny just shook his head. She won, of course, then had the guards get the guy off so she could sing her best number, "God Bless the Child." Benny leaned into me and whispered, "God bless you, child." I just grinned.

There was a crowd of people at the dressing room door and when she stepped out to shake hands, I saw she had changed into a sarong and looked small and somehow helpless amid the adoration. Joe talked with a couple of people he knew, people I didn't recognize, and Benny pointed out Tony Bennett and Billy Baldwin, whom I didn't know from Adam but probably should have. Soon Diana Ross was in front of us. Joe congratulated her, then introduced me as his nephew. She just touched my hand, not even shaking it really, and then gave Joe a little peck on the cheek. Quickly she moved on to some of the others standing behind us and we were on our way out the rear exit where the limo was waiting.

Joe was right about Benny; he had the driver drop him off at a bar called Rounds and we went on to the Village. Joe opened the car's bar and poured himself a Jack Daniels. I had a beer. "Here," he said, reaching into his coat pocket, "take this." He handed me a pill. "Jeffrey can always get the best pills."

"No. I don't do drugs, you know that."

"Just tonight. We're in New York, havin' a party."

I shook my head.

"Shit, you're worse than Benny! Now take one. You'll feel great. Trust me."

I wasn't going to swallow it, just make it look as if I did, but the tire of the limo hit a pothole in the road and the pill slipped down my throat anyway. Oh, shit, I thought, but then I was, after all, there to please him. If that's what he wanted. I put my head back and looked through the skylight of the limo. As the lights in the tall buildings twinkled as we sailed by them, I pinched Joe's knee just to reassure myself I wasn't dreaming.

Jeffrey lived on the top floor of a building he owned in the Village. On the first floor were his offices and the second and third were rehearsal halls. We went up in a freight elevator. The door opened right into a huge room, all white and chrome. There were about a dozen people there, boys and girls, all under 30. Joe found Jeffrey right away and left me with him to go directly to the bar. Jeffrey's handshake was dry and firm. He held my hand and sort of led me to the food buffet.

"Hey, you look like you're starvin'," he said. "I made all this just for you."

He didn't seem to want to stop touching me. When his hand left mine it was on my arm, then on my neck, then he squeezed me there. I turned and stared at him, as if to say, do you want something?

"You're a cute little bugger," he said, smiling.

"That's me, the bugger."

He blinked, as if he couldn't quite believe it. I knew about being bugged and being buggered. It dawned on me that he figured Joe was fucking me. Perhaps it was beyond his comprehension that Joe would take it up the ass. And he was beginning to bug me in another sense; if he showed any more interest in me and Joe saw us again, well, I didn't want to think about it. I looked around the big living room for my man. "Joe's at the bar in the kitchen," Jeffrey said. "If you want to know where Joe is, just listen for the ice cubes dropping in a glass."

He put his arm around my waist. "But we don't need him tonight, do we?"

I gulped.

"You know, you remind me of the boys in Paris. They're over 18 but they look like they're only fifteen. And they like girls as much as they like guys."

"I don't dislike girls," I muttered.

"Good."

The music blaring out of the speakers I recognized as early Skins. Jeffrey hollered to the boy at the stereo. "No, not that shit, not tonight. Put Joe's new CD on."

I shoved another one of Jeffrey's funny little gourmet meatballs in my mouth as he led me through the crowd beginning to form around the table. We ended up in a far corner of the room. "There's somebody I want you to meet," he said.

She was tiny, a little doll of a girl, with blond curls, wearing a "Bad Company" T-shirt ripped just so, enough to show a nipple, and black tights. Jeffrey introduced me as Joe Skinner's nephew and the girl, Tina, gushed, "Oh, you're even cuter than he is."

"It's in the genes -" Jeffrey snickered, slapping my ass. "All in the jeans."

"She's thinking about going to Hollywood," Jeffrey said. "Maybe you can discourage her." And he left us alone.

"It's so dark over here in this corner," I said, sitting next to her on a huge black cube.

"I don't like too much light," she said. "In fact, I don't like the sun. That's why I've turned down so many chances to go to California. Besides the radiation, it does a number on pesticides. Did you know that?"

"No."

She took a swig of something in a china cup and went on. "Besides I think things are nicer in the dark, don't you?"

"Yeah."

"I don't really plan it but I'm usually up all night. I get a lot more done that way, you know? Like, I don't need my sleep. None at all, really. And at night you pick up more signals."

"Signals?"

"Well maybe you people in California would call them vibes. I call them signals, like what's happening with us. Like when I saw you come in the door, I said to Jeffrey, that's it, that's my date for tonight. And he said, 'You mean Joe Skinner.' And I said, 'Hell, no, the cute little one with him.'" Her hand dropped to my thigh and she sighed, "It's all in the signals."

"Well, I got a date tonight, you know?"

"That's interesting, but let me go on." And she did, for what seemed like hours, talking shit, until I finally decided I'd better find Joe. But she followed along, saying she needed more tea.

"...Stimulants are important," Joe was telling some guy, "but I need to chill out sometimes, you know." He reached in his pocket and grabbed something, then opened his hand to the guy. "Red, yellow, blue. Name your flavor."

"I need a co-pilot tonight. And black. I like 'em black," the guy said.

"Oh," Joe said, reaching into his other pocket. "Here we are -"

"Yeah," the guy said, taking one of the black and white ones.

Wedging in between them, I said: "Tina needs more tea."

Joe gave her the once over with his bloodshot eyes and said, "She needs more 'n tea."

"Drugs?" the guy suggested.

"Just aspirin," Tina said, adjusting her ragged T-shirt so that both nipples showed. Her tits were small but beautifully formed. "I used to like PCP but, you know, sometimes you just come to the end of the scene."

"End of scene," Joe said, moving back to where the bottles were set up.

I went to him, touched his elbow and said, "Joe - "

Pouring another drink, he glared at me. "Hey, kid, Tina needs some tea."

I nodded, bit my lip, and went to look for the tea.

"...Let's find a darker place," Tina said, holding her china cup out in front of her and leading the way. She had me firmly by the hand. The red pill and the beer had gone to my head and my resistance was melting away. There were only two other rooms in the loft, one obviously Jeffrey's bedroom and the other a study with a wall of books and a black piano. We sat at the piano and she tried to play the song that was on the stereo, still Joe's CD, "I Remember You."

"That's such a pretty song," she sighed.

"His voice is so great; that's what makes it."

She stopped playing and finished her tea. "It puts me into a such a crazy mood. It's like I feel these terribly strong signals right now that we've got to do something. Can you feel it?" She put down her cup on the piano and pressed her body next to mine.

"No. Well, yeah, I feel strong signals like I'd better go find Joe."

"It's okay. Jeffrey told me it was cool. He said Joe'll play along.

That's what he wants, actually."

"What he wants?"

"Yeah, Jeffrey says he's got this thing about watching. He loves to watch. And it's the safest sex you can have, you know?" She kissed my chin and started rubbing my pecs. "And Jeffrey knows there's nothing I like better than an audience. That's why he invited me. I always get invited to his parties, one way or another."

"Life of the party, right?"

"Sweetie, sometimes I am the party."

As she was unbuttoning my shirt and pulling it from my pants, she asked, "What do you do for a living?"

"I hustle."

"I hustle, too, sweetie, but I'm really selling an essence. It's all essence."

"I'll have to remember that."

Suddenly, it seemed her essence was too close for comfort, but I was getting excited by the thought of it all the same. Her tit fell completely out of her ripped T-shirt and I took it in my hand. I'd seen plenty of movies; I knew how this was supposed to go, and I'd played around like this before when I was in high school with the girl who lived down the road. I'd messed around with her body, just to see what it was all about, and she really got off on it. I didn't fuck her. I didn't have to. She just went crazy without my sticking her at all.

But now I didn't feel as if I wanted to please Tina. It was as if from that point on it was as if I was pleasing Joe. That eventually he'd come in and do what she said, watch. And the thought of him watching me, for some reason, turned me on. I pulled her T-shirt over her head and threw it in a corner, then started kissing her tits, playing with her nipples, which were really hard after awhile. She climbed over me and slid her thighs around me and rubbed her crotch against mine. And there, on the piano bench in the dark, she rubbed against me and kissed me and ran her hands through my hair as if I was the sexiest thing in the world. Suddenly, the music stopped and I could hear people leaving. Then the music started again, the old Skins music again. I heard footsteps down the hall and then Jeffrey was in the room. He turned on a small lamp on his desk.

"I knew you two'd get along," he said, dropping down on the bench behind Tina.

"He's so hot," Tina gushed, pulling my shirt further apart and kissing my chest.

Jeffrey was rubbing her back and I looked at him and shrugged.

"Yeah," he said, "Joe was right about him. He's a hot little number."

As she worked her way down my chest to my navel, I leaned back on my elbows. She unzipped my pants and exposed my dick, now fully erect.

"God, sweetie, little he ain't."

Jeffrey looked around her, glanced down at my cock swaying in front of her face, and snickered, then lifted her up and started to pull her black tights down her butt. She bent over even further, took my cock in her hand and kissed the shaft. He tugged and tugged at her tights but finally just ripped them apart. She moaned and pulled my balls out of my pants.

I heard footsteps again. Just in time, I thought. I still had time to cover up and get the hell out of there. I pulled away and stood up. My cock was arching in her face and Jeffrey had his hands on her middle, pushing her toward me. Just then, Joe appeared next to me, taking me in his arms. I fell against his chest and turned my face toward him. He swayed back and forth with the music and just held me. Tina opened her mouth and started taking my cock between her lips. Jeffrey lifted her up again and got her on her knees on the piano bench, pulling what was left of the black tights down around her knees. Joe's hand moved to my balls and he played with them while she sucked me. I kissed his chest and tried to squirm away and turn toward him but he held me tight, forcing me deep into her throat. I looked over her body and saw Jeffrey undo his pants and slip out his hard rod. It gleamed in the pink light from the desk lamp, wet with his precum. It was a short dick but nicely shaped; I would have sucked it gladly. He aimed it at her cunt and just slid it in, then out again. He began ramming her with it and she started to bite my cock. I tried pulling away again but Joe held me. Tina tried to develop a rhythm but Jeffrey's plowing was erratic. For somebody who was so into fucking, I didn't think he was very good. Maybe he'd had some of Joe's pills; I didn't know and it didn't really matter because I could feel Joe's hard-on rubbing against the cheeks of my ass. Was this the way he wanted it? To do it to me while his friend did it to the girl, to somehow be linked? I didn't have a clue but her teeth were killing me and I took her head and steadied it, then tried drawing it back but every time I did, Jeffrey would ram her again. Joe was pulling my pants down the rest of the way. Then he pulled my shoes off and I was soon naked from the waist down. Finally, Tina came up for air and I yanked myself away. Joe stepped into my place and Tina unzipped his pants and his cock flopped out; it was only semi-hard. She kissed it, then played with his balls. I went around him and held him as he had held me, my erection sliding between the cheeks of his ass. I lowered his pants just enough so that skin would touch skin.

"Look at him go," Joe sighed as Jeffrey grabbed Tina's ass and really let her have it. He pulled all the way out then rammed it in to the hilt, then back out. "Music is rhythm and so is sex," Joe had said, "and Jeffrey has the best rhythm of anybody I've ever seen." I watched now as Jeffrey fucked and tried to get into his rhythm; it was too fast for me, too furious, like all he meant to do was hurt, but I almost had it when suddenly he asked, "Hey, you like pussy, don't you Willy? You gotta have some of this."

He lifted his leg over the bench and stood there, massaging his prick. It really gleamed now, dripping wet with her cunt juice. I didn't want to fuck her; I really wanted him to bring that cock over to my mouth and let me suck it, wet with Tina's juice and all, I didn't care, I just wanted to suck it, but for Joe's sake I wanted to play the game. "Joe first," I said, teasing him.

"Yeah, I'll take over there," Jeffrey said. Watching Tina devour Jeffrey's cock, I suddenly felt left out, wondering why I was there at all. I wondered how often they had done this to a girl. It seemed so natural for them, one at one end, one at the other. But Joe's cock was still limp. As he had done with me the night before, he got the head of it in but it was no use, he just couldn't fuck. I thought of all the nights, all the days when he had been hard and had come like there was no tomorrow while I was fucking him. I knew where his heart was and it wasn't in fucking this cunt. I wanted to fuck him right then but I held back. I waited for his move.

"You'd better do it, little stud," he said to me, "you and Jeffrey, fuck the hell out of her."

"In bed," Jeffrey said, pulling his cock away from Tina's mouth and having her stand up. We followed him into the bedroom. He handed me a tube of grease and then laid down on the bed on his back. He told Tina to get on her knees and squat on his prick.

"Hmmmm," she groaned as she guided it in.

I greased my cock and then her ass and got on the bed behind her. Soon we were rocking together on the waterbed, fucking her together. Joe completely undressed and stood on the bed, lowering his limp dick into her mouth. He fucked her mouth with it while she raised and lowered herself over our pricks. She moaned and groaned, going crazy with it.

Watching us below him turned Joe on and eventually his cock was almost hard. Suddenly, he knelt on the bed next to me, watching as the girl moved up and down on our cocks, Jeffrey playing with her tits, squeezing them, sucking on them. Joe put his left arm around me and with his right hand jacked off until he had a dry orgasm. I couldn't help it, I hugged him, then kissed him, then pulled out of her and told him we were going back to the hotel. He put up no resistance.

Joe dozed off in the limo on the way back to the Plaza. I struggled to get him up the steps to the lobby but then one of the bellmen helped me. We finally got him to the door of the suite, then I took over. The effects of the pill he'd given me had worn off and, after running the whole scene over in my mind while we were riding back, I made up my mind how I was going to end the night: deep inside Joe Skinner's ass.

When I went into the suite and switched on the lights, I heard voices, then, nothing. I helped Joe into our bedroom and pushed him onto the bed. Then I went down the hall and found Benny's door open. He was sitting in bed alone, naked, sipping a cocktail. I heard the toilet flush in the bathroom.

"Just in time for the party," he said, slurring his words.

Not another drunk, I thought. I shook my head and had the door knob in my hand when the bathroom door opened and a man stepped out. In the dim light it was hard to see how old he was but he was no kid., maybe in his early 30's. He had muscles for days but an angry look about him, as if I was competition showing up at the last minute. "Yeah?" he said.

"Just sayin' goodnight to Benny," I said and continued to close the door.

"Catch ya later," he said.

I hope not, I thought.

I locked the door to our bedroom behind me and got undressed. I stripped Joe and got him on his stomach. I parted his ass and laid my cock between the cheeks. I was so horny I didn't need to penetrate him; just watching myself in the mirror, I rolled over his body and I came. If he'd been awake, he'd have loved it.

*

The next morning, Joe hung up the phone and said, "My folks got back from Europe over the weekend."

"Are we going to see them?" I was stuffing my souvenirs in the new Hartmann suitcase Benny bought for me.

Joe chuckled. "No, but we won't be able to take the jet back to L.A.. We'll have to fly commercial."

"Commercial?"

I had never ridden on any plane before the corporate jet, but I'd seen them sitting on the runway. That was really as close as I wanted to get but then he said, "Well, not really. You'll see."

The MGM shuttle left from Kennedy airport and Joe was the only celebrity on the flight so we got more attention than anybody else. He said, "These flights are great fun, kid. Once Dolly Parton and I sang happy birthday to Ernest Borgnine. Shit, you never know who you're gonna to meet." Leaning back in the big lounge chair, I wondered what flying on a regular plane would be like. We sat there for the longest time together comfortably in silence, like longtime companions, watching the City across the wing as we sailed by it.

The stewards were falling all over themselves to wait on us but Joe didn't have a drink. He knew he had to be in front of the cameras the next day. "Yeah I drink," he said to the steward. "If I'm happy, I'm a happy drunk. If I'm somebody else, I'm a something-else drunk. But my drinking now is very intermittent. Like, I'll have a little something four days a week and then every once in a while, I'll binge. Shit, man, I used to binge for years."

"Yeah, I know" I said as the guy left.

"But then, one time at 7:30 in the morning I had a joint in one hand and a bourbon in the other - "

"Whose joint?"

He laughed. "Not whose, it."

"Oh."

"Anyway, I decided I wasn't gonna drink any more until five o'clock."

"It's five o'clock in New York now." My beer was gone. I needed another. I wondered where the steward had gone.

Joe leaned back in his seat, closed his eyes. "Yeah, it's all on page 449."

"What?"

"In the AA book. I'll never forget it, on page 449." He opened his eyes again and became very animated. "It says you're in the place you're supposed to be. What I'm doin' now is trying to create a whole new thing. Instead of the group it's just me and I wanted to bring my vocal out of the mix, to unclutter the arrangements, get a certain focus into it, yet cover the whole terrain. You know, a collection of highs and lows."

"I love it." I wondered how many times I was going to have to tell him how much I loved the new album. Because it hadn't "gone gold" yet, it was as if he had to be reassured every five minutes he was doing the right thing. "It's wonderful, man. Better than Randy Travis."

He chuckled. "That's important to me, to hear you say that. That's the nicest compliment you've ever paid me." He put his hand on top of mine. "Well, almost. You know, at this point, everything I do has to be important. I may be dying, for chrissakes."

"Oh?" Now he was back to dying again. I felt like saying, Give me some air, but I didn't.

"You never know these days, kid. But anyway, maybe what I tried to do wasn't that well received but I've gotta try, you know?"

"Yeah," I said as he rubbed the back of my hand. I closed my own eyes and could hardly wait to get home because there was only one sure way to get him to stop doubting himself, to stop talking, and that was with my dick in his mouth.

From the LP "I Remember You"/Sung by Joe Skinner/Side 2, Cut 4:
"More Than You Know:" "I've been looking for you / Where did you go?
...Everybody says I'm wasting my time / I must reply, the time I waste is
certainly mine."

When we returned to the special field where MGM lands, Harold met us with the limo. We dropped Benny off at his place in Brentwood, then went home.

I was exhausted but Joe had to have a soak. And, of course, as it always did with Joe, one thing led to another. He could never get enough.

And while I was watching in the mirrors as I fucked him, I realized how much I'd missed being at the house, having this routine. But even with the production being way over schedule there were now less than two weeks on the shoot at Disney. Then what? The next morning, I was determined to find out.

I had all this stuff in the computer, what was I going to do with it? Somebody would have to sort it all out, make sense of it, put it in order. As Joe was having his coffee and rolls I brought the box of computer discs into the kitchen.

"...What am I supposed to do with all these files?" I asked him.

"I've been thinking about that. I want to hire a ghostwriter and have you work with him. You might learn something. I know a guy, a screenwriter, that's great and he's available. It should be done like a movie, don't you think?"

"Yeah, I guess. Who is it?"

"His name is Rodney Templeton...oh, but he's got a problem."

"Oh?"

"Yeah, he's gay. Openly gay, I mean. Would you object to a gay guy?"

"No." I looked down at my feet.

"I would. He couldn't keep his hands to himself."

"I'd smack 'im."

"Ha! This guy you probably would. But he'd keep on trying."

Let 'im try," I said, raising my arm in a punch.

"Good kid." He kissed me goodbye. Harold was waiting in the drive with the motor running.

*

"I have a terrible sex drive," Rodney said as we were reading over an anecdote Joe had told me about a typical night on the road.

"Terrible? How?" I asked.

"Can't get enough."

"Shit, everybody has that problem."

"Except Joe Skinner. It sounds like he gets all he wants."

"Not anymore."

"You mean you play hard to get?"

"Sometimes, when I want something."

He laughed. Laughed so hard his belly shook. Joe was right, he was obnoxious, but he was very smart and taught me a lot. "Structure," he said. "You got to put all this in some kind of structure. Chapters, sub-chapters. Then we'll work with it. I don't think we need to put everything in exact chronological order. We should group it, though. There are so many things going on at the same time."

I'd sit at the desk with him as he'd edit the stories, poring over the material, hour after hour, reading it right off the computer screen. I added what I could but it was his show now. I didn't want my part to be over, though. Not just yet. So I stuck close to him. Maybe too close.

"...God, you are beautiful," he said at one point, turning from the screen and looking at me as I came into the room carrying a beer for him.

"Thanks."

"But it's odd, there's an earthy quality about you that -well, it's like you're rough, but gentle at the same time - "

"Like a farmboy?"

"Exactly. In a way you remind me of that guy on the Waltons, Richard Thomas. Not in looks, really, but in manner."

"He's an old man now, isn't he?"

"I'm sure he'd love to hear that!"

"Ever sleep with him?"

"No. And if I had he wouldn't have gotten much sleep."

Later, he asked: "...Do you have any friends your own age?"

"No. Not here. Not anywhere, really. I just came out here from Ohio."

"I was hoping you might have some friends who like to play around, some friends as cute as you are."

"Not a one."

"That's a shame. There should be more like you."

"No, one like me's plenty, believe me."

"Then if there's only one, it should be spread around."

"But I'm spoken for. But, look, I know some people, maybe I could find something for you."

"I'd appreciate all the help you can give me."

And it went on like that, day after day. It grew old fast. I ran out of ways to say no but I wasn't about to call Van. No way.

"Look," I said in the second week, "I'm going shopping; Harold's taking me." And we left. I was determined to find somebody for Rodney. He seemed nice but proud, as if he wasn't about to pay for it. So I figured I'd give him a little present, but I couldn't bring it to the house. Joe wouldn't hear of it. So I decided to buy somebody and stick 'em at the Econo Lodge and have Rodney go there. That was the plan. I made up a story that Joe wanted Harold to take the Chevy in for service. He'd done that before so it was no big deal, but I wanted to ride along. Get away from Rodney. That Harold could understand. So we took off, the chauffeur and the live-in stud in the old Chevy with the top down. It was a trip. I put on my new Ray-Bans just like Joe's and acted the part. Harold, who usually showed no emotion at all, laughed like hell.

We cruised the boulevard but I decided Rodney needed something better than street trash. No way was I going to get into a bar, though. I had no drivers license, no fake ID. We decided to just sit in the car and wait near The Pink Elephant. It didn't take long.

He was black. Rodney had mentioned he liked 'em dark. I figured that meant really dark. He said his name was Slick. Harold got out of the car to get cigarettes while I talked to the dude.

"So, what's up?" he asked. He was dressed like a businessman, without a tie. Neat, clean, almost elegant. Lots of gold jewelry.

"You a cop?"

"No. You one?"

"Hardly."

"Who's that?" he asked, pointing to Harold walking across the street.

"My chauffeur."

"Yeah, okay," he chuckled. "So then, what's up?"

"A party."

"Yeah? Where?"

"Econo Lodge up on Vine."

"I know it. When?"

"Eight. Say eight. There'll be a red Cadillac parked in front of the door."

And it went on like that. I told him I had a friend in from out of town who was a real closet case and he needed a good drilling.

"Okay. How much?"

We agreed on $150. I gave him $50 as a down payment.

*

The next morning, Benny came to the house around nine o'clock. Matty hadn't arrived yet. "We need to talk," he said. He looked awful.

"What's wrong?"

"How could you?"

"How could I what?"

"Set up Rodney like that?"

"What happened?"

"He was beaten and robbed last night, that's what happened."

"Shit."

"I was just at the hospital. He did you a favor, you know. He didn't have them call Joe, he had them call me."

My pa was right. I wasn't just dumb. "I'm so fuckin' stupid!" I screamed.

"You meant no harm; we both understand that. Rodney agreed to it. You take a chance, no matter what. But if Joe finds out -"

"I didn't think. I should've just let well enough alone."

"If you wanted to please him, you should have done the job yourself. That's your business, isn't it?"

"I retired, remember?"

"I hadn't noticed."

I walked away from him, out onto the balcony. I thought of jumping off to get away from him.

Soon he was standing behind me. "Why don't we just keep this as a secret between the three of us."

"Anything you say."

He clamped his hand on my crotch. "It's better that way, kid."

"That's what it comes down to, then?"

"Yes. And I won't hurt you. I just want to make love to you."

I gripped the railing. It was bound to happen, one way or another, I realized. They always get what they want. They have the power. What was I after all, but just a kid? And a kid from a farm in Ohio, for chrissakes.

He slid the robe down off my shoulder and kissed my skin.

"Matty's due any minute," I said, moving away from him, going down the steps. "Let's go to my room."

...I closed my eyes as his mouth clamped around my limp cock. I hadn't even taken my shower and I was sure it still smelled of the coat of cum from the night before, but that probably turned him on even more. He worked it over and I kept thinking about Joe. As long as he didn't know, know about how stupid I was, know what I had to do to stay here, maybe it was all right. I had to allow myself to let somebody do this. I had grown to respect Mr. Kaplan. And, as he worked it over in his mouth, I realized he was a good cocksucker. It could have been worse.

My cock finally rose to meet his lips and he really started to get on it. "Yeah, that's more like it," he cried, and he slid down onto his knees. Poor little man was worshipping my cock.

I remembered the rough trade in his room at the Plaza and I decided if I had to do this, I was going to have some fun with it. I began slapping his face with my cock, forcing it between his lips, into his throat. He really got off on that, cumming right away. But he didn't want it to end. He held my ass and cried, "Fuck my mouth, kid. Fuck my fuckin' mouth with that big thing." I thought, better than your ass, and I let him have it.

He was so good, I started cumming. I pulled out and he hugged me. I shot my load all over the top of his head. He cried, "Oh, no," and reached up, running his fingers through the stickiness.

"Sorry, but you can get it cleaned."

He laughed, then lifted the toupee from his scalp and threw it across the room. He pushed me back against the wall and started sucking it again, my cock, slick with cum, sliding between his lips and back down his throat.

Seizing me that way, wanting more after I'd already given everything, jolted me and suddenly, something snapped. I wanted to be mean to him. I grabbed him by the ears and forced his head back and forth the full length of my cock. The head of it popped from his mouth and it began to harden again. I kept yanking his head back and forth and the more I did, the more he seemed to love it. I didn't expect that. I wanted him to hate it, to feel some pain with this. I was now feeling terrible pain, that I'd let Joe down, let myself down. I'd been stupid. I wanted to ram my cock so far down Benny's throat that he gagged on it. I shoved him, pushing him onto his back and when he hit the floor I pounced on his chest, taking my hardon and jamming it in his mouth. I held the back of his head and began face-fucking him with a fury that I couldn't believe. This wasn't sex anymore, this was punishment. I was punishing him but also punishing myself. He bit my cock a couple of times and I slapped him on either side of the head. He began to kick his legs and his arms twisted my shoulders. He tried to pull my cock out of his mouth but it was no use, I had him pinned. And then I came again. Cum flowed down his throat and he fought harder than ever, but I wouldn't release him. Soon all the wind had been drained from him and I stood up. He lay there on the floor in the big mirrored bedroom and began to cry. "I hope to God you're not sick. I swallowed it. I swallowed it."

"I'm not sick," I said, stepping away from him, heading for the bathroom. I felt like saying I wasn't the sick one here but I didn't.

A few moments later, while I was washing my cock at the sink in Joe's black marble bathroom, Benny came in and stood behind me.

"You sure can surprise a person." He ran his hands up and down my body and brought them to rest on my balls. He kissed my shoulder. "We'll just keep this a secret between us, okay?"

I nodded but I had made up my mind that somehow I was going to find the courage to tell Joe I'd been an asshole.

*

"...The bitch is on 'Current Affair,'" Joe yelled as he came through the door.

He grabbed the remote and started scanning the channels. It was just a little after seven. The show had already started. It was the last segment so they kept mentioning it all through the other stuff about a man who murdered his wife and a son who murdered his mother.

After the show, while we ate the dinner Matty had left, he told me all about the case: "Don't worry, kid, I got my attorneys working on it right now. She'll be sorry she ever started this shit. I finally remembered. She was there the first night we played Indianapolis. She was in the room with us for a while. You know, Paulie doing his own thing, watching me. But then Luisa was coming in and I left. I never saw her again. Paulie didn't OD until two nights later, our last night there. Like I say, I've been studying all the aspects of this shit while I've been at the studio and I've been on the phone with my attorneys. The law's on our side. I know the law, kid. You know, I've always been fascinated by the law. I wanted to be a lawyer. When I was a kid, I thought F. Lee Bailey was the greatest thing there ever was. I read 'The Defense Never Rests' and his other book and I was really into it. I'd act out courtroom scenes in my father's office. His office is as big as a courthouse, for chrissakes.

"But I found out I had to have these great fuckin' grades to get into law school so then I decided I wanted to sing. I'd sung in the choir; I'd sung for my girlfriends. I sang in the shower. I sang all the time. I was like always on, so why not get paid for it? I got a lot of inspiration from the saloon singers, Tony Bennett, Sinatra, Mel Torme. I wanted to be romantic like that but I wasn't going to get anywhere with that gig in the seventies. So when Jeffrey asked me to join his band and sing, I dug it. Hell, they even changed the name because of me. Paulie came up with it. He said it was like when we chose up sides for basketball at school; one was shirts, the other was skins, and we were always skins and we so we decided with me as the singer that's what we'd be. And of course we couldn't wear shirts. That's when I went to the gym. I wanted to look better than any of the other guys with my shirt off. Well, I was supposed to. Shit, I was upfront."

"Yeah, you were upfront all right," I laughed, groping him, then clearing the table.

"That's all you ever think about, isn't it?"

"Beats feelin' sorry for myself."

"Yeah, what you got to feel sorry about?" He came up behind me at the sink.

I kissed him. "Nothin'. Right now, absolutely nothin'."

*

"Rodney's in the hospital," I told Joe after we'd fucked. I was washing myself in the bathroom; he was lying in bed, recovering.
"Oh?"
"Yeah. Nothin' serious. He just picked the wrong trick. But I want to go see him tomorrow, okay?"
"I'll have Harold come back and take you."
I walked back into the room. "I'm afraid it's going to slow up the book."
"Yeah, well, maybe we'll get away for a while."
"Serious?"
"Yeah. When they wrap the movie we'll go to Maui. You know I bought a condo over there from Jim Nabors and I've never even seen it?"
"I'd love it."
"But that's for later and we'll spend at least a week. Now, we'll just take another long weekend. They're even further behind schedule on the picture but they won't need me till Wednesday. What do you say we leave Saturday?"
"Leave for where?"
"The mountains."
"Which mountains?"
"Near Lake Arrowhead. I haven't been there since that time with Jeffrey and Luisa."
"And you want to go back?"
"Sure. Now. I've never wanted to go back till now."
"Well, okay, but on one condition."
"What's that?"
"That we do everything."
"You back on that shit again? I told you, if I wanted a woman I'd get one."
"I know, but just once...in the mountains."
"Well, I'll think about it. You be nice to me and I'll keep thinking about it." And he rolled over, exposing his ass to me again, moving his hips, wanting it. It seemed he could never get enough of my cock. It was enough for him, but it wasn't enough for me. I had to know what it would be like with him on top. Just once.

"I'm so sorry," I told Rodney. I'd brought him flowers. "Orchids," the saleslady said. "He'll love it," I said.

"It wasn't your fault, kid."

"But it was. I shoulda known better."

"It was me. I've let Joe down. I feel terrible."

"He said there's plenty of time. We're going to the mountains this weekend anyway, so when you get out, we'll start right back up again."

"Taking you to the mountains, eh? God, Joe must love having you around."

"Yeah, I'm sorta like a human dildo. Yeah, that's it, the human dildo. The dildo was a dodo."

"Don't be so hard on yourself. You've come a long way in a short while."

And I realized he was right. I closed my eyes and remembered what I'd told Joe, "I'm a fool for just about anything. Once some guy called me gullible. I guess that's what I am, totally gullible. If I'm told something I believe it until it's proved otherwise. I always wanted to believe people. I still do.

"Yeah, most of the guys I met on the street, they had hope for the future. Like the white knight was going to show up. They thought I was a joke at first. They wondered how I ever found my way home."

Now I had a home, well, sort of a home, but I couldn't forget what Luisa had said, that the bed would turn cold. I wasn't prepared for that. I needed to get my shit together. "I appreciate your not being mad at me," I told Rodney. "I'll make it up to you, I promise."

He didn't say anything for several moments, just stared at me. Then he said, "Sure. If you say so."

"Well, ya never know."

"No, kid, you never know."

From the LP "I Remember You" / Sung by Joe Skinner / Side 2, Cut 5, "Let's Get Lost:" "Let's get lost / Lost in each other's arms / Let's get lost / Let them send out alarms / Although they'll think us rather rude / Let's defrost in a romantic mist / Let's get crossed off everybody's list / To celebrate this time we found each other / Oh, kid, let's get lost."

We left in the morning, the top down, Joe's eyes hidden behind tinted glass.

When I slipped on my own new Ray-Bans, Joe laughed, "Yeah, the Hollywood kid."

Eventually we got off the freeway in San Bernadino and stopped at an Italian place, Bon Appetito, and had red wine with lunch.

He handed me a passbook. It had my name on the first page.

"You gotta have a bank account in L.A. You don't want to live like a pigeon."

"But I've got no money."

"Now you do."

I looked down at the first page. The balance was $1,000. "Wow," I sighed.

"Hey, kid, you deserve it. I'd become a real loner. I didn't intend for that to happen but it did. I didn't realize just how lonely I was until you came along. And to know sex the way a woman knows it, to have that power in my asshole, to know both sides the way Paulie did, well, you did it."

"I'm glad." I felt like continuing, that I wanted to feel that, too, if only he'd let me, but I didn't. I knew he would, once we got to the mountains.

"Yeah, I wasn't taking care of business for a long time, kid. Now I want to do this tour. I need Jeffrey on keyboard and I want you with me, to stay with me, to stay on the road with me."

I drew a deep breath, a breath of relief.

"Yeah, Eddie Van Halen has Valerie, I want my William."

"I'm glad."

"Oh, they do well, Valerie and Eddie. She comes in and stays a while, keeps him happy. That's what I needed, somebody like that." He chuckled. "Yeah, Eddie's world revolves around himself and he married himself. They're very happy with each other."

"I'm very happy with you."

"I'm happy too, almost as happy as I was when I was a kid. See, I had to invent everything I am as I went along. I created my own little fantasy world when I was a kid, populated it with characters, and it all came true. Except the women. I never really understood why but I guess I just don't really like women." He sighed. "Oh, well, now it's one big party thrown by God in our honor."

He went on about his plans for the tour. It would be different, completely different from the rock tour: "... We visualized what the kids were hearing. It was a complete experience. The minute you heard our songs you visualized what it looked like, what it represented, how it talked, how it walked. And we gave it to 'em. Now, I'm going to make it intimate, even if it's a big hall. It'll just be me and Jeffrey. Shit, I may even sit on a stool like Sinatra does."

"And you want me to tag along?"

"You bet. See, it was difficult bein' on the road. You don't make friends on the road; you just have all these people around you telling you how great you are all the time. Nobody is there to spank you."

I chuckled. "Yeah, I'll spank you all right."

"Shit, spoil me's what you do."

"No, I'm the one that's spoiled." I rubbed the cover of the passbook.

"Well, I look at it this way, you don't meet all kinds of people, just some kinds of people. You're the kind I want on the road."

We ordered another bottle of wine and he went on: "God, it was insane being on the road. I'd never do it again, like that, if I had a band. The Stones, they do it right, maybe three months every two or three years. That's the formula. You get to be saturated and people say, 'Oh, I missed them but I'll catch them next year.' It's no longer an event. Yeah, this'll be an event, only twelve cities, me and Jeffrey together again. Yeah, it'll be great." He beamed. "Hey, maybe we'll even get some mean pussy along the way, like we had in New York. What do you think?"

It was the first time he had spoken of New York. I wasn't sure he'd even remembered. I didn't know what to think, just sipped my wine.

"I loved it, you know," he said.

"Loved what?"

"Watching that gorgeous big dick of yours going in and out of that cunt. You were everything I told Jeffrey you'd be and more. Shit, he still talks about you." He thought a moment. "I think he'd like let to get it on with you. But you're mine, not his, remember that."

"How could I forget?" I slipped the passbook in the back pocket of my jeans and smiled.

When we finally left, I was high on the wine and the excitement of what was to come, his acceptance of my being part of his life for a while longer, his acceptance of my need to know the way a woman feels the same as he did. And, as we climbed higher into the mountains it got colder and, after he put the top up, I snuggled against him.

As the rich gold of the trees sailed by us, I put his new LP on the stereo, then unzipped his pants. I took his cock out and played with it until it was almost hard, then went down on it. Every time I would get him close, he'd start weaving on the curvy road and almost run us into the forest.

When we left the main road, the sun was setting and we were suddenly into thick clouds. The road zigzagged upwards, with shoulders that ended at the pine forest. The air was dry, filled with the smell of pine and what Joe said was eucalyptus. The effect of the wine was slowly wearing off but now I was drunk with other things, with the smells, the sounds and the taste of Joe's cock. I didn't want him to come but finally he just couldn't help it and when he was finished, Lake Arrowhead was in front of us.

We drove around to the south edge where the cabins were, past the piers with small boats tied up, and the water was shining, dancing in the moonlight. We got out of the car and I hugged him.

"Tonight's the night," he teased, squeezing my ass.

I could hardly wait to get undressed.

*

He made the cozy rooms even cozier. It seemed he was celebrating the taking of my cherry, getting off on it more than I was. He lighted candles in the living room and the bedroom. "This is the honeymoon suite," he kidded me when he were carrying our suitcases in.

"Only one with mirrors, I'll bet," I said.

Now he brought out a joint. "I've been saving this," he said. "I don't mess with this shit any more but tonight, well, tonight, I think you'll need this."

I didn't argue. Anything was better than his going to the bottle of Jack Daniels he'd packed. "I wish we had some of the great stuff Johnny used to get but..." He hesitated, thinking. "Yeah, there was always a history to every drug, like the hash from Turkey, the grass from Jamaica, the LSD from up north, a chemist he knew. Now, the hashish, that I could handle. It's a good thing to try. We'll do it one day. Once you make it a habit, though, I understand the boundaries begin to contract again. But there's a point when the limits vanish, the limits between reality and what isn't quite real, I mean. You perceive reality as something that might be happening inside you or outside you." He shook his head. "It's hard to explain if you haven't tried it. I just know you feel things more deeply than before, or you feel other things, other kinds of things. It's qualitative more than quantitative. But, oh God, the LSD! Did I ever tell you about the first time I did that?"

I shook my head and knew we were off on another story I would have to remember when I got back to my computer at the house. "See, Johnny was the one that was into all the exotic stuff and one night we were just hangin' out at the beach house he and Jeffrey had rented in Malibu and he got into the mind-expanding benefits of LSD. This guy could go on for hours about it. I could only imagine it. I told him that's all I wanted to do, just imagine it, but he insisted I try it. He handed me a small paper stamp and told me to swallow it. In just a few minutes I began to feel different. It was as if something had a hold of my shoulders, grabbing me, and then everything got fuzzy, like you say happens to you on grass. He told me later that I stood up and walked over to the windows and looked out at the Ocean. I just stood there. Finally, I started reacting to the rhythm of one of our songs that he'd put on the stereo. I went over to the piano where Jeffrey always practiced and started to play. But the white keys looked like they were fused together. I tried to play and only one finger would work. I ran from the house, out onto the beach and there was a man walking along with his dog. I don't know why but I thought he was God, coming to take me away. I scared the shit out of him and he called the cops. By the time they got there, I was asleep. They'd made so many calls to that house that they took it as another of our harmless disturbances. But it was funny, Johnny said that they warned him that if he didn't mend his ways - " A sadness suddenly entered his eyes. He shook his head and lit the joint. He took a toot and handed it to me. "Good stuff. Better than we used to get in the old days.

"But, anyhow, the next day was a killer. I couldn't remember the trip, I was in a panic all day. It was frightening. It scared the shit outta me. But it helped me understand Johnny. Why what happened, happened."

I nodded and handed the joint back to him. We didn't say anything for a long while, just letting the drug sweep over us.

Finally, he smiled. "They should legalize drugs, then there wouldn't be so many murders. But it's all so corrupt. I think they want to keep the people down and drugs is the best thing to do that. And it's the only way they make any money and then they get caught so then we have to build more prisons. That's all we're gonna have is prisons. One big fuckin' prison. Give me the old days, man. When we were doing it, it was almost innocent." He chuckled. "Speaking of innocent, bring your sweet virgin ass over here."

He was sitting in the largest chair in the living room and I got up from the couch and slid into his lap. Our hands seemed to automatically go to each other's cocks. Our lips met and I brought my other hand to his face. I wanted to tell him I loved him but I was afraid. Instead I just let him keep on kissing me. Finally, he asked, "You ready?"

I thought about saying, Who wouldn't be?, but I didn't. I just stood up and let him lead me into the bedroom.

From the LP "I Remember You"/Sung by Joe Skinner/Side 2, Cut 6, "A Time for Love:" "...A time for holding hands together / A time for rainbow colored weather / A time for that make believe that we've been dreaming of / As time goes drifting by / The willow bends and so do I / But oh my friends/ Whatever sky above / I'm sure, a time for spring/ A time for fall / But most of all, a time for love."

Joe pulled me tightly to his chest and I felt his prick quiver and harden against mine. He kissed my lips and I offered no resistance as he began shoving his tongue deep into my mouth. He continued shoving, then withdrawing, as if he was fucking me with it. As he withdrew his tongue, I whispered, "I want you." And soon I was flat on my stomach and he was massaging me, then he started slipping his fingers in my ass.

"You greased yourself," he chuckled.

"No, that's cum left from the last customer."

He slapped my asscheeks, first one side, then the other. "Dirty slut." He kept slapping them. It was beginning to hurt. Suddenly he stopped and began kissing them, sucking them, making a fuss over them. "Your ass is almost as nice as mine," he said.

"Better. I'm a virgin."

With that he shoved in three fingers and I screamed. He loved it. Four fingers, screwing me. I screamed again. He pulled them out and went back to kissing my ass, holding the cheeks up, shoving his tongue inside me, playing with my cock while he did.

After a few minutes, he rolled me over and got on his knees over my face. The blue veins of his cock strained against the skin of his prick, stretching up as his hand moved rapidly over it. He pulled the head of my cock with the tips of his lips, then opened his mouth and began licking it, savoring the sweet taste of my prick. The moonlight filtered through the window and blended with the glow of the candle. The beat of the music, not a Skins CD but Robert Palmer, one of his favorites, pounded in my head. The pot had its effect; it felt as if I was floating on the bed.

Slowly I moved up and down over his cock, circling the top and flicking my tongue around its head as he groaned. We stayed in the 69 position for several minutes, then he rolled over on his side and as he played with my cock with one hand with his other hand he was squeezing and pinching my nipples.

I suddenly raised my hips and brought one leg over his body and straddled him. I guided the elegant tool into my ass and sat back, feeling the hugeness of him fill me as my muscles grasped it and tightened around it. Slowly, slowly I raised myself until, when I looked behind me, I could see all but the tip of it, then I slid down on it again, and began riding him as he so often rode me. I bent forward and he took my pecs in his hands and squeezed them and began kissing me. I was drowning in his spit as he kissed every inch of my face.

As he raised me up and held my shoulders, then shoved upward, jabbing, stabbing me, my head bent forward, my hair covering his face, and I stifled a scream of pain by biting his shoulder. He rolled me over again and pushed me down on the bed and took me as I had taken him when I felt he wanted it that way. He cradled me in his arms and told me he would be gentle. I could feel him guiding his cock with his hand, increasing the pressure to get the head past my tight opening. Then came the most difficult part, his cock growing wider and wider toward the base. But he was easy with it. Suddenly, my resistance was gone. Soon the base of his cock was tight against me, completely in me, then he started moving, slowly, rhythmically, in and out. One hand and arm were under my neck, holding my shoulder, the other hand moved up to grab my balls and then my cock. I met every thrust. I contracted, sucked, squeezed, and held his cock with every stroke, then hung on as he pulled back.

He took my cock in his hands and pumped it. I didn't want to come but I couldn't help myself. I clamped my hands on his gorgeous ass and pushed it so that all of him was in me. "Oh, shit," I groaned as my cum splattered everywhere. He took my head in his hands and held it steady, then kissed me. Soon I could feel his own cum entering me. I didn't want him to wear a rubber. I had bought some spermacide at the drugstore and prepared myself so that I could take it the way it was meant to be and was glad I did. I remembered what that girl had said at Jeffrey's, something about essence, and now I had the essence of Joe exploding in me.

"Yes, yes," I cried, slapping his ass.

He rolled on his side and brought me with him. We laid there, holding each other, with his cock still in me, for several minutes and then he started again, with little movements at first, then stronger. I ground myself up against him and, crazy with it, I cried, "Oh, Joe, I love it. I love you!"

I'd never told anybody that before.

"I love you, too, kid. I really do." And then he came again, more of his essence filling me, as he jacked me off.

*

Sunday we hiked and found a place where we could get naked and it was as if he had discovered a new toy. "You're so damn tight," he said, thrusting his fingers into me before he shoved his cock in.

"See what you've been missing," I said, saying it more to myself than to him. Feeling his cock fill me turned me on like nothing ever had. And having him get off on it like he did made it even more exciting. He fucked me in the woods, then fucked me in the shower when we got back to the cabin. It was as if I was with someone completely different and I thought maybe, just maybe, he would want to keep me around a little while longer.

"...We haven't talked much about your life," he said while I unwrapped the basket of food Matty had made for us.

"Not much to tell."

"It must have been terrible, that's why I've never pushed it."

"It was," I said, opening the bottle of wine. "But you've made up for every minute of it, believe me."

"Having to go with people just for the money - "

"Oh, you meant that part of my life. Well, that really wasn't me. It was like the easiest thing for me to do when I got here. Hell, I was even met at the bus!" I munched my triple decker sandwich. "But I knew you'd get around to asking about it sooner or later. The answer is: sometimes. Sometimes I enjoyed it. Mostly not. And sometimes I hated it. Okay?"

"Okay? Okay, what?"

"Okay, do you know enough? Can we just forget about it?"

"I'll let it go, forever, if you will."

"All right," I said, pouring some wine. "All right."

*

The next morning, Joe was watching me busy myself making breakfast and he said, "You're a helluva kid, you know that?"

"Thanks."

"What I said about loving you, it's true. I really think I do love you. And I haven't said that very often in my life."

I didn't turn around and look at him, I just kept buttering the toast. "I love you, too," I mumbled. "And I've never said that to anybody."

"Never?"

"Never."

He chuckled, as if he was savoring a victory of some kind. "Well, now that we love each other, we have to help each other."

"Nobody's helped me like you have, Joe. I can read, I got a bank account -"

He interrupted me. "Hey, kid, you deserve everything you get. And now I want your help."

"Anything." I went over to the stove to check on the eggs.

"Well, I never told you this but Luisa had a kid. My kid."

"Oh?"

"Yeah. Didn't tell me. She told me she had an abortion, but I found out she didn't. She put the kid up for adoption. A girl." He paused, thinking, then went on, sadly, "God, I hope she's not having to put up with what I had to put up with. I remember when I was just getting known and these stories about the road began to appear. I went home and Daddy says to me, 'You got a smug look, you know that: your face sickens me. You've become scum and I'm tired of scum.' Can you imagine?"

I shook my head. "I can't believe fathers can be so cruel."

He came over to the stove and ran his hands up my back.

"That's why I want to find her. To help. Not to mess up her life. I don't know what her life is but it's important to me to know. She's somewhere in Georgia. I'll find her one day. I want you to help me."

"I will. I'll find her for you."

"You know, one time Luisa went so far as to come up with a death certificate, trying to tell me the baby had died. But I found out that was a lie. She was just trying to protect the kid. But it hurt me that she'd do that. But what's done is done. Now I'd just like to know, you know, that's she's okay."

"Should we put it in the book?"

"Yeah," he said, kissing me on the back of the neck. "That's the end of the book. You and I go off looking for my daughter."

We embraced and I said, "Great ending, Joe, great ending."

From the LP "I Remember You"/Sung by Joe Skinner/Side 2, Cut 7,
"Don't Explain:" "Hush, now, don't explain / I know you've raised
Cain...Quiet, don't explain / You're my joy and pain / I'm glad you're bad
/ Don't explain."

Joe started drinking wine with dinner and never stopped. Then he began reading the words Rodney had written so far. He had brought the computer printout with him. Finally he said, "This shit's good."

"And he's got all those pictures picked out, too." I started to leaf through them, admiring how handsome Joe was no matter how long his hair was, no matter what age he was.

"Pictures. You always fall back on pictures, don't you?" he said, with an anger that frightened me.

I smiled. "Oh, no, they're not for me, they're for your fans."

"Yeah, I wish I could tell my fans the whole truth. Still, he'd better call it an 'unauthorized biography,' it'll sell better." Suddenly he slammed down his wine glass. "Shit, what's this?"

"What?"

"He's got some shit in here about my not playing AIDS benefits because I don't want to be identified with gays. Where'd that come from?"

"Well - "

"Look, I'm always interested in the way people speak and what they speak about, but I don't identify with any causes. I don't want them putting something between them and the act, you know? Like with Jane Fonda, it's either this exercise guru or it's Hanoi Jane. It gets in the way. And the last fuckin' thing I need is to be identified with gays, AIDS or no AIDS." His voice trailed away. He saw I was suddenly sad. "Is that wrong?"

"No. It's just that, here we are - "

"Look, what we do here is nobody's business. I don't need to take a billboard on Sunset just to tell them we fuck, do I?"

"No. But it wouldn't hurt to do a benefit. Everybody does a benefit."

He laughed. "Okay, I'll do a benefit. For sexually abused children. Now, maybe we can agree on that."

"You were sexually abused?"

"Not really. But it was confusing. I've never understood it. My father is so strange."

"All fathers are strange, seems to me."

"Well, your father never let you crawl into bed with him I'll bet."

"No, that he didn't do. I'd be the last one he'd do that with!"

"See. That's the way most fathers feel. What my father felt I'll never know."

"He took you to bed?"

He nodded and sipped some more wine. I was sure he was going to finish the bottle all by himself. "Well, here's what happened. When he had his heart attack and was made to stay home, in his room, I'd go in there. I was only nine and I knew he didn't like me but he cared about me. He'd had a daughter and a son. Both of us had let him down. How I'd let him down was very complex. Maybe he thought I'd never be able to take over the business, that I wasn't strong enough, I don't know. I knew by then that I wanted to sing. I wanted to be a singer and I knew it drove him nuts. The more nuts it drove him, the more I wanted to be singer. " He laughed. "I remember that at the time we had three records in the top ten at once, he called me and told me I'd done good and I just said, 'I couldn't have done it without you' and I meant it. If he hadn't hated what I was doing I never would have done it.

"But, anyway, I could sense his breathing change as I stepped near him. He brushed his hair back and sat up, as if I was some important company. And he asked me to sit with him on the bed and look out, over the land, his land, the miles and miles that we own there, and he told me not to say anything, just sit there next to him. And I would cut school to be able to do that, go in his room and sit in bed with him, and pretty soon he had his arm around me and then once he said, 'I can't stand what you are, you know that? But I can't do anything for you. I can't do anything for anyone anymore.' And we'd watch the sun setting in the west across the fields like it was a show. And he would hug me, hug me so hard I could hear the thudding of his weak old heart and he would complain about mother and the people who worked for him and everything and say how nobody loved him. All the while, he would run his hands up and down my body. It gave me the creeps.

"And then he asked me why I came every day and I said I hadn't anything better to do. He shook his head in disgust and said that wasn't a nice thing to say but it was nice of me to come just the same."

"And what happened?"

"He got well and was as mean and awful as ever. We never talked about those days and I was never so close to him again."

"Still, it wasn't so bad -"

"What was bad was that I wanted him, you know, in a sexual way, and I know he knew it. That's what disgusted him. He knew my secret. Nobody knew my secret, but he knew. That's why I played football, just to please him."

"You too? I tried it, but I was always too little. I can remember Pa'd yell across the field at me, 'You're standin' up, get low,' or 'Keep your hands in, stupid!' If I knew he was going to be there, I found something else to do. That would even make him madder. Finally I quit altogether. Then he said, 'Just as well, you'd never be anything more 'n a benchwarmer. Just a goddamn benchwarmer.' It was great."

"Mine called me scum. Always called me 'scum of the earth.' Maybe I am. Who knows. I know he thought there was nothing in the world worse than being a sissy."

"Maybe it takes one to know one, ever think of that?"

"Yes, it's crossed my mind. He's probably this mean nasty man 'cause he's never had any and he's always wanted it!" He was laughing, but crying, too. "I overheard him say once that he couldn't believe he'd given birth to a son like that." Now he was crying full out. He came into my arms. "Hey, kid, you fuck me tonight, okay? I gotta feel it, and you holding me while you're doing it. Just hold me all night."

"Okay." I didn't tell him but I wanted to hold him forever.

*

He was late waking up the next day. I had fixed breakfast and was eating it when he stood in the doorway with a huge erection. He didn't say anything, just started stroking it.

"My turn?" I asked, munching my Cheerios.

He just smiled. I put down my spoon and silently moved past him onto the bed. I lay on my stomach and lifted myself up to him.

I had greased myself the night before, before he told me he wanted to get fucked, and I was ready, but still it hurt when he shoved it in. "Please, it hurts," I groaned.

"Let's try it this way," he said, yanking me over on my back.

I grabbed his arm and pulled him down on me, wrapping my legs around his waist. The small head of his cock slid in easily but the width of it stung the more he shoved. He was enjoying it, gasping as he began to move it inside me but I was still in pain. I rolled him over on his back.

And we started again. I guided his cock into me. I could control how deep it went and I got a rhythm going, ramming myself up and down on it, but still it was stinging me. I thought my insides were being torn up. I slowly rose up until the tip of the cock was at the rim of my asshole, then he began moving his hips, driving himself into me. I cried out in pain but he kept on until I felt a gusher of sperm entering me and he was shaking me.

"Oh, god, kid, god, god..." His voice trailed off as he sucked on my nipples, his spit soaking my chest.

My ass burned as his cock slid from the opening with a terrible pop. I could feel my bowels loosening and I tried to stand up. I felt dizzy. He looked at me, at himself and the bed. "Shit," he said. "What did I do?"

"Nothing. It'll be all right."

His cock and the sheet were covered with blood. "No, you won't. You're hurt. I've hurt you. Damn!" He helped me into the bathroom and washed off my skin, then his cock. "I'm sorry, kid."

"Don't worry about it. Just too much too soon, I guess."

"Fuckin' story of my life. I can't get enough and I take too much. Shit!" He slammed the wall on his way out the door.

Now there was no cheering him up. It seemed like the flood of all the memories, all the talking, maybe even his new position of being the fucker, and a ugly, messy fuck besides, had changed him and our relationship. He started drinking early and wouldn't stop. The wine was all gone but he'd brought plenty of his Jack Daniels. The more he drank, the more difficult be became. Finally, I stopped talking. I couldn't watch him just keep on drinking, out of control. I went outside and sat on the little porch. It began to rain, hard. I was miserable. My ass ached. My heart ached. I wanted to leave, but I was stuck there, with him. Finally, I begged him to take me home.

"Yeah," he said, slamming the bottle of bourbon on the table and switching off the television, "let's get the fuck outta here. I can't stand it here. I never could. I don't know why we came."

As he began to stand, I thought he might fall over but he didn't. He pulled himself together and said it: "Dammit, I can't stand being stuck here with a fucking fairy."

I felt like saying, "Dammit, man, I hate being stuck here with a fucking drunk!" But I didn't. I decided it was all my fault. I'd wanted him to be the one to fuck me. I had let him fuck me. He loved it; couldn't get enough. But that was when he was sober. After something to drink, I had turned into something he despised. I had turned into the thing he hated more than anything else: a fairy. He looked at me and saw himself.

Now I hated myself again. I'd been seduced by the dream that I was his lover, a strange kind of surrogate wife, another person that he had shared his most intimate secrets with and he was now regretting it. I had gone beyond what was intended, that I simply serve a purpose, a live-in whore to relieve his tension when he was bored after a long day at the studio. I wanted to go back to the house in the hills, to the way we were before I'd been so stupid. I wanted to go, rush back, back to the time before reality had set in, as it always has a way of doing.

And I didn't realize just how intoxicated Joe was until he started the car and we turned onto the main road. On the way up the mountain, it had been fun, seeing how fast we could take the blind curves. But going down, now, with him stoned, with the roads slick from the rain, I became terrified. If only I'd known how to drive. I had learned how to read, next was driving school. But a lot of good that did now.

I begged him to slow down. There were two hairpin curves in front of us and I looked down the mountain and for a second, through the mist, I thought I saw another car coming up on the wrong side of the road. The speedometer was hitting seventy and the second blind curve approached. Joe twisted the wheel to the right like a crazy man and we spun toward the edge of the gravel but not in time to get out of the way of the car coming up the mountain, a projectile whizzing toward us. Joe hit the accelerator, trying to get away. As the other car slammed into us, we went into a skid and I screamed...

From the LP "I Remember You"/Sung by Joe Skinner/Side 2, Cut 8,
(Reprise) "I Remember You:" "...When my life is through / And the angels
ask me to recall / That thrill of them all / Then I shall tell them / I remember
you."

They put me in a room alone. I could barely lift my arms so I kept
the remote control for the TV on the bed next to my hand. I never
saw a report on the accident. Benny had arranged everything and
Joe was being flown back to Alabama on the company plane for
burial. I wouldn't be going. I wasn't invited, of course, but I would
have to stay in the hospital for at least a week.

"You're lucky that old car didn't have seat belts," Benny said
when he finally came to see me. "You were thrown from the damn
car and ended up in some trees. Joe wasn't so lucky. He had
massive internal injuries. The steering wheel..." he started sobbing.
I felt even sorrier for him than for myself. He loved Joe more than
I ever could, I decided, and never got to express it physically.

"Get some rest," he said after he pulled himself together. Patting
my leg, he smiled and said, "I'll see you tomorrow."

Rest, shit. At that moment I wanted to die. Seeing Benny crying,
remembering the past few months, how wonderful it had been. If
I hadn't insisted we go home, none of it would have happened. It
was all my fault.

Like when I was ten and my father got drunk and told me it was
my fault Mom had died. Tumors on the brain were my fault. I must
have caused them, I figured.

And then I begged him to take me camping with him. At first it
was great; we took the old canoe and slept in tents. We ate off the
land, wild plants and berries, and caught fish and fried them.

One afternoon we stalked through the thick wood, alive to every
sound and movement. Suddenly, a rabbit appeared, its summer
coat of brown turning white for winter. "Hey, the Easter bunny,"
I whispered to my father. But my father didn't even smile. He told
me we could have it for dinner that night if I could hit it with my
.22. I did, catching it just below the eye.

My father applauding, I rushed up to it. It lay impossibly still. The eyes were still open and a trickle of blood came from one eye, like a tear. I'd tracked animals only to watch them, never to kill them. I began to cry. My father called me a "goddamn sissy." I couldn't eat that night. I'd killed the Easter bunny. It was all my fault.

*

"What's this?" I asked Benny a couple of days later as he handed me a legal-looking document with all kinds of copies and a gold pen. He said he was on his way to Alabama for the memorial service and he wanted to take the documents to the Skinners.

"This is an agreement that you'll never speak about this, any of it, ever." He called in a nurse to be a witness.

I signed all the copies without reading them and handed them back to him.

"You didn't read it."

"Doesn't matter anymore, does it?"

He dismissed the nurse and closed the door. "What it says is that you get Joe's condo in Maui," he cleared his throat, "and $50,000 a year for 10 years."

"That's a lot more than I deserve. I never should have let him drive - "

"Stop that shit!" He shoved the papers in his briefcase then looked up at me again. "And now that it doesn't matter you should know the truth."

"Yeah?"

"The reason Joe hated himself so much."

"Oh?"

"That night, the night Paulie died, Joe arranged for the boy and sent him to Paulie with some drugs. Joe wasn't there. He was with Luisa like he said, but he bought the deal and he could never forgive himself."

"I thought so. That's why you were so pissed when I did that arranging for Rodney." And I closed my eyes and began to play all the tapes over again in my mind.

"Yes," he said, starting to leave, but then he came back and stood beside my hospital bed. I opened my eyes and he looked deep into them. "You're lucky to be alive, you know that?"

"Yes."

"And there's no permanent damage. Oh, maybe some scars on your legs, but nothing permanent."

"Yeah, nothin' permanent."

"You'll be just as gorgeous as ever." He smiled. "You know, I'd like to come see you in Maui."

"Sure, Mr. Kaplan. Anything you say." I smiled back. "Anything."

"I'll hold you to that, kid." And he began making his way out of the room.

I nodded and felt like saying, "Hey, you got my signature, Mr. Kaplan. You got my fucking signature," but I didn't. I just thought, Once a whore, always a whore. But then I chuckled to myself thinking, But hey, I'm probably the best damn whore there ever was, and I knew for a little kid like me that had to count for something.

Epilogue

For the first couple of months on Maui, I waited for Benny. But he was always too busy to fly over and I was growing more and more restless.

It was a beautiful place but I was bored out of my mind. I'd sent my father a postcard every day and I was running out of things to say. He probably didn't believe for a second I was writing him anyway so it didn't really matter.

At least I'd learned to drive. I rented a jeep and drove all over, taking the Kahekili Highway faster than anybody else ever had, at least that's what the gasping instructor said. Instead of letting the accident get to me, I'd decided never to ride with anyone else again. I would do all the driving myself.

And then one day, out of the blue, Rodney showed up.

"I need your help," he said, still panting from the walk from the parking lot.

"Oh."

"Benny destroyed all the discs. 'There'll be no book,' he said. That's what the bastard said, 'No book.'"

"That's right, there'll be no book."

"But it was so important to Joe."

"No, not really. He was never going to let you tell the truth, you know that. And without being able to do that, what's the point?"

"But that's the whole idea. Now I want to tell the truth."

"Go ahead. I can't. I've signed a contract."

"I've thought about that. What if I wrote the book about you?"

"Me? What good is that? I'm nobody."

"Ha! You nearly died with him. You're somebody now. That's why Benny's parked you over here so no one can find you."

"Sure," I said.

He had made reservations at the Marriott but I told him he could stay the night, in the guest bedroom, if he bought me dinner. He smiled, "It's a deal."

I helped him carry in his luggage and then I told him he could take me to dinner at the Swan Court in the Hyatt Regency, one of the most expensive places on the Island. We had to dress and I really laughed when he said I looked so "grown up" in my Polo outfit I'd worn in New York.

I'd only been to the Hyatt once, to see the swans in the lagoon. I'd had a drink in the bar and Jim Nabors was there and sent me a second one. Although I wanted to show my appreciation to him for selling Joe the condo, I just nodded my thanks and went home. I wondered if he knew who I was. Maybe he'd seen my picture in *People* when they reported the accident. It was the only picture of me that was published; the photographer, Strange, had sold it to 'em. They cropped it at my navel and called me a "former model," which was a lot better than some of the other things they could have said. And then in the article they said I was Joe's "bodyguard." Obviously, good old Benny took care of it.

...At dinner, with wine in me, I became more agreeable to Rodney's plan, and to Rodney.

"We'd have a business relationship," he said, cutting his blackened mahi mahi.

"That's about all I seem to ever have."

He smiled. "Is that what you were? I never really knew, you know."

"Only for a few months. I didn't work the streets, though. I had an agent and a beeper. You do what you gotta do. But once you do, nobody will let you forget it."

"I understand. But I can forget things easily. I'm a forgiving man."

"I'm glad of that, believe me." He was beaten and robbed. It was all my fault.

He looked away and sipped his wine, not wanting to get his hopes up I suppose. But the more wine I drank, the better he looked. I was horny for some contact with another human. I realized I hadn't had sex with anybody but myself for weeks. Although I'd had plenty of opportunities every time I went down to Makena Beach, I kept thinking about Joe and missing him. And I kept telling myself I was saving it up for Benny, figuring it was part of the deal, but obviously I was wrong; Benny was too busy counting his royalties to worry about a piece of ass.

"I really can't cooperate with you," I told Rodney. "On a book, that is. Not openly, anyway. See, I don't want to fuck up this deal with Benny and the Skinner family."

"I understand. But I don't see any harm in your just reconstructing what was on the discs. I could say I memorized it all."

"I'll see," I said, dropping a couple of hundreds on the tray with the bill.

"But - "

I held up my hand. "This one's on the Skinners."

*

When we returned to the condo, Rodney treated me as if I was a piece of sculpture, wanting nothing more from me than to let him worship me. And I only wanted to be nice to him, to make up for my stupidity. Like I said, I learned a long time ago a lot can depend on a little.

I'd been with so many johns one more or less didn't seem to matter, but when he had removed all my clothes and was kissing me, kissing me everywhere, I gave myself up to the moment and asked what he enjoyed most. When he said he really got off on what he so seldom got, a good fuck, I told him he'd come to the right island.

It had to be in the dark for me to pull it off, but he didn't mind. "I don't think I can take it," he said as I began, carefully, slowly sliding it in.

"Sure you can," I said.

And he did. They always said that and they always took it all, all the way down to my pubes.

He loved it so much, groaning, screaming, heaving himself up to meet every stroke, that I came after about five minutes but kept on, turning him over on his back and jerking him off.

When I returned from the bathroom, he was still lying on the bed in a daze, sliding his fingers through the cum on his hairy belly.

"You are incredible," he sighed. "Did you do that to Joe Skinner?"

"Can't say."

"But you have to. That kind of fuck has to be immortalized, in a book."

I laughed. "Hey, just make it up. Doesn't matter anymore, does it? He's gone and nobody'd believe me anyway. Just make it up."
*

The next day, I took him to Haleakala Crater.

"Ya gotta see it," I said as we bounced along the mountain road in my jeep. "It's one of the biggest in the whole world."

He chuckled, "Yeah, I'm beginning to like 'em big." And he dropped his hand into my crotch and left it there. It felt good; I had missed adoration.

In the late afternoon, we stood at the Leleiwi Overlook, six miles up, and I held his arm. "Isn't this weird?"

And what they call "The Specter" occurred, our shadows showing up on the heavy cloud layer with a rainbow around them.

"Wonderful," he said, slipping his arm around my waist and hugging me to his tall, bulky body. "Simply wonderful."

And in that moment I realized I really liked Rodney. I didn't love him, not like I did Joe. But I liked him. He was so caring, so happy when he was with me. I began to think about the other men, that maybe if I'd given them a chance, some more time, maybe I would have liked them, too.

"I love you," Rodney whispered in my ear.

I chuckled, "You'll get over it."

Rodney stayed three days and when he was leaving he said, "I'll be back."

"I know."

"But I've gotta give it a rest," he groaned, "Shit, I won't be able to sit down for weeks."

"Ha! You'll get used it. My pa always said you can get used to anything."

He stopped, dropped his bag, and took me in his big arms. "I sure could get used to this."

And I closed my eyes and remembered that song, that album, that man. And was glad I'd turned down Rodney's offer. He could say what he wanted about Joe; it didn't matter. That's what they do, Benny said, after a star has died; they are free to make up anything they want.

But I was lucky. I didn't need to make anything up. Shit, I'd been there.

The Lyricists of
Joe Skinner's Songs of Love

"I Remember You:" Copyright and Lyrics by Johnny Mercer

"I Won't Send Roses:" Copyright and lyrics Jerry Herman.

"Easy to Love:" Lyrics by Cole Porter (Copyright by Chappell & Co.)

"Unforgettable:" Lyrics by Irving Gordon (Copyright by Bourne Music)

"I Could Get Used to This:" Lyrics by Ellen Silverstein (Copyright by Wild Pink Music and Never Off Key)

"What a Difference A Day Makes:" Lyrics by Maria Grever (Copyright by E. B. Marks Music/BMI)

"Impossible:" Copyright and lyrics by Steve Allen.

"Fairy Tales:" Lyrics by Anita Baker (Copyright by All Baker's Music)

"More Than You Know:" Lyrics by Anita Baker (Copyright by All Baker's Music)

"A Time for Love:" Lyrics by Paul Francis Webster (Copyright by M. Whitmark & Sons)

"Don't Explain:" Recorded by Robert Palmer, written by Holiday/ Herzog (Copyright by EMI USA)

"Let's Get Lost:" Copyright and lyrics by Jimmy McHugh.

Acknowledgements

I wish to thank Joe Leslie for his invaluable contribution to this book. His story, "Fresh," originally appeared in our anthology "A Natural Beauty" and served as the inspiration for "The Kid."

As the story developed, Joe, being an educator of many years standing, provided the background needed to make William's learning problems accurate and as poignant as they are.

I also gratefully acknowledge the assistance of our longtime editor, "Georgia John," and Art & Mike in bringing this story to life.

Thanks, too, to Brown Bag Co., Hollywood, for supplying the beautiful photography for this book.

- John Patrick

Footnote

"A Study in Sexuality: The Complexity of What We Are"

THOR PRODUCTIONS

Star of Bisexual Videos Chance Caldwell:
"I like men and women and I wanted to be in the movies.
I'm also horny all the time, so I thought, 'Why not?'"

The story you have just read is a study in the complexity of what we are sexually. William, although he had heterosexual encounters, preferred the company of men. He was not the tormented closet case Joe Skinner was. Indeed, the confused sexual feelings Joe had for Paulie, and the fact that he may have contributed to his partner's death, haunted him for the rest of his life. Eventually, he was able to seek out the company of men, but under his own conditions, his own set of circumstances. And he never uses the term "bisexuality" to describe his behavior. He simply is.

But once Joe had experienced gay sex, he joined the many who fluctuate between the gay and straight communities, in different social contexts or at different points in their lives. Many refuse to believe there is such a thing as bisexuality. Alfred Kinsey, the great sexual researcher, thought forcing a label on anyone was unnatural. In his famous 1948 book, "Sexual Behavior in the Human Male," he wrote, "The world is not to be divided into sheep and goats. Everything is not black and white. It is a fundamental taxonomy that nature rarely deals with discrete categories and tries to force facts into separate pigeonholes. The sooner we learn this concerning sexual behavior, the sooner we can reach a sounder understanding of the realities of sex."

The reality is that like homosexuality, bisexuality has been a part of things since before recorded time. In her new book, "Bi Any Other Name," Lani Kaahumanu says: "Literary and visual references to bisexual desire can be found from the Egyptians on down. Some cultures encouraged or accepted homosexuality as a natural precursor to heterosexual marriage. The Greeks developed a formal system of patriarchy around gay desire and intergenerational love; a married man with a young male lover was not unusual."

Perhaps it has more to do with opportunity than anything else. And perhaps we common folk are just finally catching up to what the rich and famous, including the rock stars in this book, have known all along, that boys will be boys and that can be fun. A recent book about Aristotle Onassis claimed that when he was 73 and married to Jackie O he would have two beautiful Italian boys regularly join him on his yacht and play around. Then, when he was finished with them, he would curtly dismiss them, well paid, we assume, for services rendered.

And then there was Johannes, Prince of Thurn und Taxis, who died in December of 1990. He was descended from Mad King

Ludwig of Bavaria and lived up to his heritage, sometimes playing noblesse oblige, sometimes Caligula. With $2.5 billion in the bank, he could afford to be a madcap consort.

John Richardson, author of the best-selling "A Life of Picasso" and a keen observer of what used to be called the jet set, said of Johannes: "Given his hatred of hypocrisy, Johannes made no bones about liking good-looking boys as much as, if not more than, good-looking girls. In the 1950s, he had a long-standing relationship with a handsome young Chicagoan who was far from poor. ("New money, I fear, " Johannes said. "His family did not get to Chicago until after the fire.") Later, there was a French boy, whose socially ambitious parents were constantly upgrading their fictious title, much to the amusement of Johannes. And then in 1979 he dropped in, as he often did, on a Munich milk bar frequented by swinging adolescents ("Schicki-Micki" kids) whom he would try to impress by driving up in a Winnebago and claiming to be a Panamanian waterskiing champion. Instead of picking up a boy, he ended up with a twenty-year-old girl, a distant cousin, the half-Hungarian Countess Mariae Gloria von Schonburg-Glauchau, who would become more familiarly known as 'Princess TNT.'"

It wasn't long before the aging bachelor realized Gloria would make the perfect consort, providing the solution to a major dynastic problem, the need for an heir. And marriage to Gloria, at that time a dynamic drama student, didn't change his sexual orientation or way of life. Gloria was a free spirit who had no problem adjusting to her husband's proclivities. Each went his or her own way, which didn't prevent them from producing a male heir and two daughters.

Besides what Richardson refers to as "childish perversity," Johannes exhibited a subversiveness and black humor that smacked of Dadaism. Like the Dadaists, he wanted to deride and defy conventional morality and trigger anarchic situations. "He put as much calculation, fantasy, and nerve into his effects as the late Charles Ludlam put into his absurdist farces," Richardson noted. Even after his marriage, Johannes continued to anchor his yacht off the gay beach on the Greek island of Mykonos so as to take his more conventional guests ashore and shock them. "Hairdressers galore," he would promise the ladies. He headed unerringly for the epicenter of the action and immediately set about fomenting a row between two petulant boys. "I saw your friend put sand in your tanning cream," he would tell one. "As for what he did to your towel..." In no time, it was reported, fights would be going on all over the beach.

A first-hand observor of high level hijinks is Liz Taylor. She's been linked, romantically and otherwise, with Rock Hudson, Montgomery Clift and notorious cheapskate billionaire Malcolm Forbes, married with children, who gave his tricks a hundred bucks for their time. When further light was shed on Forbes' bisexuality with the publication of the book "The Man Who Had Everything," Liz said: "It's nobody's business what Malcolm's sexual preferences were. It's nobody's concern. I respected him, which means I respected all of his choices, all the way around."

Speaking of all the way around, one wonders how Malcolm or Ari or Johannes would rank on Kinsey's famous scale, rating human sexuality on a scale of zero to six. Homosexuality never crosses the mind of the zeros (appropriately) while the number sixes pretty much know they are completely gay or lesbian early on. Only five percent of the population, Kinsey theorized, live at those ends of the spectrum. The rest are to be found between two and five. The problem with the scale was that it didn't take into account specific life situations, especially those that changed over a period of time. And, no matter how you look at it, you end up with six different "labels."

In my book about Tim Lowe, "Lowe Down," I quote the handsome, always horny star: "I'd love for everyone to forget all the gay and straight shit. I'm a person. That's the reality of it. I don't have time to worry about all these other things, am I this or am I that. Just let me be who I am." And I was content to do just that, with explosive results.

However, one cannot ignore the tendency to label those things we do not understand. Distributors of videos also like to compartmentalize. They like to section their catalogues so customers will be able to easily choose "young stuff" from "he-man stuff" and so on. "Labels are about confusion," Gino Colbert, frequent performer and sometime director of bisexual videos, says. "They get into a whole negative character. You don't need a film that gets into the filmmaker's personal hang ups."

Thanks to video erotica, we are permitted to live vicariously, to see what being bisexual might mean in the sexual arena.

Although lesbian scenes have long been a staple of straight tapes, because it is said men love to watch women eat each other out, films pairing men with each other, and perhaps a woman along for the ride, only started to become a staple of a video library in the early '80s. Colbert, who brought us the bisexual potboilers "The Bi Spy" and "Gidget Goes Bi," says there is a market for this: "People want to see these tapes." He admits that "biphobia" exists even in the adult film industry, though much of it may be based on homophobia. At one awards ceremony, a presenter introduced the category by saying it was for people who hadn't made up their mind what they wanted. Colbert says that he never gets into orgies. "It's usually private, intimate sex. I think I shoot the most normal erotica in the business. The women usually come out ahead in the plot, which is either detective or love stories."

One of the early successes, "Bi-Coastal," remains one of the better efforts in this category. It employs a time-worn "a star is born" theme well developed by director Lancer Brooks, who once was known as Tom DeSimone and made "The Idol," "Skin Deep," and "Bad, Bad Boys" for gay audiences. "Bi Coastal" boasts tiptop production values and chronicles the heart-wrenching adventure of an attractive little blonde waif who goes to Hollywood to live with her boyfriend and finds he's taken a powder. So, what to do? She meets a powerful agent named Vanessa, beautifully played by Pat Manning, and she becomes a top model. "I don't know how I'll ever thank you," she tells the agent. Vanessa smiles and says, "You'll find a way, darling. You'll find a way." And, of course, she does. Eventually, the heroine finds her long-lost boyfriend and, to her initial dismay and eventual bliss, discovers he's got a BOY friend. They all get cozy and, presumably, live happily ever after.

Another classic of this genre is "The Big Switch," released in 1985 from Catalina and Paul Norman's first venture as a director. The orgy sequence which, natch, climaxes the film is frenzied, with every imaginable sex act occurring at least twice. Lots of juice flows in the finale as Tex Anthony plugs Beverly Glenn while he is getting plugged by Mark Miller for the ultimate in bisexual ecstasy. As critic Robert Leighton observed, "Aside from changing sexual tastes, many of the biggest stars of gay films label themsleves straight or bisexual. That these men are all capable of enjoying sex with either men or women is obvious after viewing this production. It's a must for the hard-core voyeur."

One of our favorites from a strictly gay viewpoint is "The Switch

Is On!" written, directed, produced, and photographed by John Travis. The opus employs the same "a star is born" theme as "Bi Coastal" but, unfortunately, doesn't develop it as well. It starts promisingly: Jeff Stryker, in a performance he has yet to top, pun intended, leaves his mother back on the farm and strikes out for Hollywood. His adventures along the way make for some titillating entertainment. Travis is totally in awe of his star and the camera dotes on Stryker. There's lots of sucking on that huge dick and we even have Jeff dancing around in a big shower at a spa and playing on a jungle gym at the beach. And then, sadly, it all ends. They must have run out of money. Surely Travis could have come up with a cozy little ending to this. Couldn't he have had Stryker meeting a producer of gay films and becoming a star overnight, something borrowed from real life? But we'll settle for this as the definitive bisexual Stryker, far superior to his ego-trip "Every Which Way."

Stryker is among the many porn stars who have been forthcoming about their bisexuality in interviews. Jeff says that his cock has "a mind of its own." And with a cock like that, from which the world's most popular dildo was molded, that's understandable.

The hot blond Leo Ford, the popular star of such classic gay male porn as "Leo & Lance" and "Style," who recently passed away in a motorcyle accident, revealed in an interview that he first became aware of sex in the second grade. One day, at a picnic, he spied a friend of the family who was two years older and couldn't take his eyes off of him. "He was very beautiful," Leo said. "His body was a picture to look at and I was sitting with my grandmother. I remember whispering to her, 'That boy is so beautiful...look how pretty he is.' And my grandmother said, 'That's okay for you to think like that.' I went home and got turned on in my sleep and that's when I first masturbated. I wasn't able to come but I got a tremendous feeling.

"After that, I got into fights in school just so I could touch other boys. I first heard the word 'homosexual' in the sixth grade. I had a girlfriend who had the biggest tits in school. We would draw a lot of goodlooking guys - and there was a boy in school who was very goodlooking, and we were all skipping school together one day. We were in this attic at his mother's house and I had my first experience with this boy. We had something to smoke and the girls fell asleep so we got together at the far end of the attic. He made the first move. He wrote 'bisexual' on my arm. I didn't know what it meant and he said, 'That means you like guys as well as girls.' Then we played with each other and we sucked each other but we didn't get off.

"When my mother saw what was written on my arm, she asked, 'What's this?' And I said, 'Ben wrote that. I don't know what it means.' She didn't say anything. She didn't know what to say. Anyway, the next day, I was sitting in the living room with my brothers and my mother. I guess they were discussing what to do about me. My brother Tom, who's two years older, said, 'Well, it's his long blond hair. He has to get his hair cut.' And then they had the priest talk to me. Nothing did any good." Leo said that for years he would go "in and out," meeting someone who was "this way or that way," and having sex with them. But it was never in a menage a' trois or orgy situation as you might expect given his profession. Rather it was, in the words of the star, "very one on one."

Perhaps to make the sex more universally appealing, the orgy has become a staple of bisexual videos. My collaborator Tim Lowe has the dubious distinction of appearing in perhaps the sleaziest of the bisexual videos to date, made late in his career, "Angels by Day, Devils Bi-Night." My review of the film, as it appeared in "Lowe Down:"

"Tim keeps disappearing in this Eselle (sic) Ferrand production for Filmco and it's easy to see why. This is arguably the sleaziest video Tim ever made. The ladies (and I use that term loosely) are Bianca, Sharon Kane, Cassi Nova, Kay Sera and Rusty Chaps (no kiddin', those are the stage names). The men include Rod Garreto, Marc Radcliffe, Eric Von Buelow (no kiddin'). The premise: nurses by day run an 'emergency hotline' by night.

"Tim, studily dressed in jeans and a black tank top, and Marc drop by the girls' apartment. 'What perverted things you tellin' the customers now?' Tim asks. '...To add another man to their lovemaking,' one of the sluts replies. 'What's so strange about that?' Marc asks. Tim interjects: 'What Robert (Marc's name in this little play) means is that everyone must fantasize about it every now and then. Doesn't it kinda drive you crazy, make your nipples hard?' 'Are you crazy?' one girl laughs 'Are you kiddin' me? That's my all-time fantasy, watching two guys suck each other's cock!' 'You mean, like this?' Tim asks, zipping down Marc's pants and taking out his limp salami and jamming it in his mouth. But Marc, alas, can't get it up so he goes to Tim's crotch while Tim gives one of the babes a tongue-lashing: 'Your pussy tastes fucking good,' Tim sighs. But soon it's back to Marc's dick while one of the girls goes down on him. But Marc still can't get it hard, so Tim just lays back and enjoys it as Marc and a girl take turns sucking him. Finally, Tim slips on a rubber and fucks one of the girls but before long he's disappeared and Marc is getting finger fucked by the girls. Just as suddenly, Tim comes back (did he have to relieve himself? What's happening here?) and slips it to Marc. Tim cums, then disappears again, leaving hapless Marc to fend for himself.

"The last scene of this tedious video is the obligatory orgy and this one is held at a bar on a slow night, with customers in attendance, billed in the credits as 'The Bad Boys at the Bar, including Bruce Seven as himself.' We find Tim on stage alongside a light-skinned black (Rick Wynn), holding the black's cock while a blonde goes down on it. Then Tim disappears again while the black screws the blonde. Later, Tim comes back to screw her himself. We don't see any more of this because the action shifts to the bar where Marc is nibbling on the balls of studly Jake Larkin who is getting fucked with a string of beads. Mercifully, the whole thing simply ends and as the end title is shown, the camera pulls back to show the director and, at her side, is Tim, arms crossed, chatting with her. Perhaps that's where he was all the time, picking up pointers for a future career behind the cameras? If so, by watching this filming he certainly learned what to avoid."

Some porn stars claim they are manipulated into gay sex. In William Higgins' hugely popular 1985 release, "The Young & The Hung," gorgeous Chris Lance swaps blow-jobs with Brian Estevez (billed as Mike Raymond) through a hole. Later, after bottoming for many stars, Brian would confess: "They told me I wasn't big enough or buff enough to play a top role, so I was labeled a bottom - a small hot guy who gets dick up his ass." Now does that sound like a bisexual to you?

It doesn't to me either, but listen as Brian tells us just what it all means to him: "I jack off, even with men, you know. I can enjoy sex with a man, after doing all the movies and breaking down and breaking the ice and breaking through the sexuality thing...and the fear and everything else. If I chose to do it, I can enjoy it. It's just my genes, inside of me, something inside of me...I prefer women."

But he says he was lucky to have done the movies. "This one producer, I'm not going to say who, always says to me, 'You fucking love it -you love that dick in your ass.' He wants me to say, 'Okay, I love it! I love it!' Look, when I started out there was the pain. I was just doing it without any emotion or feeling, then as time went on, I started to let myself relax and enjoy. I mean, eventually you get honest with yourself. Sure, it does feel good, the prostate is a gland. If you massage it, of course you'll feel good. Anybody's gonna feel good. I don't care if a guy says he's the straightest guy in the world and that it doesn't do anything for him or make him feel good - if you stick a finger up his ass and rub his prostate, and he doesn't say it feels good - what's wrong with this guy? I always hear it in the business, 'Oh, I'm straight.' Then, all the gay men go: 'You're a fucking liar - you're not any straighter than we are.' It's all crazy. I don't know. I guess at this point I have to say I'm bisexual."

As renowned gaymale film critic Dave Kinnick has remarked: "It's always interesting to see someone actually coming out while in the process of making gay pornographic films. I've seen it happen a lot and it's so weird - like stripping gears on a car."

As a longtime fan of video erotica, it has been a personal source of fascination to watch boys work out their sexual confusion while making porn films. Perhaps they use it as an excuse to indulge, conveniently slipping back into a "straight persona" when the task is done.

The popular dancer and porn star Damien ("Buttbusters" and "Read My Lips") commented: "Yeah, I mean once you've done that, what is there? You're out." Being "out," if that is what it is really, is what it's all about, it seems. But even Damien, who fully admits to being gay, not bi, won't get fucked on screen. "I've never bottomed because personally it's something that is really important to me. I know it sounds stupid but in my personal life there have only been three people who have done that to me, the last being my current lover (the former porn star Tony Sinatra, a.k.a. Erickson). I couldn't even tell you what it would take for me to bottom in a movie."

When he had only two movies out, he was amazed at the incredible amount mail he got. "This is the first one I ever got, right after 'Read My Lips' came out. This guy says, 'You're a stud -a near flawless example of gentle/ masculine beauty.' Isn't that fabulous?"

"When I started out," Cameron Kelly, veteran of dozens of

gayporn films said, "when it came to sex, I had no real preferences. I just liked sex in general and I was pretty much willing to do anything for adventure." And Adam Grant, king of the sequels, including "Two Handfuls II," "Head of the Class II," and "Sailor in the Wild II," is another of this new breed of sexual athlete, able to deal with whatever comes up. Says he: "I like women, I like men. I never really put much a label on it. I'm just a very sexual being."

Another "very sexual being" is porn star Chance Caldwell, who toils in Colbert's "Bi Madness" and Catalina's "Sex Bi Lex." A former wrestler and truck driver from Czechoslovakia, Caldwell says: "I always felt this way, since I was 13. I like men and women and I wanted to be in movies. I'm horny all the time, so I thought, 'Why not? It's more variety. It's something different.'"

The fact that Chance grew up on foreign soil provides a clue to his openness.

As Grace Jones commented, "In America, bisexuality is such a big deal. Americans are so wrapped up in what is normal, what is right and pure. The only things that are pure are sex and nature. Nature doesn't argue back, it just is. It survives and evolves and returns."

Speaking of evolving, the scholar Arthur Evans, author of "The God of Ecstasy," describes the Athenian man, raised to be a warrior, the man who is now most likely to be considered homophobic, as one whose values are counter to many deeply rooted human capacities. States the author: "We are not born exclusively masculine or feminine, nor alienated from nature, nor inclined toward perpetual violence to the members of our species. On the contrary, we all have the capacity for a very wide spectrum of human characteristics, as evidenced by the glorious variety in values and behavior found in the world's differing cultures. But when we are raised in a society that deliberately delineates half of the spectrum of human abilities and feelings as taboo, every person born into that society is fated to spend a huge amount of energy denying half of his or her personality."

In America's appallingly sex-negative society, author Kaahumanu summarizes it best: "We must identify the complexity of what we are."

Afterword:
"The Hidden Handicap"

By Joe Leslie

William, the protagonist in this novel, "The Kid," possesses a "hidden handicap," a reading disorder eventually diagnosed as dyslexia.

Experts cannot even agree on a standard definition of this disability. Sylvia Farnham-Diggory, in her book "Structural Approaches to Dyslexia," published by the Harvard Press, states: "Offering a definition of dyslexia amounts to 'waving a red flag in front of a herd of bulls.' Parents and professionals alike. Far from clarifying the situation, the definition (inspires) so much snorting and ground-pawing that the conceptual dust has grown thicker than ever. Definitions are not truth: they merely set up the conditions under which particular actions are to be taken. Some of these actions may be experiments, some of which may produce results that have bearing on truth, but the definitions simply name the game."

Further, as Susan Spaeth Cherry, author of "Dyslexia: The Hidden Handicap," asserts, some learning experts even doubt that dyslexia exists, arguing that "a diagnosis of the disorder lumps together various causes of poor reading. Many schools ignore the specialized needs of dyslexics by dumping them into classrooms for children with multiple handicaps."

A lack of understanding of his abnormality on the part of parents and teachers can have a severe impact on a disabled youngster's self-worth. The ultimate irony of the story of "The Kid" is that while his parents and teachers condemned him, not recognizing his other qualities, such as his physical beauty, honesty, integrity and eventual virility, these attributes would be those that would serve him well during the time we are fortunate enough to meet up with him. And it is those qualities that come to fascinate the character of Joe, who becomes William's white knight, and cause him to fall in love with the youth.

Unfortunately, in the real world, for most dyslexics there is no millionaire rock star to lend a helping hand, no white knight, no fairy tale ending. Rather, because of tight budgets, lack of properly trained diagnosticians, and contemptuous administrators and instructors, the dyslexic generally doesn't get the help he needs. And worried and over-protective parents seem to be more at fault than anyone.

Cherry says, "Parents frequently find the dyslexic's conduct baffling, embarrassing and exasperating. Some blame themselves for their youngster's problem; others feel victimized by them."

Cheery quotes Joan Sharpe of Chicago, a mother of two dyslexics: "Having a dyslexic child is very threatening to parents' egos. There were years I felt like a failure."

This feeling of failure manifests itself in a variety of ways, most often overtly, sometimes non-verbally, but almost always in an accusatory way. Many times, those parents who do seek solutions do so to assuage their own anger and frustration rather than to aid the child, who remains a victim until some outside force intercedes to provide aid and comfort.

After reading "The Kid," one of STARbooks' long-time editors recalled: "I had a boyfriend once who, ironically, was named Billy, and he suffered the same problem as the boy in this book. I remember he would hand me a record label and ask, 'What does this say?' just because he didn't want to make the effort to read it. In the story, when William is left alone at the star's hilltop mansion, he is eager to find out about this mystery person and consequently makes an effort to read the CD covers. Later, when he is handed the tabloid, he freezes when confronted with masses of oppressive gray type. He could have made an effort to read it but it would have taken considerable time and effort, and surely Joe would have caught on. What William didn't realize is that Joe's sister had suffered the same problem and been helped by therapy."

Indeed, as we see in "The Kid," a loved one's understanding, coupled with the correct therapy, can not only help a youngster deal with the problem but also have a dramatic impact on his self-esteem. As Sharpe says, "Therapy makes all the difference in the world. It doesn't make the problem go away but it helps the child deal with the problem better."

For further information on specific language disability, you are invited to write: Ms. Rosemary Bowler, Orton Dyslexia Society, 724 York Road, Baltimore MD 21204, or call (301) 296-0232.

"The Book of the Year"*
is now even bigger, even better!

NOVEMBER 8, 1991   TWN-Florida's Most Complete Gay/Lesbian Source Since 1977

BOOK NOOK
BY JESSE MONTEAGUDO

Books of the Year: The People's Choice

The following titles were best sellers at Tampa's Tomes and Treasures, Wilton Manors' Dangerous Ideas and/or Miami's Lambda Passages during 1991. They are, in a sense, "the people's choice" for the Books of the Year:

1. *Angel* by John Patrick (STARbooks).
2. *Behind the Mask* by Dave Pallone (Signet).
3. *The Beverly Malibu* by Katherine V. Forrest (Naiad).
4. *The Big Gay Book* by John Preston (Plume).
5. *The Black Marble Pool* by Stan Leventhal (Amethyst).
6. *Brother to Brother* edited by Essex Hemphill (Alyson).
7. *The Caregivers Journey* by Mel Pohl (Hazelden).
8. *Coming Out: An Act of Love* by Rob Eichberg (Dutton).
9. *Dancing on Tisha B'Av* by Lev Raphael (St. Martin's).
10. *Death With Dignity* by Jack Ricardo (Banned Books).
11. *Halfway Home* by Paul Monette (Crown).
12. *I Left My Heart* by Jaye Maiman (Naiad).
13. *Intimacy Between Men* by John Driggs & Stephen Finn (Dutton).
14. *Lavender Lists* by Lynne Y. Fletcher & Adrien Saks (Alyson).
15. *Leathermen Speak Out* by Jack Ricardo (Leyland).
16. *Living in Hope* by Cindy Mikluscak-Cooper (Celestial Arts).
17. *Men on Men 3* edited by George Stambolian (Plume).
18. *Murder by Tradition* by Katherine V. Forrest (Naiad).
19. *My Country/Right to Serve* by Mary Ann Humphrey (Harper).
20. *Rescuing the Bible from Fundamentalists* by John Spong (Harper).
21. *Surviving AIDS* by Michael Callen (Harper).
22. *Vampires Anonymous* by Jeffrey N. McMahan (Alyson).
23. *Wish You Were Here* by Rita Mae Brown (Bantam).

The New International Edition

with even more great
reading is here...

When having it all is not enough...

*No one
can say "no"
to Angel...*

A Special Collection of the Best Erotica of JOHN PATRICK
Including:

The Romans á Clef
Angel: The Complete Quintet
The Bigger They Are
The Younger They Are
The Harder They Are
Stacy's Story
Stacy's Return

Billy & David: A Deadly Minuet

The Erotic Fables
The Boy in the Park
The Biting Tongue
The Masterpiece

The Star Essays
Excerpts from the Best-Selling Series from
STARbooks, Including:
Christopher Atkins: Chickenhawk's Delight
Vince Cobretti: A Charmed Life
Tim Lowe: Lowe Down
Tom Steele: Hard As Steele
Joey Stefano: Sex Maniac

International
Edition Includes
Material Never Before
Published

About the Author

John Patrick is a prolific, prize-winning author of fiction and non-fiction. One of his short stories, "The Well," was honored by PEN American Center as one of the best of 1987. The author's acclaimed romans a´ clef, including "Angel: The Complete Quintet" and "Billy & David: A Deadly Minuet," have now been collected into a single volume. His novels as well as his non-fiction works, including "Tarnished Angels," "The Best of the Superstars" series, continue to gain him new fans every day.

Mr. Patrick is currently at work on the anthologies "Insatiable/Unforgettable" and "Runaways/Kid Stuff," and a new collection, "Heartthrobs," which will include the novels "The Boy From El Dorado" and "Teen Idol" along with the best-selling non-fiction novel "What Went Wrong?" complete and unabridged. A divorced father of two, the author is a longtime member of the American Booksellers Association, the Florida Publishers' Association, American Civil Liberties Union, and the Adult Video Association. He resides in Florida.